W9-BPO-393

free+style

maximize sport and life performance with four basic movements

Carl Paoli & Anthony Sherbondy

Victory Belt Publishing, Las Vegas

First Published in 2014 by Victory Belt Publishing Inc.

ISBN 13: 978-1-628600-20-9

This book is for educational purposes. The publisher and authors of this instructional book are not responsible in any manner whatsoever for any adverse effects arising directly or indirectly as a result of the information provided in this book. If not practiced safely and with caution, working out can be dangerous to you and to others. It is important to consult with a professional fitness instructor before beginning training. It is also very important to consult with a physician prior to training due to the intense and strenuous nature of the techniques in this book.

Printed in the USA
RRD 01-14

contents

Let me get this out of the way first: I am an unabashed Carl Paoli fan. No other coach or athlete has had a bigger impact on the way I have come to understand how humans move and should move.

But first things first.

It's one thing to talk of bulls, and another thing entirely to be in the bullring. The first time I met Carl it was as an athlete. He'd heard about what we were doing and, like any great athlete searching for a better way, decided to see for himself. One skill set ubiquitous to nearly every working coach is the ability to spot talent. It took me all of about two minutes of watching Carl move to know that something was "different" about him. If you've seen Carl Parkour, Olympic lift, on the rings, or on a trampoline, you know exactly what I'm talking about.

It's big of me, right? Spot the freak show of an athlete among a group of mere mortals? But here's the rub: Carl was performing movements he'd never seen or attempted before. I was watching him pick up new skills on the fly. And he was doing it well.

I'm very lucky in my career. I get to go behind the scenes and exchange notes with the best coaches on the planet in nearly every pro/college/Olympic/national-level sport you can think of. This means that I'm exposed to the very best athletes in the world. I'm used to seeing mutant athletic prowess. Heck, even my children are used to hanging out with some of the greatest athletes of my generation. What I'm saying is, I'm a bit immune to witnessing the outliers of human function in their fields. It's not that being around a bunch of superwomen ever gets boring (it never does!); it's just that you start asking a different set of questions after a while. And this brings me back to Carl.

Watching Carl move, it was clear to me that he'd had formal movement coaching and training. Like the great coach Dan John says, "No one just walks in off the street and overhead squats their body weight fifteen times. No one." But what is never taught, and what is so amazing about Carl, is that he has the ability to translate his historical skill set into the successful completion of novel tasks on the spot. And here we are at the really interesting questions. What skills are transferable? How and why? Is there a root or fundamental movement language that sets up a lifetime of continued skill development? What does that program look like? What are its core elements and values? Does it explain complex phenomena outside its domain? Does it scale up and down based on ability? Is it observable, measurable, and repeatable? Can it be taught to children? In short, how do you create a human operating system that remains flexible and infinitely utilitarian—a model that prioritizes skill acquisition over raw work but allows for greater power, force, and complex task completion over the long haul without the dead-ends of injury, low skill, poor motor problem-solving, or failure to reach peak individual function?

I work with plenty of athletes who are very successful in spite of having nearly zero meta-awareness of their skill sets. They are the best in the world, and they have no idea why what they do works or how they came to understand their abilities (besides generally freakish dedication and hard work). They have even less of an idea how to transfer that information to another athlete verbally, much less communicate the many thousands of mini-steps required to build skills. And this is precisely why getting to hang out with Carl over many years at the Lab/gym is so profound. He knows how he got from A to B, and more important, he knows how to teach *you* to get from A to B.

Thanks to the Internet, we are living in an age when the training methods of the best athletes and coaches on the planet are at our fingertips. And while it's nearly miraculous that you can log on and find a 5k training program used by Kenyan runners or some secret Russian squat program to follow, it is akin to reading about how to race a Formula One car without really knowing how to negotiate the first turn at 200 kph. You can do it, but chances are you are going to end up in the weeds or worse. And this is precisely what we are witnessing in the greater athletic/competitive world. We take many millions of eggs and toss them into the first turn at 200 kph, and the ones that don't break go on to the next turn. I witness these gaping holes in the fundamental understanding of how we should and should not move on a daily basis. Ask my wife, Juliet, about the onslaught of e-mails we receive from the world's best soldiers and athletes asking us for help. The scale of the problem is far worse than you can imagine. For example, we haven't even moved the needle on women's ACL injury rates. How is it that young girls are able to get all the way to college and pro-level sports without knowing how to jump and land? It's not an issue of strength or will, I assure you. It's an operating system error. The egg finally breaks in one of the turns. The season before women's slope-style skiing debuted at the 2014 Olympics, 75 percent of the sport's top ten women sustained knee injuries. Would you let your daughter play if the odds were three out of four that she'd win an ACL surgery?

So where do we begin? Physical education in schools is practically absent. Go be a volunteer at any elementary school's field day games and be prepared to be horrified at the profound lack of movement skill. I mean basic life skills, like hopping or performing a forward roll. I've done it. I witnessed fifth graders who could not extend their hips with enough ability to hop 10 meters in a sack race. True fact. This isn't news by any stretch. Nearly every master coach I know advocates for some kind of formal movement training for developing children. Remember that kid in your class who took gymnastics/karate/dance as a child? Remember how he or she was able to backflip into the pool on the first try, or was the best athlete on the team in high school? Of course you do. And so do the master coaches. You see, after about a billion hours of clinical hands-on coaching experience, all these master coaches and movement educators noticed that these kids are very teachable.

This is all well and good, but it still doesn't get us any closer to the reality of endowing athletes of any ilk with a formal, systematized, progressive, and immediately transferable set of skills. You mean kids who climb trees a lot as children can usually perform pull-ups and are more stable, effective, and injury-proof swimmers and throwers? Sign me up! By the way, how much tree climbing? How often? How high? What if I'm not strong enough to climb a tree yet? What if I don't have a tree? How do I get a classroom of kids to climb at the same time? How do I progress tree-climbing skills? How do I not kill any kids in trees? Right?

There are no shortcuts to becoming a skillful human animal. Believe me, having spinal surgery or a hip resurfacing after years of running and picking things up like a bull in a china shop is an expensive, pain-in-the-ass way to "pay" for the privilege of playing. And the horrific part is that you still have to learn to do it correctly. There is no way out. Sure, you can stop running, biking, lifting, playing ball, surfing, or skiing. Water aerobics and gentle walking are valid solutions . . . but you know this already. That's why you are holding this book.

In the eight years that I've known Carl, I have had the incredible privilege of witnessing firsthand the coalescing and channeling of a lifetime's work and intuition into this book. And while many of today's current master thinkers in the fields of human movement and performance have been calling for simple baselines of movement competency, they are no closer to creating a curriculum to get us there. We've cracked the code on strength and conditioning. We can make people fitter and stronger than ever before. We know what the best practices in these realms look and feel like. Still, we have yet to crack the code on making athletes both resilient and ready to receive that training. There has been no blueprint for systematically teaching the building blocks of human movement—until now. We've just historically hoped that some kid would work it out well enough for the folly of chance to pluck him or her into sport. But what if we could erase the uncertainty? What if we could endow people (not just athletes) with the tools that allow them to acquire nearly any new motor skill? What if nearly every human movement could be reduced to its original source code? Fortunately, it has been. This book is the beginning of a revolution. Viva la Freestyle!

Kelly Starrett
May 2014

Photo by Maria Davey

introduction

00

Don't let other people's thinking limit yours.

My name is Carl Paoli, and here is my story.

After more than fifteen years of training as a gymnast and over a decade of coaching, I have identified four movements that will change how you view fitness and sport and how you move through life. If you are eager to jump straight into those movements, feel free to turn to part 2 of this book. Otherwise, let me tell you a little about myself in order to help you understand where my training philosophy and methods originated.

During my gymnastics years, I realized that physically I wasn't the most naturally talented athlete. It may have had something to do with the way I learned gymnastics in elementary school. Back then, my coach sat on a bench, smoked cigarettes, and yelled out orders. The older kids would then perform based on her instructions, and we younger kids would try to mimic them.

When I moved on to become part of a competitive team at a local gymnastics club, the kids who surrounded me were much more advanced than I was. Despite the competition, or maybe because of it, I fell asleep nearly every night dreaming about going to the Olympics one day, and this dream fueled me to try to close the gap. Even though I managed to keep up with the other kids, I always felt like I didn't quite measure up.

By the time I was seventeen, I had tendinitis in both elbows, multiple sprains in both ankles, torn trapezoids, a broken neck from the year before, scars on my head from having had twenty-eight stitches, and the usual sexy torn-up hands and bruised legs from the day-to-day practice. I felt like the system was wrong. By then, I had earned respect among my peers in the gym and in the gymnastics community in Spain, but I was still nowhere close to my dream of making the Olympics.

I remember my coach trying to come up with new techniques and talking to other coaches to bring home new knowledge, but his efforts always ended up being one-size-fits-all. One method works for everyone, the story went, and I was usually the guy who couldn't get it. It could have been my fears or simply me being unable to adapt, but I felt like something was missing.

Eventually I left gymnastics behind and transitioned into snowboarding and wakeboarding. My on-ramp to these two sports was exponentially faster than it was for the people around me, which I believe was due to the significant overlap of fundamental skills between the disciplines.

Action sports gave me a sense of freedom and allowed me to develop my own style. No one told me what to wear or how to perform. There was no real method of learning; it was simply you, your vision, and your body. Anything goes! You knew things were moving in the right direction when your friends got excited about you landing a new trick or simply by the way you felt while performing the moves.

As time went on, I picked up trampolining, hand-balancing, Olympic weightlifting, and kettlebell training. Through the exploration of these different disciplines, I found that each one was simply a matter of training my body for a specific purpose. I also noticed that the leaders in these disciplines often developed a stubborn mentality. Their way was the one and only right way—the same thing I had heard in gymnastics. One size fits all! Once I experienced this sense of limitation, it was only a matter of time before I moved on to a new sport.

return to my roots

Training in various styles eventually led me back to the sport I had left behind. I started teaching a recreation-level gymnastics class, but on the condition of doing it only for fun. Despite my desire to make it just about enjoyment, I found myself falling into the same rigid approach to coaching in which I had been brought up: "You are going to line up small to tall and do this movement until it's perfect, and we'll move on to the next thing only when you can do it eleven out of ten times."

Even though it was a noncompetitive program and limited to a couple of hours a week, I crushed those kids and believed that they should thank me for it. After a few months, I could tell that they didn't really like me, and truth be told, I didn't like them, either. I started having the same negative feelings I'd had when I was pursuing gymnastics as a career.

One day I came in and decided to skip lining them up small to tall. I sat them down and asked, "What would you guys really like to learn? Why are you here? What motivates you?" Knowing me and wanting to please their coach, the kids replied that their dream was to be great at gymnastics, of course. I knew that they had no clue what they were talking about; greatness was not going to come from participating in a recreational program a couple of hours a week. I told them the truth: "You guys are here because your parents want you to be here. So what do you really want to learn?" One kid shyly raised his hand and said, "I want to learn to run up a wall and backflip off." Then another kid said, "I'd like to be able to jump out of my tree house and survive." So I offered them a deal. Every week we would pick a movement or trick of their choice and use traditional gymnastics training to develop that movement.

After a couple of months, I started seeing huge gains in the kids—and both the kids and I were excited to be there. I was loving my job! Everything became a little looser, and everybody was having a good time. Soon the parents sitting in the bleachers noticed this progress and asked if they could join in the fun. "Of course," I said. "Just sign this waiver. . . ."

The adults were a different story than the kids. They knew that they weren't there to be Olympic champions; they simply wanted to have fun and learn cool tricks that they could practice on the trampoline at the gym and then bring home to their backyards. I tried to explain to them that it's best to learn to walk before you run, but they managed to convince me otherwise. So I gave in, and we'd start to practice some cool trick.

The problem came the next day when one of them would call and say, "Hey, Carl, I had a great session with you yesterday, but my arms are so sore that I can barely reach to wipe. I can't move my back from my butt to my head, and I'm walking around like a T-Rex with my arms curled up to my chest." The message was loud and clear: We needed to prepare their bodies for the tricks. And I had the solution: strength and conditioning! Not just any strength and conditioning, but gymnastics strength and conditioning.

"I'd like to be able to jump out of my tree house and survive."

The gymnastics strength and conditioning actually worked for them, and they improved. After some time, though, another slight problem developed: Their joints started to ache. I didn't really know what to do, so again I did what I'd been taught as a young gymnast: "If it hurts, tape it up!" Hundreds of rolls of athletic tape later, my clients looking like stiff mummies, I thought to myself, "Maybe gymnastics is not for adults."

For some reason, though, I chose not to believe that adults shouldn't be allowed to move in any way they want. I knew that these adults had more potential, and I simply needed to figure out how to connect them to the ways they wanted to move. Not to mention that I was really enjoying my job and didn't want to give up.

This was the moment I discovered my philosophy of coaching.

My number-one priority as a coach is to help people achieve their dreams by:

1. Helping them define their goals, as was the case with the children
2. Finding a practical solution that guides them toward those goals as safely as possible, as demonstrated by the adults

coach carl

Having defined my coaching mission, I found the hard part of my job laid out before me. How was I going to help these adult athletes learn to perform the gymnastic tricks that they wanted to do despite the lack of information about how best to prepare adult non-gymnasts for this type of movement?

My search took me from the gymnastics gym to one of the fanciest health club chains, where I became the top-selling personal trainer, and all the way to a shared-business basement gym in the heart of San Francisco, where I started each day reading and researching lifting workouts. This intense study and the interactions with my most dedicated clients who had followed me led me to the discovery of my framework on teaching human movement. I call it Freestyle Connection.

I always want to give credit where it's due, so it's important for me to note that I made the biggest leap by far in my thinking when I began studying CrossFit. Before diving into it, I had checked it out several times only to dismiss it, partly because I thought the form and technique looked awful. CrossFit seemed dangerous to my gymnastics-trained eye; watching those crazy Kipping Pull-ups made me cringe. Luckily, my fascination with Olympic-style weightlifting finally drew me into a local affiliate called San Francisco CrossFit.

CrossFit has since become a very popular fitness program, and with this popularity comes many different ways of defining it. CrossFit is "fitness for elite athletes," "all about the culture," "a cult," "about moving large loads over long distances quickly," "just a lot of fun," and "dangerous." What is most important to me is that CrossFit is the culmination of an enormous experiment on how the human body can address various challenges and which adaptations are the most successful at helping people move better. CrossFit finds the answers by creatively introducing an incredible array of challenges to the body, meticulously measuring how people perform, and then continuing to change the stimulus based on the performance it elicits.

The biggest challenge I faced while coaching CrossFit was managing the pressure of trying to ramp people up to movements they weren't familiar with in order to make their training sessions both safe and useful. For example, one day we would perform heavy Olympic weightlifting combined with running, and another day we would perform technical gymnastics movements at high speeds. This is like asking people to become competent in two very different Olympic sports at the same time.

This environment was an ideal breeding ground for understanding and developing movement just below the specificity of a particular sport, but not far from the sport itself. For example, athletes would be asked to learn a Clean and Jerk as seen in Olympic weightlifting, but would perform it in circumstances not seen in that sport. My focus in training my clients shifted slightly toward understanding specific techniques for the sake of learning better general movement patterns rather than understanding specific techniques in order to fulfill specific performance requirements—for example, we worked on the deadlifting technique required for multiple repetitions in order to develop cardiovascular endurance rather than focusing on lifting the most weight, as seen in the sport of powerlifting.

In addition, the act of scaling movements by finding the variation or style of each movement that best fits an individual's performance level allows for innovation—a process of finding the optimal yet safe training stimulus. At first, I thought this flexibility in standards was dangerous, but now I know that, with the right coaching, it is safer and more effective in the long run.

This new approach to training, in combination with my previous experience in gymnastics and personal training, helped my clients see immediate results. These results encouraged them to give gymnastics another shot, or to try it for the first time. I was astonished to see how the more basic movement patterns I was teaching carried over into the gymnastics gym better than the gymnastics-specific training did. My clients really got it, and they didn't feel sore and miserable the next day.

While I was thrilled with these results, they also confused me. How was it possible that the students were able to get better at gymnastics without training in specific gymnastics movements? Even though I was confident in my skills as a trainer, I couldn't put my finger on what I was doing that was so special.

Then one day I was listening to a neuroscientist from Sweden talk about child development, and he said, "Kids need to learn to read, and then they use their ability to read to learn new things. You need to learn to read so you can read to learn." BINGO! That's what we've been doing, I realized. I teach people how to move so they can use that movement to learn new things. We must learn to move so we can move to learn! For these athletes, I had found the right balance between general movement preparedness and sport-specific training.

My confidence in teaching a foundation of movement with methods for creating individual movement styles on top of that foundation only strengthened over a decade of coaching athletes who had failed to find success with previously prescribed programs from their sports. I firmly believe that getting an education across multiple styles of movement and understanding how to use those styles to your individual advantage is a better approach to maximizing your performance in a particular sport.

I think it's important for me to clarify that my advice is not simply to do CrossFit or any other program out there. The idea is to pursue a balance between general movement preparedness and sport-specific training. CrossFit simply gave me a lot of tools and evidence that tweaking this balance was the best way to enhance individual performance. As athletes and coaches, we must constantly work to balance movement ability with sport-specific or goal-specific progress.

Let's look at a specific example: lack of balance. In my gymnastics career, my preferred event was vaulting, but I had problems generating enough power in my jumps to fit in the extra movements I needed in my routines. My coach and I worked hard in the gym on generating more power, hitting harder, and jumping higher. Those solutions didn't work for me, though. Only after many years, when I took a step back and thought about my performance from a more basic understanding of movement, could I figure out what was missing and correct it. I was missing some fundamental jumping movement patterns that were difficult to expose in the gymnastics-specific training.

To increase power in my jump, I realize now that I should have introduced a style of training that matched the jump movement but helped fill the general holes I had rather than simply continue to practice the more specific act of jumping seen during vaulting in gymnastics. Even though every sport has drills that are simpler versions of the complete movements that are specific to that sport, those drills sometimes fall far from the essence of the actual problem you are trying to solve. Only a better understanding of human movement will enable you to decide how to choose among all styles to solve the movement problems you face. This is how I justify practicing a style of movement that at a glance may seem unrelated to the style you need to perform in your sport.

It drives me nuts thinking about all that I might have missed out on by following only one program and not understanding some fundamental principles of human movement. I'm not saying that any person or program is dumb because it follows the results seen before. In fact, I'm saying just the opposite: Most programs contain some essential truths about human movement. And that's what I'm saying is the answer: We need to enhance our ability to see across disciplines with a proper education on fundamental movements. I'm not suggesting that this is easy to do or that it is the first time someone has attempted it. As athletes, we always have to trade off between exploring different styles of movement and preparing along our specific disciplines.

My greatest pain from the past is knowing that, locked within other styles or disciplines, there were known solutions to the obstacles I faced in gymnastics. I just didn't have the education in human movement that I needed to understand how to use other styles to improve my own. Freestyle is my approach to helping you avoid my mistake by giving you the ability to effectively select and combine styles to fit your specific purpose.

what is freestyle?

I define Freestyle as a strength and conditioning approach in which you cross over and practice other disciplines in order to develop a foundation of skill, and then use that skill in the most effective way for your specific sport or discipline. What I present in this book is the culmination of my knowledge and experience in building and using an effective skill base to reach specific goals.

The Freestyle approach is focused on studying multiple disciplines and styles of movement, but also on moving as efficiently as possible toward specific goals. It's difficult to get into the mindset of living at the crossroads of multiple styles because you can get locked into the notion that you shouldn't waste time away from your chosen discipline. But remember that every discipline can trace its origins to a crossover of styles. Formal practices in sport are important, but if you don't find the balance between exploration and progress that Freestyle suggests you should have, it is hard to create, define, and evolve sports or styles of movement.

All sports are based on bodies interacting with the environment and each other. Often these interactions come out of a free exploration of movement that starts as a form of play or just messing around. Eventually, benchmarks, standards, and rules are developed, packaging a discipline so that it can be shared, regulated, and advanced. In this sense, Freestyle can be thought of as finding movements that are fun to do or inspired by friendly competition and eventually become part of a formalized sport.

Freestyle also plays a crucial role in evolving existing sports. For example, wrestling is an art of combat that dates back to the ancient Olympics. The original, extremely violent style practiced in Greece was used for training and in combat. Through the exploration of a less violent yet still effective way to train and compete, this original style evolved into a less brutal form: Greco-Roman wrestling. The Greco-Roman style, which didn't allow wrestlers to use their legs, became so regulated that it limited a person's natural ability to use his entire body to perform. Once again, the act of exploring human movement led to a less formal and more open style of wrestling that allows the use of the legs as well as the arms, becoming what is known today as freestyle wrestling. This exploration only happens when we can step away from the approaches that are already established in a sport, which is critical for the sport's evolution.

Sometimes a sport evolves as signature movements are created. When specific demands are placed on athletes who are then given room to innovate, they often take their learned movement vocabulary and construct something new. Let's take swimming as an example. In particular, the 400-meter medley race includes the formal styles in the following order: butterfly, backstroke, breaststroke, and freestyle. I want to believe that the last leg of the race was originally presented to participants as "finish as fast as you can in whatever style you prefer," the idea being to test them on each of the different styles and then demand that they swim for their life in the last leg, letting them and their bodies figure out what's best. Most people ended up picking the forward crawl because it is the fastest, and it eventually became known as the freestyle stroke.

The natural adaptation that our bodies use to select the optimal solution within set standards is Freestyle. This exemplifies how the body makes unique adjustments based on specific demands, which creates signature movement patterns within an individual discipline and further defines a discipline or sport.

Freestyle is my philosophy of how best to enhance human performance. Regardless of your chosen style or discipline, you can always improve your performance by looking across styles or disciplines and spending time working on styles that complement your own.

Through Freestyle, you can develop signature movements that express the optimal way of moving for a specific purpose, as in the swimming example. These signature movements can come to fruition after you train and practice the foundation of human movement and later combine it in creative ways in order to apply it in situations that require precise action and the highest levels of performance, such as competitions.

In terms of movement, Freestyle is freedom of physical expression and the unlimited number of styles that the human body can adopt. I see Freestyle as an essential part of the learning and development of any sport or physical activity. By trusting what you have learned and allowing Freestyle to occur, you put yourself in a position of constant growth. Freestyle is progress.

four key elements of freestyle

Because you are reading this book, I can safely assume that you hope to improve as an athlete, a fitness enthusiast, a trainer, a coach, or simply a healthy person. It is difficult to understand how the body works, let alone know how to further develop it. In training, it is not uncommon to run into roadblocks or make poor decisions that lead to injury or limit performance. This is the main purpose of this book: to help you feel confident that you are taking the right steps regardless of your specialty, ability, or goals.

I am fortunate to get to travel the world coaching and working with talented athletes and coaches. At a CrossFit Athlete Camp in San Diego, where athletes from around the world gather to meet their

freestyle in hip-hop

In the world of hip-hop, freestyle is used in rapping and b-boying. In rapping, the meaning of the word freestyle has changed over the years; it used to mean going from a prewritten rap to showcase skill but with no particular subject matter, and nowadays it means "off the top of your head." Even though the performance of freestyle rap is spontaneous, there is a formal foundation that involves training and rehearsing. The key to the collaboration between the rehearsed foundation and the spontaneous presentation is to combine the rehearsed units in creative ways that allow for self-expression through music. Artists often showcase these skills in "battle" or competition.

I became familiar with freestyle in hip-hop when a dancer named BBoy Wicket invited me to join him on a trip to South Korea. There, he was going to battle with his crew—the Renegade Rockers—at R16, one of the biggest annual b-boy battles in the world. During the event, I learned that even though all b-boys share the same set of basic movement patterns, the way that each b-boy expresses those movements during battle defines his style and allows him to have his own individual expression of the dance.

competition, improve their performance, and gain insight into what they need as individuals to take their performance to the next level, I worked with a group of athletes on Muscle-ups. For those who don't know, a Muscle-up is a gymnastics movement that has been adapted to CrossFit, and you perform it by swinging and pulling yourself up over a set of rings. In my group, one woman was known for having the best and most efficient Muscle-ups in the world. I wondered, "How am I going to add value or insight to her performance?"

I proceeded to present the Muscle-up progression that I teach in all my seminars, which is focused on ramping up beginners as quickly as possible. Specifically, it's designed to help people get the Muscle-up for the first time. Surprisingly, the woman came up to me afterward and said, "That was so much more efficient! I love it!" The funny thing was that I had created the majority of the progression by watching a video of her Muscle-up in slow motion.

I always tell the coaches and athletes I work with, "I didn't invent this; I'm just talking about it." In other words, I am simply observing someone's performance and then describing what I saw, but always in terms of how an athlete might sense the movement based on her experience and background instead of in technical terms that are specific to the movement itself. Describing movement in this way is essential to bringing self-awareness to athletes. It marks the transition from a state of exploration to a state in which the body and mind meet and help performance reach new heights. This process of guiding athletes to explore their own movements and behaviors enables them to self-coach and better solve their own performance problems.

The story of the woman improving her already top-notch Muscle-up with so little coaching demonstrates how the presentation of knowledge can mean more than the quality and quantity of that knowledge. Over the years, I have come to realize that sometimes it is not so much the amount of knowledge we have of a particular subject, but rather how we gather and influence the information we deliver.

I have found that four key elements shape how we collect information in order to share it in a constructive fashion:

1. ***Observation and description:*** We have an instinctive ability to observe, assess, and describe our movement. As a coach and teacher, I want to keep this in mind because it is highly informative.
2. ***Sense:*** We have the ability to sense our bodies in relation to our environment, which is a great tool for self-assessment. Even though this sense is subjective, it can provide unique information about how and why someone behaves and responds to particular situations.
3. ***Motivation and purpose:*** The drive to survive, be rewarded, or be the best at something, or even sheer curiosity (to mention a few motivators), keeps us alive and moving. Without being aware of what drives an individual or a group, it is impossible to create a plan for growth and development.
4. ***Technology:*** We are products of our environment, but we also mold and develop our environment. Technology is heavily influenced by how we move, and it is essential to understand this in order to develop ourselves and develop technology based on ourselves.

Even though these elements may seem obvious, they are often overlooked. They are the most effective tools for understanding who we are as individuals, why we move the way we do, how our performance is affected by the people with whom we surround ourselves, and how we are influenced by new technologies.

Let's take a closer look at each of these four elements.

observation and description

movement is the most fundamental form of communication

Our ability to read body language lies deep within our genetic code. It has developed over millions of years of human evolution. Communication has been an essential tool for survival. For example, humans are known to use body language as a tool to find mates to procreate.

Fifty to seventy percent of all communication is nonverbal. A person's posture, facial expressions, eye movements, and gestures, when kept in context, are often enough to convey a message. Body language is intuitive and universal.

If you see someone smile, you don't need a degree or a translator to understand that she is happy. Your ability to process this information in a split second is exciting; it reminds you that you are naturally gifted with a powerful tool for studying and developing the human body.

As a popular hip-hop artist said, "School is easy. Why? Well, the answers are in the book." What he is saying is that the answers are usually right in front of us. In terms of studying movement, if we just stop and pay attention to what's happening with our bodies, we can discover a lot of answers to our questions.

I chose to focus on the mechanical aspects of human performance because movement is right there in front of us. We can measure, manipulate, and test it in many ways. Even though I am well aware that the physiological and psychological aspects are important, I have come to realize that when we focus on the physical aspect, the other two tend to follow.

As a coach, I strive to make the most accurate decisions on how to improve someone's performance. This requires learning how to process the information gathered through observing the movements and describing what we see by using our knowledge, personal experience, and, most important, intuition.

Due to the complexity of human performance, it is difficult to get a complete picture, but by mastering the physical aspect and having a basic understanding of the physiological and psychological aspects of the human body, we will have enough information to make rational decisions to guarantee ongoing progress.

sense

true human performance can only be measured through feel

When I first started coaching, I often performed movements and described them to myself while I moved. In this way, I became my own observer. This practice not only improved my own performance of those movements, but also enhanced my ability as a coach to observe and instruct others.

Because you are an observer wired for understanding movement, becoming a student of movement is relatively easy, but how do you observe yourself? Well, thankfully, you have your senses to guide you. The ability to feel is a powerful tool that you can use to assess yourself in much the same way that an outside observer would assess you.

A challenge that you are likely to run into when you self-assess is that most of the movements you perform on a daily basis are automated; you don't have to think about them before you perform them. This can be especially problematic if you have developed bad habits, such as slouching while sitting at work. These habits may be causing some aches and pains now or setting you up for injury later. Simply being aware of what you are feeling can inform you of what is wrong and how to correct it.

You can use all of your senses to guide your body in relation to the environment, but I focus mostly on the awareness of pain, balance, and position of your body and its parts in space. These are collectively known as the proprioceptive senses.

I focus on proprioception being the sense of position and movement of the parts of the body in space. As mentioned in the Muscle-up story, simply having someone describe what you look like while moving can enhance your performance. By making a conscious effort to describe how you feel while moving, you can increase your proprioception and thus your performance.

By training your senses, specifically at a physical level, you can make a fairly accurate assessment of your own performance. This assessment is critical for improving your ability to move.

motivation and purpose

sharing is progress, progress is success

In order to create the most effective plan for individual growth and development, we need to understand what motivates us. The three primary motivators I focus on are survival, reward, and innovation.

The industrial and scientific revolution and the introduction of new technologies shields us modern men and women from the need to protect ourselves from nature. Today, "survival" is predominantly motivated by reward or fear of punishment.

Consider an athlete training for the Olympics. This athlete, who wants to be the best at his sport, is driven to train and willing to invest his entire life to make his goal of winning a gold medal a reality. Once the athlete wins the gold, he gets to share his victory with the rest of the world. Without this moment of celebration, the Olympics—and competition in general—would not exist, and that victory would die with the athlete without becoming part of history and human evolution.

The moment of sharing a victory is essential to establish a point of reference for everyone in pursuit of a similar goal. Such points of reference are benchmarks that become targets for the next athletes to aim for, reach, and eventually surpass. The need to transcend one another's accomplishments is part of our natural drive to compete and grow, not just in sports, but also in nature and the rest of society. By understanding that it is human nature to constantly set new performance benchmarks, you can build more effective road maps or progressions to further develop your performance.

Finally, as Daniel H. Pink states in his book ***Drive,*** another motivator beyond survival and reward drives humankind, but often goes unacknowledged. This driver is the desire to create or do something new and share it with the world. I like to think of this drive as being motivated by a need to grow and expand our horizons.

technology

technology is a product of how we move and vice versa

Steve Jobs, the late founder of Apple, said during a presentation in 1980: "Man is a toolmaker [who] has the capacity to make a tool to amplify the amount of inherent ability that he has." This statement was in reference to a study done on the efficiency of locomotion of a number of species of animals moving from one place to another. The condor came out on top, with the human falling somewhere in the thirties. Then someone decided to do the same test but with the human on a bicycle. This time the human came out on top, winning by a huge margin. The way we make and use tools sets our species apart from others in the animal kingdom.

Growing up doing gymnastics, I took for granted that we had to perform on different pieces of equipment and that every two to four years we would see new designs of this equipment. It never really dawned on me until I got into the fitness industry later in life that these tools were designed to maximize our ability to showcase what our bodies are capable of doing. For example, the high bar was made a little more elastic to generate more power and speed; and the vault horse became a table, which allowed new and higher levels of skills

community

During my coaching career, as I travel from one country to another and one gym to another, I see one similarity that repeats itself over and over. Every gym has a similar group dynamic, with a leader and a group of people organized and ready to accomplish something. Usually, they are trying to improve themselves and the performance of their sport or craft.

The beauty of this group dynamic is that it allows the participating individuals not only to be led, but also to have the opportunity to tap into the irrational or instinctive side of their performance with minimal risk. As in most professional coaching establishments, every participant survives the experience and comes out on the other side a better athlete and person. This dynamic of a coach leading a group of athletes achieves two fundamental things:

1. It makes the athletes feel more alive by tapping into a more primal and irrational state governed by natural instincts, and therefore makes them feel human.
2. It moves the athletes toward their goals with the support of a community, essentially giving them an education on physical culture.

to be developed. This is a great example of how technology influences skill development for a sport. This happens in daily life as well, and it's helpful to keep in mind in order to understand who we are today as physical beings. These tools have greatly influenced our culture and how we transport ourselves, care for ourselves, play, and move on a daily basis.

As powerful as technology can be for enhancing performance, it can also be harmful. We tend to easily adapt to what is comfortable in terms of energy expenditure, which can physically hurt us. Take sitting, for example. The caveman sat to rest and eat and stood on two feet to work. Nowadays, we sit to work, rest, and eat and stand for very few tasks. In sports, we see how technology has evolved to enhance athletes' performance dramatically, but in fitness what was intended to enhance physical health and general preparedness is often confused with comfort and has turned most of the fitness world into gimmicks that are wasting more time than they are doing good.

Keeping in mind how we can use technology to enhance performance and how technology affects how we perform gives us a more detailed perspective on how to further develop our bodies with purpose and how our bodies, in turn, will further develop new technologies.

An interesting interpretation of the evolutionary history of human movement, according to the book ***The Story of the Human Body,*** by Daniel E. Lieberman, is that the human being seems to be the only mammal capable of running extreme distances in the heat. This crucial adaptation appears to have been gained around 2 million years ago, when it is theorized that humans began to exploit a hunter-gatherer culture.

The book suggests two key adaptations:

1. The many sweat glands across the human body
2. Our ability to walk on two legs, making locomotion more efficient and effective in terms of energy expenditure as compared with walking on four legs as other mammals do

technology vs. performance

Every four years, my gymnastics teammates and I were excited not just for the Olympics but for everything that came about after the Olympic cycle. We would usually see a change in the scoring system at this time, but we were mostly excited about the advancements in the technology implemented in the different gymnastics apparatus. The reason we were excited was because every improvement in the equipment changed our performance and enhanced our ability to perform higher-level skills.

One simple change that I got to experience while growing up was a suspension system integrated into the rings at the anchor point that connected the ring cables to the rig. The suspension system reduced the impact on the shoulders and facilitated the performance of the more advanced swinging movements. The parallel bars also became more flexible, allowing for easier swinging, and the design of the legs that held up the bars became less sharp and more rounded, making them safer and less scary. I also got to experience how the vault transitioned from a hard wooden horse covered in leather to a more impact-friendly horse, which eventually took the shape of a table that allowed for a safer and higher level performance.

Technological advancements implemented in the development of the equipment used to practice a sport play a big role in the progress we see in human performance.

how to use this book

Freestyle is the culmination of my experience as an athlete, coach, and person. My goal with this book is to help you discover what is most relevant and useful for advancing your performance toward your goals. This book is an interactive way to learn how your body is designed to move through space and interact with your constantly changing environment. Consider it a practical manual for developing a blueprint for human movement. By understanding the essence of the Freestyle philosophy and being unafraid to study, practice, and train in different styles and disciplines, you can find potential solutions to your performance problems and get closer to your specific goals.

This book is equally applicable to veteran athletes attempting to analyze their performance in order to perfect their practice, recreational/weekend-warrior athletes looking to train for a better surfing experience by gaining new movements, novices looking to pick up a skateboard for the first time, and even athlete-parents racing around the grocery store "track" while carrying a baby, holding the hand of an older child, and pushing a full cart at the same time. No matter who you are, your purpose for training and your ability to perform are unique, and that is Freestyle.

The main takeaways from this book are to:

1. Select a specific movement in a specific discipline, like Shaun White's Double McTwist 1260.
2. Use the Freestyle approach to balance exploring a foundation of human movement across all styles with progress toward a specific goal.

When I talk about specializing, I mean being specific about who is training or trying to develop human movement and when, where, and how that training or development is happening. To understand your specific needs, you must have a purpose. What is yours? Because everyone has a purpose, there is a vast array of expressions of human movement. These unique expressions are known as ***styles,*** and together they form the concept of Freestyle.

As someone who has explored a wide variety of training methods, I realize that wide exposure is great for building a broad base of experience and knowledge, but trying to master all styles is impossible. Therefore, your approach will always have to find a focus on some set of styles or specialty.

Instead of helping you specialize, I will open your eyes so that you can more clearly understand what specialty you should use to fit yourself and why you might go along with a defined specialty and tailor it to your own needs. It is like explaining how to select a tailored shirt rather than having to select between large, medium, and small. If you get only one thing out of this book, that should be it. Become a specialist, learn to see across other specialties, learn to tailor them to your goals and purpose, and do not be afraid to innovate!

This book is not specific to gymnastics, CrossFit, or any other program or sport. It is my take on how I discovered, study, and teach human movement and how you can better understand how to move within your own specialty.

Having grown up a gymnast, I find that bodyweight or calisthenics movements are in my nature, so I use some formal fitness movements to explain my theories and discoveries on developing human performance. I take four movements that I have found to be extremely powerful tools and use them to teach you the foundation of human movement. I then help you dissect these movements and fit them to your needs.

This is not the Carl Paoli program. Whatever you want to get out of this book, you will get by engaging with the material. To help you do so, I will teach you the basic frameworks that represent my thought process. This will help organize your own thoughts and practice and give you a vocabulary to describe your level or stage of movement and specific goal, its focus, and how it fits in with a progression plan. The frameworks are developed around mechanical movement, but you will also see how the frameworks relate to the physiological and psychological aspects of human performance.

The best way to interact with this material is to read about a new concept, put the book down and experiment with that concept, and come back and learn movements that you can use to diagnose, experiment, and build your individual practice. The experience will be interactive: You will read something, which will generate a plan to reach a movement goal or lead you to form a new goal. At that point, you should immediately put down the book and start making progress toward that goal. The book will always be there as a tool to help you focus and work toward your goal; come back to the book when you're ready for the next step or when you have the time to continue your education. The journey must be iterative and ongoing—a lifestyle. I will provide the tools; you just need to bring an open mind to see your own style and that of others and a willingness to work toward your goals, which you must continue to communicate to yourself and the rest of the world.

Through my philosophy on training, my framework for creating a better understanding of human performance, and the use of four basic movements, I will teach you how to navigate any sport or physical activity and assist you in building your individual path to success.

The book is organized into three parts. Part 1 discusses my Freestyle Connection framework for observing and progressing movement. This part is the most theoretical; the theories simply serve to explain the thought processes that I have come to use based on my experience. Chapter 1 gives my simplified language for describing the body and movement and can be thought of as a super-simple summary of anatomy and biomechanics. Chapters 2 and 3 are probably the most important in terms of describing the theory behind the rest of the book. These two chapters are all about movement progression, or improving your movement ability. Here, I define movement ability, movement strength, and how I come up with plans for improving movement.

Part 2 details my Freestyle Four movements. Chapter 4 covers the Pistol, chapter 5 covers the Handstand Push-up, chapter 6 discusses the Muscle-up, and chapter 7 is about the Burpee. This section is driven by careful explanations of the movements and uses the theory developed in part 1 to help you understand how to progress these movements as well as how they can enhance your specific sport or life pursuits.

Finally, part 3 gives you tools for incorporating Freestyle into your life. Chapter 8 covers many movements that are important for assisting the development of the Freestyle Four. Chapter 9 offers theory and practical examples for programming (creating training schedules to reach your goals). Chapter 10 explores the athletic lifestyle through nine athletes who help inspire my pursuit of Freestyle.

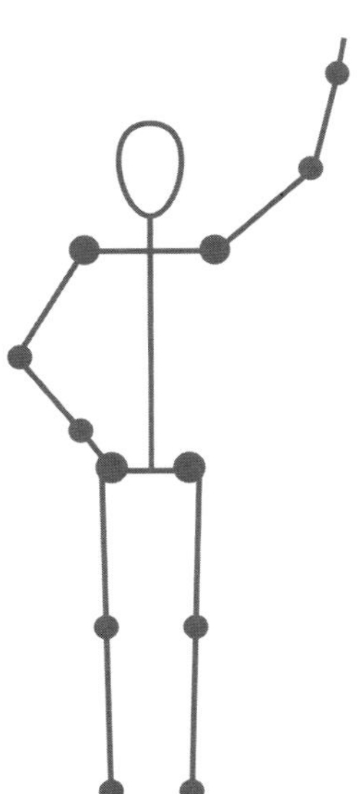

Meet Sticks. He'll be taking you on some anatomical adventures, laying some groundwork to talk about all this Freestyle jazz.

we are the product of who we are surrounded by

The pursuit of mastering the foundation of movement is an essential part of a successful physical education practice. This is something I have learned over the years of working with great coaches and athletes. This book is my approach to teaching and learning the foundation of movement, which has been influenced and molded by the people with whom I have surrounded myself over the years. As I have mentioned already, I didn't invent the foundation of human movement; I am just talking about it.

Every teacher, coach, athlete, coworker, and student I have ever had the opportunity to work with has made an impact on my life and my professional career as a coach and teacher, especially my gymnastics coach, Javier Amado, the most committed and determined coach I have ever met. He sacrificed everything in his life for the well-being and success of my teammates and me. The way I look at and coach movement is a reflection of his teachings and philosophy. To this day I strive to make him proud, and I am reminded of him every day as I see his coaching traits in myself.

The biggest influence on my work and who I am as a coach was my mentor and friend Kelly Starrett. Kelly brought my thinking full circle. He taught me how to make connections between athletics, life, and strength and conditioning. He gave me a language for better expressing my ideas and philosophy on training. In this book you will notice the influence of Kelly's teachings in the way I speak of movement and the principles and solutions for constantly pushing human performance to the next level.

1

freestyle connection

Watch it. Describe it. Do it.

After more than a decade of coaching, teaching, and talking about physical development, I have created a framework for approaching human performance through the lens of movement. My goal with this framework is to help you connect all the fundamental aspects of human movement in order to better define your goals, find the right place to start your training, and ultimately create and practice a plan to further develop your physical abilities. I call it Freestyle Connection.

This part of the book is composed of three chapters:

01 **observation:** I give you a simple and specific language for describing the complexity of the human body in motion. Every discipline has a number of fundamental movements containing the roots of other disciplines. The observation language helps you identify these fundamental movement patterns and tailor them to your performance goals.

02 **movement ability:** I describe how to measure your ability to move in a way that allows you to focus on your progress toward your individual goals. You will learn my definitions of strength, skill, skill transfer, fitness, and athleticism.

03 **progression:** I explain what is behind the most successful progressions and how essential efficient progression of your physical ability to move is to life and sport.

observation

01

Everyone cares about physical performance. The medical field and the fitness and sports industries offer an infinite number of solutions to improve it. But which solution do you choose, and how do you know if and why a particular solution is working for you?

The fact that the human body has 206 bones and more than 600 muscles interacting in a constantly changing environment makes this task extremely difficult. As a coach, I have spent a lot of time thinking about why a movement is good or bad and which patterns within that movement can hurt or help. After ten years of coaching, I have developed simple approaches to observe and describe the basics of how the human body functions. My goal in this chapter is to give you insight into these approaches that you can use to better understand how your body functions physically and apply that knowledge in your specific field: fitness, sport, or medicine.

This chapter gives you a basic overview of anatomy and biomechanics. It also teaches language that you can use to connect the human movements and athletic positions that you observe to your purpose. I like to call this language Position-Movement-Purpose:

Position refers to the basic body shapes we see in movement; ***Movement*** is the change from one body shape to the next; and ***Purpose*** is the motivation for movement.

Charles Darwin

An important approach to identifying and describing movement in a thorough way is to break the movement down into the most obvious or predominant shapes the body goes through while in motion. I call these body shapes ***positions,*** and I use a Global-Local language to describe them. ***Global*** refers to the shapes that the whole body can adopt, and ***Local*** refers to the shapes that the major joints adopt.

The Global-Local language is commonly used in the health and fitness fields to describe systems at the micro and macro levels. I will present a simplified version of this language by relating your midline to your extremities.

global

Your ***midline*** is the imaginary line that crosses your body from head to toe, representing your spine. There are several important reasons to address movement based on the spine, the first and foremost being movement control, which I will introduce in chapter 2. Even though the spine is a complex system composed of twenty-four vertebrae and four different curves, it is useful to think of it as a single unit or as the midline, as shown in the illustration at left.

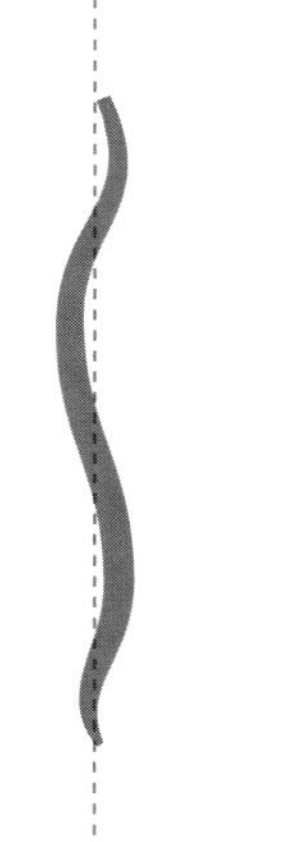

When the spine is stable and aligned, it creates a solid base for movement in the extremities. This stable spine position is the best foundation for performing and learning most other movement patterns. As I will explain in chapter 2, the stable spine position is critical for movement control. In his book *Becoming a Supple Leopard,* Kelly Starrett presents his One Joint rule, which states that being able to globally control your spine as one unit allows for optimal motor control and performance at a local level.

When observing and describing the midline, there are two key properties: orientation in space and shape of the midline.

global orientation in space

The orientation of the midline in space is a simple concept that gets its importance mostly from the fact that gravity is a fundamental part of our lives. As you change orientation in space, gravity creates varying challenges on your midline that you need to address in order to maintain the desired global shapes throughout an entire movement.

There are four key orientations that I like to think about:

1. Standing
2. Inverted (upside down)
3. Supine (faceup)
4. Prone (facedown)

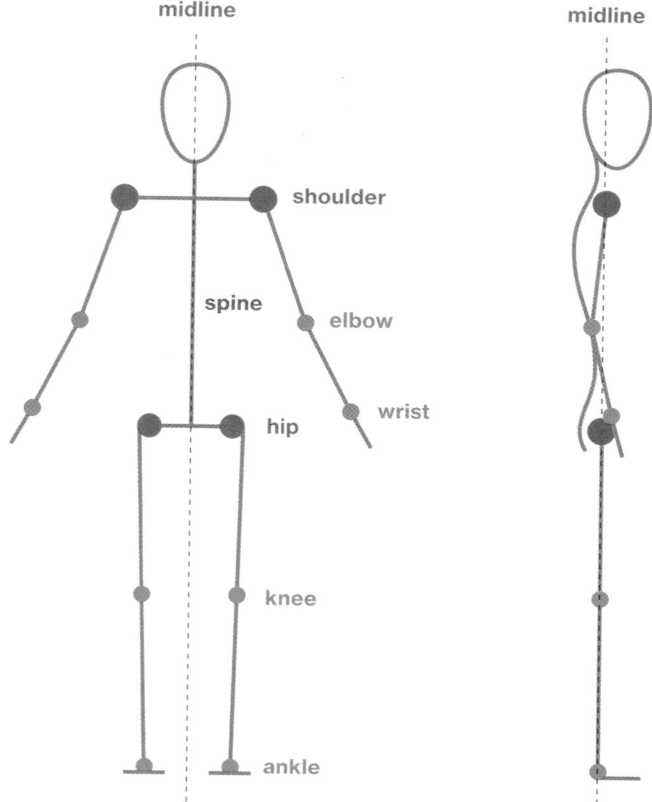

global/local coordinate system

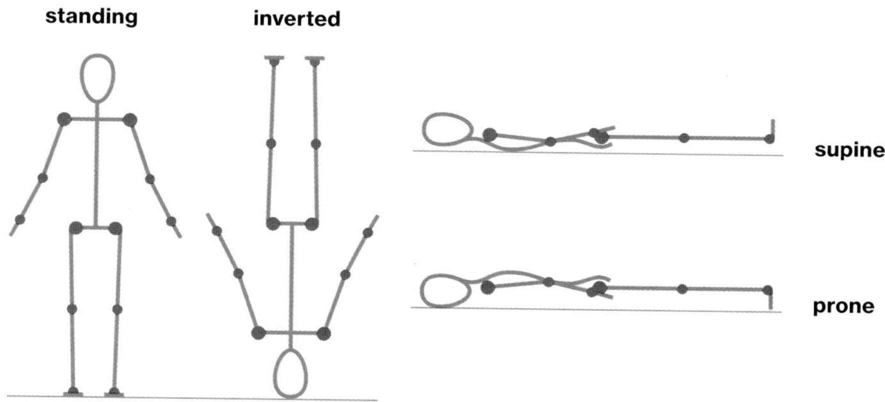

global orientation in space

global shapes

The shapes that your midline creates as you move are another key aspect of the global system. I use a simple coordinate system composed of three planes, where each plane defines a position of the midline and therefore a global shape. Be careful: It's easy to confuse body position with the direction of a particular movement, so I will note potentially confusing descriptions in several places.

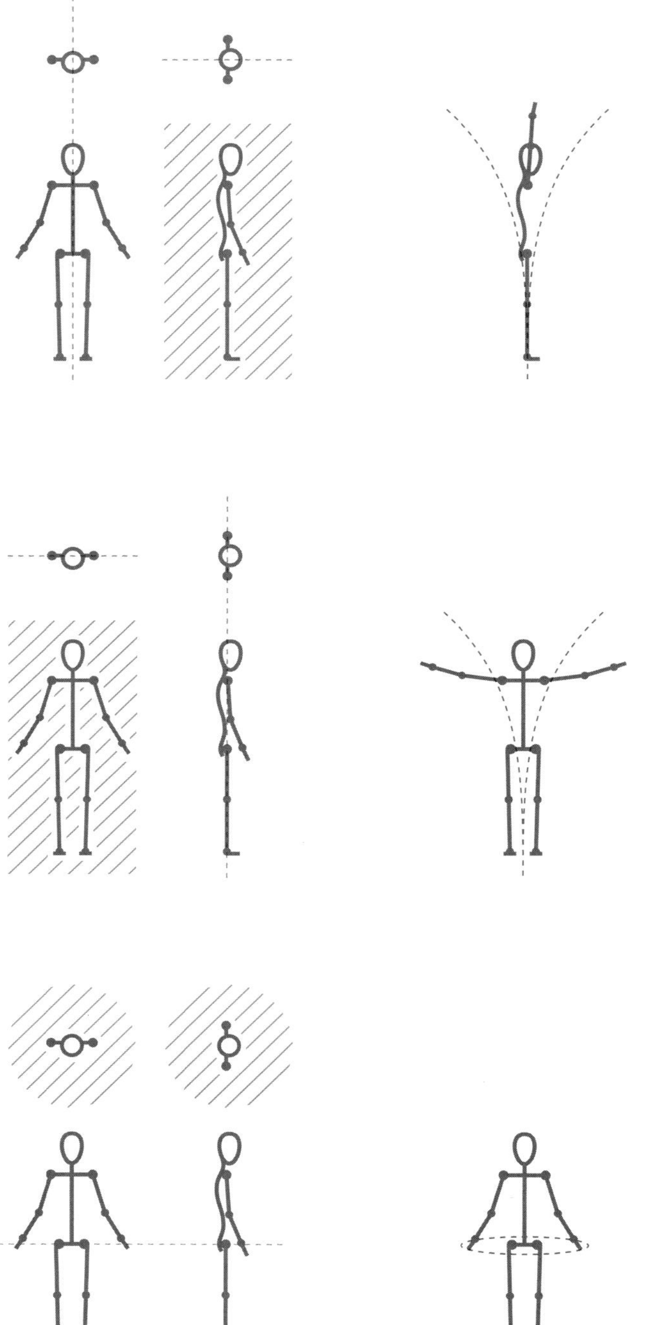

The sagittal plane divides your body into left and right halves. A common movement within the sagittal plane is walking.

Flexion/extension occurs in the sagittal plane. You are in a position of flexion when your spine bends, moving your face closer to your toes. You are in a position of extension when your spine arches, moving the back of your head closer to your heels.

The frontal plane divides your body into front and back halves. A common movement within this plane is a cartwheel.

Lateral flexion occurs in the frontal plane. You are in a position of left lateral flexion when the left side of your head bends closer to your feet. The same is true for right lateral flexion on your right side.

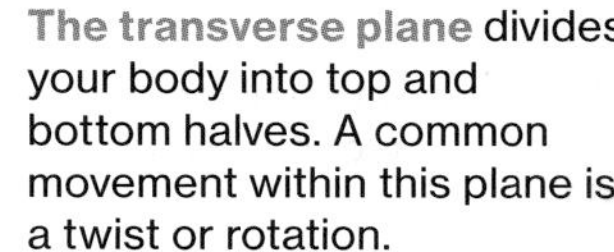

The transverse plane divides your body into top and bottom halves. A common movement within this plane is a twist or rotation.

Rotation occurs in the transverse plane. You can rotate to the left or to the right.

global examples

Looking at a few examples, we can practice using the global language to describe the body's positions and directions of movement. Although most movements are not isolated to one plane of motion in real life, the following examples bias one plane of motion for illustrative purposes.

overhead throw in soccer

Plane: sagittal

Global movement: flexion and extension

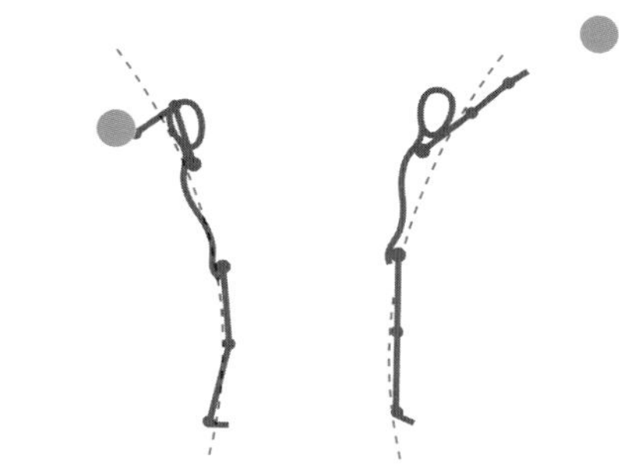

cartwheel

Plane: frontal

Global movement: lateral flexion and extension

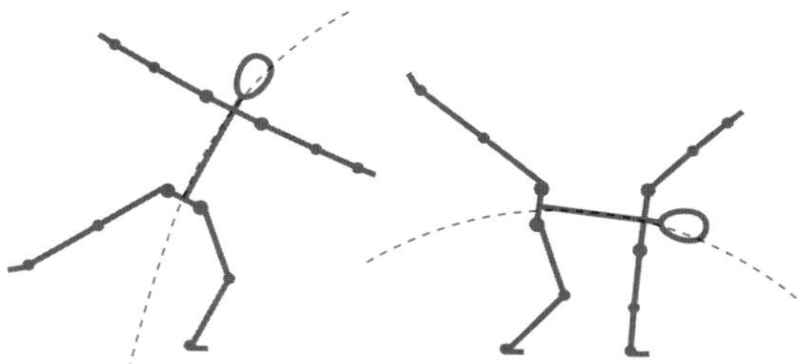

pirouette

Plane: transverse

Global movement: rotation

baseball throw

3D movement combines all planes and global movements

local

At the local level, I focus on the major moving joints: hips, knees, ankles, shoulders, elbows, and wrists. Even though there are 360 joints in the human body, focusing on the prime movers (the hips and shoulders) and their respective assistants helps us observe and describe what a body is doing while in motion.

There are two very important properties of the local system:

1. Primary versus secondary movers
2. Positions of joints

primary versus secondary movers

The property of primary versus secondary movers is easy to define and extremely important, but as you will see throughout the book, it is sometimes difficult to detect in certain complex movements. I define primary movers as the major joints that are closest to the midline—for the lower body the primary mover is the hips, and for the upper body it is the shoulders. Secondary movers are farther away from the midline—for the upper body, the secondary joints are the elbows and wrists, and for the lower body, the secondary joints are the knees and ankles. There are times when we need to compare the relative order of motion for the hips and shoulders, and in that case the hips are considered the prime mover.

shoulder: The shoulder socket is commonly described in the fitness and medical fields as a golf ball on a tee. Notice how the head of the humerus, which has a spherical shape, sits on the shoulder socket, which can be seen as a tee. This is one of the reasons the shoulder is more sensitive to injuries such as dislocation and cannot generate as much power as the hip.

hip: The hip is seen as a ball in a socket, where the head of the femur sits deeper in the hip socket. This is one of the reasons the hip is more stable than the shoulder and is the main power generator in locomotion.

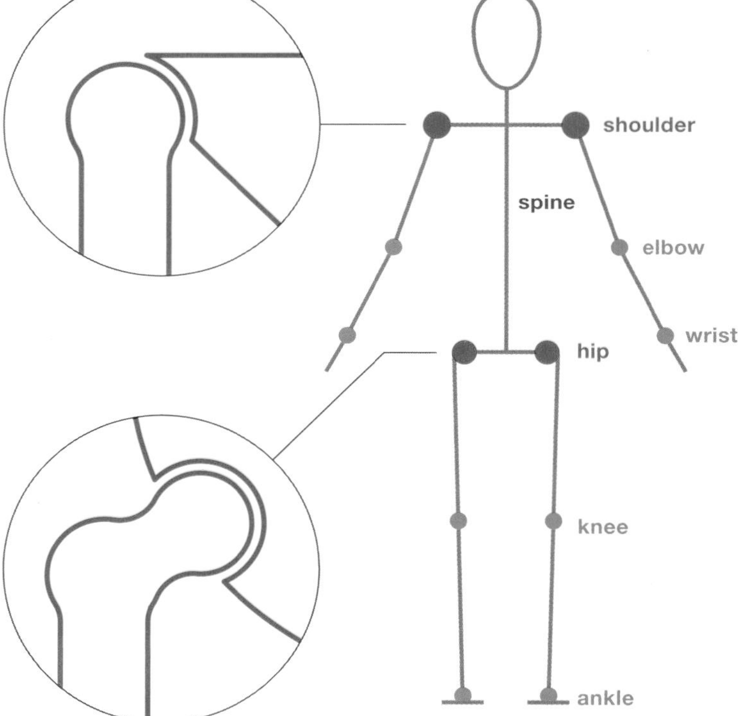

local coordinate system

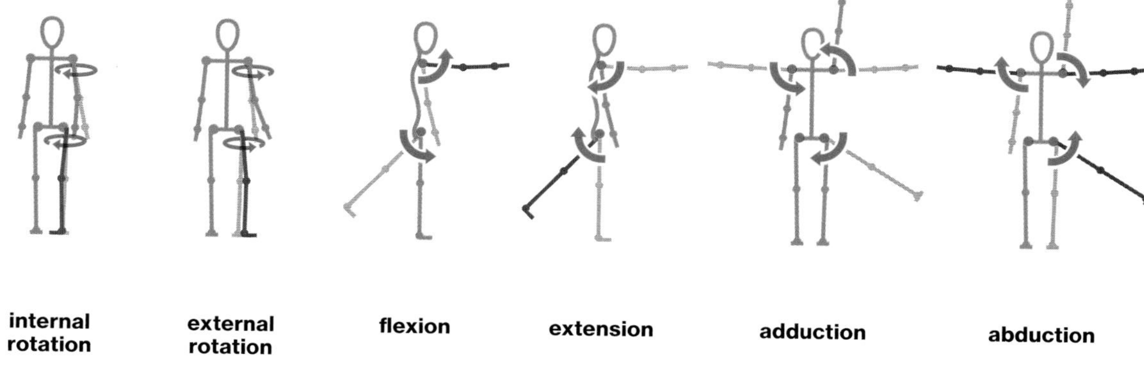

positions of joints

The position of a joint can be described based on three simple variables:

1. Internal/external rotation
2. Flexion/extension
3. Adduction/abduction

I did not invent this material, so you'll find definitions for these terms in many places, but I will explain the way I like to think of them.

I like to think about the joints' positions based on a body in the anatomical stance (page 53). From there, ***internal rotation*** is motion that rotates the joint toward the midline, and ***external rotation*** rotates the joint away from the midline. ***Flexion*** closes the angle of the joint with respect to the midline, and ***extension*** opens up the angle. ***Adduction*** brings your limbs toward the midline of your body. Adduction can happen in different planes of motion. For example, it occurs in the frontal plane in a jumping jack, when your arms move to your sides and over your head. It can also occur in the transverse plane, such as when you reach out and bring your arms in to grab something directly in front of you. Finally, ***abduction*** brings your limbs away from the midline of your body. Abduction can happen in different planes, just like adduction, but in precisely the opposite manner.

These three variables define a nice coordinate system for explaining the positions that the body's extremities can adopt. Note that people commonly confuse a joint moving in the direction of a position with the joint being in a particular position—for example, the shoulder extending versus being in a position of extension, as shown in the figure above.

local examples

Let's look at the major joints in the body. Even though the joints move together to accomplish most tasks, these examples bias isolated joint motion.

extension

A Push-up starts in a position of shoulder extension and finishes in a position of shoulder flexion. Note that you are moving in the direction of flexion as you are coming out of the bottom of the Push-up, although you are in a position of extension.

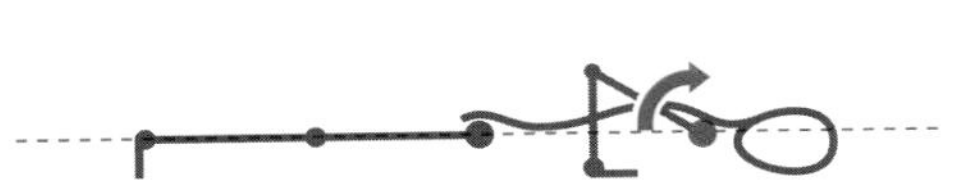

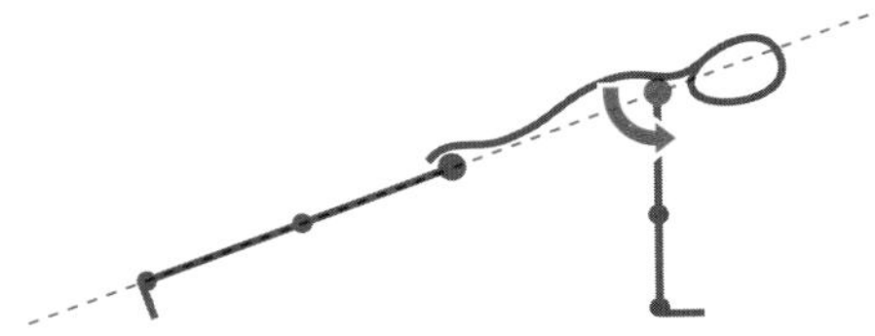

adduction

Adduction is the act of bringing your arms or legs toward the center line of your body. Adduction can happen in different planes of motion. In the jumping jack, it occurs in the frontal plane when your arms move to your sides and up over your head. Adduction can also happen in the transverse plane, when you reach forward to grab something directly in front of you.

abduction

Abduction is the act of bringing your arms or legs away from the center line of your body. Abduction can happen in different planes, just like adduction, but in the precise opposite manner.

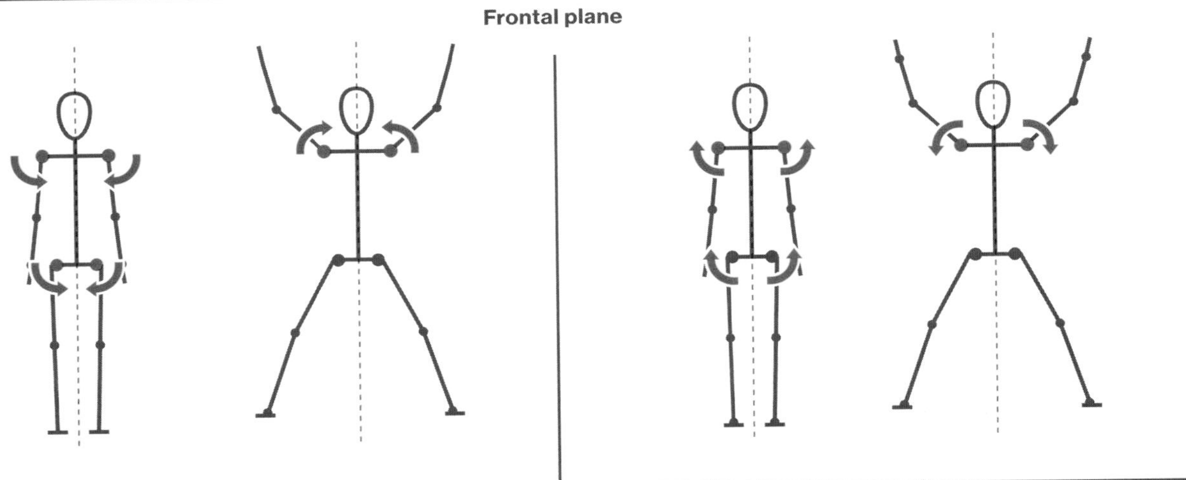

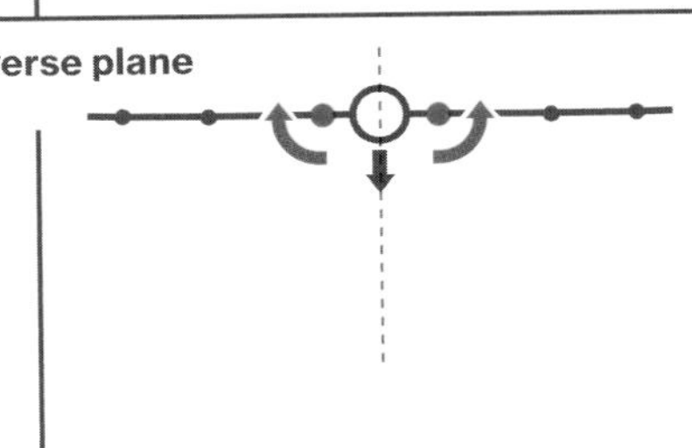

position hierarchy

When observing and describing how our bodies move, we should start at the spine and move out toward the extremities, or start from the global level and move to the local level. As discussed previously, starting at the global level focuses us on the overall shape of the body based on the midline. Starting this way is also key for creating safe and effective progressions, or methods for learning movement. Progressions are one of the most important parts of this book and will be described in detail in chapter 3.

As stated earlier, when looking at the local (joint) level, we want to distinguish between primary and secondary movers. For example, as shown below, for a Push-up the primary mover is the shoulder and the secondary movers are the elbow and wrist, and for a Squat the primary mover is the hip and the secondary movers are the knee and ankle.

Looking at movement from a global approach enables you to focus on the midline of your body and on movement control. A local approach gives you details on what a movement looks like at joint level and how to relate one movement to another, even if they do not appear similar at first. While these two approaches can be talked about separately, I always consider global and local together when describing a movement.

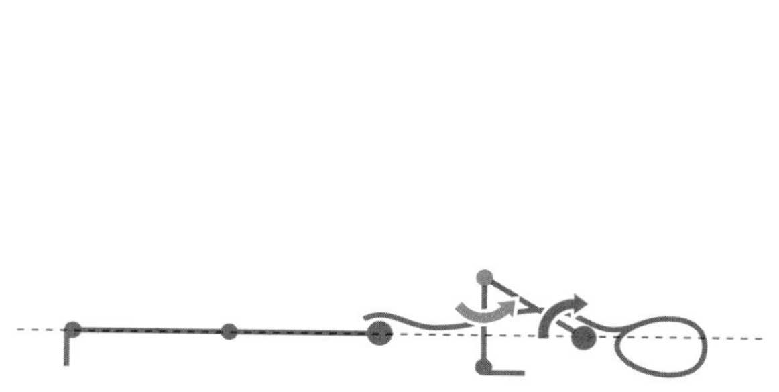

The Push-up shows the primary mover at the shoulder, putting you in global extension. The secondary mover is at the elbow, putting it in local flexion.

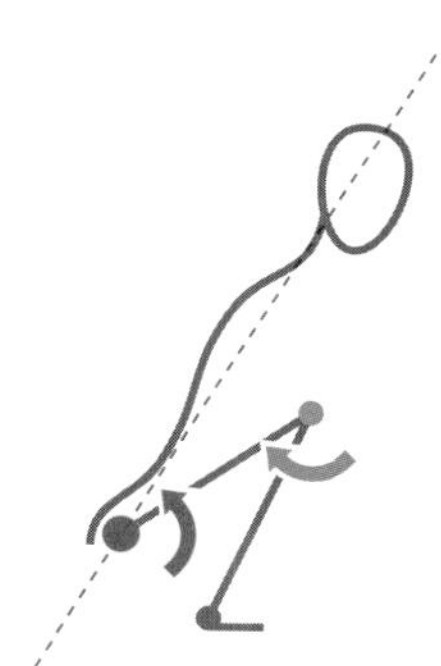

The Squat shows the primary mover at the hip, putting you in global flexion. The secondary mover is at the knee, putting it in local flexion.

In the previous section, we began our study of movement by looking at the global and local positions of the body. The human body does not remain at rest, however; we are always in motion. So this section focuses on how the body moves from one position to the next. To get us started, I will use four simple approaches to observe and describe movement:

1. Start-Transition-Finish (STF)
2. Pushing and Pulling
3. Shift-Connect-Flow (SCF)
4. Functional Movement

In the Start-Transition-Finish approach, start, transition, and finish are the major positions the body goes through as it moves. Using these three positions to anchor a complex movement pattern helps us understand what we observe and create better progressions.

Next, a look at pushing and pulling mechanics helps us understand how we move without getting too bogged down in biomechanics and anatomy.

We cannot fully appreciate how we move without understanding the body's relationship to its environment. The Shift-Connect-Flow (SCF) approach helps us understand how gravity interacts with the body's center of mass and base of support to create unique expressions. This approach is especially helpful for creating and developing new movement patterns.

Finally, we can all agree that we are interested in "functioning" well, and the term "functional movement" has been kicked around the fitness industry for quite a while. I will conclude this section of the chapter with my definition of functional fitness and my perspective on a universal approach to prioritizing movement.

start-transition-finish

Any movement, such as standing up, picking up a child, brushing your teeth, or driving a car, can be broken down into master positions, which are the most critical shapes that the body goes through while performing that movement. The master positions are start, transition, and finish.

Take, for example, sitting down in a chair and standing back up, which is a style of squatting. In order to do it, your body must go through the three master positions.

The start position is important because it is the only shape that you have the opportunity to set up for good movement and performance. It is also not influenced by the other positions. Errors in the setup are normally exaggerated (sometimes exponentially) in the transition and especially in the finish.

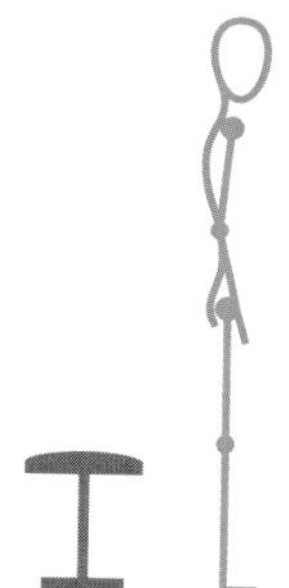

1. Start

The first shape you get into before performing a movement. Here, it's the standing position.

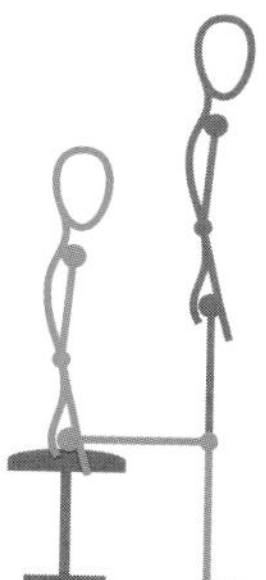

2. Transition

A signature shape that you adopt within the movement, often at the midpoint, between the start and finish positions. Here, it's the sitting position on the chair.

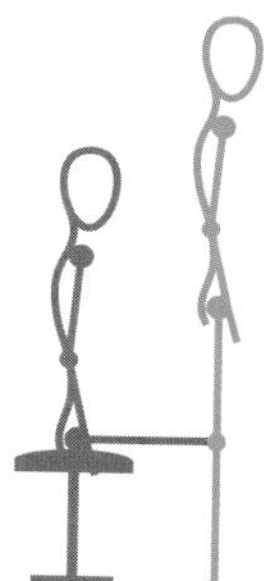

3. Finish

The shape in which you end up. Here, it happens to be the same as the start (standing) position.

The transition is the most important position, as it often helps differentiate one type of movement from another. For example, the difference between a Squat and a Deadlift is best explained by the transition position of each movement. Even though these movements serve different purposes, they share many common traits from a local (joint) perspective; for example, the hips and knees flex and extend, and the ankles dorsiflex and plantarflex. Despite these local similarities, in the transition position the hips are below the knees in the Squat and above the knees in the Deadlift.

As another example, walking and running differ in that walking always has one foot on the ground during the transition, while running has no feet touching the ground during the transition.

Studying the transition position doesn't just help us differentiate movements; it also helps us find key similarities between them. As a strength and conditioning coach, I care about finding similarities because I want to be able to take any movement seen outside the gym and relate it to any movement that can be trained in the gym. And the best place to start is to match up movements based on their transition positions. For example, running can easily be matched up with squatting, as the hip, knee, and ankle functions in the transitions correspond.

It's also in the transition where things go wrong. For example, knees usually cave in at the bottom of a Squat. And athletes miss their Muscle-up somewhere between the pull and the dip. So when it comes to helping you move better, movement progressions must focus on these crucial sticky spots. This is a big focus of chapter 2.

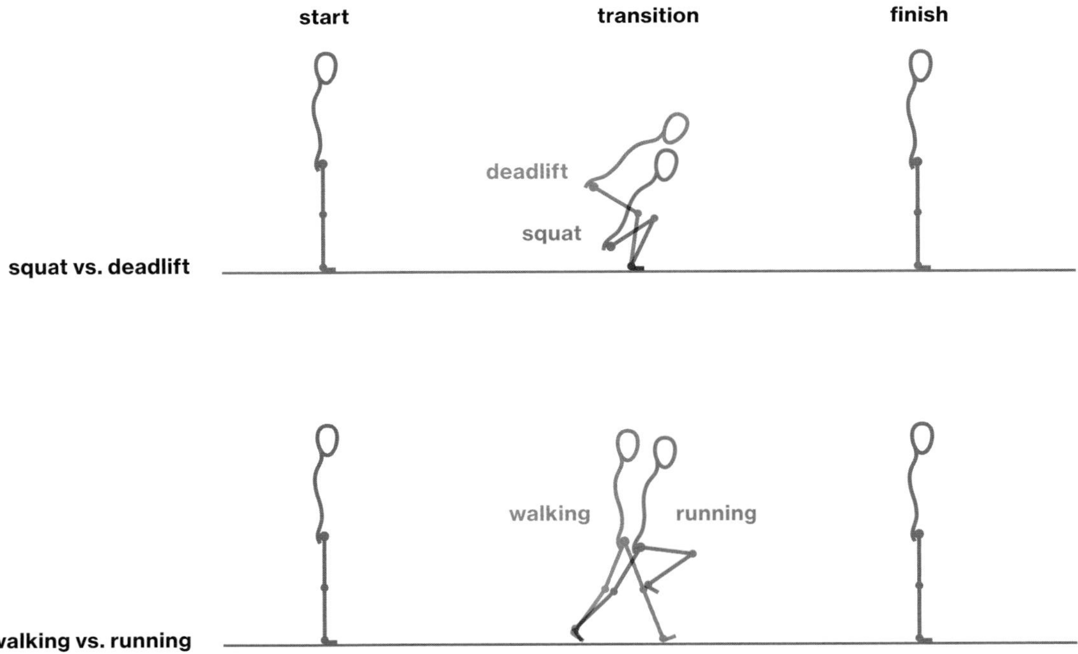

in the world

in the gym

study the transition

When looking at movements outside the gym, such as running, it is helpful to use Start-Transition-Finish as a way to identify the positions the body goes through and how they relate to movements seen in the gym.

In this running example, Sticks' arms swing from front to back. This swing can be looked at from a pushing and pulling perspective in the gym. The most obvious pushing movement you could use to develop the arm swing would be the Push-up, and for pulling it would be the Ring Row. As the arms swing from front to back during the run, they also alternate, creating a rotational component and a single-arm movement if you look at it from one side of the body or the other. In the gym, a One-Arm Push-up mimics and helps develop the independent arm movement and rotational forces created around the body.

The lower body works the same way. In this case, the Squat could be used as a way to further develop the basic lower-body mechanics, a Pistol or single-leg Squat to develop the single-leg movement and the challenges created by the rotational forces during running, and finally an Olympic lift to improve the hip extension and explosiveness required to run faster, longer, and stronger.

The finish position of a movement can be used to diagnose what happened during the start and the transition. For example, while performing a heavy Snatch, if your hips rise first, the bar will likely shoot forward, with the bar received in front. This forward finish position tells you most of what you were missing in the transition: you lacked external rotation and stability at the hips, so your hips shot upward, looking for the muscular tension required for you to stand.

So, by studying these master positions, we can break down any movement into its most essential parts. As you will see in chapter 2, this breakdown becomes especially useful when we are developing how best to learn a movement.

If an Olympic weightlifter performing a Snatch loses position by lifting his hips before his shoulders during the first pull, the path of the bar deviates away from the body, which could cause the lifter to miss the lift or even cause injury.

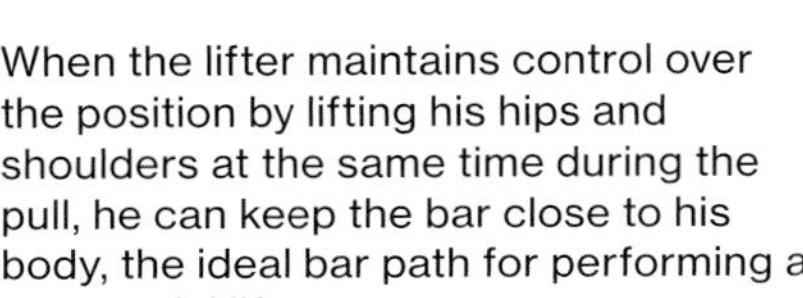

When the lifter maintains control over the position by lifting his hips and shoulders at the same time during the pull, he can keep the bar close to his body, the ideal bar path for performing a successful lift.

it's not always what it looks like

On one of my visits to the C.A.R. de Madrid (the Olympic training facility) in Spain, I had the opportunity to sit in on a gymnastics national team training session and saw one of my childhood friends working on his floor routine. He was having problems with his takeoff while performing a tumbling pass. He kept jumping off to the side rather than straight up, and his coach kept cuing him on the takeoff. The coach was yelling out instructions, such as "arms up" or "take off first, then flip."

After watching my friend struggle to correct his takeoff, I noticed that the problem didn't lie in the actual takeoff position, but instead in the movements leading up to the takeoff. As he initiated his tumbling pass, he was placing one leg at an angle that enabled him to enter the pass at a higher speed and with more power. Although this gave him the sensation of better performance, this subtle angle shift led to his off-axis takeoff. Once he realized this, he was able to correct the angle of his leg in the movements leading up to the takeoff, and the problem was solved.

The finish position is great because it is the most obvious way to determine whether a movement was successful. Did the gymnast land correctly on the tumbling pass, or did the weightlifter make the lift? Unfortunately, though, when the focus is drawn completely to the finish position, it is easy to lose track of the full movement from start to finish. This is especially problematic when dealing with complex movement patterns that involve sequences of multiple movement patterns. This was the case when my friend was having trouble with his takeoff. The Start-Transition-Finish approach helpfully reminds me to make educated decisions about where the finish position comes from by backing my focus away from the finish through the transition and back to the start.

pushing and pulling

When moving from one position to another, a complex sequence of musculoskeletal interactions occurs that could be described as the muscles elongating and contracting, resulting in tension differences that cause your skeleton to move. I like to simplify this complex biomechanical process by saying that either your extremities or your whole body is being pushed or pulled either away from you or toward you. Regardless of whether the body is pushing itself away from something or is pushing something away from itself, it can be called pushing.

Simply:

1. ***Pushing*** is the act of exerting force on something in order to move it away from yourself or the origin of the force.
2. ***Pulling*** is the act of exerting force on something in order to move it toward yourself or the origin of the force.

Pushing and pulling are the forces we use to change from one position to another. As we know from physics, forces are essential for movement. There are many complicated ways to describe all the forces that are in play during a movement, but I rely on a very simple way to name the two categories of forces: pushing and pulling. And this simple language for understanding the forces behind our movement can explain most movements seen in sport and life.

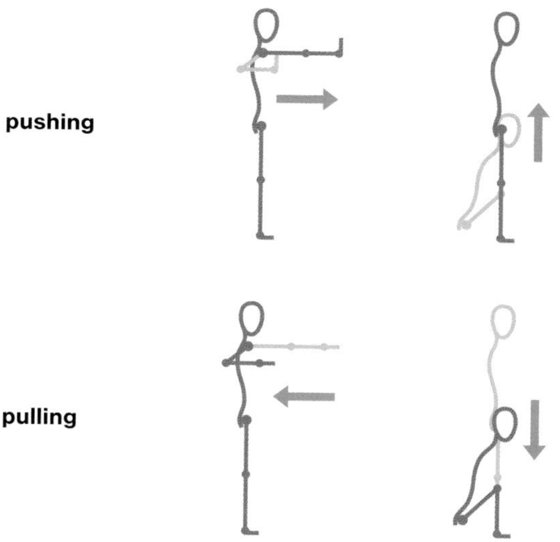

The concepts of pushing and pulling can get complicated, especially in the fitness industry, as the acts of pushing and pulling are usually associated with the upper body. Even though the lower body is also trained to push and pull, it is usually approached through hinging at the hip and squatting. This relates well to the importance that coach Dan John gives to pushing and pulling in both the upper and the lower body as seen in his five basic human movements—Push, Pull, Hinge, Squat, and Loaded Carry. As long as we remember that pushing is away from the body and pulling is toward the body, we can easily relate them to the upper and lower body and apply them to any movement pattern.

shift-connect-flow

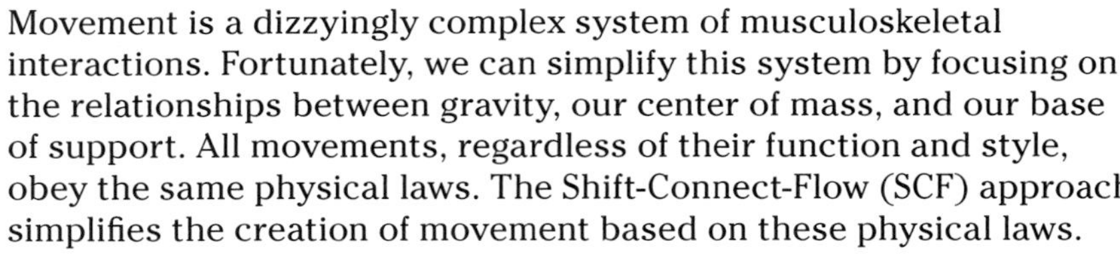

Movement is a dizzyingly complex system of musculoskeletal interactions. Fortunately, we can simplify this system by focusing on the relationships between gravity, our center of mass, and our base of support. All movements, regardless of their function and style, obey the same physical laws. The Shift-Connect-Flow (SCF) approach simplifies the creation of movement based on these physical laws.

shift

Shifting is the act of displacing your center of mass (your hips if standing) over your base of support (in this case, your feet) to create movement. Any movement involves this shift. An obvious example is walking. A more extreme example of this shift occurs when you use it to change orientation in space, as seen in gymnastics, where athletes create full revolutions around a point of contact or their center of mass.

We take for granted that gravity largely influences how we move through space, yet it is an extremely important tool to keep in mind while learning and developing new movement patterns. This will be explored further in chapter 2.

connect

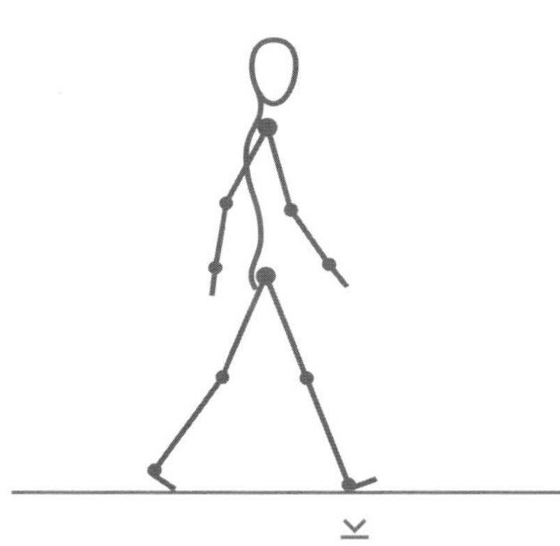

Connection refers to physical contact with an external object—for example, the ground, a piece of equipment, or even a cane. Because humans have evolved over millions of years under the influence of gravity, we have developed natural behaviors that are influenced by our environment—that is, the points of contact that our bodies have with the ground and the objects around us. The more points of contact or the larger the surface area of contact, the more stable and comfortable we feel.

Have you ever thought about why you sleep lying down? For this exact reason: when you lie down, your spine, which contains your central nervous system, doesn't have to be 100 percent protected by the muscles surrounding it, allowing you to relax. You are in a more stable position due to the high amount of contact you have with the surface area of your bed.

Why is running a more advanced movement than walking? Because walking has a constant point of contact with the ground, while running has a moment of no connection, making the body more unstable and thus requiring a higher level of movement control.

This increasing complexity introduced by changes in connectivity is a key topic that will be discussed further in chapter 2. Basically, more points of contact equate to greater stability.

flow

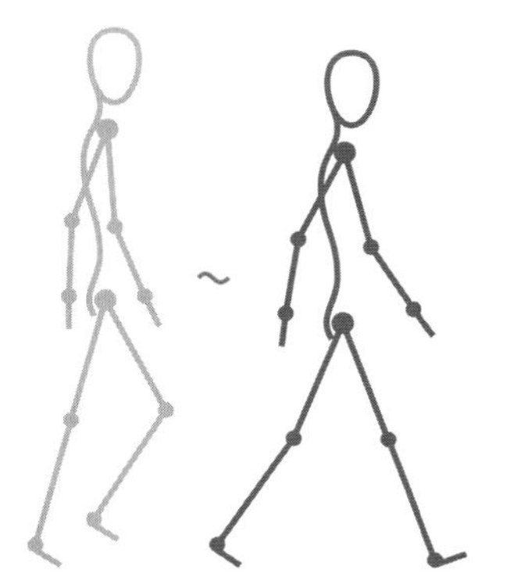

Flow describes steady and continuous movement. It is commonly expressed as rhythm, tempo, efficiency, or cyclic movement. The way I look at it, flow is the ability to recycle a movement over and over again for as long and as efficiently as possible.

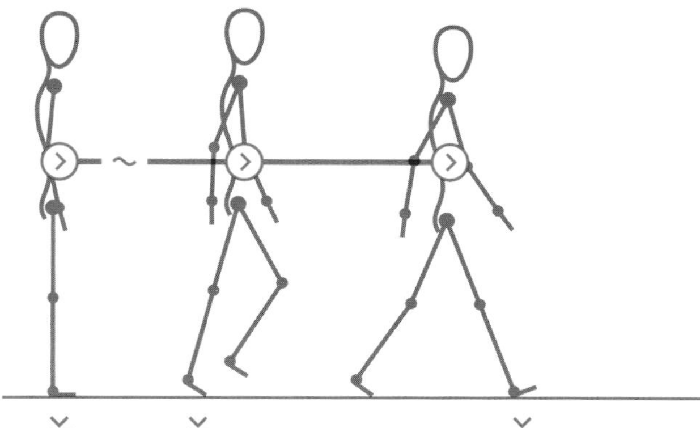

walking: Walking starts in a static position, with both feet on the ground. To start the movement, a shift of the center of mass occurs, which causes a controlled fall of the body over the front edge of the base of support. In order to walk rather than fall, one foot is lifted off the ground, creating a change in connection with the ground. The foot that leaves the ground moves forward until it reaches a point where it can reconnect with the ground and create the next base of support over which the center of mass will have to shift. As this cycle repeats itself over and over, having a fluid motion is key for efficiency. This style of Shift-Connect-Flow showcases no change in direction of the shift.

standing up out of a chair: Just as in the walking example, in order to start the movement of standing up out of a chair, there has to be a forward shift of the center of mass toward the feet. As the body shifts the center of mass by bending in the hips and leaning forward, it gets to a point where most of the weight is over the feet and the hips come off the chair, changing the points of connection. As this happens, the legs simultaneously push away from the ground in order to finish the stand, causing the shift of the center of mass to change to a more vertical direction to finish in a balanced standing position. This style of Shift-Connect-Flow showcases a change in direction during the shift.

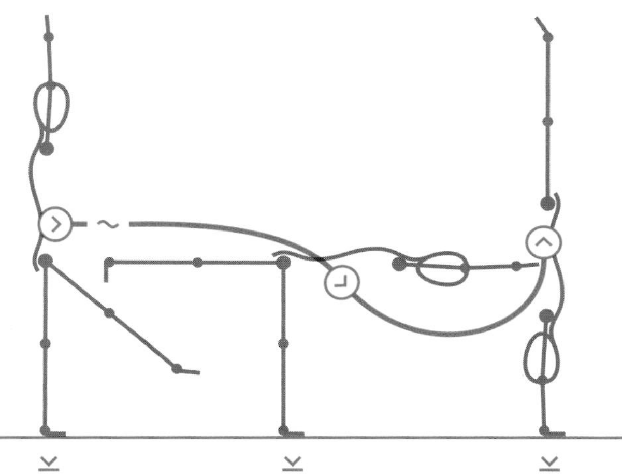

kick up to handstand: Kicking up to a Handstand is an example that combines the two previous examples. The first part of the movement requires a forward shift followed by a hinge in the hips, which causes the shift to curve downward. As the inversion of the body occurs, the shift changes direction again when the hands reach the ground in order to move away from the ground in a vertical fashion to finish in a balanced Handstand position. This style of Shift-Connect-Flow showcases multiple changes in direction during the shift.

balance in motion

Shifting has a lot to do with the concept of balance, but when shifting your center of mass in relation to your base of support, the balance is dynamic. For example, standing takes balance, as it requires you to keep your center of mass completely static on top of your base of support. While walking or running, you continuously shift your center of mass on top of a constantly moving base of support underneath it, which requires balance in motion.

Flow is being able to perform the shift of your center of mass in relation to your base of support while changing points of contact with the surfaces around you in a fluid manner.

functional movement

When I first started coaching, functional movement was the big trend in the fitness industry. Each discipline, whether it was kettlebell training, TRX, or even BodyPump, would advertise its "functional" training benefits. But the big question is, what exactly is functional movement? A lot of definitions exist, such as "movement that goes from core to extremity," "multi-joint movement," "movement that applies to daily life," and "moving large loads, long distances, quickly." All these definitions are great, but I don't think they quite capture the true meaning of functional movement.

For me, there are three aspects that define functional movement:

1. ***Safe:*** You must be able to perform the movement and finish unharmed.
2. ***Useful:*** The movement must help you achieve a goal.
3. ***Long-lasting:*** The movement must be the most efficient way to perform a task.

I will describe each of these aspects individually, but it's important to recognize that they overlap and depend on one another. For instance, a long-lasting movement such as walking often is considered to have high degrees of safety and usefulness.

safe

Sal Masekela, a good friend, athlete, inspiration, and mentor of mine, once told me a story about training to hold his breath underwater for safer big-wave surfing. It is common for surfers to be held underwater from ten to upwards of thirty seconds, which can feel like an eternity. Breath-holding is a critical, lifesaving skill for all big-wave surfers. After several sessions with his buddies, Sal's lung capacity and breath-holding ability had improved. But he felt limited by a lack of oxygen and the inevitable biological alarm that would go off after around two minutes, telling him to breathe at all costs.

It wasn't until his more experienced peers encouraged him to work through that desperate feeling of discomfort that he made another attempt to go longer. They asked him to take a premeditated, conscious risk to push past that two-minute biological alarm to breathe. When that feeling came again and Sal simply would not let his body give in, it was like a switch had been flipped. It was as if his body had walked into a new room where he was suddenly filled with more oxygen. At that moment, he realized that he had a far greater capacity than he thought, which ultimately gave him the confidence and sense of calm to blow by his previous record.

My number-one priority as a coach is the health and well-being of the people I work with. Anytime we try to improve human performance, there is inherent risk. Deliberately pushing past your biological alarm to breathe, as seen in Sal's story, can be quite dangerous. But when Sal practiced, he made sure that he was surrounded by experienced athletes and coaches who guided him. They knew CPR, and they practiced in the controlled environment of a swimming pool—in other words, they had an appropriate safety protocol. Ultimately, they helped him understand, accept, and mitigate the inherent risk of deliberate breath-holding. Remember, it is the coach's job to make sure that the athlete both feels comfortable with the amount of risk he is taking and is capable of continually improving the assessment of that risk.

Pushing the limits of human performance always involves some discomfort. This feeling of discomfort can act as either a limiter of your current capacity or an indicator of pain and future harm. Fortunately, through experience and knowledge, you can assess this signal and make an informed decision. Being able to understand the differences between mere discomfort and potential harm is critical for anyone trying to improve their physical performance over the long term.

Sal's story demonstrates that even though safety is our number-one concern, having an experienced coach and group of people to work with helps you simultaneously control risks and push your limits. If you learn to observe and describe your current state as well as the next state that you might be capable of, you can more easily chart a path to get there.

useful

As a young gymnast, when my gymnastics facility closed for the summer, I spent my summer strength-training sessions at a bodybuilding gym. One day, my program involved a set of elbow extensions to build my triceps. As I pulled on the rope attached to a cable, extending my arms from chest to hips, a large man approached and said, "Hey, kid, flatten out your back." I turned my head around my caved back and gave him a "Who are you?" look. He said, "Yes, I know you are a gymnast. You need to think and look like a gymnast performing while you train." Basically, he was saying that every movement has to transfer, or at least has to look like the other movements you care about and want to improve.

A movement is useful if it helps you achieve a goal. To do so, a useful movement should give you information about the progress you are making toward your goal. Say I am an Olympic weightlifter, and I am squatting in order to get stronger. The Squat is useful because it improves my squatting mechanics in the Clean and the Snatch. Squatting helps me measure my progress toward this goal because I can quantify it. In fact, many people look at their squatting weight to determine their potential in the Olympic lifts. By using the positional and movement approaches (Global-Local, Start-Transition-Finish, and Shift-Connect-Flow), it is easy to see the high degree of overlap between the Olympic lifts and the Squat.

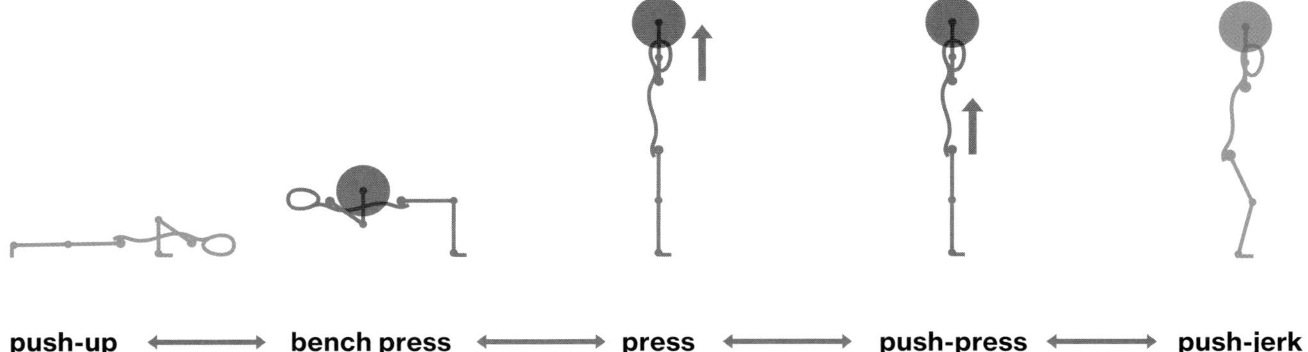

The Push-up offers a simpler expression of the same pushing mechanics seen in advanced pushing movements, such as the Push-Jerk in Olympic weightlifting. Understanding the basics of pushing mechanics is useful for creating progressions that can help improve your movement patterns and also for observing inefficiencies.

One of the movements in Olympic weightlifting is the Jerk, where the barbell travels from the shoulders to a locked-out overhead position. Interestingly, even though many talented Olympic weightlifters have high numbers in the Jerk, if you examine their Push-ups or Pull-ups, you can easily spot inefficiencies and dysfunctions in their basic movement patterns. These same inefficiencies likely appear in the Jerk because of the high degree of overlap in the positions and mechanics of the movements. But while the Jerk is complex and lightning quick, the Push-up is a simpler expression of the same mechanics and therefore is a great way to observe inefficiencies, improve movement patterns, and measure progress toward the weightlifter's goal.

We all diagnose problems around what we know, and usefulness may mean different things to different people based on our goals and backgrounds. This chapter will help you grow your ability to observe and describe movement in order to more closely match it to your goals.

long-lasting

Anyone watching a top-level athlete perform has probably said at some point, "Wow, that person is really efficient." But how do you really know how efficient an individual is? Do you examine her energy expenditure? Are we all biomechanics experts? Or is there something about efficiency that simply looks and feels right?

The word efficiency is thrown around a lot in the fitness and sports industries. But to what is it referring? Well, efficiency is usually used to describe top performers—those who perform at the highest levels, with high success rates and low injury rates. These individuals usually look good during their performance, too. We naturally see what looks good or bad and use it to gauge efficiency. But you need to understand the best way to perform a specific movement in order to address its efficiency. In this book, I focus on the physical and mechanical aspects rather than the physiological and psychological aspects of efficiency, using the language of movement found in this chapter. They all tie in together.

When looking at a movement, you may naturally ask, "What is the most efficient way to do it?"—or, in other words, "What's the fastest way to get from point A to point B?" To figure this out, you may find it important to ask more specific questions: Are you carrying a large load? What is the distance? What is the time requirement? These varying demands suggest that one style of movement may be more efficient than another. They can even lead to something new, such as when new demands or a renewed understanding of existing demands result in brand-new styles of movement! This is where efficiency leads to innovation.

The most functional movement for a task is the one that you can do over and over again for a lifetime. Interestingly, we all have a natural ability to recognize this efficiency, even if we can't explain it. Sometimes, though, recognition alone isn't enough to further develop a movement; you need to deliberately work on a movement's development. I will discuss the relationship between long-lasting movements and progression in chapter 3.

functional movement summary

Say I'm installing a wood floor in my house. I have the wood and a bunch of nails to hammer it in and keep the floor together. As I start hammering the nails into the wood, I naturally tend to hit straight on the nailhead to drive each nail directly down. Depending on my experience and the amount of force I can apply, it will take me more or fewer hits to drive each nail all the way down. If I don't hit the nail straight on its head, though, the nail could bend or break, and the floor wouldn't look as good or last as long.

Because we all want to live longer, perform better, and feel good, we must optimize the way we move. I like to look at functional movement as the hammer and nails in this story. When faced with a task (installing the floor), I prioritize safety in order to avoid harming myself. I have a specific reason for performing a movement (hammering the nail) in order to guarantee utility (a finished floor), and I focus on how to perform this movement efficiently (straight hammering for a stable and durable floor). The goal is always to chase the best way, not the most familiar way. Maintaining this relationship between functionality and health helps you map out the optimal way to do something. Keep in mind that every movement is a functional movement as long as it fulfills these three criteria: it is safe, it serves a purpose, and it is long-lasting.

Everyone has a reason to move. You may be sitting down in a chair at your office, getting into your car, or using the act of sitting as a training tool (squatting) to get stronger and fitter. The reason for and style of sitting/squatting may be different, but the general movement as described in this chapter is the same.

The act of squatting is general. We could say that it is the act of lowering the body to the ground by bending the hips, knees, and ankles without the rest of the body touching the ground. Squatting becomes very specific, however, when we inject the concept of purpose. Purpose defines a style of movement. Let's take three squatting styles as examples: powerlifting, Olympic-style weightlifting, and the Poop in Woods Squat (see illustrations on the opposite page).

There is a great deal of overlap between these three squatting styles, but the specifics of each one are very different. The differences are derived from their different purposes. As simple as this concept may be, I see coaches, athletes, and health practitioners get caught up in arguing about who is right, who is wrong, and what is the best way to perform a movement all the time. Especially in the strength and conditioning world, egos fly high, with everyone believing that they have found the perfect way of performing each movement. Truth be told, they may be doing nothing wrong and may even be getting amazing results. But is there really only one way to perform a movement? Is it one style among and above many? Or could it be a style of the movement that is a part of the movement's constant evolution? You must keep these questions in mind if you want to break down the walls of dogma, benefit from all styles of movement, and enhance your individual performance needs.

As a good friend and former athlete of mine always says, "Everyone is right, everyone is wrong." The purpose defines the movement, and the body adapts to it. This mental model of Position-Movement-Purpose plays an important role in my coaching career. If you can learn to see movement for its purpose, you will succeed not only in seeing further down the line of the development of all movement, but also in adding value to your sport, your community, and yourself.

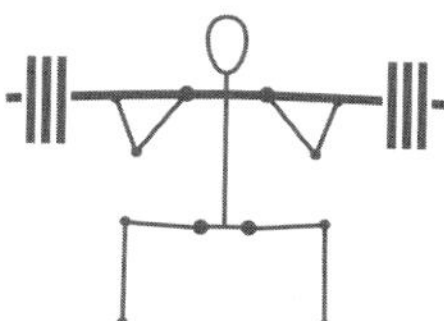

powerlifting

The style adopted is a wide stance, with the knees over the ankles, the bar racked on the shoulders behind the head, and the chest in an upright position for the best line to apply force. The purpose of this style is to take the heaviest possible amount of weight on your back while going from standing to squatting position and back for one repetition.

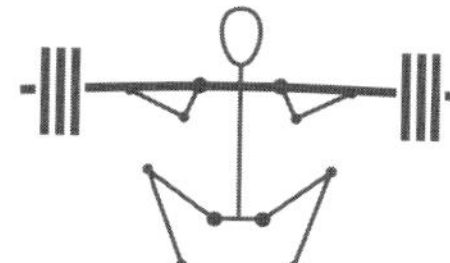

olympic weightlifting

Here the stance is narrower, the knees track outside the ankles, and the bar is racked on the shoulders in front of the head. The purpose of this Squat is to pick the heaviest possible weight off the ground into either a front rack or an overhead position. This style gives lifters the increased range of motion needed to apply the most force for this purpose.

poop in woods squat

The back may be rounded so that the butt can drop much closer to the ankles, and the feet are far enough apart to avoid the mess. The purpose of this Squat is to poop, and, believe it or not, these mechanics allow the body to relax so that the poop comes out more easily.

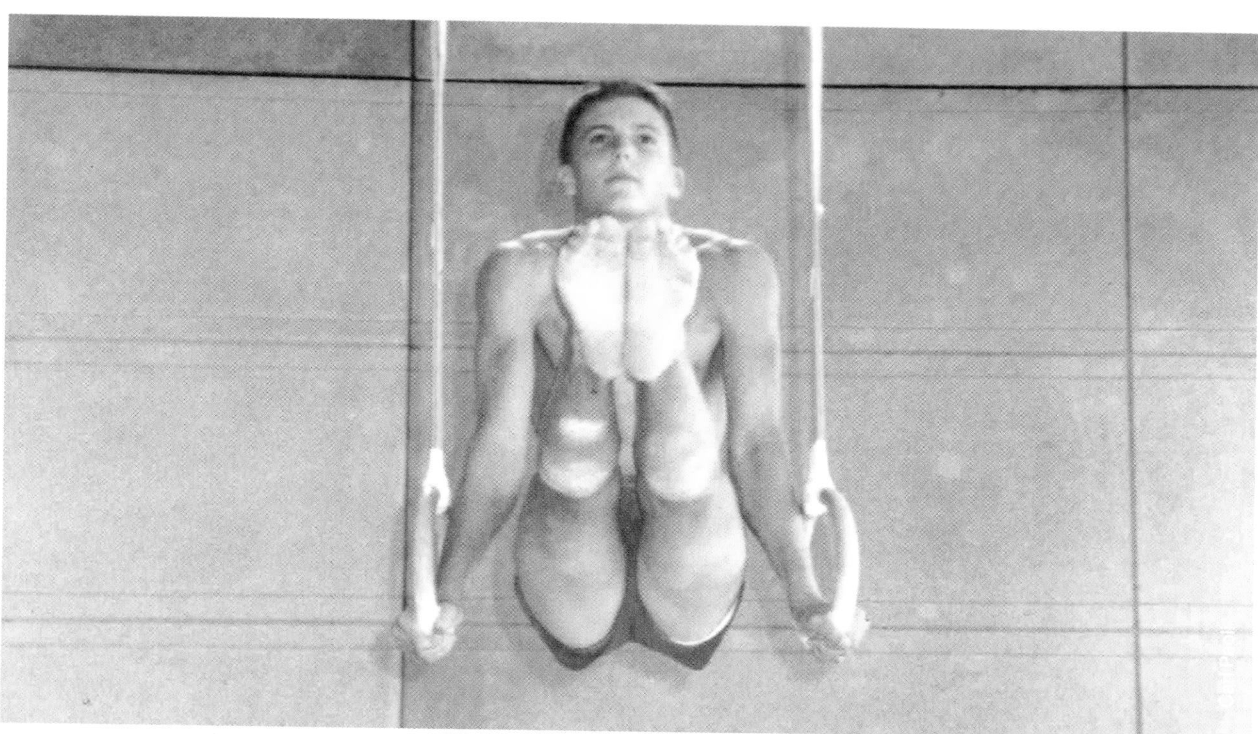

When I look at movement styles across different sports, I believe that the standards for those movements can typically be determined by three characteristics:

1. The mechanics are safe and efficient.
2. They fit a point system that encourages optimal performance.
3. They succeed aesthetically and "look sexy."

For example, let's examine why gymnasts turn their hands out when they support themselves on the rings, as shown in the photo above. This is the anatomically safest, most stable, and most efficient position for supporting the body on the rings. It is the best way to avoid touching the straps that hold the rings with any part of the body other than the hands, which is part of proper execution of ring work as stated in the gymnastics code of points, and at the same time it happens to be the most aesthetically pleasing body position to be in, representing power and grace.

This doesn't happen just in the sport of gymnastics, but in other games and sports as well. If you stop and look at these three characteristics, they tend to show up in every discipline—and if they don't, it may be time to rethink the way that discipline is performed.

movement ability

02

"When you want to move, you're moving." —Bruce Lee

We all want to be able—physically capable of doing many different things. I think this drive is best summarized in a three-layer model that describes our desire to improve our ability to move. These three layers make sense especially when you look at the industries that have been created to help us develop them.

health / wellness / well-being: Well-being is everyone's number-one priority. We want to feel good and hope to live long lives. This is a field in which we see many health practitioners—doctors, physical therapists, chiropractors, and massage therapists, to name a few—offering solutions. They are the students of human health and longevity, and their goal is to help us make better decisions at both the personal and the community level to maximize our time on this planet and feel like we are in control of our lives.

fitness: The fitness industry is focused on achieving and maintaining health. Exercise has always been a part of our lives, but the fitness field didn't become important until the human population developed into a formalized society in which the physical requirements of day-to-day living were vastly diminished. The resulting sedentary lifestyle has led to the creation of a more formalized way of developing and maintaining our physical culture.

athletics / sport: As physical education developed beyond the need to prepare for war or for natural threats, play became a tradition, and sports came into existence. We can consider athletics our ability to apply the health we achieve through fitness to specific tasks. Traditionally, we think of athletics as being related to sports, but in daily life, athletics is really the ability to respond to random physical demands—for example, having an object thrown at you without warning and being able to duck before it hits you, or tripping and falling and rolling out of it without getting hurt.

BBoy Kid David – Photo by Glen Co Photography

Isaac's story

Beyond understanding what motivates us to move well, we also need ways to assess how physically capable we are. Some sports, gymnastics in particular, try to come up with rigorous definitions in order to compare athletes' abilities. Despite our intuitive sense of movement ability, establishing clear definitions is actually quite challenging.

A good friend of mine, Isaac Botella, is someone who can move very well. As an accomplished member of the Spanish gymnastics team, Isaac won many national and European championships, even placing sixth in the vault event in the 2008 Olympics. But on the rings, the category he was most known for, Isaac felt that something was missing.

One day, I was hanging out with Isaac during one of his practice sessions, and he casually mentioned to me that there were certain elements on the rings that he couldn't do. Specifically, he was bothered by not having the inverted cross. To a non-gymnast, this feat may seem impossible, but in men's gymnastics it is a common skill, and a person at Isaac's level should have it mastered. The really unfortunate part is that, despite all the accolades Isaac had accumulated, this missing piece negatively affected his psyche and how he measured his own ability to move. Beyond that, he felt that he might simply have weak or incapable shoulders that made him an inferior gymnast, especially after having two major shoulder surgeries.

I asked Isaac to show me his Push-up. He performed several strong Push-ups with the ease that you would expect from any well-trained gymnast, but I noticed something that seemed dysfunctional in his basic shoulder pushing movement pattern. To test this theory, I placed him in a position that would expose the possibly faulty mechanics. From this position, Isaac couldn't do a single Push-up! An elite gymnast was unable to access this fundamental movement pattern.

As I hope you are learning by now (and you will learn specifically in chapter 5), there are many ways to perform a Push-up, but the style I asked him to attempt contains an essential movement pattern that is required to perform the higher-level movements he was lacking on the rings. After pinpointing this potential hole in his basic movement mechanics, I went on to show him how it connected to the inverted cross and other ring movements.

A few months later, after the 2012 Olympics, Isaac and I were chatting, and he brought up that he wished he had worked on training this basic movement pattern earlier, because it had made a significant difference in how strong his shoulders felt through many advanced movements. He also wondered if focusing on basic movement patterns later in his career would have enabled him to go further or avoid setbacks like the surgeries. In gymnastics (and many other sports), advanced athletes end up focusing almost entirely on performing very specific movement patterns for their sport and then assisting them with equally specific movement patterns to further develop them. For example, while training to do an Iron Cross, a gymnast typically assists that movement pattern with a gym variation of a cable fly that mimics it. These athletes often overlook how crucial holes in basic movement patterns can be when performing the most advanced movements and don't give those basic movement patterns nearly as much attention as they deserve.

The most fulfilling part of this story for me was that I was able to help my friend, even for a moment, regain his vision of his amazing movement ability. It even inspired him to see further toward another level of untapped performance.

This story also helps me define fitness. I define it as the ability to move in order to accomplish the specific tasks that make us successful in sport and in life. In Isaac's case, many people would have used his gymnastics medals to conclude that he was a success. But success is measured both by others' observations and our own internal feelings, and Isaac had not yet satisfied his internal standards.

This simple definition helps me address a common question that is asked throughout the fitness world: Who is fitter, stronger, or more skilled? Is it the powerlifter who can squat 500 pounds, or the gymnast who can perform seemingly impossible feats of bodyweight control, or maybe an insanely fast sprinter, or perhaps a tireless long-distance runner? At first, you may believe that I am avoiding the question. But because I define fitness as the ability to move to perform a specific task, fitness simply cannot be compared across disciplines. This question can't be answered, because fitness depends on the task you care to use to define your success, and the ultimate measure of success is whether you can perform that task. Did you run a sub-three-hour marathon? Did you squat 500 pounds? Then you are fit for your purpose.

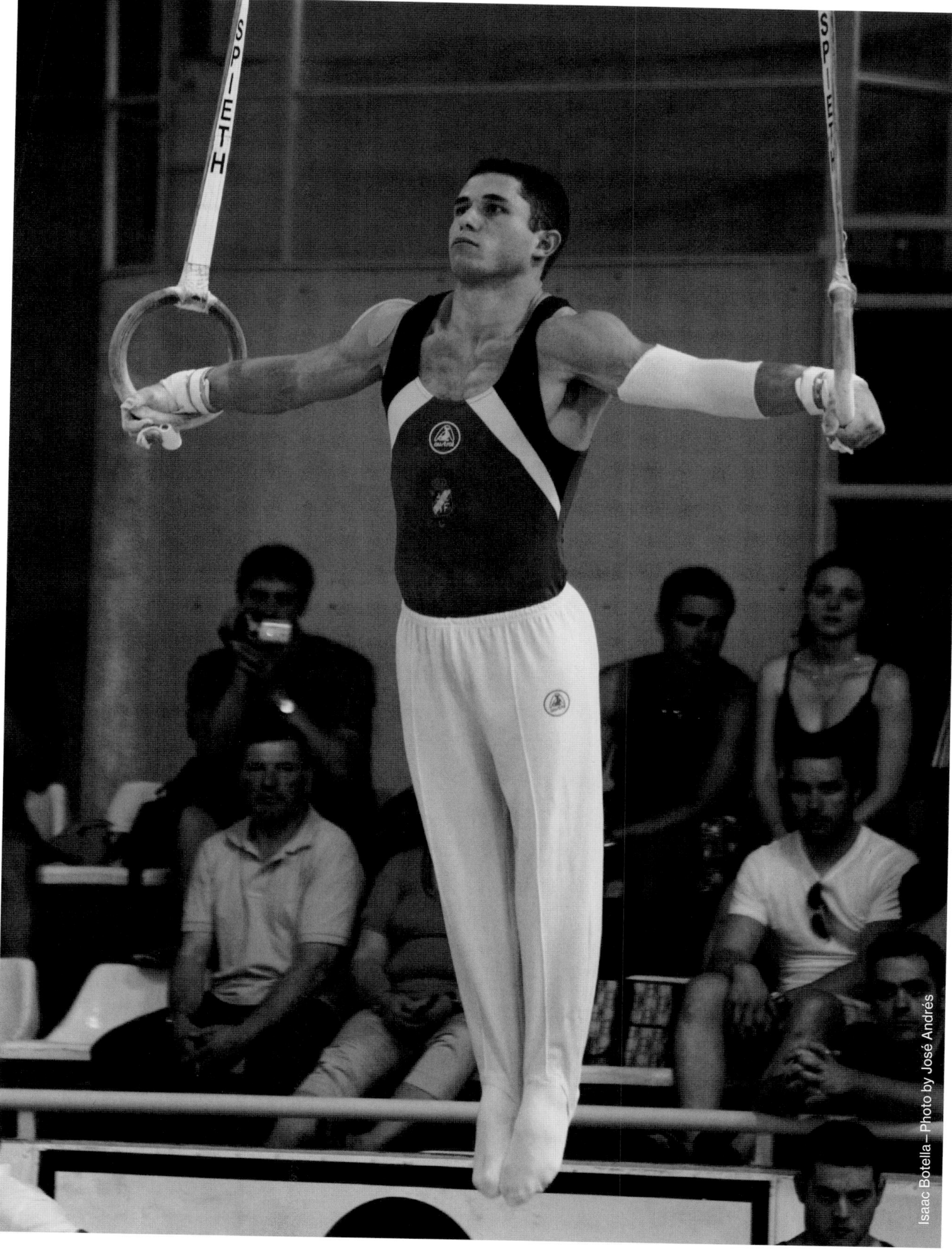

Isaac Botella—Photo by José Andrés

When I talk about movement ability, I avoid comparing different athletes' life pursuits. This perspective is useful for building progressions to make you successful at what you care about. As you will learn in chapter 3, progressions are all about breaking down movements into stages that take you from one level of ability to the next. When developing progressions, I always look at the task being performed in terms of movements that you are already capable of and ones that are slightly beyond your current capabilities.

In fitness—and really any field—we get carried away with measurements that are easy to acquire rather than ones that say something meaningful about our goal. I see so many athletes get caught up in shaving time off a clock or adding a pound to a bar without thinking about the movement ability they need to get closer to the movements that define success for them.

In this chapter, I describe how to measure your ability to move in a way that allows you to focus on your progress toward your individual goals. In the first section, I explain the difference between form and movement control. Following that, I discuss movement strength, which I define as the physiological capacity to move. Next, I introduce skill, which I define as the ability to apply that physiological capacity through movement performance. Finally, I define skill transfer as the ability to use the foundation of movement strength and skill that you have developed on some movements and apply them to other movements, sports, or disciplines. Even though most of us can observe human movement and intuitively know what movement ability is, my goal is to help you know why and how to move better through training.

I don't care what you do as long as you know why you are doing it.

Two of the most common words used to assess the quality of a movement observed in the gym or a sport are ***form*** and ***control.*** I like to think of form as the optimal technique and mechanics of a movement and control as the ability to execute those mechanics properly. Being able to perform a movement with form and control is like saying that you have mastered that movement.

Chapter 1 is devoted to observing and describing what I refer to as form. When describing control, many fitness experts look to motor control, or the process by which the nervous system stimulates the muscles and allows them to fire, contract, and move the skeleton. I prefer a more pragmatic approach that I call movement control: the understanding, practice, and development of motor control as seen in complete human movement. In other words, it is the ability to maintain form and control throughout the full range of motion and across different time and load demands. Movement control is the mechanical or physical result of motor control.

You can use this simpler definition of control to understand, measure, and train movement ability. Since movement control is grounded in motor control, I will first describe a simplified picture of the nervous system. The rest of the section discusses movement control by observing and challenging it in basic physical shapes: standing, hollow body, and plank.

summary of the nervous system

Movement involves a complex coordination of signals flowing through your nervous system, sometimes processed by your brain, and physical or mechanical actions in the musculoskeletal system. While it can be complicated, I find that it's necessary to have a basic understanding of the nervous system in order to discuss movement control.

Fortunately, the basic picture that I learned as a young gymnast is sufficient for my needs even today. Movement control can be thought of as a two-sided system: one side is the central nervous system (CNS), or brain and spinal cord, and the other is the peripheral nervous system (PNS), or the projections that innervate all muscle tissue. This model helps us understand that there are mechanical actions that we want to be as limitless as possible, and then there is the processing and networking (CNS) side that we need to be as stable as possible.

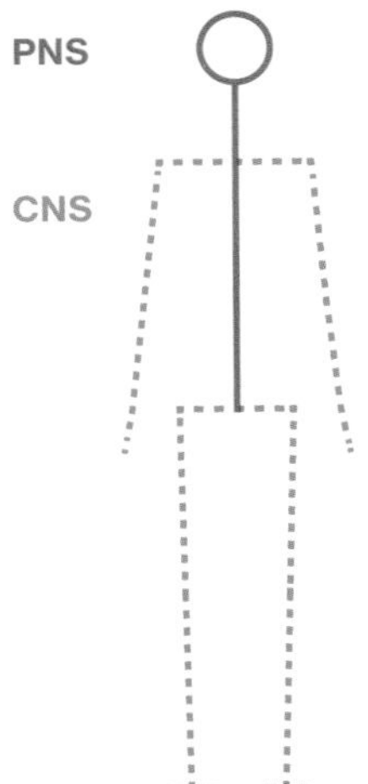

Given the conflicting demands placed on the nervous system, I see the spine as a mediator between these two sides. The curvature of the spine (refer to the illustration on page 24) seems to have naturally adapted over thousands of years of human evolution to allow us to move at different levels of the spine. Human spinal composition allows for head movement, arm movement, and rotation, to name a few examples. Most important, the spine moves to accommodate maintaining connections throughout the peripheral nervous system, while still protecting and stabilizing the central nervous system. Although the spine is an extremely complex system composed of bones, soft tissue, and many other things, we are going to eliminate all those variables and think of it as a simple rod called the ***midline.***

This simplified understanding of the nervous system as a two-sided system with a rod that balances the CNS need for stability and the PNS need for mobility allows us to approach and challenge movement control through basic shapes.

basic shapes

I like to introduce movement control by using fundamental shapes that the human body needs to have with respect to global position and orientation in space. These shapes are fundamental because they seem to be required for every movement you may need to do. I take these shapes and challenge them in ways that allow you to develop the movement control that is crucial for the proper execution of the movements throughout the rest of the book.

The Global-Local language outlined in chapter 1 (beginning on page 24) overlaps well with this two-sided picture of the nervous system and our understanding of movement control. The global system focuses on the position and shapes of the midline, or rod version of the spine. The local system concerns itself with the mobile peripheral nervous system.

First, I introduce standing, our starting point for movement based on human evolution. Next, I introduce the hollow body position, which adds a change of orientation in space (lying on the ground). This change of orientation requires using muscular tension to control the shape of the spine. This tension is the beginning of developing the control of our global position throughout movement. Finally, we flip the body around to a prone (facedown) position and continue to develop muscular tension to control the spinal shape using a different strategy.

standing

The first thing a gymnast learns is how to stand. We stand tall with legs straight, chest up, back flat, feet together, and arms to the sides. My gymnastics team started every session this way, standing in formation to be told what to expect for the session. This is also how we finished each day. The simple act of standing was a way of establishing form and power from the beginning of the session. And no matter how beat we were at the end, we had to finish strong!

The beauty of the human body is that it isn't limited to one plane of motion or movement. It is capable of any combination of these, which gives you an unlimited number of movement and position options. This concept should get you excited because it's your first glance into the world of Freestyle.

You may not think much about the act of standing, but standing dictates and influences movement control. You can observe a body standing tall at spinal level and see how the position of the spine affects the movements that follow. As a retired gymnast who now focuses on strength and conditioning, I have come to realize that the utility of the gym is that it exaggerates reality. This exaggeration applies to everything, even standing.

standing points of performance

01 Stand tall with your feet together and both your heels and your big toes touching.

02 Lock out your knees, squeeze your butt, suck in your belly, lift your chest, and pull your shoulders back.

03 Lengthen your neck by imagining a string being pulled from the top of your head, and tuck in your chin without looking down.

04 With your arms straight and your hands by your hips, turn your thumbs out so that your palms are facing forward.

If you think about the anatomical stance that you might see on a poster at the doctor's office, it is a position of strength and control. It is strong because the spine is stacked up vertically to the ground, the position in which it is the most stable. This stability exists thanks to the surrounding musculature, such as the back muscles pulling in toward the spine to keep the shoulders back and down. The butt is also tucked in, leveling the pelvis. The abs are engaged to create an imaginary protective belt around the lower back. This standing position is relatively easy to adopt, and with practice you can transfer it to many movements.

Standing also happens to be the position in which you (should) spend most of your day. In the gym, you can work on an exaggerated view of standing for training.

As a strength and conditioning coach, I do not encourage a lot of change in spinal position, regardless of the movement you are performing, even though I am aware that this is not the natural or real behavior seen on the field or in life. Your spine needs to be protected and set up to send the necessary signals to facilitate optimal movement. This is where the fitness community's obsession with core strength and midline stability comes in. A very basic way to challenge these two things is to learn how to keep your spine in the most neutral, stable position possible—the anatomical or stacked spine described earlier. Kelly Starrett, my mentor and author of the book ***Becoming a Supple Leopard,*** refers to it as an organized spine.

Even though you spend most of your day upright, whether you are standing or seated, your spine changes orientation in space every time you move. It leans forward, back, and side to side, as well as combinations of those. These changes of orientation in space create different stressors on your spine due to changes in muscular tension around the spine and, most important, to the orientation of your spine in relation to the pull of gravity. So you could say that simply moving while keeping your spine in this neutral or anatomical position gives you feedback for understanding what movement control is and how it relates to common concepts in the fitness industry, such as core strength and midline stability.

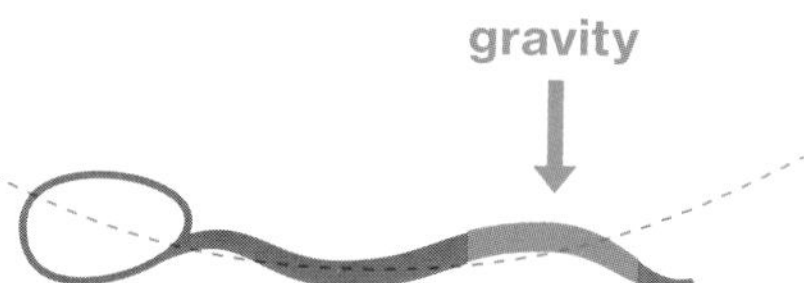

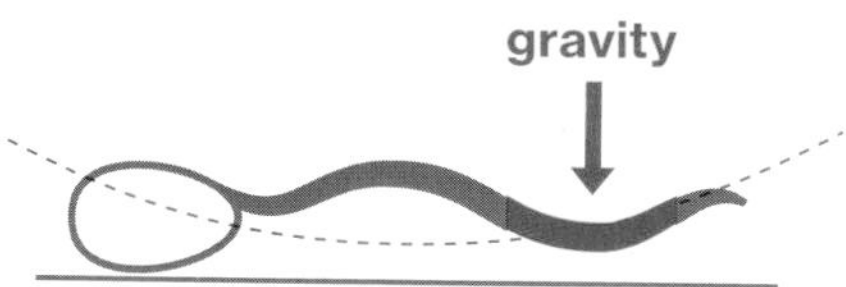

hollow body

Few of us experience much of a challenge in maintaining a neutral position while standing, or even as we vary our upright position. Understanding and advancing your movement ability happens best under a stressor or stimulus, so it helps to challenge the neutral spinal position by introducing simple demands on movement control. As your spine changes orientation in space, it is affected by gravity, and this seems like a natural challenge to start with. Simply changing your position in relation to the ground, such as lying down on your back, adds a controlled challenge.

Getting into the hollow body position is hard for some people and easy for others. Regardless of where you fall, if you hold the hollow body position at peak tension, you will quickly fatigue and have to come out of it. Your goal is to be able to hold this position stable for as long as possible. A simple test is to see how little muscular tension you can use while maintaining the structure of the hollow body position. When I test this important concept of consciously changing the amount of muscular tension required to hold this shape, people start shaking. This shake is a flinch response that will be described in the Flinch section (page 56).

The lumbar spine, which is the segment that connects your upper body to your lower body, is the most important part of the spine to address in movement control for adults. The cervical spine, which controls your neck, is the most important part of the spine to keep in mind for infants. The lumbar spine is dedicated to motor control, and the cervical spine to proprioception and orientation in space.

hollow body 01 Lie on your back with your knees tucked in toward your chest, grabbing your shins.

02 In the same tuck position, extend your arms straight out in front of you.

03 Extend one leg, keeping the other leg bent.

creating tension

Why pointed toes? Pointed toes are a common expression in gymnastics, but that expression has a greater meaning than simple aesthetics. Pointing your toes is an expression of pushing, which your body is wired to do to create tension and movement. A simple question I like to ask is: If your car breaks down or runs out of gas and you have to move it off the road with your own body, do you push it or pull it? Obviously, you are going to push it. There are many reasons for this from an anatomical or structural perspective, but in terms of movement control, it is because elongating the nervous system creates more tension in the body and allows for a greater application of force. If you watch someone jump, you see her push away from the ground with her legs, and as she pushes off, you see her hips and knees extend, followed by her feet pointing away from her body as an expression of finishing the push and reaching the full potential of mechanical work output through range of motion and muscular tension from the point of extension.

Loading order: The order in which you get into positions is quite important to the story of movement control. It is referred to as loading order, or the order of adding load to a movement by changing your position without adding an external load like a barbell in order to get to the final position (or often the starting position). In the hollow body progression, you load up your spine by bringing your legs and arms in first. This creates muscular tension around your abdominal area but no stress around your lumbar spine. As you drop your legs down, you steadily increase the amount of pull on your hips, which increases the muscular tension around your lumbar spine. This increased lumbar spine tension requires a compensatory increase in abdominal tension to maintain the neutral position. The same thing happens as you move your arms to your ears, but on a much smaller scale due to the size and length of your arms in relation to your legs.

Even though the hollow body position is a great way to work on movement control at spinal level, it is important to understand that this global body shape is not applicable to squatting or deadlifting, or even the Handstand. But it is a great way to learn how to load up your lower back or lumbar spine, which is very sensitive to going into even more extension and wants to trigger the flinch. The tremor you see in the hollow body position when backing off the tension is a series of micro-flinches, which is a very basic expression of physiological motor control. If you can't control this spinal position while moving, it will affect all other movements as you progress into more complex and advanced ones.

The gym is an exaggeration of reality, and you can train movement and position at peak tension to develop motor control. As your body adapts and becomes more efficient, achieving the same tension no longer requires as much energy expenditure. This is a fundamental concept in training and therefore in progression.

04 Extend both legs so that they are completely straight, with your feet together and your toes pointed.

05 Bring your arms overhead. This is the hollow body position.

We are natural pushers. Imagine you are driving your car it runs out of gas just a few hundred feet from a gas station. Would you get out and push or pull your car to the gas station?

flinch

When I asked you to explore the amount of tension necessary to maintain control over your hollow body shape, you probably found a point where tremors or shaking challenged your control of that shape. Why did you shake?

You shook due to a lack of stability at lumbar spine level under tension or load. But what does this mean? Your central nervous system is like a command center, and it has an extremely complex design to communicate with your body. One of these elements is a sophisticated and powerful protective mechanism called the flinch.

I like to bring up the flinch (or spinal flinch) in order to get you to understand movement control, because this protective mechanism kicks in especially when you lack stability at spinal level.

The shaking that you experience in the hollow body position is just one example of this flinch. The flinch at this scale is a series of micro-flinches—which is essentially like an on-off switch of the nervous system trying to protect you from injury.

The micro-flinches occur due to a loss of neuromuscular control. In this case, because you are in global flexion, you are loading up the lumbar region of your spine. Around this section of your spine, all you have is muscle tissue to support the structure. In other sections, such as the thoracic spine, you have ribs and shoulder girdle that provide extra stability. This freedom around the lumbar spine is important because it facilitates the transmission of locomotion driven from the lower body into the upper body and from the upper body downward.

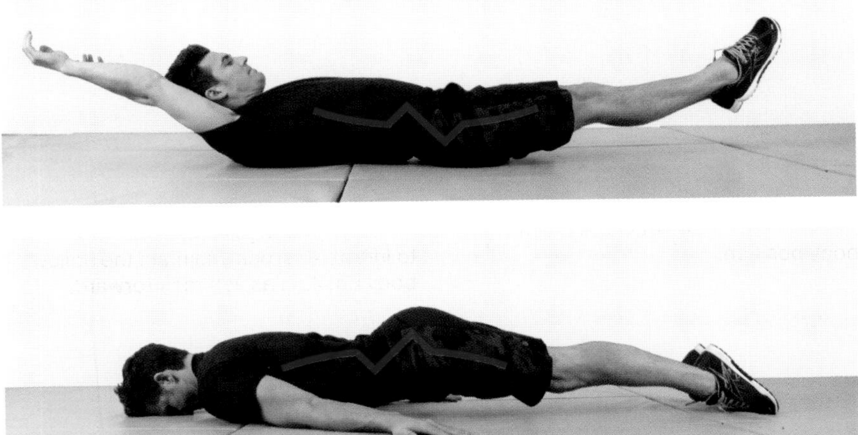

I am in the hollow body position. If I lose engagement of my belly and butt, gravity pulls down my upper body and legs, placing my spine in local extension.

I am in a supine position. As I press my hips and belly away from the ground, gravity pulls my lumbar spine into extension.

hollow rock

Static positions like the hollow body are great for developing awareness of motion what your body feels like under certain demands. The hollow body shape is designed to teach spinal stability, which translates to better spinal position while performing movements. The key phrase here is other movements. To further progress this ability to stabilize your lumbar spine for better overall movement control, you can add a little motion: a rock. The tension around your spine shifts as you rock back and forth.

Notice that I used the word shift. As you rock, your center of mass shifts from the front of your base of support (your lower back and butt) to the back of your base of support (your upper back). Especially when performing the Hollow Rock for the first time, you may find that the shifting back and forth causes problems, even if you are really good at holding the static hollow body position.

The rocking motion itself is not necessarily difficult, but it does cause changes in tension at different levels of your spine as you rock. As you rock forward, your legs pull your body forward and down, and your upper body follows by performing a Sit-up. Even if you never do traditional Sit-ups, you perform the same movement seen in the forward rock every time you get out of bed or stand up off a chair, which is an expression of pushing. It is usually on the backward rock that the spine tends to deviate in shape, where the hips and legs are left behind and the spine starts to reverse into a more extended position, especially at the top of the lumbar region or ribcage. This happens because as you rock backward, you progressively load your spine with the weight of your legs pulling down, which requires you to perform a pull with your hips toward your face and up. As simple as it may seem, we have lost some of our ability to perform this movement due to our modern environment.

hollow rock 01 Start in the hollow body position.

02 Drop your legs toward the ground to initiate the rock. Maintain the hollow body position as you rock forward.

03 Descend backward by dropping your shoulders to the ground and pulling your legs away from the ground. Continue rocking backward by allowing your arms to reach for the ground, and emphasize picking up your hips in order to maintain the hollow body position.

This is one of the main reasons people get injured when running. Every lift of the foot causes over-tension and therefore stress on the spine, leading to injury.

Every time you sit down on a chair, you perform a pull from your legs. But because the chair is stable, is high up, and has a backrest, you don't usually pull yourself into the chair with control; you just drop. This convenience has led to underdevelopment in our ability to pull from our lower extremities, which causes extension at the lumbar spine and a subsequent loss of motor control, which is expressed as a loss of movement control.

By adding this Hollow Rock, you learn not just how to change tension around your spine, but also the basic principles of pushing and pulling from your lower extremities.

plank

A basic understanding of the hollow body position is a great foundation from which to add movement to the spine, such as the Hollow Rock. Now think a little further. While sleeping, you may be comfortable on your back, and then you perform a Sit-up to get up, but anytime you squat and stand back up or bend over to pick something up, your spine rotates in space to the point where it is no longer supine or upright, but is moving into a prone or facedown position. This brings us to the infamous Push-up position, known as the plank in the fitness community and Chaturanga in the yoga community.

plank position

In plank position, your arms are locked out and your shoulders are right above your knuckles. Your body is a straight line from head to toes, your legs are straight, and your feet together and flexed, with the balls of your feet supporting your body and your butt and belly tight.

The plank position is important because the gravitational forces on your spine are coming from the opposite side—the front. These forces cause your lumbar spine to want to sag and extend, and you must pull your spine away from the ground and focus on squeezing your butt and pulling your belly in tight in order to neutralize your pelvis for better alignment.

As easy as this control may seem in a plank, try the prone test, pulling yourself into this position by supporting yourself with only your forehead and feet. For most people, this effort causes a noticeable deviation in the spinal position.

From the prone position, it's important to understand how to adopt an extended global shape, also called the Superman position, and an extended global shape with motion, the Superman Rock.

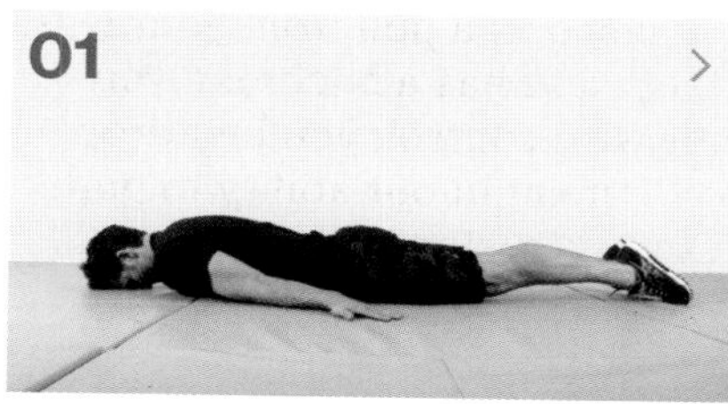

prone test 01 Lying facedown on the ground with your arms at your sides, lock out your legs and squeeze your butt and belly tight.

02 Pull your hips and belly off the ground while keeping your upper back and neck aligned with the rest of your body and adopting slight global flexion.

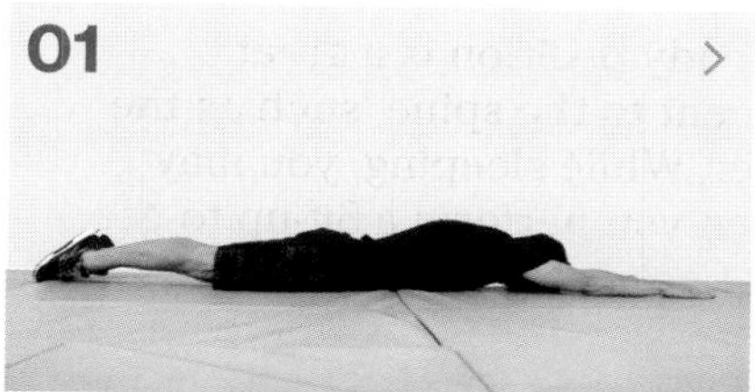

superman 01 Lie facedown on the ground with your arms overhead and close to your midline, with your palms facing the ground. Your chin is tucked in, and your legs are straight and held together.

02 Pick up your legs by pushing your hips into the ground and driving your heels up and behind you. Lift your arms, face, and chest off the ground. You should feel a lot of tension around your spine.

superman rock 01 From the Superman position, initiate the rock by dropping your chest to the ground and driving your legs up to the sky. The leg drive facilitates staying in the Superman shape.

02 After you reach the top of your forward rock, hold that position until gravity takes over and starts pulling your legs down. Progressively pick your arms and shoulders off the ground in order to maintain the Superman shape as you rock backward.

03 Using the momentum created in the transition, allow your legs to drop to the ground. Pull your chest and arms up away from the ground, maintaining Superman position throughout the full rocking range of motion.

Even though the focus in this section has been on the lumbar spine, it is extremely important to keep your neck and head position in mind as you move due to its effect on your relative orientation in space for movement control. The position of your head usually determines where your body is going to follow, but when your head is moving independently of your body, or with muscular tension connecting your head and neck to the rest of your body, you lose your ability to create spatial awareness, and thus you lose movement control. This is proprioception, which is the sense of the relative position of neighboring parts of the body and the strength of effort being employed in movement.

Focus on being movement strong, not numbers strong.

How strong do you need to be to squat 500 pounds? We could study this movement and talk about contractile forces at muscular level, but we can also simply say, "Strong enough to squat 500 pounds." This may seem like circular logic, but strength is where we can really get lost in fitness, and where I find my task-focused definition of fitness especially useful for keeping me on track. After all, what is a better measurement of how "strong" someone is than the accomplishment of an amazing feat?

To perform a 500-pound Squat, you need to have the skill to perform the style of Squat required to lift 500 pounds as well as the physiological capacity to support this movement.

I define ***movement strength*** as the physiological capacity to support a movement and ***skill*** as the ability to apply this capacity to your performance.

I think it's important to separate movement strength and skill because in the gym we are always working to understand our current ability in terms of adaptations that we know how to progress. For example, knowing that you ran a marathon in three hours is a fantastic measurement, and a well-known way to improve your performance is to start with physiological adaptations. But what are these physiological adaptations, and how do they relate to your ability to move?

movement strength

I believe that the physiology underlying an individual's current capacity to move, or movement strength, is best described by four of CrossFit's ten aspects of fitness:

1. ***Strength*** is the contractile potential of muscle and its application to moving the skeleton for the completion of a task.
2. ***Stamina*** is the ability to sustain muscular strength.
3. ***Endurance*** is the cardiovascular system that allows us to perform for long periods of time.
4. ***Flexibility*** (also known as mobility) is the physiological capacity to move the body with minimal restriction at joint and muscular levels.

These physiological aspects are important for improving performance. They can be observed, measured, and repeated, and many formal methods for creating these adaptations already exist in fitness and athletics. Unfortunately, the fitness community often gets lost in the most obvious measurements—for example, adding one more pound on the bar. If this training does not translate to actual progress toward your goal, then it is useless. Just because something can be measured doesn't mean that it is the most important measurement.

My job as a coach is to identify specific movement patterns in life and sport and bring them into the gym to train and progress them. I enhance performance by challenging those movement patterns in different ways. To translate the gains from these challenges back into real life and sports performance, I need to understand the language of human movement as presented in chapter 1. If you stop and think about it, the data you collect are products of how you move and therefore are extremely important.

Movement strength is about not just developing the physiology, but also developing the movement quality that then allows you to tap into the physiological adaptation you truly want, the one that supports quality movement.

The concept of being movement strong, as simple as it may seem, is about having the physiological capacity to support the highest-quality movements. Measuring your movement strength progress based on the quality of your movement will help you maximize your efforts to train your body in a way that will be most transferable to other aspects of life and sport.

skill

As stated earlier, I define skill as the ability to apply movement strength to perform a task. This definition of skill is easily confused with the term "technique," which describes a way to carry out a particular task.

A Carl Lewis long jump and a Parkour artist's jump from one building to another share similar mechanics that make them both jumps, and the approaches in chapter 1 enable you to identify those shared mechanics. I define being good at jumping as skill and the specificity required to perform each style of jump as technique.

To further understand skill and technique, it is helpful to distinguish between the general and the specific mechanics of a movement. Take, for example, a Squat. You can perform a Squat in many different ways according to your purpose, even though squatting is a general movement pattern that involves lowering your center of mass toward the ground by bending your hips, knees, and ankles. We can say that squatting is general, but the style of squatting is specific. Skill refers to general squatting mechanics, while technique refers to the specific requirements to perform a certain style of Squat.

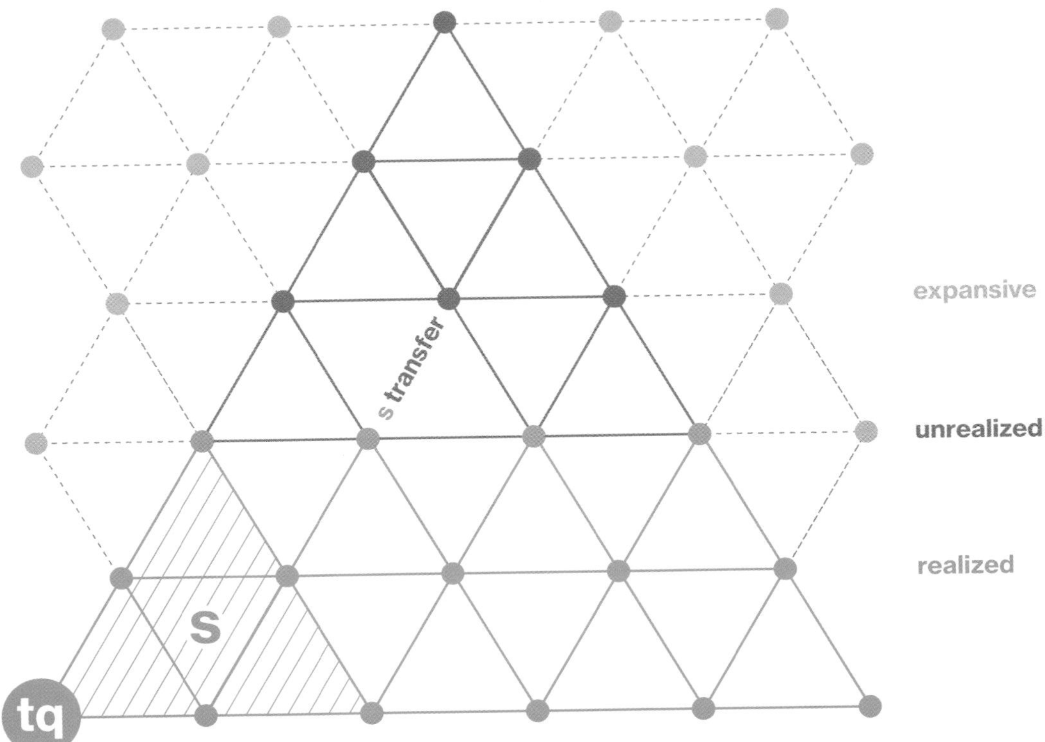

This diagram illustrates how I view movement ability. Each node represents a specific movement technique; clusters of techniques can be considered skills; and the lines that connect one technique to another are what I like to think of as skill transfer. Notice that the diagram takes the shape of a pyramid, representing how building a strong base of realized movement ability will determine not just the height of the techniques you can reach, but also your ability to transfer the skill gained from learning one technique to other unrealized, yet close, techniques. Also notice that the pyramid is not limited to one direction, but instead creates an infinitely expansive movement ability blanket.

There are an infinite number of styles of every general movement pattern. Think about throwing an object: All styles of throwing involve similar mechanics, but their differences have important implications that define them. For example, pitching is general throwing mechanics in baseball, but the styles of pitches (curveball, knuckle ball, and so on) require different techniques.

The difference between skill and technique can get even more confusing because the most straightforward way to assess skill is to observe the performance of various techniques. So keep in mind that technique is the specific details of each individual style, while skill is the general mechanics.

As for movement strength, it is important to identify the physiological foundation of skill in order to train it. Again, I find CrossFit's definitions of fitness aspects useful, and I believe that four of them represent the basis of skill:

1. ***Balance*** is the ability to control your center of mass or combined center of mass while moving or lifting in relation to your base of support.
2. ***Accuracy*** is the ability to move exactly or correctly.
3. ***Agility*** is the ability to change the direction of movement.
4. ***Coordination*** is the ability to perform complex movement patterns in a way that flows.

These fitness aspects allow you to mechanically perform complex movements in an accurate, balanced, smooth, and sequenced fashion. Skill is what brings the complexity of human anatomy to work together in a way that makes the extreme complexity of the human body seem simple.

Although understanding movement strength and skill separately is important for understanding the roles they play in the development of progressions, they can never be separated during actual movement. The magic of training the human body is that when you develop and progress movement strength and skill, you see an increase in your ability to perform basic movements, which increases your capacity to perform in specific life and sport scenarios. Furthermore, I believe that an understanding of skill as the application of movement strength to a specific task is crucial for understanding how to optimize your performance in order to see progress.

skill transfer

We all have that one friend who is just all-around good at everything. Besides being annoyingly good, this superstar makes you wonder how it is possible. If you asked him about his background, you would probably quickly realize why he is so good.

I have been fortunate to work with one of these athletes very closely. Her name is Annie Thorisdottir, aka Iceland Annie. She has won the CrossFit Games twice, and I was lucky to be a part of her team. When I first started working with her, she was that person—she just got it! And even though she felt that her learning curve was slow compared with everyone else's, she was actually far better. She was unstoppable.

As I got to know her, I began to understand why. Her track record was insane. She grew up in Iceland on an island in the middle of the Atlantic. Her family was extremely active; Annie practiced several sports and liked to dance and perform. She did artistic gymnastics for many years and eventually went into track and field and focused on pole vaulting. Her training involved rigorous metabolic conditioning in a boot camp type of environment. It wasn't a fluke that she was able to learn new things faster than everyone else: she had the movement foundation, had an amazing engine to do work, and was always mentally ready to learn.

Annie's story of athleticism relates to my own coaching story, and although I already described it in the introduction, I find it so fundamental to my approach that I want to highlight it again. When I first got into coaching, I coached noncompetitive gymnastics to a group of young boys. Eventually, their parents wanted to participate as well, and it didn't take me long to realize that I had to put a strength and conditioning program in place to help them survive the challenge of doing gymnastics as adults. After failing several times at implementing a good program, I found CrossFit. The implementation of the CrossFit method made a big change in the way my athletes performed. Even though I understood the movements and challenges, I had a voice in the back of my head that kept telling me, "Carl, you still don't have a clue!" Truth was, I didn't, but it was working anyway.

A few years later, I was listening to a neuroscientist from Sweden talk about child development, and he said, "Kids need to learn the basic skill of reading so they can later use this skill to learn new things. You need to learn to read so you can read to learn." BINGO! It hit me right there and then. That's what I do! This is who I am! I teach people how to move so they can learn to use that movement to learn new things. We must learn to move so we can move to learn! This is what the concept of skill transfer is all about: learning how to move so that we can use movement as a tool to progress and optimize our life and sports performance.

applied athleticism

I coached "Iceland Annie" Thorisdottir during the 2011 CrossFit Games. I knew that being able to climb a rope was going to be one of the challenges, especially after seeing everyone struggle and fail miserably in 2010. A couple of days before the competition, I decided to spend five minutes teaching Annie a very basic rope-climbing technique. This technique was an adaptation of how I had taught her to perform a Muscle-up on the rings, which is simply the act of getting over an obstacle by rotating around the rings. Because we had worked on this Muscle-up technique for so long, the rope-climbing technique came easily to her.

On the first day of the competition, Annie had a difficult start. Toward the end of the day, the final event was announced, and of course it included rope climbs, which were combined with heavy Clean and Jerks. This was the moment of truth: we hadn't practiced the rope-climbing technique, but would Annie be able to apply what she had learned? The answer was yes. She didn't just apply it and win the event; she changed the game. Annie introduced to the world of CrossFit a new style of movement that served a purpose and didn't require specific training, just a foundation of performance and an understanding of how the body naturally moves—a clear example of skill transfer.

If movement strength is the physiological capacity to move your body and skill is the application of this strength to your movement performance, then skill transfer is your ability to use your foundation of strength and skill developed on some movements and apply them to other movements, sports, or disciplines. Skill transfer can also mean creatively enhancing a particular technique.

If we go back to the physical aspects of fitness as defined by CrossFit, there are ten of them. I use four of them to define movement strength:

1. Strength
2. Stamina
3. Endurance
4. Flexibility

I use another four to define skill:

1. Balance
2. Coordination
3. Agility
4. Accuracy

The remaining two are speed and power, which in CrossFit are referred to as the result of the other eight aspects. And this result always occurs and is learned through movement.

Without skill transfer, I don't believe that we can take advantage of the gains we make in movement strength and skill and use them to fully express speed and power in the broadest circumstances.

With skill transfer, one of my goals is to show you that regardless of the style or discipline of movement you choose for your training, if you master the basics of human movement, you will maximize your ability to translate your performance from one discipline to another, or simply from the gym to the field of sport and life.

The sum of all movement styles is Freestyle, and the ability to connect these styles through training is the most important benefit of my Freestyle Connection framework.

Without an understanding of the concept of skill transfer, we can't maximize training the basic movement patterns for the purpose of athleticism. The physiological adaptations are important, but the movement patterns are king! Freestyle is connected by skill, applied through skill transfer, and expressed as athleticism.

progression 03

The best progression will ramp up the most novice and challenge the most advanced.

Progression is the ultimate focus of the Freestyle Connection framework. It is the act of building a road map to advance your performance. A progression is good if it has a high likelihood of success for maximizing your performance in your sport and also in your life.

Chapters 1 and 2, while important in their own right, merely develop the language needed to create these progressions. In this chapter, you will learn what is behind the most successful progressions and how essential the progression of your physical ability to move is to life and sport.

Photo by Sevan Matossian

We all have an intuitive ability to move and to advance that ability. Take a child learning to walk for the first time, for example. When babies are born, they can only lie on their backs and move their arms and legs. Eventually, they acquire the ability to sit, helped along by adults moving them around. From there, all babies go through the same progression: rolling, creeping, crawling, kneeling, squatting, standing, stepping, walking, climbing, and finally running.

Let's look at the stages of how a child learns to walk. As she transitions from crawling to squatting, she gains the strength to pick up her hips from a crawl on hands and knees to a Downward Dog position on hands and feet. She looks for something to hold onto and begins to stand upright. That "something" she looks to hold onto is you, specifically your hands. You begin to pull her around a little and teach her how to pick up her feet, even though she naturally does it on her own. As she takes these assisted steps, she gains the strength to walk.

Our experience as parents or family members of young children makes it easy to see that a child naturally progresses from a more elemental state of movement to a more advanced one. A child's parents and community formally facilitate this natural progression to help her adapt more quickly. This formal progression is an instinct we carry inside us from millions of years of evolution. The sooner the young become self-sufficient, the easier it is to survive. This urge for survival is not something we consciously think of; it is part of who we are.

Our bodies are in a constant state of evolution, both as a species over millions of years and at the individual level in the span of one lifetime. The human body has evolved specifically to survive. Over the years, humans have become well-engineered systems in which our minds direct our bodies to move in order to protect ourselves and each other and ultimately to continue the propagation of our species. Historically tough living circumstances have driven the development of how we move to accomplish these tasks. And those tough conditions helped keep the body in check physically.

Unfortunately, this is not the case today. We have ready access to all of life's needs—all the food we need can be found at the supermarket, and long-distance travel is effortless thanks to our vehicles. Ironically, the modern body pays the price for these comforts and technological advancements.

Thankfully, the human species is smart enough to acknowledge this fact. We have even developed ways to engineer tough living conditions back into our lives by creating facilities dedicated to progressing our physical abilities for health, higher-level play, and sport. As these facilities multiply and grow, a structured system to mimic the demands for survival is being put into place. Never before have we had a more formalized "physical education." As time has gone on, though, the motivations behind why we created these artificial facilities have been lost.

If we want to keep advancing physically, we must remember where we came from and how the human body has evolved. This is especially important if we want the full use of our knowledge and experience, as well as modern science and technology, to find new and creative solutions to continue our natural adaptation to our environment and the potential survival demands that we may be exposed to in the future.

As I mentioned earlier, the way we formally address movement at these facilities is influenced by who we are, which in turn is a product of millions of years of evolution. To further adapt, we must understand this important truth.

The million-dollar question we ask at these facilities has become, "Why do we move the way we do, and are these movements 'correct'?" Why are we doing what we're doing? Is it to get ourselves to improve a movement for the sake of it, or is that movement a stage of a larger progression?

This chapter gives you several essential tools for answering these questions and building successful progressions. I organize progressions into three types: natural, formal, and creative. These types give us a larger context to appreciate the purpose of creating road maps for enhancing movement. Then I share the principles and methods I use to understand and develop progressions. Understanding these principles is crucial not only for developing progressions yourself, but also to fully appreciate the progressions seen in the rest of the book.

We can improve our understanding of how to advance movement by considering the three different ways we can progress: naturally, formally, and creatively.

1. ***Natural progressions*** are based on the ways we evolve to move in response to the demands and purposes placed on us. In the natural progression of a child learning to walk, we see the same steps taken all over the world. Parents don't have to do much to encourage those steps.
2. ***Formal progressions*** are purposefully constructed, usually based on natural progressions, to train and advance movement and make it more efficient. As a gymnastics coach, I may teach you the steps that the community has evolved in order to raise your chance of success at learning to perform a Handstand.
3. ***Creative progressions*** come from the drive to surpass our current limitations and share that progress with others. For example, think about a freestyle skier working to create a new trick or jump that takes his sport to the next level. There is a natural cycle among these progression types; once at least one skier has discovered a new creative progression, it often turns into a natural progression as others learn of its existence and attempt it themselves. As I've already described, this now-natural progression informs and shapes the next formal one in an effort to get more skiers to learn this new trick.

natural progressions

Strength training was a big part of my daily routine when I was a kid doing gymnastics. As kids, though, we don't give much thought to why we are doing whatever it is we are doing. We just do! I vividly remember doing Pull-ups and getting tired and starting to swing and kick in order to get my chin up over the bar. This was considered cheating, of course; it was not going to increase my strength as a gymnast. But this style of kicking and swinging, called a Kipping Pull-up, has become a legitimate style in the CrossFit world. I probably wasn't the only gymnast struggling on the Pull-up bar. This innate tendency to swing and kick demonstrates how one style of movement can naturally progress into another style when influenced by fatigue, stress, or desperation.

Natural progression happens constantly in life and sport. Often it is a simple result of having to go from point A to point B, only faster, farther, or more frequently. If I were walking and had to get to my destination faster, for example, the walking would eventually turn into jogging, running, and sprinting.

formal progressions

Imagine that I'm a creative coach and I see one of my athletes start to adopt the Kipping Pull-up style as he fatigues. I make a mental note of the fact that despite being unable to do one more strict Pull-up, he could kick up another ten without much difficulty.

So I might allow my athlete to kick up during the Pull-up. In fact, I could encourage it by saying, "I don't care what your form looks like; just get your chin over the bar as many times as you can." Then I would record the commonalities between the athlete's Pull-ups using the observation and description language covered in chapter 1. Seeing the abilities that it seems to impart based on the demand—in this case, doing as many Pull-ups as possible in the allotted time—I formalize this Kipping Pull-up as a new style of movement, and I begin instructing other athletes on how to move this way. And thus a formal progression is born.

Studying natural progressions is a powerful tool for developing movement. The act of taking a natural progression created by the body's instinct to perform a movement, developing a new style based on those natural tendencies, and creating a road map with formalized steps to teach that new style is what I consider a formal progression.

creative progressions

We all have a creative side that we can express through making art, performing, innovating, or exploring answers to difficult problems. In the world of physical performance, creativity is an essential part of continually developing and adapting our bodies and coming up with new movement progressions.

The late Shane McConkey, who was a skiing and overall action sport legend, had the bright idea of using water skis rather than regular skis on the mountain for deep-powder days. Because a water ski is wider and fatter than a regular snow ski, it provides a different experience, allowing the skier to float on top of the snow rather than sink into the snow and slow down. The word on the mountain is that with this simple idea, McConkey influenced the ski industry, introduced a new way of looking at the experience of skiing, and changed the game.

The creative aspect can blur the lines between the different types of progressions. A creative progression could be called an accident or a natural adaptation. For example, in 2008 a video of a new style of Kipping Pull-up appeared online and became popular within the CrossFit community. This style is called the Butterfly Pull-up today. To me, it seems to have come about naturally because of the demand to perform Kipping Pull-ups at high speeds for long periods of time. I refer to this movement progression as creative rather than natural because there is a strong component of originality to it. Only a few athletes had come upon this Butterfly Pull-up; it was not a style that others naturally progressed to as they did with the Kipping Pull-up.

Creativity doesn't just happen in the world of fitness. I have also seen it in b-boying. This style of dance, which is a branch of hip-hop that originated in the Bronx, is heavy influenced by gymnastics and kung fu, and it was the ability to pull from and implement those different disciplines that made it original. This process, though it may seem natural in retrospect, required creativity and therefore developed creative progressions.

Signature movements are original and specific movements or styles of movement that belong to unique disciplines, such as the Butterfly Pull-up in CrossFit, the knuckle ball pitch in baseball, and the high jump in track and field.

Similarly, one of my favorite gymnasts of all time implemented the windmill seen in b-boying into his gymnastics floor routine. Not much later, another gymnast implemented the airflare, which was without a doubt an original movement created within the b-boy community. The originality that I assign to creative progressions is not solely an act of creating a new way to move; it can also involve borrowing and repurposing a movement for use in another discipline or area of life.

The creative process is fueled by our ability to see natural progressions, explore the frontiers of human ability, and ultimately push past the boundaries of what our bodies are able to do without having to stay within the formal standards that someone else established. Looking beyond the rules of a game or sport helps us inject originality into our performance and allows us to come up with new ways of improving our performance. Creative progression is the act of taking an original movement, formalizing it, and introducing it as a unique style or new discipline.

progression principles

If you are like me, you may have wondered: How does a basketball player jump up and dunk a ball? How does a gymnast perform a double backflip with a few twists in there? How does a surfer manage to stand up on the board and ride a wave so seamlessly amid all the chaos? Besides asking yourself what steps they take and how they go about learning those steps, you may have thought, Where do I even start if I want to learn these things? The answer is always to start at the beginning. This may seem obvious, but you must start with the foundation of any movement and inch your way toward the movement you're interested in. Few people would disagree with this statement, but most have a hard time figuring out where the beginning actually is or how to make the most effective progress or inches toward the end goal.

You now know that I define progression as improving your movement ability for sport or life. I have discussed three progression types, but I have yet to introduce the actual creation of a progression. In this section, I discuss my principles for creating formal progressions. I believe that this is the most important thing I do as a coach, and I spend most of my time consciously or unconsciously using these principles to build progressions.

Similar to disclaimers I've made before, I did not invent these principles. I discovered them by studying many disciplines of movement and sport and have refined the list based on what has been the most successful for me in my years of coaching. The first thing you will learn as you use these principles is that there are many ways to successfully progress movement ability.

Unfortunately, there are many experts out there who state that their method is the only way to learn how to do X movement correctly. This often comes from an inherited worldview where the expert has been taught a certain method, and that method's correctness is reinforced when the expert sees success. Just because a method has been successful, however, does not mean that it is the only successful method or even the most effective method for any individual.

The truth is, there is no set structure or single best progression. It is much more productive to think of creating progressions as an ongoing process of taking measurements and constructing road maps than to think of it as being about finding the right progression off a shelf of progressions.

My goal is to help you learn the art of creating formal progressions. As discussed in the progression types section, a formal progression is one that is constructed for the purpose of making a natural progression more efficient. I see the art of building progressions as constantly alternating between:

1. Defining your purpose or goal
2. Measuring your current level of performance or movement ability
3. Creating a road map or sequence of carefully crafted stages that takes you from your current ability to your goal

There are so many systems, methods, disciplines, and styles of training. So which one do you pick? Which is best? Well, the truth is that you can find success with almost any road map; there is not just one solution that will work for you, and certainly not for everyone. However, after years of developing progressions as both an athlete and a coach, I have found one truth underlying the most successful progressions that come from any discipline: They balance your chance of success with the amount of progress you make toward your ultimate goal at every stage of development.

No matter how advanced you are as an athlete or a mover, the best way to keep improving is to master the basics.

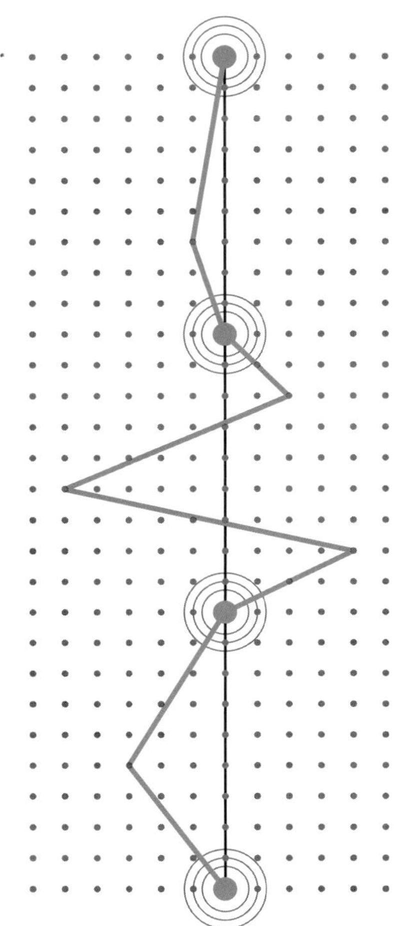

universal skills / path

your skills / path

styles

Although certain milestone progressions have organically created a universal path toward a movement, we all begin and progress with different skill sets and styles. The fact that there are an infinite number of styles of any given movement allows us to reach that end goal in a personal way.

This balance ends up being an important navigation aid because it helps you make well-informed decisions. It might also be considered a "minimum effective dose"—the smallest amount that will produce the desired outcome (see Timothy Ferriss' book ***The 4-Hour Body***). The bottom line is that a progression is designed to get you from one stage of physical performance to the next as fast as possible while keeping each stage safe, useful, and long-lasting—in other words, functional.

Telling you the secret that you need to build progression stages that offer the minimum effective dose of movement ability doesn't actually make your job of finding these stages much easier. Most of the work in creating progressions is using creative exploration to find these balanced stages. Over the years, I have collected principles that help me explore and build progressions with well-defined and balanced stages. These principles are not meant to be followed like an instruction manual for building furniture, but instead are more like guidelines you can use to solve a complex puzzle. Think of a Rubik's cube: it is a completely integrated system, yet there are strategies you can use to simplify solving it, such as picking a color to focus on or looking for patterns. In the end, you are creating your own unique decision tree, and these are just tools to use for that purpose.

Before diving into these principles, I want to make it very clear that my intention is not to say that you should ignore expert guidance and always build your own progressions from scratch. It would be ridiculous for any athlete to ignore generations of knowledge of the human body, and in particular the performance of the human body within a specific discipline or sport. I simply want to give you tools to help you understand the experts' progressions better, thus letting you get more out of these tried-and-true methods in addition to enabling you to deviate from them when necessary.

The experts have a good reason to push their methods: these methods are the ones that work most often in their disciplines. However, every good coach knows that even in the most trusted progression plan, it is easy to get lost; our bodies plateau or stop progressing, and the biggest contributor to failure is giving up the journey because we distrust the map. So I give you these progression principles as tools for constantly evolving even the most trusted road map, even if they just give you more confidence about the path you're on.

By now, you should realize that this section is not going to give you a million different progressions to build any movement you might want to learn. As I just mentioned, most of the existing progressions out there are great. Instead, I offer some fundamental progression principles to help you create road maps and get the most out of the ones you're already using. In this section, I list principles for building progression stages that balance progress toward your goal with the chance of success. In the following section, I introduce the methods that I use to put these principles into practice and create sequences of progression stages to build a complete road map. These are the progression principles and methods that I used to create all the progressions you will see in part 2 of this book.

pushing and pulling

Pushing and pulling are some of the most common concepts in the gym. As mentioned in chapter 1 (page 75), these are simple ways to look at all forces related to the body. Performing any movement involves components of both pushing and pulling. If you are working toward a movement that falls outside of your current movement ability, you will want to consider working on similar movements that overlap with the global and local shapes, but with an emphasis on pushing rather than pulling.

Concentric loading is usually related to creating movement. The force generated is sufficient to overcome the resistance, and the muscle fibers shorten as they contract. This is what most people think of as muscle contraction.

Eccentric loading is usually related to cycling from one repetition of a movement to the next while maintaining the optimal position for the best application of force, usually seen in the push. The force generated is insufficient to overcome the external load on the muscle, and the muscle fibers lengthen as they contract. An eccentric contraction is used as a means to decelerate a body part or object or to lower a load gently rather than let it drop.

Let's look at an example of a beginner trying to get his first Pull-up: a classic pulling-dominant movement in the gym. One obvious starting point would be a less-demanding pulling movement, such as a Ring Row (see page 229 in the Muscle-up chapter). The athlete may be able to perform this row, but if his mechanics are poor, then a Push-up would be a better place to start. The Push-up offers similar global and local movement mechanics, but with pushing being more of an emphasis than pulling. Most athletes find it easier to maintain the desirable global and local positions while pushing rather than pulling. Because these positions are similar to that of the Ring Row, the athlete will find more success with this movement pattern and be able to transfer the adaptations from the training to the Ring Row and eventually to his first Pull-up.

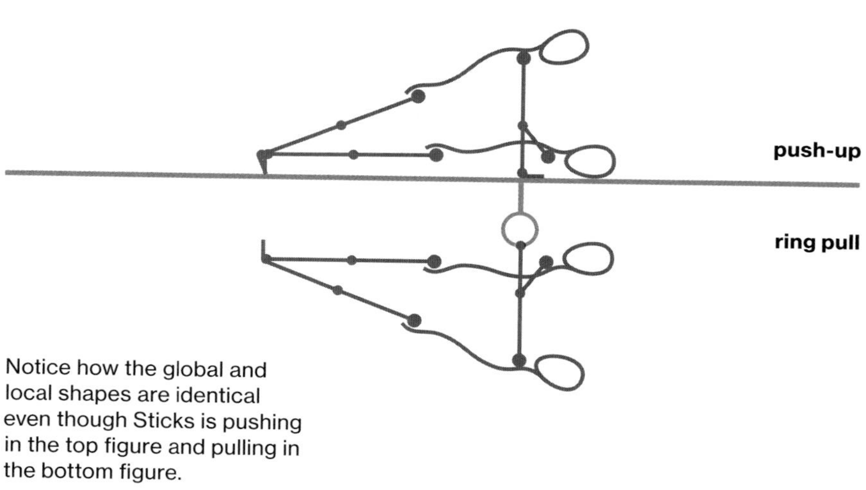

Notice how the global and local shapes are identical even though Sticks is pushing in the top figure and pulling in the bottom figure.

Another interesting thing to consider when building progressions based on pushing and pulling is whether you are struggling with your form in a movement. Let's look at a Squat, for example. When standing up out of a Squat, the main force is pushing away from the ground. This pushing can be more or less effective depending on the integrity of your transition position, or the bottom of the Squat. Your shape in the transition is a product of how you pull yourself into the bottom position. If you don't understand how to pull your body as you lower yourself to the ground, you will lose form in the descent and will be less prepared for the main push from transition to finish. So if someone is having problems finishing the ascent of a Squat, I often start by working on the pull required for the descent (see the negatives aside on page 231).

The example of developing pushing before pulling in the Squat to improve the descent also applies to the Dip. A common mistake that people make when performing the Dip is to let their bodies collapse to the bottom position with their shoulders on top of their hands (shown in red) rather than pull their bodies into position with vertical forearms and shoulders optimally set up for the push back to the top position (shown in green).

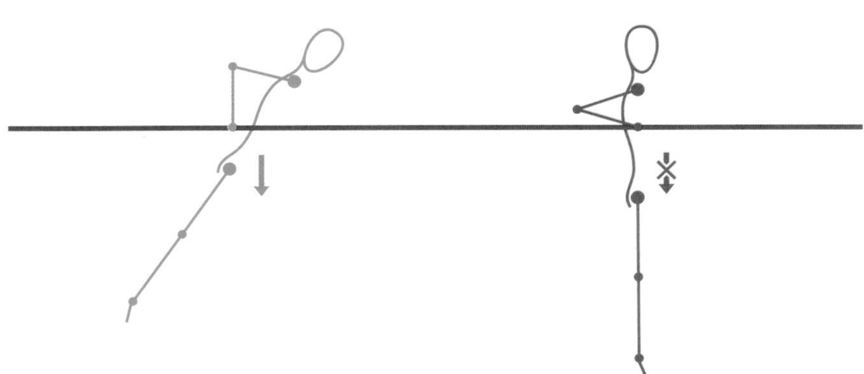

adaptive technology

In the Paralympics, advancements in the technology and design of prosthetics are enabling athletes who have lost their legs to run the 100 meters in as fast as ten seconds. A well-known prosthetic is the Flex-foot Cheetah, designed by a medical engineer named Van Phillips, who lost a leg and wasn't satisfied with the technology available for the high-level performance of adaptive athletes.

One of the main features that Phillips introduced was the capability to store kinetic energy in the prosthetic. This allows an athlete to take advantage of the powerful foot strike seen in sprinting in order to explode off the ground and assist the subsequent leg pull to perform the next step of the run. This is an example of understanding the importance of pulling in a movement that seems to be pushing dominated. Previous devices that did not emphasize the pull are inferior.

2:1 pull:push

During my gymnastics years, one of my teammates and I would do some of our off-season strength training in a small bodybuilding gym. This is where I first heard of the concept of working on pulling exercises twice as much as pushing exercises. This idea of a 2:1 pull:push ratio wasn't just an idea they had in this small bodybuilding gym; it also showed up years later when I was working as a personal trainer. The common justification I would hear for this 2:1 ratio is that if you trained pushing much more than this, specifically for your upper body, you would develop bad posture by developing your chest muscles too much. This overdevelopment of the chest muscles could eventually start pulling the shoulders forward.

Back in those days, this logic was enough for me, but as I learned more about the human body, I began to doubt this concept. Some of my experiments led me to believe that pushing could be more fundamental than pulling for posture. For example, being able to stand tall is facilitated by pushing away from the ground with the lower extremities. Proper posture in a Handstand, just as in standing tall, requires pushing the hands into the ground.

My belief is that pushing and pulling go hand in hand and must be trained equally for developing the movement I care about. We always need to be careful about adopting standards or training without understanding where they come from and how they fit our purpose.

global-local

In the movement control section of chapter 2 (page 51), I discussed how the integrity of your spine is critical for establishing control over your shape throughout any movement. This is the motivating factor for the Global-Local principle, which essentially prioritizes your global shape, or projection of your spine, over your local shape, or projection of your other joints. This principle extends in a continuum away from your midline. So, after the spine position, you prioritize hips over shoulders. Next, when looking at the upper body, you prioritize shoulders, then elbows, and then wrists; and when focusing on the lower body, you prioritize hips, then knees, and then ankles.

This principle also deals with the prioritization of the different shapes you can get into at either a global or a local level. For global shapes, I prioritize establishing a neutral or anatomical shape, then move on to flexion, extension, lateral flexion/extension, rotation, and combinations of these. For local shapes, I prefer to establish external rotation, flexion, extension, adduction, abduction, and internal rotation, in that order. Finally, I discuss the importance of establishing the shapes of a movement before developing range of motion.

prioritization of joints from spine to extremities

Only after establishing effective global positions can you maximize your efforts at local levels. As Kelly Starrett often states, "Our bodies are built for establishing a solid platform from which we can generate explosive movement." The prioritization of joints flows from the midline out to the extremities. So, after your spine, the next priority is your hips, even if your hips are simply acting as a support for the rest of your body.

Your hips are your body's main power generator. They are the most stable joint and the joint closest to the pelvis, which is the base of your spine. Your hips are also closest to your lumbar spine, which, as discussed in the movement control section of chapter 2 (page 51), is extremely important to keep stable in order to optimize performance.

Your shoulders are your body's secondary power generator. I like to think of the body as a hybrid car, with the hips as the gasoline engine and the shoulders as the electric engine. Your hips, similar to the gas engine, are most useful for big-performance-course movement patterns. Your shoulders, similar to the electric engine, are for lower-power and often more technical movement patterns, such as cooking, writing, or brushing your hair and teeth. If your hip movement is not optimized, the transmission of power through your spine will be limited, and because you won't be able to generate as much force at shoulder level, your performance will be limited.

When looking at the upper or lower body, the same order of spine-to-extremities priority continues. So, for the upper body, you prioritize shoulders, elbows, and then wrists, and for the lower body, it is hips, knees, and then ankles. This prioritization defines the progression; I am not ignoring the fact that as you move, these joints are operating at the same time in perfect harmony. So when developing a movement progression, start by prioritizing the movement at the joint closest to your spine and follow with the rest down to your extremities. For a full-body movement, do the same, but prioritize hips over shoulders.

For example, a Backflip requires you to prioritize hips over shoulders due to the hips' importance in performing the jump for the takeoff. Even though the shoulders are secondary, they still play a huge role as a follow-through to maximize the jump effort, the direction of the jump, your ability to control your body in the air, and even stability if your hands meet your shins to increase stability and rotation.

Pressing a barbell from your shoulders to overhead, on the other hand, doesn't require your hips to move, but it is still important to prioritize the hips, as they act to stabilize your spine and therefore affect movement control at a global level.

prioritization of global shapes

I prioritize developing global shapes in the following order:

1. ***Neutral:*** In the anatomical (standing or upright) position, gravity affects the spine and for the most part creates compression and no other forces. Think about a stack of quarters. If you stack them perfectly on a flat surface, the force of gravity or the load placed on the column reinforces its strength.
2. ***Flexion:*** Going into spinal flexion is the natural path that the body tends to take due to the spine's architecture and how gravity affects it. Flexion also goes in the direction you can see. It is the first movement most people perform when they get out of bed or bend over to tie their shoes.
3. ***Extension:*** I pick extension next because it allows you to emphasize movement control at spinal level. To compensate for the natural movement into flexion caused by gravity, you must move into extension in order to find a neutral spine position. Learning how to go past neutral into extension can help increase your overall mobility because extension is where you naturally run into movement restrictions due to the architecture of your spine. Especially at the thoracic level (upper back), the spine is naturally flexed, and it becomes pretty rigid due to the stability it has because of the ribs, the shoulder joints around it, and its job of supporting the cervical spine or neck and controlling the arms.
4. ***Lateral flexion and extension:*** Many people focus on bilateral movements in the gym and neglect the unilateral movements that occur frequently in real life. I see lateral flexion and extension as a bridge between bilateral and unilateral movements. Performing any movement loaded off-axis causes your spine to want to flex laterally, so to maintain a neutral position, you must resist that load by pushing into extension. In addition, having good lateral flexion is important for a healthy spine and the muscular functions around it.
5. ***Rotation:*** Rotation is seen in most human movements but appears near the bottom of this list because it is the most complicated global shape due to the spiral shape the spine takes. The natural curvature of the spine and the great number of vertebrae and joints in the spine make rotation pretty complex to "master."

6. ***Combination:*** You can maximize your ability to combine these global shapes by focusing your movement progressions in this order. Combining the shapes seen at spinal level produces sport and life movement patterns such as walking, running, and lifting your kid with one arm as you fry an egg with the other and tilt your head sideways to squeeze the phone between your shoulder and ear.

prioritization of local shapes

I prioritize developing local movements for primary movers (hips and shoulders) in the following order:

1. ***External rotation:*** This joint movement comes first because it helps set the joint closer to your spine in a stable position, ready to work. It also affects global position as it sets your thoracic spine in a more neutral position.
2. ***Flexion:*** One of the reasons I put flexion second is that it channels movement in the direction you can see. (Being able to see how you move is great feedback—why do you think mirrors are so common in fitness clubs?) Another reason is how often flexion occurs in the most common movements.
3. ***Extension:*** Extension comes next as an expression of taking your extremities behind you. The fact that you can't see this movement visually makes it a little harder. On top of this, in our modern environment we don't spend enough time naturally moving in and out of extension, and our ability becomes limited. Extension must be addressed in order to optimize movement in flexion.
4. ***Adduction:*** In the anatomical position, you are naturally in adduction. It is important to train adduction in order to reinforce the anatomical position, which is the most fundamental position for developing most movements.
5. ***Abduction:*** Abduction occurs later in this list because, as your limbs move away from your midline, your primary movers (hips and shoulders) often become secondary movers. For an example, see the Abduction Push-up in chapter 8 (page 318).
6. ***Internal rotation:*** Internal rotation comes last because it does not occur in the anatomical stance and therefore is used less frequently for setting up proper movements. Of course, we cannot completely ignore it, because this movement is required for all other movements, especially while the joint is in extension.

position over range of motion

It is sometimes easier to think of a movement in terms of its static positions or freeze-frames. In fact, I have already suggested the Start-Transition-Finish language for observing movement (page 33). ***Position*** refers to the shapes that you can get into, as described in the Global-Local section of chapter 1 (page 24)—for example, flexion and extension. ***Range of motion*** simply describes the ability to move your joints within a plane of motion. Common terms are end range and midrange. ***End range*** refers to the farthest a joint can move along a plane of motion without changing the shape of any other joint. So each person's end range of motion may differ based on their mobility. ***Midrange*** is commonly used to refer to any position at less than end range. We naturally feel more comfortable working at midrange of motion.

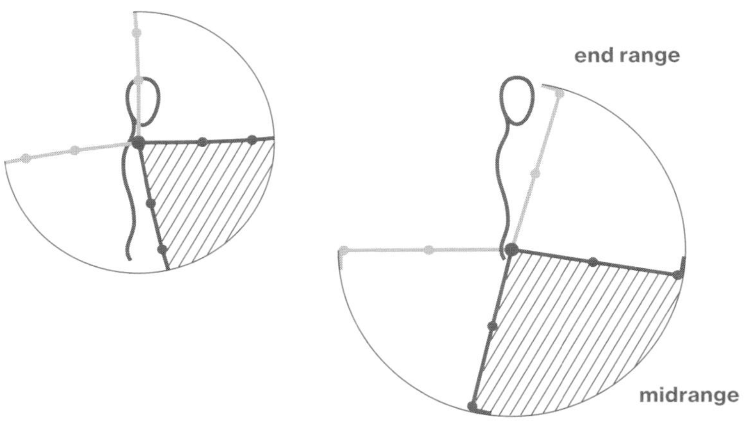

For example, when working on a Burpee, which is the act of getting facedown on the ground and back up again to a standing position, it is important to start in the most anatomical position possible to reinforce better movement globally and locally. But if asked to perform a Burpee in a strict anatomical position, most people would run into trouble simply because they can't touch their toes and would have to compromise their mechanics in order to perform the movement. Decreasing the range of motion of the hip movement, such as by placing a plate or box in front of you, can solve this problem and reinforce your position until you achieve the optimal range of motion required to perform the movement pattern effectively. See the Box Burpee progression in chapter 7 (page 280).

Let's return to the example of trying to get your first Pull-up. In the pushing-pulling principle, I discussed using the Push-up as a tool to develop the Pull-up. In addition to moving from pulling to pushing, the Push-up changes the range of motion that the shoulders go through. This is motivated by the principle of establishing position before range of motion. I would start with the Push-up rather than the press, even though the press seems more mechanically similar to the Pull-up, because it is easier to examine the integrity of the anatomical position as you go through midrange of motion rather than end range. See how the Row comes before the Pull-up on page 224.

stability

Stability is the physical result of maintaining form and balance—in other words, keeping your center of mass over your base of support—whether you are static or in motion. For example, think of a Cirque de Soleil artist performing a One-Arm Handstand without any noticeable wobble versus a football running back, who resists falling down while running at high speeds with several people trying to tackle him. Both actions require stability, even though the circus performer is static and the running back is in motion. I like to break stability into two types: points of contact with surface and physiological stability.

points of contact with surface

The more points of connection with a surface you have, the less muscle tension you need to maintain stability. Let's take the simplest example: lying on the ground. This is an extremely stable position from a points-of-contact perspective, so it makes sense as a position for rest and sleep. When progressing movement in the gym, the first thing I like to address with respect to this type of stability is the base of support. The bigger your base or the more connection you have with a surface, whether it is the ground or some external object, the more stable you are. When creating a progression, start with a big base and decrease it—for example, standing to walking to running.

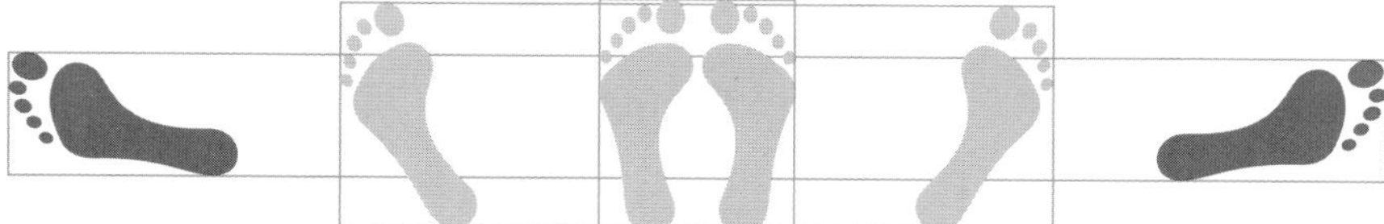

Changing the position of your feet changes the shape of your base of support, and various shapes lead to various levels of stability—for example, a board versus a balance beam.

One thing that may seem surprising is that you continue to lose stability the farther you remove yourself from a surface. For example, when training on a trampoline, the higher you go in the air, the less stability you have, and the more muscular tension you must use to compensate.

In terms of the base of support, it is ideal to start with a static surface (such as the ground or a Pull-up bar) over a dynamic or moving surface (like roller skates or a trapeze). Prioritize connected dynamic surfaces, where your two extremities are bound to one object (such as a trapeze, snowboard, or barbell) over non-connected dynamic surfaces, where your two extremities are attached to two separate objects (such as rings, skis, or dumbbells).

physiological stability

Physiological stability is a result of the muscular tension placed around a joint. More muscular tension equals greater stability. While performing a Handstand, for example, gymnasts are taught to straighten their legs and point their toes in order to generate greater muscular tension throughout the body to increase the stability of the position. Also think about the difference between being pushed when you are tensed and ready and being pushed when you are relaxed and not expecting it.

Let's take a Push-up and look at how increasing the degree of freedom, and therefore dispersing the muscular tension, decreases stability in the shoulders. The most stable starting position brings the arms as close to anatomical position as possible. The farther away from the midline the hands travel, the more freedom is imparted to the shoulders and the more unstable the shoulder position becomes.

Another important concept is the creation of additional points of contact with yourself. The more points of contact you have with yourself, the more stability you often have. Let's look at a Pull-up, for example. Some people perform a Pull-up by wrapping or hooking their legs around each other. Doing so increases the surface area of the legs in contact with themselves and creates a position in which these athletes feel more stable.

The third type of physiological stability to consider is bilateral versus unilateral loading. When you lift one foot off the ground (which creates a unilaterally loaded body), you experience a significant physiological change in addition to the obvious change in points of contact with the surface. In order to maintain stability, you must change the muscular tension throughout your body. When learning to balance on your hands, the best practice is often to work on stability when balancing on two hands before moving to one-handed balancing. You use this same progression principle when working on the Pistol (page 127); it is important to work on the stability of the Squat before you move to one leg.

The main challenge of unilateral loading, or loading laterally off the spine, is that you have to deal with the rotational forces that occur as you try to maintain the desired global shape. A clear example of how gravity affects the body under the rotational forces caused by unilateral loading is to hang from a bar with one arm. Any off-axis or off-midline loading due to the setup of the body does not just cause a lateral displacement of the other side of the body; it also causes a rotational displacement due to the body's anatomical design.

The Hang Test requires a fixed bar; it will not work with a dynamic piece of equipment like the rings. Hang from the bar with two hands, let go with one hand, and completely relax without letting go of the bar. After getting a good grip and relaxing your shoulders, belly, and body, you'll notice that your body rotates away from the direction your palm is facing. This is natural internal rotation occurring at shoulder level. But in the context of developing movement control, this internal rotation is not ideal for creating an optimal movement pattern to which you can add load, speed, cardiovascular demands, or other kinds of stressors later.

If you simply reach forward with your opposite arm (the arm that is not grabbing the bar) and tighten your belly while hanging, you'll immediately notice a fix in the shoulder you're hanging from. This fix occurs in the form of external rotation—a position in which the shoulder is stable, mechanically sound, and ready to work. The real purpose of this test is to show you that if you look at the body from the Global-Local perspective, you can see how the global side of things affects how the local side works.

In other words, if you can't create enough tension around your spine by squeezing your belly, you can assist yourself by reaching with the opposite side of your body. The Hang Test is a great way to show how unilateral or off-axis loading creates rotational forces that you must address in order to remain efficient or mechanically effective at performing a movement. It also shows how your body requires you to compensate globally by tightening everything around your spine in order to put your shoulder (or whichever local joint is active) in a better position for movement.

When a gymnast performs a twisting maneuver, we sometimes see her cross her legs during the movement. This tendency to cross the legs occurs because the gymnast lacks the movement strength required to maintain the anatomical position (legs side by side) by resisting the rotational forces in the movement. Because she is unable to create the stability she needs with muscular tension, she makes up for it by crossing her legs. Doing so compromises her performance because:

1. She loses points for poor execution.
2. She is not in the best position for landing.

A great way to improve this is to work on developing muscular tension in a position of adduction and especially unilaterally loaded with adduction, which can be done by squatting with a load on one shoulder.

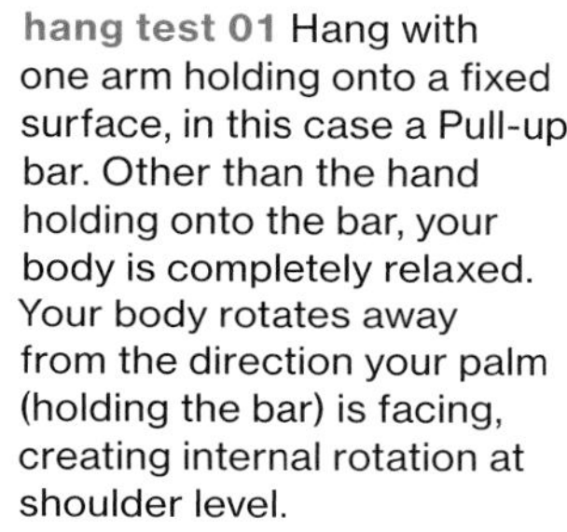

hang test 01 Hang with one arm holding onto a fixed surface, in this case a Pull-up bar. Other than the hand holding onto the bar, your body is completely relaxed. Your body rotates away from the direction your palm (holding the bar) is facing, creating internal rotation at shoulder level.

02 Reach forward with the arm that is not holding the bar, and squeeze your abs. Doing so causes your body to rotate so that the arm hanging from the bar has external rotation at shoulder level.

Internal rotation doesn't just happen while you hang from one arm; it also happens when you stand on one leg. I do the Hang Test simply because it exaggerates what happens at a local or joint level while walking, running, throwing, or doing any other unilaterally loaded movement with one side working and the other side posting.

orientation

When learning movement, it is always easiest to start where you feel the most comfortable. Most daily life functions happen while you are upright, either sitting or standing. Even though the principles don't always align here—for example, you just learned that the lying-down position is where you probably feel the most stable—common sense tells us that since most activity happens we are upright, it's probably not the best idea to start a progression of movement lying down.

When we talk about orientation in space from the perspective of an outside observer, we are usually doing so with respect to the ground. However, when trying to determine your own orientation in space, your head is really the key. If you simply tilt your head back or down, you create the orientation perspective of being either horizontal or upside down, even though an observer would simply state that you are bent over. So it is important to keep control of your head position if you want your best estimates of your body's orientation in space. As the saying goes, "Where the head goes, the body follows."

So, to prioritize orientation in space in terms of the starting position for movement, I typically follow this order:

1. Upright
2. Supine or prone
3. Inverted

We can further refine our prioritization of orientation in space by looking at orientation changes within different planes of motion.

sagittal plane

The sagittal plane, which divides your body into right and left sides, is the plane within which you move most frequently. As an axis of rotation, it allows you to rotate forward and backward. In terms of the movements performed in this plane, regardless of what is happening at the global or local level, I prioritize forward movement over backward.

1. ***Forward rotation*** goes from upright to prone position. As explained in the Global-Local principle, forward rotation is natural; plus, you can see where you are going. It can be as simple as bending over to tie your shoe. If you went further, you could take it to full inversion, doing a Handstand or Headstand, and eventually all the way to a supine position, like a ¾ Front Flip onto your back, or a full revolution, such as a Forward Roll.
2. ***Backward rotation*** goes from upright to supine. It comes second even though it is such a basic thing to do. When you lie down in bed, you rotate to the most stable position, which is supine. From there, you can continue rotating backward to inversion, like a Back Extension Roll; rotate backward to prone position, as in a ¾ Backflip or a Back Extension Roll to Push-up position; or do a full revolution back to an upright position, as in a Backflip or, a more stable version, a Backward Roll.

When learning how to progress a movement, we begin with forward rotation. Eventually we get to movements in the forward rotations, such as a Front Flip, that may be more difficult than their backward-rotation counterparts, such as a Backflip. This is mostly due to the fact that spotting the landing is more difficult.

transverse plane

The transverse plane divides your body into top and bottom halves. Its axis of rotation allows you to rotate left and right. It can get tricky because your upper body can move independently of your lower body, but, just as I explained for the sagittal plane, I am going to focus on the global aspect to help you understand this plane a little better.

Throwing a ball or a punch with your right hand causes your body to spin to the left.

Your ability to turn left or right depends on who you are. Lefties tend to turn right, and righties tend to turn left. The rotation can occur 1 degree at a time, but we can take a four-part approach and start with quarter-turns: 90 degrees, 180 degrees, 270 degrees, and 360 degrees.

frontal plane

The frontal plane divides your body into front and back halves. Its axis of rotation allows you to rotate sideways or laterally, as you would when doing a cartwheel. You can look at the amount of rotation by quarters: upright to right or left side, upright to inversion in either direction, upright to right or left side, and finishing in a full lateral revolution.

combinations

Looking at these planes of motion is a simple way of studying and understanding movement, but your body is a designed to move through all three planes and can emphasize one plane of motion over the others according to the task being completed. Here are a couple of interesting combinations to think about, as long as you understand that all planes of motion are working to some degree:

1. ***Sagittal + Transverse:*** A forward rotation with a full twist (called a Full in gymnastics). You could perform this movement over and over down an aisle; your body would never deviate from the line and direction of the movement.
2. ***Sagittal + Transverse + Frontal:*** Most life functions involve all three planes of motion, but, as stated earlier, one plane may be expressed more or less than the other two. Take walking, for example. All three planes are working: sagittal = swinging the arms and moving the legs, frontal = resisting the rotation caused by the unilateral loading created by picking up one foot at a time, and transverse = moving the legs and swinging the arms in the opposite direction in order to create positional stability and maximize efficiency. In this example, the frontal plane has the least amount of movement expressed.

misty flip

A Misty Flip is an off-axis Front Flip with a 180-degree twist. It is an example of a movement that occurs in all planes and has an interesting history. The Misty Flip is the result of a creative progression that evolved from the natural progression of a Front Flip. Imagine the original progression being your friends teaching you the Front Flip by telling you to just "chuck it." What added the twist to this movement was the inability to spot the landing during the flip, which caused the person practicing the Front Flip to look over his shoulder to see the ground. When the athlete turns his head from this position, it pulls the rest of his body into a twist, making the movement a Front Flip with a half twist. So the Misty is essentially a natural progression that developed because an athlete was trying to see the ground early during a Front Flip. Once this natural progression was introduced and mastered, action-sports athletes used creative progressions to introduce off-axis rotation by experimenting with purposefully controlling the head turn at different points in the flip.

central-peripheral

The basis of all human performance, regardless of specialty and therefore regardless of specific physiological demands, is that we all want to last longer! We want to be able to lift more longer, we want to play better and longer, we want to go faster and longer. "Longer" can define one set, one day, days, weeks, years, or a lifetime. This goal involves two key physiological aspects:

1. The ***central engine*** is the ability to distribute the necessary fuel for movement to the entire body. The capacity of the central engine is often referred to as endurance.
2. The ***peripheral engine*** is the ability to use that fuel at the local level to create motion or maintain the integrity of the structure. The capacity of the peripheral engine is often referred to as stamina.

I often prefer to start with the central engine. The reason for this bias is that most people lack central ability more than peripheral, which stops them from doing the amount of work they might otherwise be capable of. After this initial bias, either engine may become the focus of a particular progression stage, depending on the desired outcome.

Let's take a runner, for example. If the goal is simply to complete a 5k, most people have the peripheral engine or stamina to go that distance, even if it takes them all day. If the runner's goal is to complete a 5k in thirty minutes, then his central engine or endurance may have to be developed in order to achieve that target. If the runner wants to be even more competitive and complete a 5k in less than fifteen minutes, he may need to increase his stamina as well as his endurance. I like this example because it demonstrates the delicate balance and constant decision-making we all need in order to be successful. Goals change constantly, and with them the strategies and tactics you use to reach them.

speed continuum

The Swedish word ***Lagom*** means "just right." It comes from ***lager*** ("beer") and ***om*** ("around"). Essentially, to get a single glass of beer all the way around a table, everyone has to drink just the right amount. I hope it's clear by now that when developing movement progressions, the principles are never black or white; they need to be applied in just the right way. The ability to figure out what "just right" means in a particular situation comes from experience in training and testing with these methods, and how you balance principles or focus on one principle over another is really what makes any progression just right.

This concept of "just right" is highly applicable to speed. There is a relationship between the speed at which the body travels and the amount of stability required to maintain form at that speed. The interesting thing is that the relationship is not linear—it is parabolic. We often experience high stability demands at very low speeds and then again at very high speeds, and a sweet spot when the speed is just right. For example, if you go too fast, like if you're bombing a hill on your skateboard, you may get the death wobbles, and if you go too slow, such as when biking up a hill or doing a really slow Push-up, you can get the slow wobbles or shakes.

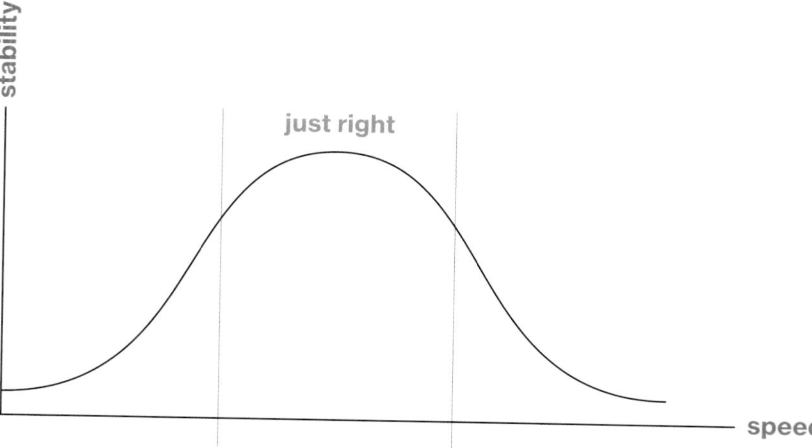

Speed is an important factor in working out. A coach's job is to use speed to create just the right dose.

Sometimes the best position to focus on is a static position. After all, the position over range of motion principle (page 80) suggests that mastering a position typically precedes maintaining the quality of that position while in motion. This advice to practice position quality statically before controlling that position in motion may seem obvious, but let's look at a few examples where a little motion is the best way to maintain a position.

Think about riding a bike. When a kid gets on a bike for the first time, she can't put both feet on the pedals and balance without moving forward; she falls to one side or the other. Finding stability requires a little forward motion. This is a case where an increase in speed makes the movement more successful.

Similarly, if you ever tried a Handstand and thought that you could stand completely still like an Olympic gymnast, you probably quickly realized that in order to stay inverted while balancing on two hands, you had to move around. Or if you tried a Pull-up and weren't strong enough to get your chin up over the bar, you probably added some kicking or swinging action to try to get yourself up there. The extra motion results in speed, but it's not completely clear whether it's the speed or the extra degrees of freedom, thus distributing the load, that makes the movement easier. Static position is usually harder and isn't always the best place to start. Remember, you must always balance the success of a stage with your progress toward your end goal. Sometimes principles conflict, and you have to experiment to find the sweet spot.

The progression principles outlined above are truths that I have learned over years of coaching. In this section, I introduce the strategies that I have collected to put those principles into practice.

Most of us believe in the statement "practice makes perfect," or the general idea that you need to put in your time in order to perform at the level you desire. Or perhaps you think of it as accumulating your 10,000 hours to master a concept. You also understand that you can't simply jump into accumulating 10,000 hours of a movement you want to perform. For example, if you desire a career in hand-balancing and want to become proficient at one-handed balancing, you wouldn't have an easy time starting with 10,000 hours of standing on one hand. Instead, you must move in a way that gives you a chance of success as well as being somewhat close to the edge of what you are capable of and where you are heading. This concept is found across disciplines. In fitness it is considered scaling a movement; in gymnastics we talk about levels; for mogul skiers there are degrees of difficulty.

Whatever you call it, most people focus on the chance of success, or easiness of the movement, without fully understanding how to balance the chance of success with progress toward a goal. This section introduces my methods for using progression principles to create progression stages that achieve that balance. You can use these stages to accumulate hours of practice or training.

blocking

Blocking is the act of setting an anatomical standard for a movement that helps you maximize your performance. Setting a standard forces you to perform the movement in the optimal fashion without having to be conscious of some of the mechanics, because you are using your anatomy to restrict the degree of freedom you can move in.

Let's look at a Push-up. When performing a Push-up, you are primarily concerned with the mechanics of your shoulders moving from flexion into extension, as well as the form that enables your shoulders to move effectively through those positions. To reduce the degree of freedom that your shoulders can move in, you can bring your arms closer to your midline, or closer to anatomical position. Or you can reduce the degree of freedom around your elbows by rotating your hands 180 degrees so that your fingers are pointing behind you. This reduction in the degree of freedom allows you to focus on the shoulder pushing rather than on form. See the Anatomical Push-up in chapter 5 (page 164).

If you are having trouble figuring out how to block a particular movement, it's helpful to go back as close as possible to anatomical position and then use the progression principles outlined earlier to rebuild the movement in incremental layers that let you limit the mechanics that you consciously control.

I typically use three blocking techniques: anatomical, external, and distance. Anatomical refers to keeping your body as close to anatomical position as possible throughout the movement. External blocking takes advantage of objects or friends to maintain positions. Finally, distance blocking sets distances that the movement must cover to limit positions.

anatomical blocking 01 Stand in an anatomical stance.

02 Change your orientation in space to horizontal, and put your arms in plank position without changing your anatomical shoulder position.

external blocking 01 Adopt the plank position with a dumbbell placed behind your forearm.

02 As you initiate the descent, the dumbbell blocks your forearm from deviating from vertical.

03 When you reach the bottom of the Push-up, your forearm is still blocked vertically.

distance blocking 01 Start in a Lunge with your back leg straight and your arms straight overhead, preparing to kick up into a Handstand.

02 Reach out as far as possible with your posting leg, keeping your body in a straight line.

03 Continue to reach and place your hands as far away as possible from your posting leg. This reach will prevent your global position from changing.

60 percent rule

The 60 percent rule states that once you achieve 60 percent of success at any stage of a progression, it's a good time to introduce the next stage into your training. This isn't an exact science; it's about intuition.

My experience is that once you succeed more often than you fail, it is better to introduce the next stage than to wait for more success in the current stage.

Introducing the next stage does not mean that you are done with the current one. When you can perform 60 percent of the movement well, you add new movements or move on to the next stage. However, you continue to start with the 60 percent version to prepare yourself for the more advanced movements, thus bringing the 60 percent movement closer to 99 percent perfect over time.

position-range of motion-load-speed-freestyle

I often recommend prioritizing your positions first, then working on the range of motion you cover, then handling the muscular tension or load on your body to maintain form throughout the movement, and then efficiently performing the movement with speed. The final component—which I call Freestyle—refers to the act of finding the next position or movement that gets you closer to your purpose.

Let's take learning a Handstand Push-up, working backward through many progression stages and beginning with a regular Push-up (page 157):

1. Start by examining the Push-up at the three master positions: start, or top of the Push-up; transition, or bottom of the Push-up; and finish, or top of the Push-up.
2. Examine the range of motion of the shoulder pressing mechanics, going from midrange extension to flexion.
3. Add load by increasing the number of Push-ups you do or by putting plates on your back, and assess your ability to maintain your form despite the increase in muscular tension.
4. Increase the speed of your Push-ups to see if you can continue to perform the movement efficiently.
5. Freestyle is your opportunity to take a broader perspective and consider why you are after the Handstand Push-up with respect to all the goals you have established. For example, an Olympic weightlifter may be after the Handstand Push-up as an assistance tool to perform the Jerk better, while a baseball pitcher may be trying to enhance his throw by improving his pushing mechanics. In the case of the Olympic lifter, the next stage may be to move to a different type of press, perhaps the Bench Press, or to a more vertical press, adapting the pressing mechanics closer to the purpose. For the pitcher, the next step may be a unilateral or One-Arm Push-up or perhaps a Push-up with a wider base to bring the pushing mechanics closer to the throwing shape.

I believe the Freestyle step is the most important because it emphasizes the process of looking at all the possible styles of movement and then selecting the one that will get you closer to your personal goals.

simple-complex-simple

Simple-Complex-Simple is a method of introducing variables of movement and intensity. At the first simple step, the movement has fewer variables and less demand; at the complex stage, it has many variables and higher demand; and at the last simple step, it has fewer variables again but the highest demand.

The way to progress something from start to finish is to start with very simple and angular shapes, work into very complex and circular shapes, and eventually work back into very simple and angular shapes. The simplicity-to-complexity of a movement is defined by the joints moving and the planes of motion utilized.

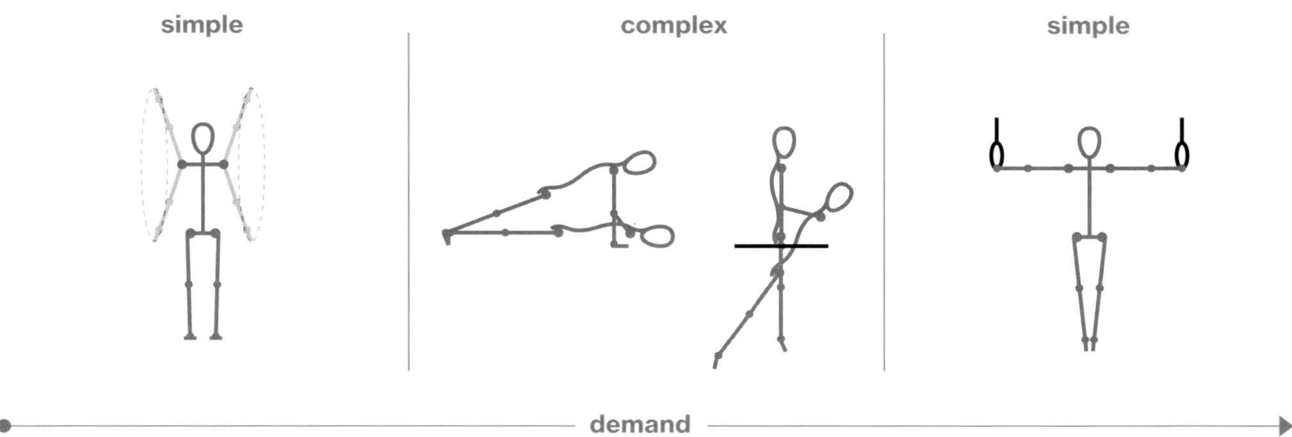

During a natural progression related to any major movement pattern involving pushing, pulling, squatting, and/or jumping and landing, the mechanics can usually be considered complex movement patterns with a lot of moving parts. But once formalized, the training for these complex movement patterns usually involves working with many simple movement patterns. Take running, for example, as a movement that I consider both arising from a natural progression of locomotion and a complex movement pattern, which is often trained using formal progressions that use simple movement patterns such as the Squat and the Pistol.

If you are working on the Push-up, for example, the first simple step may be arm circles or arm swings. In this case, your shoulders are going through the ranges of motion that would be involved in the Push-up but without any load, not necessarily much speed, and without the complexity of the elbows and wrists being involved. The complex step may be a Push-up, where the intensity or load of pushing your body off the ground and maintaining positional integrity throughout the movement requires muscular tension and places demands on the movement. The variables of movement are also high here, as the Push-up requires the synchronized motion of the primary mover (shoulder) and the secondary movers (elbow and wrist). Finally, the last simple stage may have you get on the rings to do Press-outs. In this stage, you are again removing variables of movement by moving only your shoulders to perform the Press-out, as your elbows and wrists create a static arm position, but unlike the arm swings, a great deal of muscular tension is required to maintain your position throughout the movement.

Eventually movements progress to a point of simplicity where I consider them to be "dead-end" movements. A movement is a dead-end when you have taken some variable of it and moved it so far outside the most common movement pattern that there is nowhere for that variable to continue. For example, consider a Push-up in which you are progressively widening your grip. Eventually your hands are so far apart that your chest reaches the ground. These dead-end movements may be useful for training the Push-up, but I consider them dead-ends because the movement patterns you work in those positions are far from where you perform most of your work in sport and life. Remember, when looking to progress movement, we are constantly considering the anatomical position and the most common shapes.

Let's say you are a powerlifter, and one of the movements you have to perform is the Bench Press. This lift involves shoulder pressing, elbows, and wrists. For your warm-up, you might start in a simple stage where you do arm circles to prepare your shoulders. During the workout, you may use a complex stage that includes some style of Bench Press. Finally, you may move to an advanced simple stage where you work on assistance movements, such as curls and elbow extensions.

As another example, a gymnast working on an Inverted Cross is working toward a low-variable, ultra-high-demand goal and may use complex movements to improve his stamina and general movement ability. Anytime you do a simple movement with high demands, you need a certain amount of overall movement ability (strength and skill) that doesn't seem to be effectively trained by repeating just this one movement. This seems to be the case because your body is under such a load that it brings out any holes in your movement ability, and those holes may be filled with less desirable positions. So general movement ability that is trained in the complex realm seems to be necessary even for high-level athletes.

General life seems to be mostly in the complex realm.

shift-connect-flow

How a movement is created is an important way to think about progression stages and movement ability at each stage. I discussed my simple language for describing the creation of movement in the Shift-Connect-Flow section of chapter 1 (page 38). Creating progression stages based on shift, connect, and flow can be very effective.

Let's take a Handstand Push-up. I have worked with many athletes who seem to be right on the edge of their first Handstand Push-up from the ground, or perhaps they've done one ugly one, barely surviving. Despite that huge grin of success, the athlete knows that something is missing. Usually he is missing the understanding of movement creation that he needs in order to utilize the movement ability he has effectively.

In this situation, you can use the Shift-Connect-Flow principle to develop the following progression stages and train this understanding. A Handstand Push-up is a lot easier to perform when it starts with a shift of the body toward the ground. So the first stage of the progression might be to get into a static Headstand and then work on shifting your body toward the ground in a controlled fall.

Next, you might shift your body forward without falling and then shift back to center. Working on getting in and out of the shift without falling enables you to increase the amount of stability you have as your center of mass translates around the edges of your base of support.

shift with fall 01 Start in a balanced Headstand.

02 Allow your hips to fall slowly over your hands without changing your global position.

03 Continue the controlled fall until your feet reach the ground. Keep your head down the entire time to simply experience the fall.

shift with control 01 Start in a balanced Headstand.

02 Shift your center of mass to the back edge of your base of support.

03 Shift your center of mass from the back edge of your base of support back to the most balanced position.

04 Continue to shift forward until you find the front edge of your base of support.

Once you understand shifting, you can add the concept of connection, which refers to the change in the points of contact of your body, in this case your head on the ground. As you pass the point of no return in the controlled fall created by the shift, your head will leave the ground if the integrity of your body remains stable. Your head leaving the ground after the shift can then be considered a new movement ability or stage of the progression.

At this stage, you may want to play with simultaneously adding points of contact at the finish and removing points of contact from the start. For example, you might have your feet connect with the ground or a wall. This allows you to remove stability from the beginning of the movement while adding it at the end in order to intuitively remain at the same level.

connect 01 Start in a balanced Headstand.

02 Shift your hips over your hands. As you feel a sense of weightlessness, push off the ground with your arms, using the momentum of the fall to assist in removing your head from the floor.

03 Continue to use the push and fall until your feet reach the ground and your body is in plank position.

After you see success with changing points of contact by lifting your head off the ground to connect your feet to the wall, it is often a good time to introduce a progression stage based on flow. You can do so by working on cycling between the starting points of contact and the finish as smoothly as possible, then adding speed between them. You should feel like each step of this cycle connects so well to the next that it starts to feel like one continuous motion. See page 183 in chapter 5 for more on this progression.

flow 01 Start in a balanced Headstand.

02 Allow your hips to shift over the heel of your hands as you push away from the ground.

03 Continue to push away from the ground as you shift your hips back over your hands.

04 As you reach full lockout, shift your center of mass back over the center of your base of support.

start-transition-finish

When beginning to work on the Handstand, many people start at the bottom, or Headstand, and then push up and fall off. If I ask them to do two repetitions, they can't, because they don't have the Handstand position. If there is a position you don't have, then you need to work on that position. The transition position is often the one people have the most trouble with.

When thinking about a movement in terms of the master positions discussed in the Start-Transition-Finish section of chapter 1 (page 32), it can be effective to focus your training on the transition position. As previously mentioned, the transition is often the signature of the movement, as you can see when comparing a Squat and a Deadlift. It's also the key to understanding the essence of the movement you're working toward. The transition position often contains the most complex part of the movement and is where the body hits end range of motion with a high level of physical demand.

I like to say, "Build the beginning, build the end. Work on the middle!" What I mean is that the start and finish positions require a lot of conscious effort. The start position requires conscious effort to set up, and the finish position benefits from serious, conscious effort to measure, but the transition position is where your sweat efforts really pay off.

Build the beginning, build the end. Work on the middle!

progression summary

I consider the material in this chapter to be the most essential part of what I do as a coach. These are the principles and methods that I use to understand and improve movement ability. These tools enable me to build effective road maps to make my athletes successful. As I've stated, these tools are not just for creating brand-new road maps that ignore the progressions offered in specific disciplines. Instead, I believe that one of the most beneficial ways to use these tools is to combine them with established progressions in order to get even more from the progressions that are known to work. In addition, when you understand the fundamental principles underlying the best progressions, you are better able to recognize the commonalities and subtle differences between progressions.

Without understanding the fundamentals, most people get confused when they see differing progressions to achieve similar outcomes. Take learning a Handstand, for example. Chinese hand-balancing, break-dancing, and artistic gymnastics all use different progressions, but at the end of the day, they all finish in a Handstand. The reason each discipline has a unique progression is that the athletes come from different places and are heading for different purposes. When we look back at the progressions, we can often see where these differences came from and how they affect our movement ability depending on our purpose.

freestyle four

Master the basics and you will be a master at the most advanced movements.

My Freestyle Connection framework gives you a foundation for observing, describing, and progressing movements. As you learned in chapter 3, building road maps for improving movement ability is the heart and soul of my framework and my career as a coach. This part of the book shows you how to utilize that framework to assess and progress the four movements that form my foundation for enhancing all other movements in sport and life—the Pistol, the Handstand Push-up, the Muscle-up, and the Burpee. I call them the Freestyle Four.

The Freestyle Four evolved from the tasks that we all must perform in everyday life: getting up, moving around, pushing and pulling to manipulate objects, and sometimes clearing obstacles. Even though the fitness industry and the strength and conditioning community have known about and utilized these movements since the beginning, I present them in a way that will help you understand why they are the way they are and how they apply to other movements. After observing and performing thousands of iterations of these movements, I have found what seem to be the most universal forms. The forms of movement discussed in this part are the ones that I believe are the most functional and applicable to your tasks.

In the gym (or any place we train), hundreds of years of evolution have led to my Freestyle Four:

1. ***The Pistol*** is the evolution of a Squat and a more challenging way to get up off the ground.
2. ***The Handstand Push-up*** is an exaggeration of your capacity to push objects and yourself away from something. The inversion is critical, as it teaches you to take your natural state of standing to its highest level of awareness by flipping it upside down.
3. ***The Muscle-up*** develops your capacity to get over an obstacle, which is done on the rings in the gymnastics world.
4. ***The Burpee*** is a formalized way of getting up off the ground from a prone or facedown position and then getting back down.

I travel the world conducting seminars and coaching sessions with various athletes. When I ask, "What is the hardest bodyweight movement?" the answer is usually some variation of one of these four. Sometimes there is doubt as to whether these four movements truly encapsulate all bodyweight movements, but often a "new" movement either is a subset of one of the Freestyle Four or requires one of the Freestyle Four in order to perform it. For example, the Push-up is part of the Burpee, Muscle-up, and Handstand Push-up. The Pull-up is in the Muscle-up, and the L-Sit is in the Pistol. The Burpee could be a requirement for popping up on a surfboard.

Despite being ubiquitous, these movements are considered the most challenging. Why is that, when almost anyone can do some variation of each of them? For example, my high school football coach punished his athletes with either a mile run or an up-down (a Burpee). But why would the up-down, something an athlete does constantly in a game and in practice, be a punishment? I think it's because it is inclusive yet challenging. Although we are wired to do these basic movements and they are the foundation for so many activities, everyone can benefit from spending more time practicing them. If you train to be an expert at the basics, you can apply that foundation to anything.

Together, the Freestyle Four form the blueprint for human movement. Although they offer the vocabulary for all the movement that I want to describe, I will describe them with other fundamental, lower-level movements that I use to construct the Freestyle Four.

TRAINER

Photo by Paolo Sanchez

the pistol

04

One day after taking a break-dancing class, I was sitting on the floor, physically and mentally exhausted. The session had been the most intense one of the week. I remember looking up and telling one of the younger kids there how I'm always mind-blown by how many layers the craft of b-boying has. Once you think you have it down, another layer is added, and then you don't. The kid looked at me and said, "Of course it is, Carl; you are working through many generations of b-boying evolution."

Simple as this statement was, it was refreshing to hear a young person so in tune with the depth of his craft, and to see the excitement in his eyes as he embraced the past in order to develop the future. Furthermore, he was able to state so clearly how relevant an understanding of the history or origin of a movement is in order to either implement it as a tool to improve oneself or simply be able to place it in a bucket of knowledge.

As a person who both coaches and practices movement, I am always intrigued by the complexity of the body, how it is designed for motion, and its capability to express motion in such a simple form. Through my exploration of different movement disciplines, I have realized that regardless of sport, activity, or physical life requirement, training should always come back to a focus on the basic movements that are the foundation of all disciplines.

As a coach, I look at some of the most basic physical requirements for human survival or independence. You usually need to get up (from sleeping) and move around (walking, running, and sometimes jumping) before performing any other tasks. The act of getting up requires the use of your lower extremities to push yourself away from the ground, a bed, or a chair. These tasks are really the equivalent of squatting.

This association also makes sense from a fitness and movement ability perspective. Squatting is king, and locomotion is one of the most basic functions that the human body is designed to perform. Excelling at squatting and moving from one place to another (locomotion) requires the efficient use of the hips, which are the body's main power generator. Therefore, I think the Pistol is the most universal movement for developing hip mechanics.

I can't tell you who was the first person to perform a Pistol, but I can tell you that the specific technique required to perform the Pistol is simply an evolution and a variation of basic squatting mechanics.

This movement is something that many people overlook and may not consider a tool for achieving elite fitness or general preparedness. While it is easy to create effective training plans without the Pistol, you should not underestimate this movement, because it has a lot of great features. The features are not just within the movement itself, but are present especially in its progression. They are extremely important, and you can use them to change your game from a movement standpoint.

This chapter starts with a universal Squat that everyone can do. I use the progression to a Squat as an introduction to basic hip mechanics. After the Squat, I introduce the concept of unilateral loading by using a Lunge progression. Next, you will learn a progression for the actual Pistol shape in order to further challenge the unilateral loading and hip squatting mechanics. Finally, I introduce rolling as a way to connect the Pistol mechanics to other movements as well as exiting and entering the Pistol itself. I consider each of these stages individually as a movement in order to build up to the Pistol.

shooting the duck

As a kid, you may have attended a birthday party at a roller skating rink where, if you were one of the "cool" kids, you got a chance to learn how to shoot the duck. Shooting the duck is a simple yet relatively challenging trick in which you squat down while balancing on one leg as you cruise around on your skates. Being able to shoot the duck had the potential to make you the king of the rink, or at least of the party.

Shooting the duck is not just a trick that roller skaters do at parties. It is also a shape seen in the sport of figure skating. Even the highest-level athletes perform it as part of their routines, usually with a spin or pirouette.

SQUAT

The Squat is the act of lowering your body's center of mass as close to the ground as possible, flexing your hips, knees, and ankles to the ground and then pushing back up without assistance from your upper body.

Most coaches, myself included, could go on a rant here, describing the importance of the Squat for making you stronger and more prepared for any physical endeavor. Take powerlifting, for example. The Squat comprises a third of the sport, being one of the three movements performed. The Squat is a key to success in all the lifts performed in Olympic weightlifting. Beyond sports, anytime you get out of bed, get off the toilet, or get out of a chair, you are performing a variation of the Squat.

So, in addition to being the essence of the Pistol, the Squat is a fundamental movement pattern for life.

Following the Global-Local progression principle, I consider it important to prioritize from the midline out to the extremities. The Squat is a wonderful movement because it emphasizes these priorities.

old man squat

While training my dad, I discovered a Squat progression that I like to call the Old Man Squat. Before using the Old Man Squat, I had tried several scaling techniques, such as having him sit on a chair, squat with a wall as a support, or cue his chest up. None of these methods worked well for him.

After failing with those Squat methods, I decided to explore some different avenues. My observation of his performance on the previous Squat tests led me to believe that one of the things he lacked was an understanding of the basic act of squatting. This lack of understanding led him to make obvious awkward moves, including lifting his heels, bending at the knees first, not using his hips, and extremely rounding his back. I came up with a simple way to demonstrate the importance of prioritizing hips over knees, knees over ankles and hips, and knees and ankles over spine. These are the basic mechanics of the Squat.

I wanted a Squat progression that first developed an understanding of how to move the hips. Next, I developed the pattern of moving the hips in coordination with the knees and ankles. Finally, I was able to combine hips, knees, and ankles and focus on developing a better spinal position while performing a Squat. This progression may seem contradictory to my Global-Local progression principle, where I prioritize spinal position over joint movement, but because there is no load on the spine, this type of spinal position is safe.

By following the principle of position over range of motion (page 80), and in this case focusing first on the prime mover, or hip, I was able to progressively layer more joint range of motion on top of the developed position. In other words, I start with the hip position, then address range of motion of the hip, and finally the knee and ankle position with range of motion of these lower extremities. Once the full range of motion at hip, knee, and ankle level has been achieved, I can focus on getting the spine in a more neutral position for better overall squatting mechanics. The three stages of the progression are:

1. Hinge & Touch
2. Hinge, Touch, & Drop
3. Hinge, Touch, Drop, & Lift

cuing the hips

Many coaches cue their athletes to push their hips back in order to flex the hips before bending in the knees and ankles. Even though this cue is effective for assuring that the primary joint is moving first and effectively, it can be problematic.

The cue is potentially problematic because, in reality, the hips, knees, and ankles need to move at the same time during the Squat. Usually, the hips-back cue is paired with a chest-up cue, which could cause the person performing the Squat to lose the lower-back position.

So these cues, which were meant to simplify the coach's instruction, can confuse the athlete and compromise his performance. Rather than asking the athlete to focus on his hip movement during a Squat, we can instead simplify or block the Squat in a way that almost forces the athlete to focus on the hip movement pattern. The Old Man Squat is a progression that I developed specifically to prioritize parts of the fundamental movement patterns found in the Squat.

hinge & touch

This first stage simply involves bending over and placing your hands flat on the ground with as much knee bend as needed. Your hips should always stay above your knees. In order to keep the focus of this movement on the hips, you perform it with your feet together so that your knees are forced to track correctly when they bend. This is a great example of the blocking progression method (page 88).

In this book, I make it a point to discuss neutral global position as the safest and best position for performing most movements. This progression allows for a natural bend in the spine because it is safe—and it's better than not being able to learn how to squat.

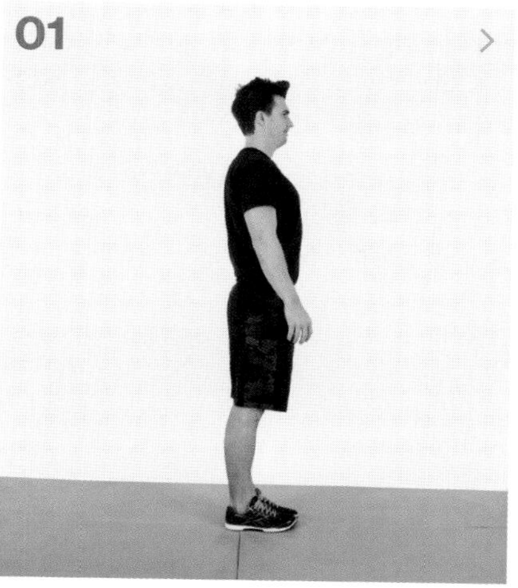

stand 01 Stand tall with your feet flat on the ground and your big toes facing forward. You are as upright as possible, with your knees locked out. Your hips are completely extended or neutral, with no hinge. Your shoulders are back and down, and your arms are hanging relaxed at your sides. Your back is flat with your neck long in the back. Your chin is slightly tucked in, but you are looking straight ahead.

hinge 02 Bend over as you slide your hands down your legs toward your knees. Think of it as a hinge in your hips while you're pushing your hips back behind you. There is no rounding of your back during this bend. Because your feet are together as your hands reach knee level, your knees will naturally fall out to the sides. Fight the knee fall by keeping your big toes nailed to the ground so that your feet stay completely flat.

touch 03 Continue hinging forward until your hands are flat on the ground. Your hips remain above your bent knees, and your feet are flat. Your spine is rounded and your head is tucked in.

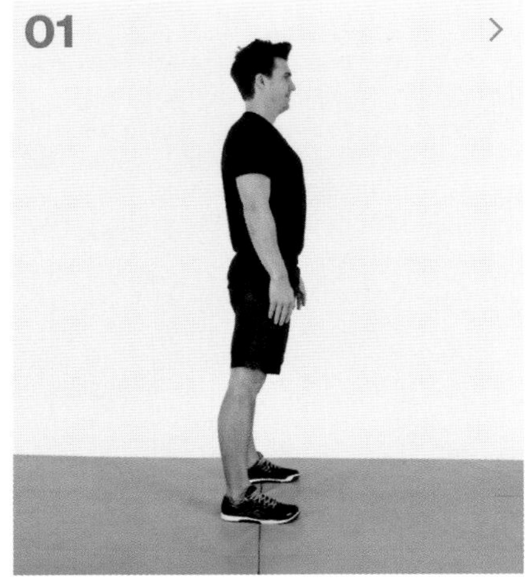

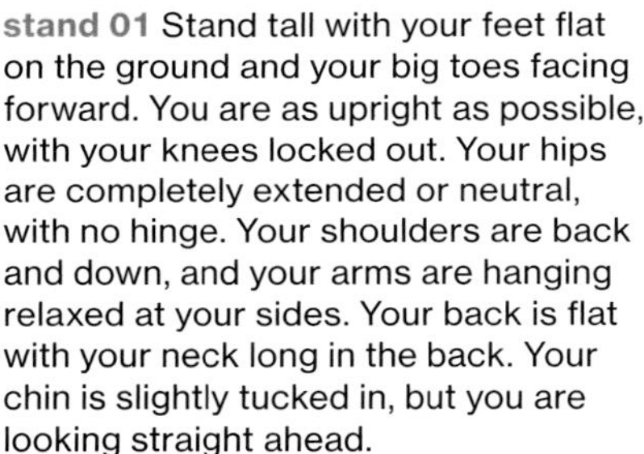

stand 01 Stand tall with your feet flat on the ground and your big toes facing forward. You are as upright as possible, with your knees locked out. Your hips are completely extended or neutral, with no hinge. Your shoulders are back and down, and your arms are hanging relaxed at your sides. Your back is flat with your neck long in the back. Your chin is slightly tucked in, but you are looking straight ahead.

hinge 02 Bend over as you slide your hands down your legs toward your knees. Think of it as a hinge in your hips while you're pushing your hips back behind you. There is no rounding of your back during this bend. With your feet in a wider stance here, you initiate the Squat by sliding your hands down your legs while keeping your hands inside your knees, which helps you push your knees out.

touch 03 Proceed until your hands are flat on the ground. Your hips remain above your bent knees, and your feet are flat. Your spine is rounded with your head tucked in.

hinge, touch, & drop

This stage adds a hip drop to the Hinge & Touch. Once you are at full hinge—in other words, when your hands are flat on the ground—you can simply lower your hips toward the ground. This movement can be performed with feet together but is easier to do with feet apart, as it starts to resemble the desired squatting mechanics. Any hip flexion creates external rotation at the hip, so the knees naturally track outward.

for hinge, touch, & drop, reverse steps 4–1

for hinge, touch, drop, & lift, reverse steps 5–1

drop 04 After you reach a full hinge of your hips, drop your hips down as low as you can go without allowing your heels to come off the ground. Your hands can remain flat on the ground, although this is not a requirement, as the focus is on hip mechanics. Tuck your head in by bringing your chin to your chest to create a uniform flexed spinal position.

lift 05 Without moving your hips, knees, or feet, lift your arms over your head. As your arms come overhead, you will feel a lot of muscular tension in your back and shoulders. Try to exaggerate this tension by lifting your arms as vertical as possible. With your palms facing each other and your thumbs pointing back, you can create good external rotation at shoulder level. You've found the finish position when you reach end range of motion at hip, knee, and ankle level and your back is flat with your torso upright.

hinge, touch, drop, & lift

Now that your hips, knees, and ankles are reaching the bottom of the Squat position, you can focus on your spine by lifting your arms overhead, or as far overhead as you can reach according to your movement ability. You can see in the photos that my back is rounded, which is OK because I am not carrying a load and the stress on my spine is not harmful. Depending on your mobility, you will have more or less rounding in your back and straightness in your legs. Finishing with your arms overhead is beneficial because it relates to many movements, and the tension it creates in your back reinforces a neutral spine.

box squats

As you learned in the discussion of the Start-Transition-Finish progression principle in chapter 3 (page 96), most of my progressions focus on the transition position. The Old Man Box Squat is a progression that can be used to add or remove stability in the transition or bottom position of the Squat. You can use the added stability, which comes from increasing the points of connection, to work on position before you worry about range of motion. Adding points of connection at the transition also breaks the transition into a finish and a start so that you can work on each position before turning it into a transition.

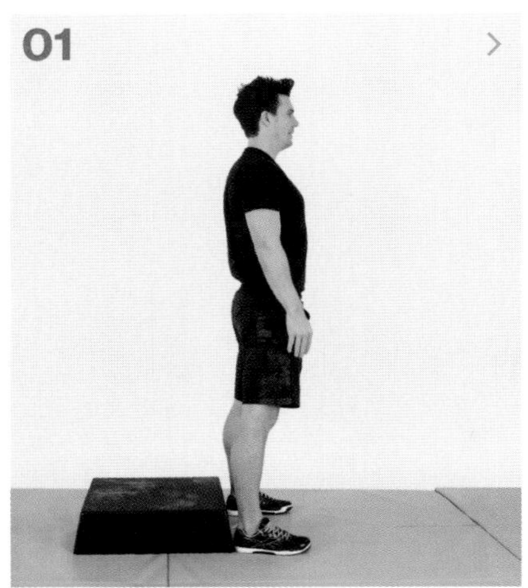

old man box squat 01 Stand directly in front of a box. Your feet are pointing straight forward, and the box is right up against the backs of your heels.

02 Slide your arms down to your knees, similar to the previous Squats.

03 It is OK to allow your back to round as you continue to drop your hands past your knees and lay them flat on the ground.

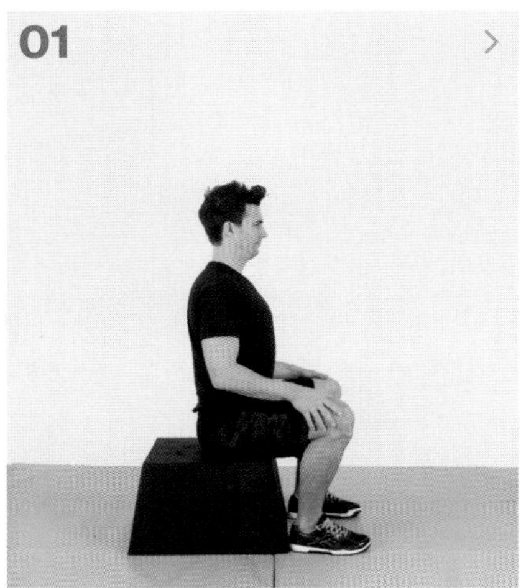

tired man box squat 01 Sit on a box with your feet under your knees, your chest upright, and your hands resting on your thighs.

02 Bend over and lift your hips as you press your hands into your thighs and push through your legs into your feet, which remain flat on the ground. Your arms are in the same shape as they would be at the bottom of a Push-up. Make the line from your head to your hips as straight as you can get it.

03 Instead of driving through your legs, push yourself away from your legs by extending your arms. This pushing is similar to a Push-up and is an interesting way of scaling Push-ups or Dips.

If you take the Old Man Squat progression, for example, and simply add a box at the bottom of the Squat, you can create a position of high stability that assists with the understanding and development of the Squat.

In addition to learning the Squat through the Old Man Squat progression, you can use a blocking method as an assistance tool to improve the Squat. In this case, I am referring to the typical tired man standing up out of a chair by placing his hands on his thighs and using his arms to assist in the Squat, as seen in the Tired Man Box Squat.

reverse steps 5–1

04 Rather than drop your hips as low as possible, target the box and drop your hips toward the ground until you gently reach the box. The box creates stability in this position, so it is important to reach it with control rather than just plopping onto it.

05 Even though you are supported by the box, you can lift your hands off the ground to mimic the ideal shape of the bottom of the Old Man Squat while flattening your back.

04 Finish by standing all the way up.

plate squats

A Plate Squat is a Squat performed with an external load in your hands. This plate variation is a great way to bridge the gap between the Old Man Squat and the universal Squat.

There are two main reasons to implement this progression:

1. Holding onto a plate increases the muscular tension around your midline and especially engages your posterior chain. This relates to the physiological stability progression principle explained in chapter 3 (page 82).
2. This weight allows you to shift your body's center of mass to the back edge of your base of support. This shift reduces the range of motion required for the Squat in your lower extremities, and it allows you to focus on finding a better squatting position with reduced ankle range of motion.

The Plate Squat progression has two stages:

1. ***Plate-Out Squat:*** Hold the plate out and away from your body
2. ***Plate-In Squat:*** Hold the plate close to your body

Both stages of the progression facilitate better squatting mechanics for the two reasons addressed above. The two stages differ mainly in the amount of weight shifted to the back edge of your base of support. The Plate-Out Squat reduces the range of motion requirement more than the Plate-In Squat because it shifts your center of mass farther back toward the back edge of your base of support. This is due to the combined center of mass of the body and the plate being displaced farther away from the body's center of mass in the Plate-Out Squat.

It is important to choose a weight for the Plate Squat progression that allows you to adopt the best body shapes without the load inhibiting your ability to perform the Squat. A great way to progress this movement closer to the universal Squat is simply to reduce the weight of the plate. The lower the weight of the plate, the higher the level of movement ability required to complete the task with proper mechanics and body shapes that are as close to optimal as possible.

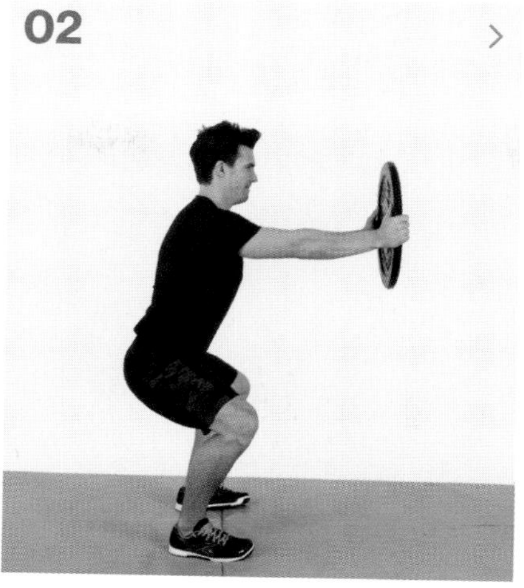

plate-out squat 01 Stand tall with a plate in your hands and your arms fully extended in front of you.

02 Hinge at your hips and bend your knees in order to lower your hips toward the ground in a partial Squat. Your feet stay flat on the ground, with your heels and big toes firmly connected to the ground.

03 You reach the bottom of the Squat when your hip crease is below your knees or you reach full hip flexion. Your shins remain as vertical as possible. Holding the plate out makes it easier to keep your weight toward your heels and your chest up.

plate-in squat 01 Stand tall and hold a plate against your chest. Pull the plate toward your chest and bend your elbows to increase the muscular contraction around your spine.

02 Hinge at your hips and bend your knees in order to lower your hips toward the ground in a partial Squat.

03 You reach the bottom of the Squat when your hip crease is below your knees or you reach full hip flexion. Your shins remain as vertical as possible. With the plate closer to your body than in the Plate-Out Squat, you must work harder to keep your weight toward your heels.

squat

Once you have mastered the Plate Squat progression, it's time to take the squatting mechanics that you've learned and apply them to what I believe is the most universal style of squatting.

This style of squatting will vary slightly from one individual to another, but the principles of squatting are the same for everyone. I like to see the spine in the most neutral position possible, as this shape develops the best movement control and can be placed under load safely. The lower-extremity mechanics require the hips to go from neutral to full flexion, the knees from extension to flexion, and the ankles from a neutral foot position to dorsiflexion.

squat 01 Stand with your feet flat on the ground about shoulder width apart. Start from the base up, locking out your knees, then getting your hips neutral by squeezing your butt and abs tight. Then get your shoulders in line with your hips, your chest facing forward and your back flat. Your neck is long in the back with your chin slightly in, while your face looks straight ahead.

02 Hinge at the hips while bending your knees and ankles in unison. This drops your center of mass directly below you while keeping most of your weight toward the back of your body. Drop your hips backward while keeping your chest upright as if you had a wall in front of you. Lift your hands straight out in front of you for balance as well as to increase the tension around your spine for better positioning.

03 Your Squat reaches full depth when you are as close as you can get to the ground or you reach end range of motion at hip, knee, and ankle level, which would be hip flexion, knee flexion, and ankle dorsiflexion. Your arms are now directly overhead, palms facing each other, to facilitate better positioning of your spine.

Your foot position is determined by the position of your hips, as shown on the following page.

In addition to your foot position, another thing to think about is your upper-body position. Even though your arms do not participate in the act of squatting, having a good shoulder position is extremely important for skill transfer. This is especially true as you try to transfer this ability to some sort of object manipulation, or if you need to use your upper body for locomotion, as seen in running or walking. Here, my arms are internally rotated at shoulder level, which compromises my lower-body pushing efficiency.

04 Initiate your return to standing by pushing through your legs and hips to drive your body away from the ground while extending your knees and hips. Your main goal here is to keep your torso upright or your chest up. As your chest rises, your hips rise, and your arms slowly descend.

05 Finish in a fully upright standing position with your arms back down at your sides. It is important that your hips return to a position of full extension when you complete the stand.

hip to foot relationship

The position of your hips determines your foot position. If you think about the anatomical stance, your feet are together and facing forward. If you were to abduct or separate your legs from your midline in order to adopt a wider-stance Squat, as seen in powerlifting, for example, your foot position would change. This change happens because any abduction at hip level is combined with external rotation of the hip and therefore affects the direction in which the feet are pointing. The closer together the feet, the more straight forward they are, such as in running, and the wider the legs, the more the feet turn out, such as in the middle split position (page 306).

Your feet should remain flat on the ground with your weight evenly distributed. You will see some shift in weight distribution in relation to your feet as they move through the different ranges of motion at hip, knee, and ankle level. The amount of shift depends on your experience in performing the Squat and/or your mobility.

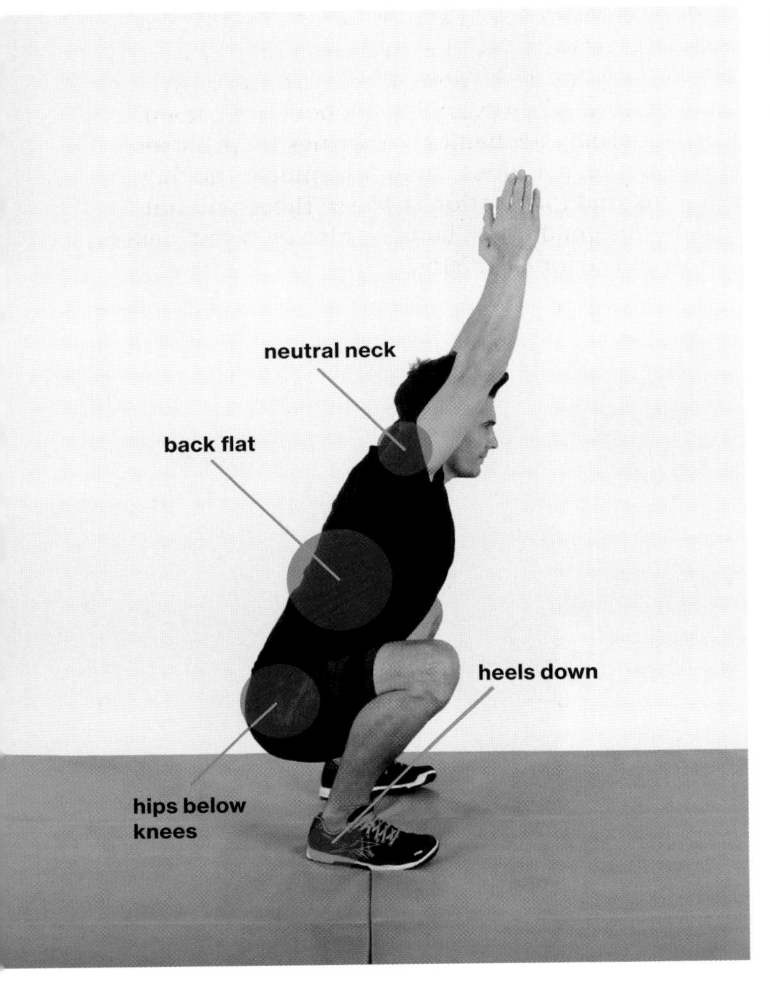
neutral neck
back flat
heels down
hips below knees

chest up
knees out
toes down

L U N G E

A Lunge is a Squat performed with a split stance in the sagittal plane, where one leg is performing a Squat and the other leg assists by dropping a knee. Another way to think about it, and the reason you might see this exercise performed by every high school track team, is that the Lunge takes squatting mechanics and brings them closer to an application to locomotion activities, such as running, walking, and skipping. I like to think that locomotion is one of the most vital activities we humans are designed to do. Lunging also gets you closer to a one-legged Squat, required for the Pistol.

lunge

I use three primary stages in the Lunge progression:

1. Flexed-Foot
2. Pointed-Toe
3. Knee

In the Flexed-Foot Lunge, your back foot is flexed so that it can provide a lot of assistance to your posting or lunging leg by enabling you to push away from the ground with the ball of your foot. The Pointed-Toe Lunge is the first step toward removing the assistance from your back leg. The back leg with pointed toe can still act to balance with extra points of connection to the ground, but it offers less pushing assistance as you stand. The Knee Lunge variation removes more points of connection with the back leg on the ground, further reducing stability. More important, without your back leg assisting with the push off the ground, your front leg is the primary driver for standing back up.

These three stages for progressing the Lunge assist you in developing the movement ability to perform the Pistol. It's important to keep in mind the main differences seen in these three stages during the transition position.

In the Lunge progression, try to maintain a straight line from your head to your back leg. This is not just for aesthetic purposes, but also for movement control, as it guarantees that your pelvis and spine are in the most neutral position. In addition, this alignment transfers nicely into a Lunge required for the kick up to Handstand that you will learn in chapter 8 (page 338).

flexed-foot lunge

When your back foot is flexed with the ball of your foot on the ground, you can push off your back foot in order to take some of the load away from your front leg.

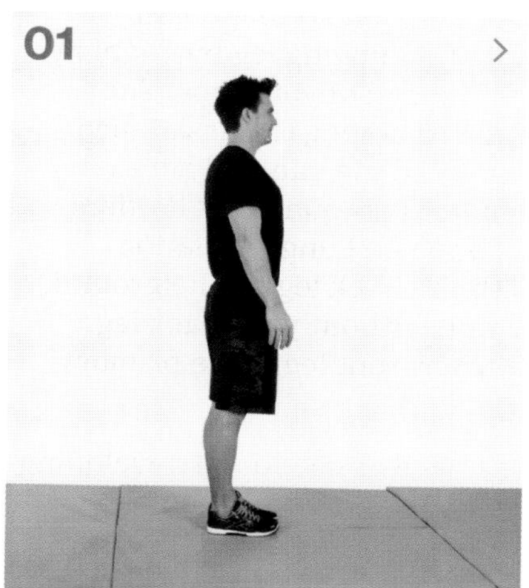

flexed-foot lunge 01 Stand tall with your feet together and flat on the ground and your arms at your sides.

02 Reach one leg as far back as possible. Lean forward to counter-balance that leg and maintain control. During the lean, your spine remains flat. Your posting foot also remains flat while resisting the slight rotational forces being generated from the unilateral (single-leg) support. This reach creates the same hinge in the hips that is seen in the Squat.

03 Touch your back knee to the ground, keeping your front or posted shin as vertical as possible. Flexion in your back ankle increases as your knee touches the ground. Your chest is slightly up so that you can get your center of mass comfortably over your base of support.

04 To stand back up, hinge in your hips as you reach with your hands toward the ground. This type of hinge creates tension in the back of your hips, and that tension plus pushing away with your back foot allows you to transfer your center of mass onto your new base of support. This new base of support is formed by your front (posting) foot as you get all your weight on top of that foot.

05 Pick your back foot up off the ground and return to the original hinging position. Try to create a straight line from your foot to your head.

06 To finish, bring your back foot all the way in, next to your planted foot, and stand tall with fully extended hips.

pointed-toe lunge

In this version of the Lunge, you point the toe of your lunging leg and lay the top of your foot flat on the ground. I like to think of the pointing of the toes, or plantarflexion of the foot, as resting your shoelaces on the ground. On the way up from this position, you perform the same hinge in the hips and the same transfer of your center of mass toward your new base of support, which is your front foot. This Lunge requires more strength from your front, or posting, leg to get you to the original standing position.

pointed-toe lunge 01 Stand and balance on one leg, reaching your opposite leg in front of you and slightly off to the side. Your arms are straight in front of you for balance.

02 Swing your elevated leg down and back.

03 Continue to swing your elevated leg as far back as possible. Lean forward to counterbalance the leg sent behind you and maintain control. During the lean, your spine remains flat. Your posted foot remains flat while resisting the slight rotational forces being generated from the unilateral (single-leg) support. This reach creates the same hinge in the hips that is seen in the Squat.

04 Touch the ground with the top of your back foot in a plantarflexed position.

05 Touch your back knee to the ground, keeping your front shin as vertical as possible. Your chest is slightly up so that you can get your center of mass comfortably over your base of support.

06 To stand back up, hinge in your hips while you reach with your hands toward the ground. This type of hinge creates tension in the back of your hips, and that hip tension plus pushing away with your back foot allows you to transfer your center of mass onto your new base of support. This new base of support is formed by your front foot as you get all your weight on top of that foot.

07 Pick your back foot up off the ground, swing your back leg forward, and return to the starting position.

knee lunge

In this version of the Lunge, your back foot is completely off the ground, so your knee is your back support. To stand from this position, your torso has to lean much farther forward than in the two previous Lunges. That lean is more exaggerated because you need to shift your center of mass toward the center of your new base of support created by just your front planting foot.

knee lunge 01 Stand and balance on one leg, reaching your opposite leg in front of you and slightly off to the side. Your arms are straight in front of you for balance.

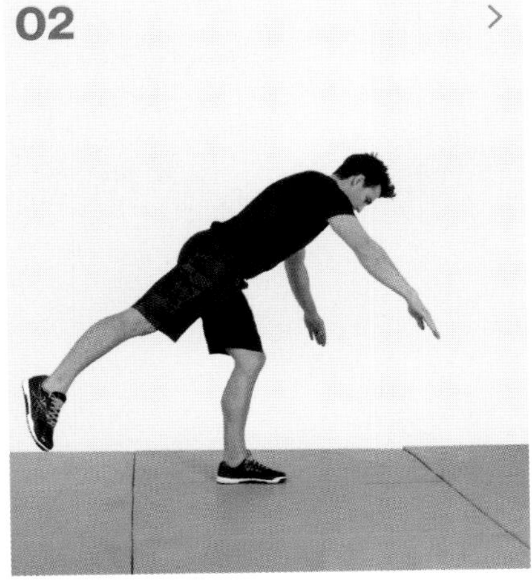

02 Reach your elevated leg as far back as possible. Lean forward to counterbalance the leg sent behind you and maintain control. During the lean, your spine remains flat. Your posted foot remains flat while resisting the slight rotational forces being generated from the unilateral support. This reach creates the same hinge in the hips that is seen in the Squat.

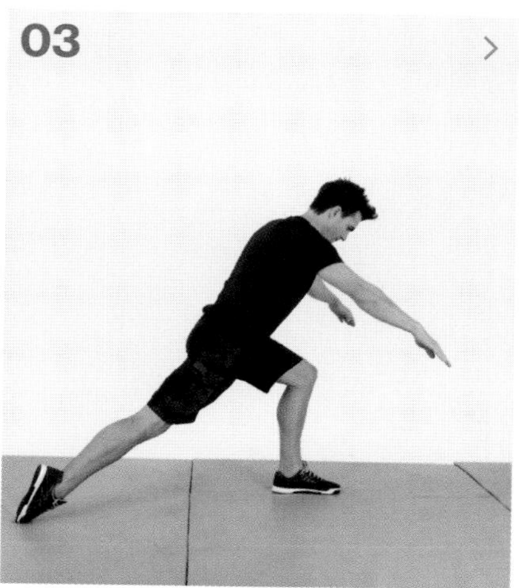

03 Touch the ground with the top of your back foot in a plantarflexed position.

04 Touch your back knee to the ground, keeping your front shin as vertical as possible. Your chest is slightly up so that you can get your center of mass comfortably over your base of support.

05 Lift your back foot off the ground so that only your back knee and front foot are on the ground. To stand back up, hinge in your hips while you reach with your hands slightly toward the ground.

06 Continue to hinge forward by reaching toward the ground with your arms while pushing away from the ground with your posting leg. Fight to keep the shin of your posting leg as vertical as possible as you maintain balance over your base of support.

07 Keep pushing away from the ground until you reach a standing position while still balancing on your posting leg.

08 Once you have found your balance, extend your elevated leg and return to the original starting position.

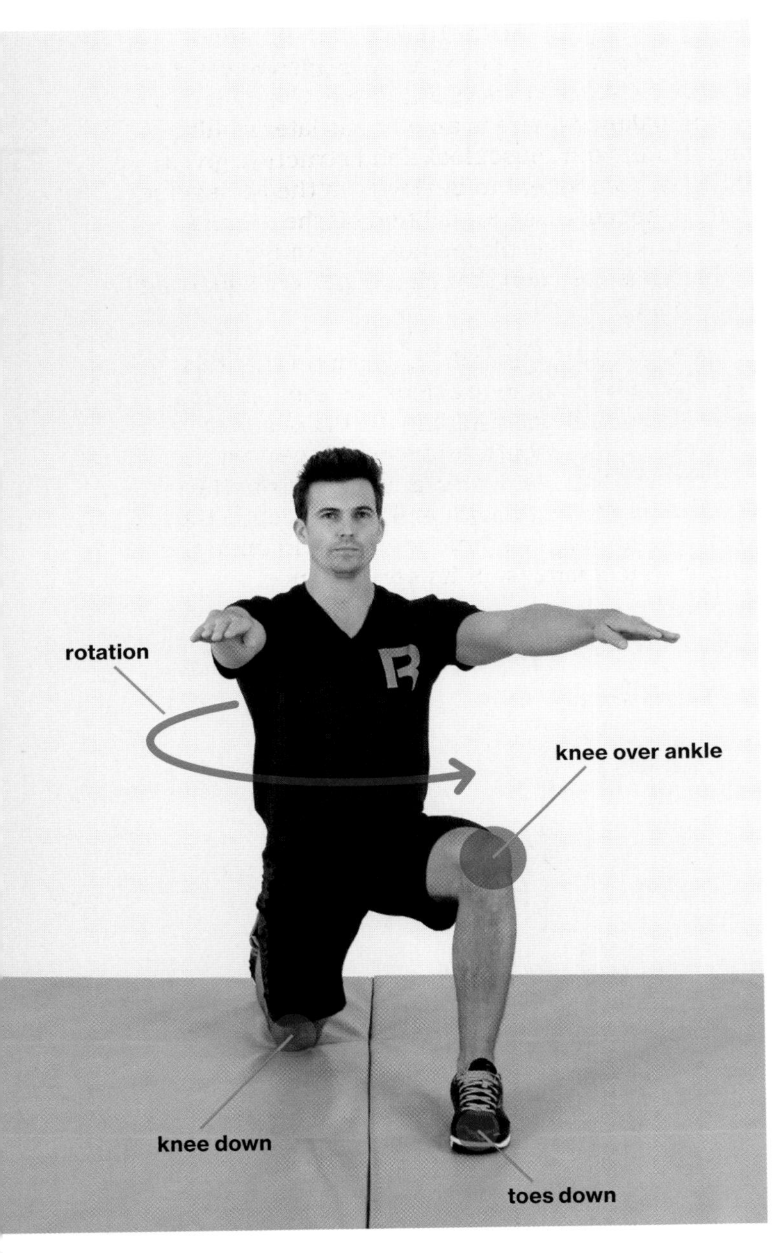
rotation
knee over ankle
knee down
toes down

neutral neck
hip over knee
vertical shin
flexed foot

PIS TOL

The Pistol is a single-leg Squat with the leg that is off the ground projected in front of your body. As simple as a one-legged Squat may seem, the single-leg stance changes everything due to the unilateral loading involved. To find balance, there is an obvious lateral shift of the body. More important, your musculoskeletal structure gives you a significant rotational component to deal with in the transverse plane (see page 26). Plus, because one leg is lifted off the ground throughout the movement, one hip is placed near end range of motion. This creates increased tension that challenges the squatting leg's range of motion capabilities.

To develop the capacity to perform a Pistol, I have found that taking the lunging mechanics described in the previous section, applying them to a Step-down on a box, and later adding the Pistol shape during the transition allows for a smooth bridge from one style of single-leg squatting to the other. And later, adding a box to the transition and/or performing the Pistol with a plate, as seen in the Plate Squat progression (page 112), is a great way to build up to the Pistol and maintain optimal mechanics for its performance.

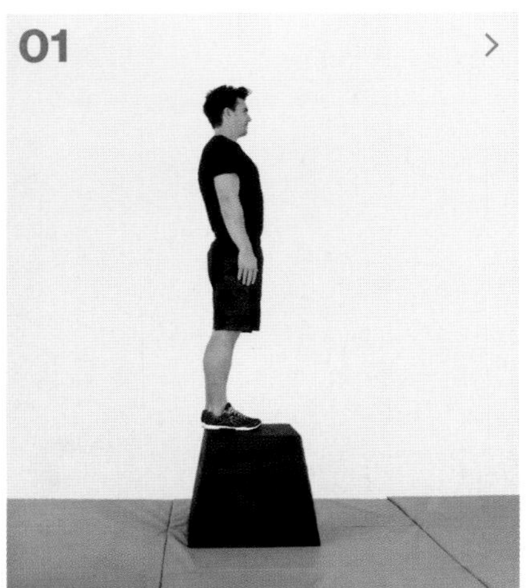

step-down 01 Stand on a box.

02 Kick one leg back as if you were performing a Lunge. Bend your planted leg as you reach forward with your upper body. You should almost reach your arms past the box in front of you for better balance.

03 Lower yourself by hinging at the hips and bending the knee of your planted leg. Keep your knee on top of the middle of your planted foot during the descent. Descend until your back foot touches the ground.

step-down

The Step-down is a Lunge performed while standing on top of a box. By performing this Lunge on a box, you are able to maintain a more vertical path during the descent/ascent as compared with the Lunge. You remain vertical because the shift in your center of mass is reduced because you can drop your leg almost underneath you.

This progression also removes the back-leg assistance during the ascent seen in the Lunge progression. It also allows you to focus on your squatting leg rather than your elevated leg. You use a box as your base of support so you don't have to worry that your elevated leg will touch the ground. But of course, you can change the box size to vary and progress the amount of ground support you have.

The two primary stages of this progression are the Step-down and the Pistol Swing.

The Step-down is a great place to start for two reasons:

1. It reduces the range of motion challenge by allowing your elevated leg to hang below or even behind you, thus enabling you to focus on positional integrity without worrying as much about range of motion.
2. It allows you to break up the transition position into a start and a finish, giving you an opportunity to pause and reset if needed.

04 Once you reach the bottom, you have the option to raise your torso so that you are standing straight up in order to establish a better position for initiating the ascent. This is not a requirement for performing the movement correctly, just an option for creating a better position. This could also be considered the starting position if you were performing a Step-up.

05 Bend over, reaching for your planted leg's thigh with your chest. This reach creates tension in the back of your planted leg, especially because you keep your planted leg's shin as vertical as possible.

06 As you continue to press your chest over to your thigh and accumulate more tension, the tension and hip hinge pivot you over your planted leg and allow your back leg to start rising off the ground. You are not jumping with your back leg; you are simply pushing on the box with your front leg.

07 Continue to drive your foot into the box while reaching farther forward with your upper body in order to maintain balance with your posting leg.

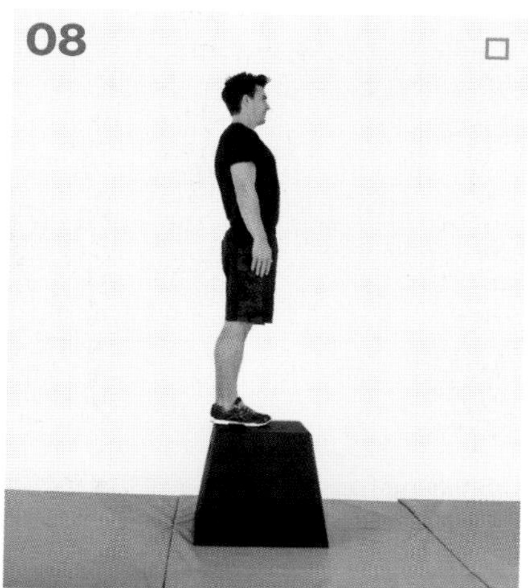

08 Continue to push and maintain balance until you reach the standing position.

pistol swing

The Pistol Swing is a Step-down, but instead of placing your foot on the ground at the bottom of the step, you swing your back leg in front of your body and adopt the Pistol shape.

The Pistol Swing is a great way to remove the challenge of maintaining the Pistol shape through the descent or ascent. By standing off to one side of the box rather toward the back edge, you can perform the same Step-down and take advantage of the height of the box to clear the floor as you swing your leg forward in order to adopt the transition position for the universal Pistol.

pistol swing 01 Stand on a box with one foot planted flat toward a side edge and your other leg elevated in front of you and slightly off to the side. Your arms reach straight out in front of you, and your torso is slightly rotated at the same angle as your elevated leg.

02 Drop your elevated leg, bringing it down next to your planted leg.

03 Continue to swing your elevated leg behind you. Maintain balance by reaching forward with your upper body. Try to keep both legs as straight as possible.

07 Follow the leg swing through until you reach the bottom of the Squat, which is also the bottom Pistol position. Your elevated leg is parallel to the ground. Your arms continue to reach forward for balance.

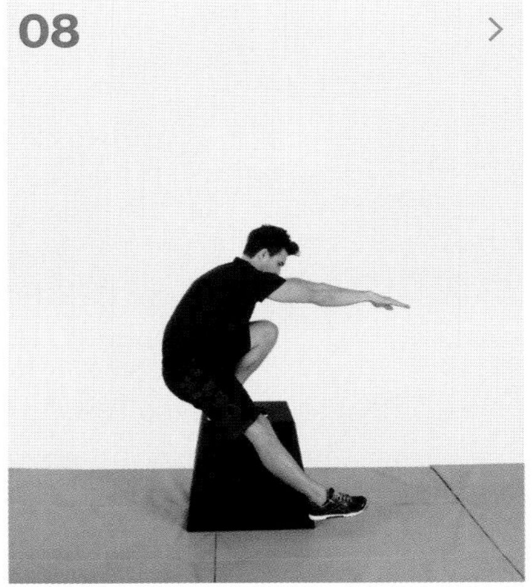

08 Initiate the back swing by dropping your elevated leg toward the ground.

09 As your leg swings underneath and starts to go behind you, make a large effort to reach forward with your arms to maintain balance as you press your heel into the box.

04 Hinge at the hips and bend the knee of your planted leg to lower your center of mass. Reach out with your arms and back with your elevated leg to balance.

05 Reach toward the ground with your free foot and start shifting your torso back toward the back of your planted foot to initiate a swing with your hanging leg.

06 Swing your hanging foot toward the front of the box without letting it touch the ground. Reach your arms out in front of you to maintain balance.

10 Continue the back swing as if you're driving your swinging leg's heel into the sky and pushing through the box with your posted leg.

11 When your posted leg reaches full extension in the knee, drop your swinging leg as you continue to stand up.

12 Return to the starting position.

box pistol

Once you feel comfortable with the Pistol shape at the bottom of the Pistol Swing and can perform several repetitions, it's time to start working on maintaining the Pistol shape throughout the full range of motion. I have defined three stages to help you do so:

1. Box Pistol
2. Plate Pistol
3. Toe Pistol

The Box Pistol is a Pistol performed on a box. The benefit of performing a Box Pistol is that it creates a position of high stability during the transition. This stability allows you to adjust your body shape during the movement and gives you an exit strategy in case you run into balance, strength, or mobility roadblocks.

box pistol 01 Stand in front of a box and balance on one leg, reaching your opposite leg in front of you and slightly off to the side. Your arms are straight in front of you for balance. The heel of your planted foot should be directly in front of the box.

02 Initiate the descent by hinging at your hips and bending the knee of your planted leg. Your elevated leg stays off the ground, and your back stays flat in line with your neck.

03 Continue to descend until your hip reaches the box. The box allows you to keep the shin of your planted leg vertical because you can hinge your hips farther back without fear of falling. Resting on the box at the bottom gives you an opportunity to reset your position if you lost it during the descent.

04 Initiate the ascent from the seated position by shifting your upper body forward and over your posted leg.

05 After shifting your weight forward, push with your posted leg to lift your hips.

06 Finish in the same starting position.

plate pistol

Sometimes the balance and/or mobility roadblocks are too big to solve with just a box. In this case, it's appropriate to introduce the Plate Pistol, which can be performed on a box or freestanding, depending on your level of experience and comfort.

The Plate Pistol is a Pistol performed with an external load in your hands. The style is a plate-out style, as seen in the Plate Squat progression (page 112). The plate is helpful for the same reasons introduced in the Plate Squats.

The key to the Plate Squats is that you can adopt the general master position of hips below knees without having to cover the same range of motion at hip level because of the shift of your body's center of mass. You use a Plate Pistol for the same reasons, but in this case the

plate pistol 01 Start by balancing on one leg and reaching your opposite leg in front of you and slightly off to the side. Your arms are fully extended in front of you and holding onto a plate.

02 Initiate the descent by hinging at your hips and bending the knee of your planted leg. Your elevated leg stays off the ground, and your back stays flat in line with your neck.

03 Continue to descend until your hip goes below your knee. The bottom position is at full hip and knee flexion. The heel of your planted foot remains flat on the ground. Your upper body is rotated toward your planted leg, and your planted knee has shifted to the outside of your planted foot as a result of the combination of shifting your center of mass and rotating your torso. Your elevated leg is in front of you and slightly off to the side for balance. Keeping the plate straight in front of you makes it easier to keep your chest upright, keep your planted heel on the ground, and lift your elevated leg.

plate offers even more assistance because the rotation of your torso combined with an elevated leg creates a situation where your hip reaches end range of flexion sooner in the Pistol. More specifically, I am talking about the relative internal rotation that occurs at hip level, but a less formal way to describe it is that you don't have to flex as much to lift your leg if the shift of your center of mass, or tilt, also lifts your leg.

As you work your way through this progression and get to the point where you can remove the box, reduce the weight of the plate, and feel capable of attempting the Pistol without assistance, the Toe Pistol is a great way to bridge the gap between the Plate Pistol and the universal Pistol.

04 Initiate the ascent from the seated position by hinging at your hips and directing the plate toward the ground, which assist in shifting your upper body forward and over your posted leg.

05 Push away from the ground by pushing your hips back and up while maintaining an upright chest position.

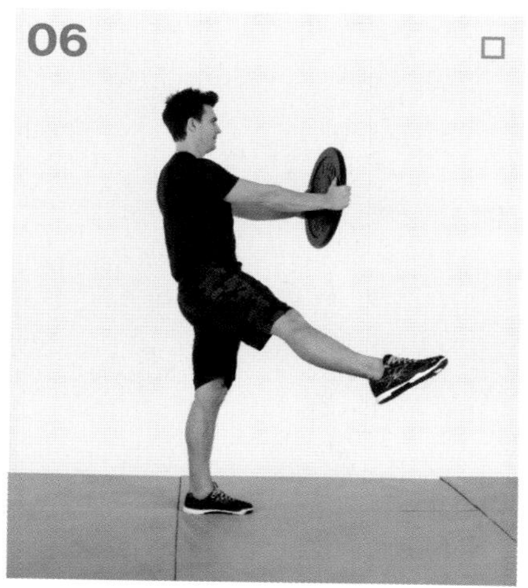

06 Finish in the same starting position.

toe pistol

The Toe Pistol is a Pistol performed while holding your elevated leg. It is a great bridge between the effect of the plate and the actual Pistol. The connection between your arm and your elevated leg introduces the same muscular tension that increases stability, and at the same time that tension relieves the flexing of your hip while keeping your elevated leg up. No longer holding onto a plate also shifts your center of mass, or tilt.

Even though it is a great style to get you closer to performing the universal Pistol, performing the Toe Pistol correctly requires a good amount of mobility and movement control. Once you have mastered the Toe Pistol, it's time to attempt the Pistol.

toe pistol 01 Start by balancing on one leg and reaching your opposite leg in front of you and slightly off to the side. Your elevated leg should be high enough that you can grab your toes firmly with the same-side arm without having to bend over.

02 Because the Toe Pistol does not emphasize the hip hinge seen in the Plate and Box Pistol, you initiate the descent simply by squatting with your planted leg. Holding onto your toes while keeping your leg straight and elevated helps block your upper body into a desirable upright position.

side scale

A scale in gymnastics is the act of balancing on one leg as you hold your elevated leg off the ground in front, to the side, or behind you. The side scale is usually performed while balancing on one leg and holding the elevated leg. The start/finish position seen in the Toe Pistol, if performed correctly, is very similar to the position a gymnast would adopt while performing a side scale.

03 Continue to descend until your hip goes below your knee. Maintaining your grip on your elevated toes in the bottom position makes it easier to keep your elevated leg off the ground and creates more muscular tension around your hips for better balance.

04 Initiate the ascent by pushing away from the ground with your posting leg as you continue to hold onto the toes of your elevated leg.

05 Finish by fully extending your posting leg and hip and lifting your chest into a fully upright position.

pistol

The Pistol is a single-leg Squat with the leg that is off the ground projected in front of your body. As simple as the single-leg stance may seem, the unilateral loading involved changes everything. To find balance, there is an obvious lateral shift of your body. More important, your musculoskeletal structure gives you a significant rotational component to deal with in the transverse plane (page 26). Plus, because one leg is lifted off the ground throughout the movement, one hip is placed near end range of motion, creating increased tension that challenges the squatting leg's range of motion capabilities.

To develop the capacity to perform a Pistol, I have found that taking the lunging mechanics described in the previous section, applying them to a Step-down on a box, and later adding the Pistol shape during the transition allows for a smooth bridge from one style of single-leg squatting to the other. Later, adding a box to the transition and/or performing the Pistol with a plate, as seen in the Plate Squat progression (page 112), is a great way to build up to the Pistol and maintain optimal mechanics for its performance.

pistol 01 Start by balancing on one leg and reaching your opposite leg in front of you and slightly off to the side. Your arms are straight in front of you for balance.

02 Initiate the descent by hinging at your hips and then bending the knee of your planted leg. Your elevated leg stays off the ground, and your back stays flat in line with your neck.

At the bottom of the Pistol, your planted foot should remain flat, with your knee falling off to the side at a natural angle because of hip flexion. Your chest is upright in order to adopt a close-to-neutral spinal position, with your hands reaching forward to assist with balance and your shoulders positioned around your spine. Your elevated-leg side should be the mirror image of your squatting-leg side in terms of hip abduction, with your elevated leg projecting slightly out to the side. This helps you resist the natural tendency to bring your elevated leg toward your planted leg or toward the center of your body, which creates a soft hip position and therefore gives you less movement control and ability to apply force.

To maintain proper movement control and resist the rotation created by the unilateral loading, your upper body must rotate into your squatting leg to create the optimal position at spine and hip level. Your torso should point in the same direction as your posting-leg knee, projecting laterally over your foot.

03 Descend until your hip goes below your knee. Your back is slightly rounded, but the load on your spine is safe. Keep your foot flat. Rotate your upper body toward your squatting leg. Keep your elevated leg in front of you and slightly off to the side for balance.

04 Initiate the ascent by driving your hips back and up, keeping your chest facing down.

05 Continue to extend your hips and knees until you reach a full standing position.

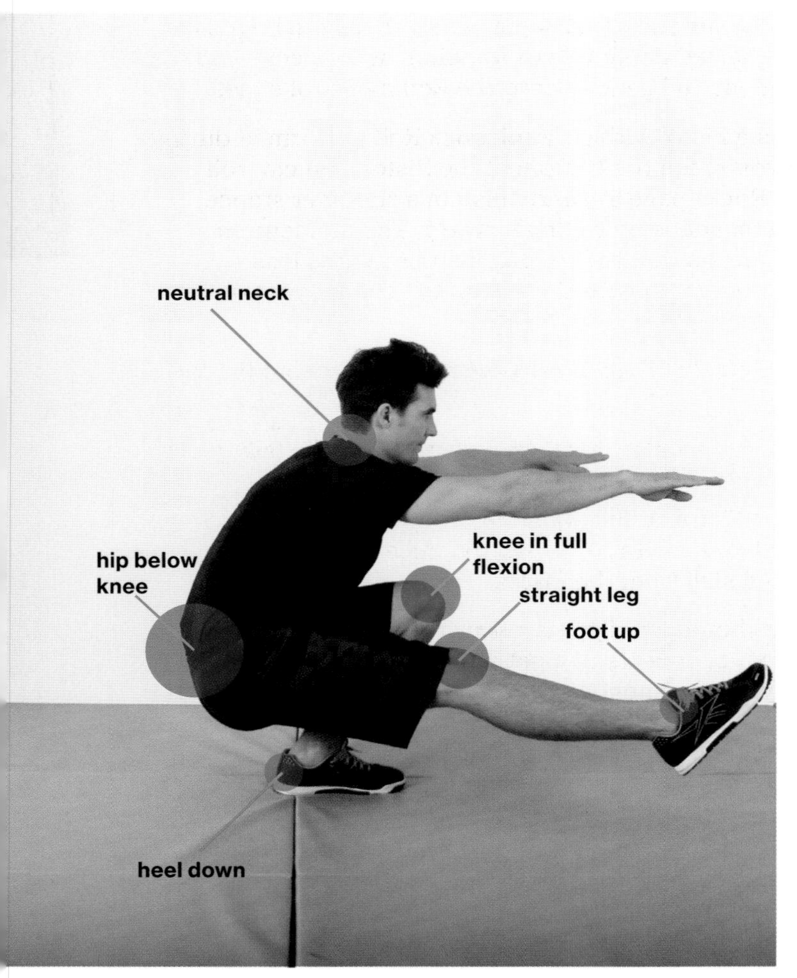
neutral neck
hip below knee
knee in full flexion
straight leg
foot up
heel down

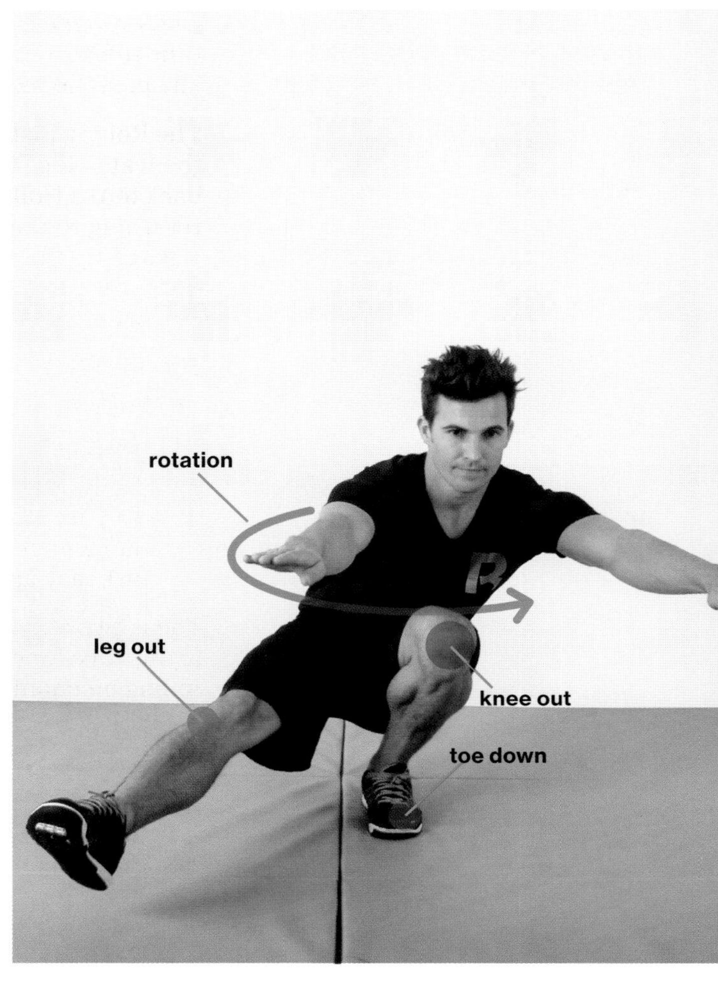
rotation
leg out
knee out
toe down

ROLLING PISTOL

Once you have developed the squatting mechanics for the Pistol, it's time to start adding speed and changes in points of connection to advance the movement and get closer to the Rolling Pistol style.

The Rolling Pistol is a Pistol with a Candlestick Roll performed during the transition. As you reach the bottom of the Pistol, you can roll back into a Hollow Rock (page 57) and finish in a shoulder stance, returning to the Pistol shape by rolling forward. The momentum created by the roll means that the Rolling Pistol requires less muscular strength compared with the Pistol, but challenges you in a completely different way.

Specifically, the Rolling Pistol helps you develop movement ability in two critical ways:

1. Rolling is a fundamental movement pattern to handle falling out of the Squat.
2. Rolling into the Pistol adds a dynamic component to the movement that helps with skill transfer, since locomotion is a primary applied skill from the Pistol.

These two features should be of great interest to anyone looking to improve fundamental aspects of most sports. Exploring these rolling mechanics yields tremendous benefits, too. You may find this exploration complicated, but if you perform the movements while varying the momentum from the rolling motion, you'll be able to find traction and stability. You will also come to further understand how the hip mechanics that are central to performing a Rolling Pistol overlap with most other locomotion activities.

candlestick roll

The first roll that I teach is the Candlestick Roll. It is great for learning how to fall or roll out of a Squat and, even more important, for learning how to use momentum throughout a Squat.

This momentum adds speed to the movement that facilitates the mechanics. In other words, the speed of the roll masks some aspects of strength needed in the universal Squat. The roll requires less muscular tension and even less mobility. Because you're moving so fast through the movement, you are able to plow through those sticky parts of your body that could limit your mobility.

candlestick roll 01 Stand with your feet together and your arms overhead.

02 Start the descent by squatting with an exaggerated hip hinge, keeping your arms overhead.

03 Descend in a controlled fall and get into a tucked position at the bottom, with your back rounded.

07 Initiate the forward roll by maintaining the rounded or hollow body shape in your spine and progressively bending your legs.

08 As your hips reach the ground, continue to bend your legs, with your feet reaching for the ground.

09 Plant your feet firmly on the ground and perform an aggressive Sit-up as you reach forward with your arms.

The momentum created by the Candlestick Roll is also an important way to scale the Squat. This concept is similar to riding a bike, and how much easier it is to balance on a bike when it is moving than when it is static. Also, when learning how to stand on your hands, freestanding is harder than Handstand walking. Motion helps balance.

As basic as it can seem, the Candlestick Roll is difficult for many people to learn, depending on their experience with tumbling movements, strength, and mobility. People who can perform a Squat but have some mobility limitations or who can perform a Squat but cannot perform a Candlestick Roll due to the speed added to the squatting mechanics are great candidates for another stage of progression for the Candlestick Roll, such as the Plate Roll.

04 Transfer the momentum from the fall smoothly into a Hollow Rock by slowly separating your chest from your thighs as you maintain a uniformly rounded back for better rocking.

05 As you continue to roll backward, progressively extend your legs while lifting your hips off the ground.

06 Roll to the top of your back, reach with your arms over your head, and plant them firmly on the ground. Tuck in your chin to protect your head and neck. Fully extend by reaching your hips and legs toward the sky without allowing your toes to break your eye line.

10 Transfer the momentum from the Sit-up to lift your hips. You are reaching away and down.

11 Continue to lift your hips by pushing through your legs as in a Squat.

12 Finish in the same standing position with your arms overhead.

plate candlestick roll

The Plate Candlestick Roll is a Candlestick Roll performed with a weight in your hands. This roll is performed in plate-out fashion, and it provides the same benefits of displacement of the combined center of mass as seen in the Plate Squat progression.

Even though a lot of people feel comfortable performing the Candlestick Roll, they sometimes lack mobility and get a little stuck in the transition. Adding a plate in front of you facilitates that movement. The plate acts as a counterbalance in the same way it does in squatting. The counterbalance creates better movement control for a better movement pattern.

This counterbalance doesn't apply just to the Candlestick Roll, but also to the Rolling Pistol. Simply by putting a little weight in front of you and extending your arms, you can create the same effect and facilitate the movement. The Plate Candlestick Roll works especially well for people who have a bigger build, who are Olympic

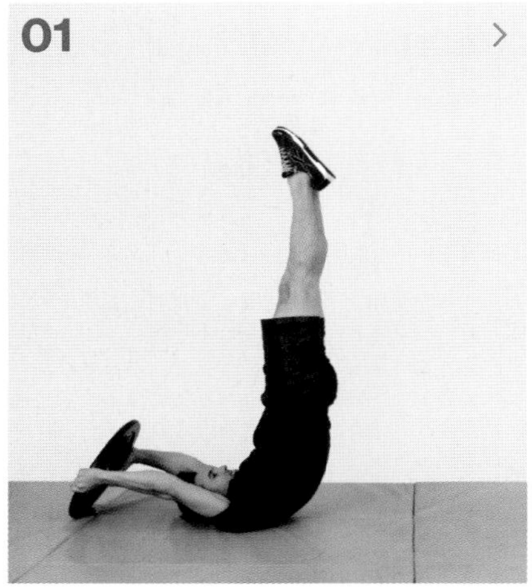

plate candlestick roll 01 Assume the candlestick position with a plate resting on the ground overhead and behind you. Your feet are not past your eye line, and your hips and legs are fully extended, reaching for the sky.

02 Rock forward and bend your legs, smoothly pulling the plate in front of you, making sure to extend your arms to keep the plate away from your body.

03 As your feet reach the ground at the bottom of the roll, make sure your feet are together and you are reaching forward with the plate.

weightlifters or powerlifters, or who have extremely long limbs, like tall basketball players. Additionally, it's a great drill for learning how to get off the ground without using your hands. A good way to scale it up and make it more difficult is to bring the plate closer to your chest or to use a progressively lighter plate.

It's important to keep in mind that anytime you do a dynamic motion that requires a change of orientation in space while carrying an external load such as a plate, you have to perform the movement at a slower speed and with a higher level of movement control. As long as you can control the weight, the counterweight of the plate picks up the slack by shifting your center of mass where you want it to go.

Once you have mastered the Candlestick Roll, it's time to add the Pistol progression seen in the previous section by transitioning from the Candlestick Roll with a Squat to a Lunge and eventually to a Pistol.

04 Continue to reach the plate down toward the ground without letting it touch the ground. This helps you lift your hips up and back with vertical shins for better squatting mechanics. It's OK to have a slightly rounded back here with a small load.

05 As you ascend away from the ground, progressively flatten your back for better spinal position.

06 Finish standing tall with your feet together.

rolling lunge

The Rolling Lunge is a Candlestick Roll in which you adopt a Lunge position in order to stand up. This movement can be performed from standing but is best learned from the Candlestick Roll itself. The Rolling Lunge is a great stage of the progression to focus on the ascent of the Pistol.

rolling lunge 01 Assume the candlestick position with your shoulders, head, and arms acting as your base of support. The rest of your body is completely stacked above your base. Your arms are glued to your ears and straight because you want to have the biggest base of support possible, and your arms touching the ground creates a stable surface. It also provides more protection for your head and neck. Your hips and legs extend straight up to the sky to create tension throughout your body. Your toes never go past your nose.

02 As you roll forward, begin to perform a Lunge by crossing one leg below the other in a figure-four, driving one of your heels toward your butt.

03 Your crossed legs will allow you to plant your lower leg or shin on the ground. Your foot is not flat; the outside of your foot rests on the ground. Reach with your lunging leg in front of you.

Once you have mastered the Rolling Lunge, you can move on to descending into the Candlestick Roll as if you were performing a Pistol and ascending in the lunging shape. Once you have mastered this move, instead of ascending in a lunging shape, you can ascend in a partial Pistol shape or, as I like to call it, a Moonwalk Pistol.

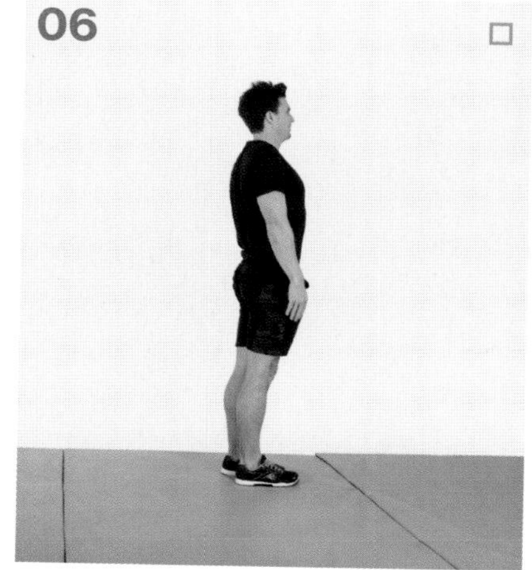

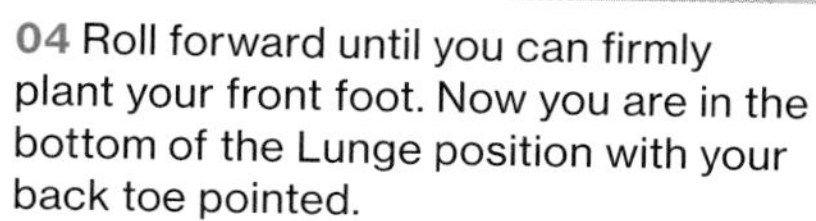

04 Roll forward until you can firmly plant your front foot. Now you are in the bottom of the Lunge position with your back toe pointed.

05 Rather than pushing with your back leg, use the forward roll momentum to lift yourself off the ground while posting over your front leg.

06 Continue to push away from the ground with your front leg until you finish in a standing position with your feet together.

moonwalk pistol

The Moonwalk Pistol is a Rolling Pistol, but during the ascent you allow your elevated leg to post on the floor in front of your body and assist the movement by planting both hands on the ground on either side of your front leg.

This stage of the progression allows you to descend in a Pistol shape and ascend with more points of connection and stability. I call it the Moonwalk because the elevated leg that posts on the ground slides back toward the planted leg, mimicking Michael Jackson's famous dance move.

Once you have mastered the Moonwalk Pistol and you feel comfortable separating your hands from the ground and making the slide of your front leg as light as possible, it's time to try the Rolling Pistol without using your hands or allowing your foot to touch the ground.

moonwalk pistol 01 Assume the candlestick position with your shoulders and arms as your base of support and your legs and hips fully extended and reaching for the sky without your toes breaking eye level.

02 Start rocking forward out of the shoulder stance. Halfway through, initiate a bend in one knee by driving your foot toward the ground. This helps you prepare for the Pistol.

03 As your foot touches the ground, perform a rapid Sit-up while reaching your arms up and forward.

“Just because it’s in print doesn’t mean it’s the gospel.” —Michael Jackson

04 >

04 Use the momentum created by the roll plus Sit-up to lift your hips off the ground and plant your front leg and hands directly in front of you. Your front leg is straight.

05 >

05 Slide or sweep your front leg back to match your posting leg. Your hands never leave the ground.

06 □

06 Stand up with your feet remaining together.

rolling pistol

The Rolling Pistol is a Pistol with a Candlestick Roll performed during the transition. As you reach the bottom of the Pistol, you can roll back into a Hollow Rock, finishing in a shoulder stance and returning to the Pistol shape by rolling forward. I believe that the Rolling Pistol is the most universal style of lower-body squatting mechanics and provides a number of movement ability resources that are useful in maximizing sport and life performance.

rolling pistol 01 Assume the standing Pistol position.

02 Start the descent by pushing your hips back as you keep your elevated leg up and your arms in front of you.

03 As you reach the bottom of the Pistol, allow yourself to start falling backward. Basically, you are falling with control.

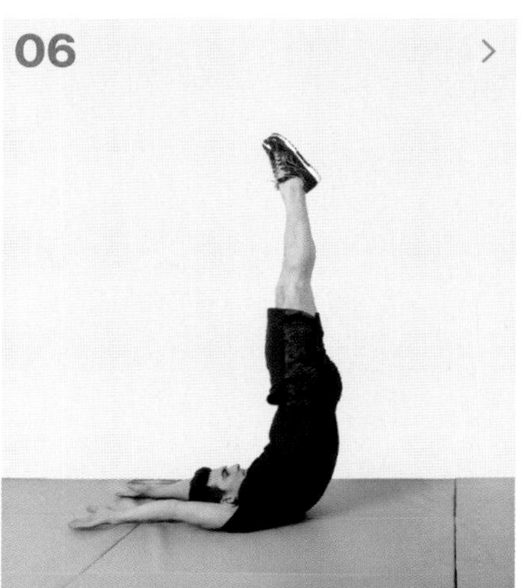

06 You reach the top of the Hollow Rock when your shoulders come in contact with the ground. Extend both your legs and your hips and point your toes to the sky. Make sure that your feet never go past eye level.

07 Start rocking forward out of the shoulder stance. Halfway through, initiate a bend in one knee by driving your foot toward the ground. This helps you prepare for the Pistol.

04 As your hips reach the ground, allow your upper body to start rolling backward. As your body starts to unfold, think about getting into a hollow body position.

05 Perform an aggressive Hollow Rock up onto your shoulders. Your arms reach over your head.

08 As your foot touches the ground, perform a rapid Sit-up while reaching your arms up and forward. This will return you to the bottom Pistol position.

09 Use the momentum created by the roll plus Sit-up to lift your hips off the ground and initiate the ascent. Continue to reach forward for balance. Your elevated leg should remain straight and off the ground.

10 After finding balance on your posting leg, push through your posting leg away from the ground until your hips and knees are fully extended and you have returned to the original standing Pistol position.

rolling pistol

points of performance

hollow body position

arms straight by the ears

This chapter introduced you to my favorite Freestyle movements for working on the fundamentals of lower-body pushing. I favor the Rolling Pistol because it is the most universal movement for skill transfer to other movement patterns involving locomotion. It also teaches you to use your hips effectively, which all strength coaches recognize as the primary power generator for human movement.

In addition to detailing the Pistol, I reinforced the Freestyle progression principles, using them to develop the Pistol progressions in this chapter.

Photo by Paolo Sanchez

handstand push-up

05

The Handstand Push-up is one of those movements that could be considered a party trick or a feat of strength that only a gymnast, diver, or circus performer would do for the sake of strength development or show. For most people, this movement seems unattainable and even unnecessary to learn. But the truth is, the Handstand Push-up is great for developing many aspects of movement ability and can bring huge benefits to your overall life and sport performance.

I often wonder who performed the first Handstand and why. I don't think I will ever know for sure, but the best answer I can come up with is that the first Handstand was performed by accident or for fun. It may have been during a moment of play; perhaps someone tripped, landed on his hands, and felt something special or was messing around in a field while running and jumping and tumbling and the Handstand came about naturally.

No matter how the first person stumbled upon the movement, I want to believe that it was further developed by an innate drive for competition. Two people may have been trying to one-up each other and somehow managed to make the Handstand a "thing." Well, however it happened, I'm glad it did!

Even though the Handstand Push-up is most commonly associated with gymnastics, it is fundamental to the circus, break-dancing, and many fitness disciplines, including CrossFit and calisthenics. Because each practice has different purposes and therefore a unique style of performing this movement, they all approach the Handstand Push-up in a slightly different fashion. Despite these style and progression differences, the general mechanics and movement pattern remain the same. For example, a gymnast might perform a Handstand on a set of rings, demonstrating control as he slowly moves from one position to another while maintaining the nice straight lines that gymnasts are known to have. In contrast, a break-dancer might use her legs to pop her body off the ground into a Handstand, and a CrossFit athlete might use a similar pop, but against a wall.

The style of Handstand Push-up that I present in this chapter is the Kipping Handstand Push-up seen in CrossFit. I believe that this style is the most universal and therefore provides the best benefits from a movement ability perspective. In addition, I believe that this style is a natural adaptation; I've seen it occur in a large number of people performing this movement over thousands of repetitions at high speeds and varied loads.

The Handstand Push-up, being a Push-up performed while balancing on the arms, requires a high degree of upper-body pushing mechanics. The Kipping Handstand Push-up is even more complex, as it adds an additional push of the lower body to facilitate the upper-body pushing.

To help you develop this movement, I have divided this chapter into four sections:

1. Push-up
2. Handstand Push-up
3. Kipping Handstand Push-up
4. Ring Handstand Push-up

the roots

Gymnastics was introduced in early Greek civilization to facilitate the development of the body through a series of exercises that included running, jumping, swimming, throwing, wrestling, and weightlifting. Essentially, it was a collection of basic movements as opposed to the complex and artistic form of gymnastics seen today. Physical fitness was highly valued in ancient Greece, and both men and women participated in vigorous gymnastic exercises as a way to develop body and mind and bond with others in the community. In later periods the Romans advanced these activities into a formal sport that more closely resembles the modern form of artistic gymnastics.

PUSH UP

The Push-up is one of the most well-known exercises in the world. In case you don't know, it is basically the act of holding yourself in plank position facing the ground, then lowering your body toward the ground by flexing your elbows and extending your shoulders. After your body reaches the ground, you press yourself back up and away from the ground by flexing your shoulders and extending your elbows.

The Push-up is the most basic form of pushing mechanics you can perform in a gym setting. I say this because the Push-up, the way you may have learned it in PE class or the way you understand the technique based on your experience in performing it, is not limited to one style; it occurs in many different aspects of life and sport. The Push-up has transferability to everything else you do in life. Think of pushing a cart at the grocery store, pushing a baby stroller, or getting your car to a gas station if it breaks down, for example.

Just as the Squat is the foundation of the Pistol, as addressed in the previous chapter, the Push-up is the foundation of the Handstand Push-up. It is the most fundamental movement for developing pushing mechanics at shoulder level. The Push-up movement requires your shoulders to go from near midrange of motion almost to full extension, your elbows to go from full extension to full flexion, and your wrists to remain in extension, creating a flat base of support with your hands.

plank position

Before I dive into the Push-up progression, I want to take a moment to address how to properly set up for this movement by reminding you about the hollow body and plank positions, introduced in chapter 2 (pages 54 and 58, respectively), that are required for maximizing pushing mechanics. Most important, if you are unable to stabilize yourself in a neutral global position in the hollow body and plank positions, then your upper-body pushing mechanics will be compromised. So refer to chapter 2 if you have problems maintaining a neutral shape throughout the progressions in this chapter.

Beyond the primary responsibility of establishing a stable neutral global position, the plank position is where I want you to start addressing the details of your base of support for the Push-up and for pushing mechanics in general. You start improving the base of support created by your hands and feet by addressing your hand position first. Having your fingers splayed out and your index fingers facing straight forward creates a bigger base for your hands and helps you put your shoulders in a better position for movement. Your feet can be in a dorsiflexed position, where the balls of your feet are on the ground, allowing for good support and balance. Your feet can also be in plantarflexion, or pointed. The pointed-toe style of plank is common in gymnastics. The flexed-foot style is more universal, as it relates to other positions in life and sport that adopt similar shapes, such as the starting blocks of a 100-meter race in track and field.

Finally, your arms should be practically vertical. Your elbows should be straight, with the creases facing forward, in the same direction as your index fingers. Your shoulders should be on top of your knuckles, which puts your shoulder joints right over the center of the base of support created by your hands, plus adds muscular tension around your joints, which facilitates better shoulder mechanics during the Push-up.

plank position Start facedown, with your weight on your hands and the balls of your feet, your arms locked out, and your shoulders right above your knuckles. Your body is in a straight line from head to toes, and your butt and belly are tight. Your legs are straight, feet together and flexed.

Your fingers are splayed to create the broadest base of support, and your index fingers are facing forward. Use muscular tension around your hands to stabilize your base of support.

push-up

The most common style of Push-up I see beginners instructed to perform for the first time is the classic Wall Push-up. The Wall Push-up is (surprise!) a Push-up performed while leaning against a wall rather than against the ground. This style is typically seen in health clubs and group classes full of middle-aged women who either have no experience in physical training or are trying to get back in shape after a hiatus. The Wall Push-up captures some of the concepts that the Push-up develops, but unfortunately leaves out many of the important ones. Mainly, the Wall Push-up does not help you address proper global positioning or develop the shoulder mechanics required to learn higher-level pushing movements.

The secret to mastering the most advanced movements out there is not just to start with easier movements, but to start with easier movements that capture the essence of the movements you are working toward.

The Push-up, a simple movement pattern, can be broken into two points of performance:

1. ***Global position:*** The global position, in this case flexion or hollow body, doesn't change and must be maintained throughout the full range of motion of the Push-up.
2. ***Local mechanics:*** The local movement pattern can be broken down into start, transition, and finish positions. Focus on the positions that your shoulder and elbow joints go through. It is also important to prioritize the primary mover (shoulder) over the secondary mover (elbow) in order to maximize the efficiency of application of force in relation to your base of support.

These two properties are key because they make the Push-up relevant to many other movements found in sport and life. If you don't know how to perform a Push-up based on these two key points of performance, don't worry, because every stage of the Push-up progression outlined in this section focuses on these key elements while getting you closer to the universal style.

box push-up

The Box Push-up is a great way to get started with Push-ups. Its simple setup decreases the load simply by changing the angle of your body, thus reducing the effect of gravity. The taller the box, the more your feet support your body weight, and the easier the Push-up is to perform. The more your upper body must support your weight, the harder it gets. This style of Push-up can also be performed on a bar or any other raised platform that can act as a safe base of support for your hands.

box push-up 01 Start in plank position with your hands on a box. Your elbows are locked out, and your midline is straight from head to toes. Notice that my body is at a 45-degree angle to the ground. Anything higher than 45 degrees would likely end up being detrimental to your shoulder mechanics, so a 45-degree angle is the best place to start.

02 Initiate the descent with your shoulders traveling forward while keeping your elbows in line with your wrists and the line from your head to your toes straight.

03 When you reach the bottom of the Push-up, your chest is in contact with the box and your hips are in line with the rest of your body. Your head is off the box, and your neck is in line with your spine in a neutral position.

Two effective ways to assure that you are addressing global position and local mechanics at shoulder level are to:

1. Respect the plank points of performance at the top or start position.
2. Keep track of your forearm position with respect to your midline at the bottom or transition position.

04 To perform the press-up, simply reverse the movement, pressing into the box until you reach full plank position. In this position, your elbows are right on top of your wrists and your forearms are perpendicular to your midline, obeying the rules of pushing mechanics.

05 Finish with your elbows completely locked out, having returned to the starting position.

If you look at the body in profile, at the bottom of the Push-up your forearms should remain perpendicular to your midline. If you look at the body from the front, your forearms should be perpendicular to the ground. In other words, you don't want to see elbows flaring out or in. These points of performance help make the shoulders' application of force as efficient as possible.

As mentioned above, try not to start with a body angle higher than 45 degrees in plank position. Any higher angle turns it into a Wall Push-up and typically offers very little load on the shoulders. With such a light load, you struggle, because the lack of feedback makes it hard to teach your shoulders the proper pushing mechanics.

You can incrementally increase the level of performance for the Box Push-up by lowering the box height, progressing the movement until your hands are on the ground. Often, this increase is not as incremental as some people need—going from the last box to the ground can be a very big jump. And as good a tool as the box is for progressing the Push-up, you probably don't have access to enough boxes at enough heights to progress smoothly through every Push-up angle. An easy way to address this is to change your stance.

wide-stance push-up

The Wide-Stance Push-up is a great way to close the gap between the Box Push-up and the real deal. It works simply by widening your stance, as seen in the photos on the right below, which shortens the distance from your feet to your shoulders and therefore takes load off your shoulders. The change in stance can be very gradual to facilitate a smooth progression.

As useful as this scaling is, the wider stance means that you need to contract your butt muscles more in order to control your pelvis and spine for better movement. Despite this challenge, I prefer this style to the more common Bent-Leg or Knee Push-up. In the Bent-Leg Push-up, your anterior thigh muscles contract and pull your lower back into extension, which puts your spine in a compromised position for optimal pushing mechanics.

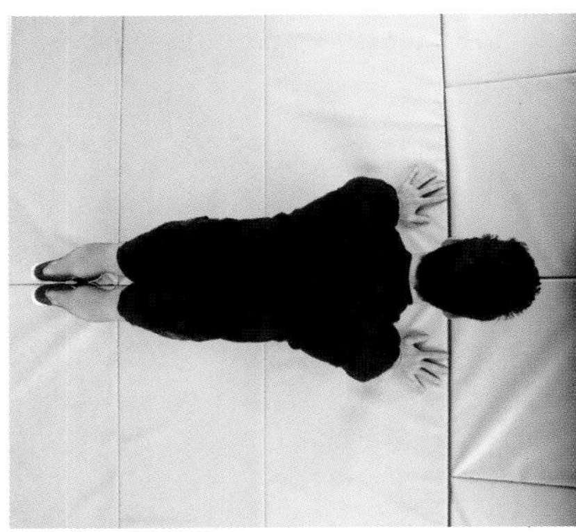

normal stance Start in plank position, with your shoulders right above your hands.

wide stance Widen your stance. Your legs remain straight, and your arms remain in the same position. You can see that the distance from my head to my feet is reduced due to the wide stance that I have adopted. If you look at the bird's-eye view, you can see that the straddle position simply abducts my legs away from my midline—nothing else changes.

band push-up

If neither the Box Push-up nor the Wide-Stance Push-up removes enough load for you to perform the ideal positions and work on the optimal shoulder mechanics, I suggest using a Band Push-up progression. The Band Push-up is a great way to scale the load by adding a band around your waist, hooked up to a bar, rings, or an anchorage point above you.

I recommend that you place the band around your hips, which provides additional stability to your pelvis. This setup offers great stabilization throughout the full range of motion of the Push-up, but not so much that you don't receive feedback if you have not engaged your butt and belly to maintain good spinal position.

band push-up 01 Start in plank position, with a band around your hips or low abdomen.

02 Perform the same descent seen in the previous Push-up progressions.

03 At the bottom position, the band is supporting you more than it was at the top of the plank. There's a progressive deloading of the body as you move through the full range of motion.

04 Ascend through position 2.

05 Finish in plank position with your elbows fully locked out.

anatomical push-up

Depending on each person's previous exposure to the Push-up, I see a wide variety of ability in this movement. For some reason, the most common thing that even some very experienced athletes lack is the ability to maintain proper shoulder positioning throughout the full range of motion. One of the biggest tells is the elbows flaring back and forth in the press off the ground. If I see this flare, I might cue you to keep your elbows glued to your body. If that fails, I might grab your elbow and hold it against your body myself so that you have no choice but to keep your forearms vertical and stationary. As discussed in the progression methods section of chapter 3 (page 88), this technique is known as blocking.

Another way to block the forearms in a vertical position is to perform an Anatomical Push-up. I give this Push-up style this name because it addresses the Push-up from the anatomical position. You start in plank position, but with your hands flipped so that your fingers are pointing toward your feet, as seen in the anatomical stance. Starting with your hands turned (externally rotated at shoulder level) blocks poor movement patterns or poor shoulder mechanics, allowing you to perform the Push-up without having to focus on shoulder mechanics as much as on the anatomical structure of your body. The remainder of the Push-up progression is the same.

anatomical push-up 01 Start with your hands right over your shoulders in plank position, but with your fingers facing your toes. Notice in the frontal view that my elbow pits are facing forward and my fingers are pointed straight back.

02 Initiate the descent exactly the same way that you initiate the descent in any other Push-up. You will notice a fair amount of tension around your wrists and forearms due to the blocking of the movement.

This setup works because your wrists are near end range of extension and your shoulders are as close to end range of external rotation as you can get them. As you bend your elbows to initiate the Push-up, your wrists act as blockers, forcing your shoulders to travel forward, engaging the primary mover for optimal pushing mechanics.

Blocking is a powerful progression method that is great for any movement, but I find it particularly useful for the shoulders. Compared with the hip joint, the shoulder has many more degrees of freedom. Blocking can help you establish a desirable position by incrementally limiting that freedom.

Blocking a Push-up with this setup doesn't always work—if you lack shoulder and wrist mobility, the position is practically impossible to adopt. But this version of the Push-up is a great tool for assessing mobility and providing a solution for people recovering from injuries related to poor mechanical movement patterns. Also, for hypermobile individuals, I have found this setup extremely beneficial not just to set up better muscular tension around the joint for movement, but also to create awareness, as one of the problems hypermobile individuals run into is a lack of proprioception.

04

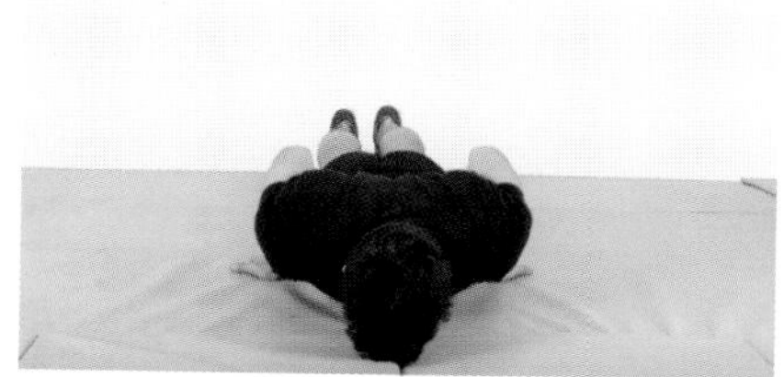

03 As you reach the bottom of the Push-up, you have created a lot of tension around your shoulder, elbow, and wrists. Even though there's a lot of tension, this position is facilitating better shoulder mechanics.

04 To press yourself back up to the plank position, reverse the motion by following steps 2–1.

05 Finish in plank position with your elbows locked out.

Hypermobility describes joints that stretch further than normal. For example, some hypermobile people can bend their thumbs backward to their wrists, bend their knee joints backward, put their leg behind the head, or perform other contortionist "tricks." Hypermobility can affect one or more joints throughout the body.

Proprioception is the sense of the relative position of neighboring parts of the body and the strength of effort being employed in movement.

kipping push-ups

The Kipping Push-up is another great way to progress the Push-up from the floor. Similar to other kipping movements, it adds a dynamic full-body movement to assist with the shoulder pushing.

Although the Kipping Push-up is useful, I keep it in my back pocket for as long as possible, because adding degrees of freedom while reducing the load on your shoulders can make it more difficult to be aware of your shoulder position, which is a fundamental error. However, similar to other kipping movements, the Kipping Push-up is great for adding speed and volume in terms of repetitions and for skill transfer to pushing mechanics during dynamic movements.

In this section I consider two kipping styles:

1. Bow-up
2. Kip-up

bow-up push-up 01 Start at the bottom position of a Push-up, with your arms in full flexion and your forearms perpendicular to your midline.

02 Push away with your arms and lock out your elbows, keeping your hips glued to the ground as your body goes into global extension.

03 Lift up your hips until you reach plank position.

kip-up push-up 01 Start at the bottom position of a Push-up, with your arms in full flexion and your forearms perpendicular to your midline.

02 Extend your body slightly globally by picking your legs up off the ground and keeping your hands flat.

03 Drop your legs toward the ground with your feet flexed to allow the balls of your feet to make contact and support your body. The momentum created by this snap elevates your hips, and your hips initiate the drive into the next position.

bow-up push-up: You perform a Bow-up Push-up by allowing your global position to change as you ascend from the ground. You initiate the ascent through your upper body by pressing away from the ground and locking out your elbows the same way you would in a strict Push-up, but you allow your global position to go into extension. Essentially, your hips and lower extremities remain in the bottom position. Only after your arms are fully locked out do you lift the rest of your body off the ground by picking up your hips and returning to a neutral global position. The descent looks just like a Push-up, where the midline stays in a straight line from head to toes rather than bowing.

You can progress this movement to the strict Push-up by incrementally reducing the amount of bowing on the ascent.

kip-up push-up: The Kip-up Push-up adds even more degrees of freedom to facilitate the pushing. You descend to the bottom of the Push-up in the same way as before. At the bottom, you pick your feet off the ground and lift your chest slightly, placing your body in global extension. From this globally extended position, you snap into a globally flexed or hollow body position. This snap creates an upward drive of your center of mass, and you can use this momentum to facilitate the press.

You can progress this movement to the strict Push-up by incrementally reducing the intensity of the snap from extension to flexion.

04 You're now off the ground and halfway through your press, with your hips lifted off the ground.

05 Lock out your elbows and finish in plank position.

push-up

With the previous progressions in this chapter, you have been working on the points of performance required to execute the Push-up. Globally, you have established stability in multiple shapes during pushing, such as neutral, extended, and flexed. Locally, you have focused on getting to a stable shoulder position, loading the shoulder, and achieving the mechanics required for the best application of force. The strict Push-up allows you to combine these points of performance into the style that I believe is the most transferable to life and sport.

push-up 01 Start in plank position with your hands flat on the ground, your elbows locked out, and your shoulders right above your knuckles or at mid-hand. Your body is in a neutral global position, making a straight line from head to toes. Your neck is neutral. Your back is flat. Your hips are in a neutral position or in slight extension. Your knees are in full extension, and your ankles are in dorsiflexion, with the balls of your feet supporting your body.

02 Bend your elbows to initiate the descent, fighting to keep your elbows right on top of your wrists. If you look at the frontal view, my elbows do not flare out or in; they stay perpendicular to the ground.

The Squat is king, the Push-up is queen.

03 As you reach the ground, your head remains in line with your global body position. Your forearms are perpendicular to your midline, and your body is completely straight. Allow your belly, hips, and thighs to touch the ground, but keep everything else except your feet off the ground.

04 Initiate the ascent by pressing away from the ground, fighting to keep your elbows in the same vertical position seen earlier.

05 Finish in full lockout, again adopting the plank position.

neck neutral
hips neutral
legs straight
hands flat

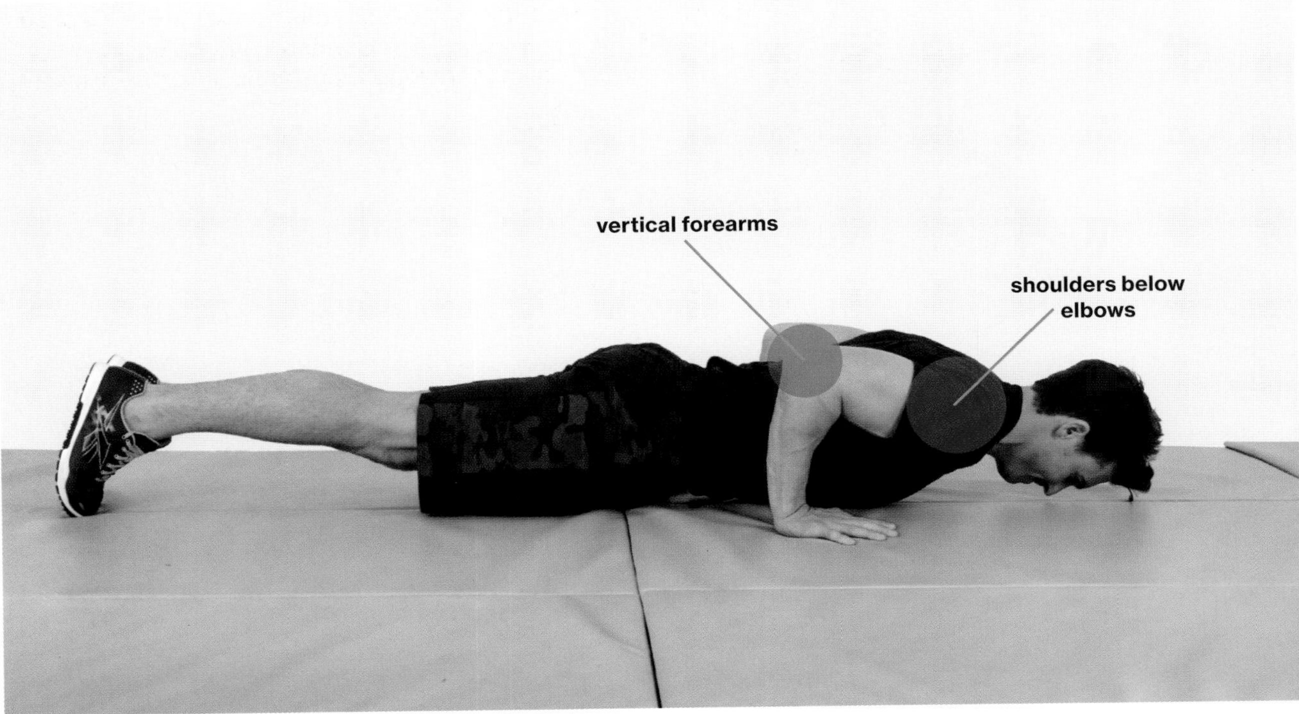
vertical forearms
shoulders below
elbows

HAND STAND PUSH UP

Once you have developed a foundation of strength and pushing mechanics with the Push-up, it is safe to begin developing the Handstand Push-up.

The Handstand Push-up involves a higher level of pushing mechanics for the following key reasons:

1. It is performed in full inversion.
2. You must balance on your hands.
3. The load is heavier because your arms must support your entire body weight.
4. Your shoulders reach near end range of flexion.

Being at near end range of shoulder flexion presents further challenges because the end range of motion of a joint is a position of high tension. For the shoulder, the muscular tension acts as a band, trying to pull your arm back down into a more anatomical position. This tension adds a load to the movement that makes it more difficult, as seen in the progression principles section of chapter 3.

This style of pushing mechanics starts in a Handstand, with your shoulders at near end range of flexion and your elbows and wrists in extension, creating the same flat base seen in the plank position. It finishes in a Headstand, with your shoulders near midrange of motion but still in slight flexion (in front of the frontal plane), your elbows close to full flexion, and your wrists remaining in extension, as seen in the Handstand. In the strict style of Handstand Push-up, your global position remains neutral throughout the full range of motion of the shoulder.

feet on box handstand push-up

In the Push-up progression, you progressed your body from a more upright position to a horizontal position. You can think of the Handstand Push-up progression as a continuation of changing your orientation in space, leading you from horizontal to the final inverted pushing position. So you can use a box progression here, too, but instead of placing your hands on the box, you place your feet on the box. This allows you to create incrementally more inverted positions while pushing.

For some people, this box progression may seem obvious, but if you lack experience with the pushing mechanics addressed in the Push-up section, the pushing mechanics required for the Handstand Push-up will be hard for you to achieve. Plus, the Handstand Push-up requires two master positions that are kind of out of the ordinary for most people: the Headstand and the Handstand.

feet on box handstand push-up 01 Place your feet on a box with your legs straight and your hips in flexion and directly over your hands.

02 Without losing the upper-body position, extend one leg over your head, adopting a Handstand position, but with your opposite leg still in hip flexion and on the box for balance.

headstand

The Headstand is one of the two master positions found in the Handstand Push-up. It is found either at the start and finish or in the transition position, depending on whether you choose to start your Handstand Push-up from the ground. Regardless of how you start, understanding the basic setup for the Headstand heavily influences the efficiency of your pushing mechanics for the Handstand Push-up.

Similar to the plank position in the Push-up (page 158), the Headstand position can be considered the base of the Handstand Push-up. In addition, the Headstand is a great way to progress into the Handstand position, which often takes great effort and patience to master.

tripod

The best way to get familiar with the Headstand is to start in what is known as a Tripod. The Tripod is a Headstand performed with your legs resting on your arms. The top of your head and your hands form your base of support, which takes the shape of a triangle and gives this Headstand style its name.

The Tripod and Headstand positions share the same points of performance seen at the bottom of a Push-up. Specifically, your forearms should be perpendicular to the ground when viewed from both the front and the side. Another way to think about this position is that your elbows should be right above your wrists.

In the Tripod, your hips are in flexion and placed right above the center of the base of support created by your hands and head. Your knees are in full flexion and resting on the backs of your upper arms, with your toes pointed in plantarflexion. Your arms are at midrange of flexion at the shoulders and near full flexion at the elbows.

Since our bodies are not identical, the triangular shape created by the hands and head is unique to each individual. Despite our differences, there are some very good rules for making sure that you are setting up an optimal Tripod.

First, you should always be able to see your hands, which prevents you from adopting many bad shoulder positions.

Next, try to refine the position of your hands in front of you by doing the following:

1. Perform a Push-up. Wherever your face touches the ground at the bottom of the Push-up is where the top of your head should go in relation to your hands in the Tripod.
2. Apply the same vertical-forearms concept introduced in the Push-up section (page 158). If your forearms remain vertical with respect to the ground and, in this case, are parallel to your midline, then you are in a good position, as long as your head is placed such that you can see your hands.

Once you understand how to establish a proper base, you can begin learning how to establish the Tripod position as shown on the next page.

The Tripod progression follows the progression principles addressed in chapter 3. You start by establishing the right position, which in this case is your base. You load up that position by shifting your center of mass above your base of support, walking your feet toward your hands and elevating your hips above your head. Once your legs are close enough to your body that your knees can reach your upper arms, you start bending your legs, placing one knee on one elbow and following with the other knee. As you lift your knees, keeping your feet in contact with the ground increases the points of contact you have, imparting more stability while you are setting up. Once your knees are resting comfortably on your arms, you can pick up one foot, followed by the other.

This progression is a basic way of adopting the Tripod shape. It is also the safest, based on the progression principles discussed in chapter 3. Even if you forget those principles, remember that human movement is mostly intuitive, and you can typically trust your body to find the easiest way to get into the Tripod position.

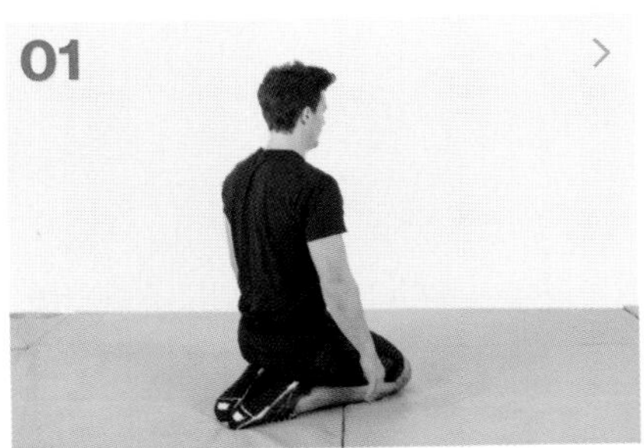

tripod 01 Start in a kneeling position.

02 Bend over and place your hands flat on the ground, where you always have visual contact with your hands. Keep your forearms vertical, with your elbows right on top of your wrists.

03 Continue to bend forward and place your head flat on the ground in front of your hands.

04 Extend your knees and lift your hips. You should still be able to see your feet and hands from this position.

05 Walk one leg and foot into one arm and position that knee on top of that elbow or at the back end of your upper arm. In the photo, my right leg is coming into my right arm. The knee that is in contact with the arm has the ball of the foot on the ground.

06 Perform the exact same movement with the opposite leg. The balls of your feet remain in contact with the ground.

07 Pick up one foot.

08 Pick up the other foot, adopting the Tripod position. Throughout the motion, fight to keep your elbows over your wrists and your hips above your hands, keeping your center of mass above the center of your base of support.

tripod finish profile

band tripod

If the Tripod position is hard for you to get into, you can add a band around your hips as you did for the Band Push-up (page 163).

band tripod 01 Hook a band to an anchorage point overhead, in this case a bar.

02 Grab the inside of the band with both hands, with your thumbs pointing down, and make a loop or triangle shape.

03 Extend your arms, pressing the band down to your hips.

04 Bend over to thread your body through the band and place it flat across your hip crease.

05 Continue bending over, let go of the band, and place your hands flat on the ground.

06 Get into the Tripod position with the band pulling as vertically as possible.

07 Lift your knees slowly off your elbows using the support of the band.

headstand

When you use the Tripod as a starting position, getting into a Headstand is relatively simple. All you really need to do is extend your legs in order to achieve the universal Headstand shape seen in picture 6.

Start by lifting one leg at a time to slowly increase the load on your spine and progressively remove the points of connection that were providing stability. The key to this progression is to remove your knees from your elbows and adopt a neutral spine while keeping your legs in a tucked position.

This first step of the progression focuses on:

1. Changing points of contact, thus increasing muscular tension around your spine
2. Establishing a more universal or neutral spine position

headstand 01 Start in the Tripod position.

02 Pick up one knee off of one elbow. You can bring it back down and perform the same movement with your other knee and leg for training purposes.

03 Once you are comfortable lifting and lowering one knee and then the other, pick up both knees at the same time.

The next step requires you to bring your legs together to adopt a more streamlined body shape. This shape also adds tension around your hips for better movement control.

Once you can bring your legs together and maintain balance, you can proceed to extend your legs until you reach the full Headstand position. While extending your legs, it's easy to lose balance, as the tendency is to want to place your legs and feet directly over your head. In reality, the Headstand position requires a slight lean in your midline to maintain proper balance and ensure that your center of mass falls on top of the center of your base of support. A good way to avoid losing balance is to think about keeping your feet above your hands, which keeps your hips approximately over your base of support.

A spotter can be useful for progressing your body into these positions with balance. Having a wall behind your back can also serve as a safety net in case you lose balance.

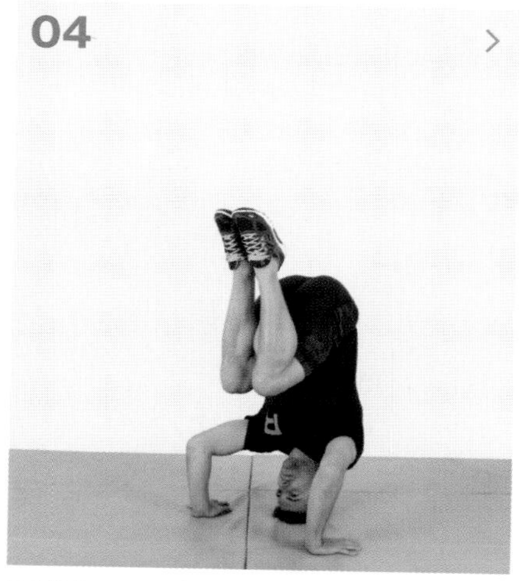

04 Bring your knees and feet together, creating a more streamlined body position. This position will help you execute any movement related to Handstand Push-ups or inversions later.

05 Start to extend your legs, reaching them toward the sky. Your feet should always remain above your hands.

06 Continue to extend your legs until you reach the full Headstand position, where your body is in a straight line from head to toes. Your elbows remain directly above your hands, and your shoulders are at midrange of flexion. You have a slight lean from head to toes, which allows you to place your center of mass, which is around your hip area, right on top of the center of your base of support.

A Handstand should be seen as a perfect pillar.

Once you've developed the proper base Headstand position, strength, and balance and you feel comfortable with being inverted, you have the option to learn the Handstand or start developing the Handstand Push-up. The Handstand progression that I present in this chapter allows you to develop the Handstand position as you develop the Handstand Push-up. This doesn't mean that you will be able to master the Handstand just by working on the Handstand Push-up progression presented in this chapter, however.

The Handstand is a beast of its own to master, and reaching a level of competence takes a long time. In my many years of gymnastics, the Handstand never got old; I needed to train and practice it daily. I could have dedicated this entire book to developing the Handstand, but instead I have opted to give you a few points of performance to help you understand the principles behind this position and how it relates to the Handstand Push-up and other performance aspects seen in life and sport.

There are many ways of getting into a Handstand, such as kicking up, jumping up, and pressing up. In this chapter, I show you how to perform a Handstand Push-up as a way to get into a Handstand.

The Handstand requires you to maintain a straight body position from head to toes while balancing on your hands, with your arms acting as two posts that support your body. The details of your hand position in the Handstand are very similar to the Push-up (page 158). Your arms should be shoulder width apart. I think it's helpful to compare the Handstand to normal standing position. When you stand, your feet are directly under your hips; therefore, in the Handstand, your hands should be placed directly under your shoulders. To keep your body in a straight line, your legs remain together with toes pointed. Your belly and butt stay tight to establish proper spinal position for balance and movement control. A Handstand should be seen as a perfect pillar.

floor handstand push-up

Now that I have covered the fundamentals for pushing mechanics and introduced the two master positions required to perform the Handstand Push-up, I am going to dive into the Handstand Push-up progression. This section covers what is sometimes considered a strict style of Handstand Push-up, where your global position remains neutral throughout the full range of motion of the Push-up or pushing mechanics for the shoulder.

You start the Handstand Push-up progression from the Headstand position and build up to the Handstand as you move toward the higher-level stages of development. As previously mentioned, the Handstand will be built up as you progress the Handstand Push-up. Keep in mind that the Handstand is so fundamental and challenging in its own right that, if you're interested, you can and should develop the Handstand constantly with other practices; some options are shown in chapter 8.

fall-pause-press

This progression starts in the Headstand position. You initiate the movement by falling out of balance with intention and directing your feet toward the ground. This act of falling or shifting your center of mass to the edge of your base of support and beyond is the most fundamental form for creating movement, as discussed in the Shift-Connect-Flow section of chapter 3 (page 92).

Once your feet reach the floor, your body adopts the bottom position of a Push-up, while your head remains in contact with the ground. Basically, you are in a very-large-base Tripod. This position allows you to pause and find stability, which is especially helpful for beginners.

In addition to creating stability, this progression is another type of movement blocking. Keeping your head on the ground blocks your arm position from changing, which keeps your elbows on top of your wrists and your forearms vertical. It is up to you, though, to fight to maintain lateral (in-and-out) control of your elbow position. Performing a Push-up from this position is the final step required to complete the progression.

fall-pause-press 01 Start in a balanced Headstand.

02 Allow your body to fall into a hollow body position off the back edge of your base of support, meaning that your hips fall toward the ground in the direction you can see. Fight to keep your elbows on top of your wrists and your head glued to the ground.

03 When your feet reach the ground, adopt a hollow body position with your feet, hands, and head creating your base of support.

04 Pick your head up off the ground and perform a partial Push-up.

This progression also allows you to break the Handstand Push-up into two parts. In the first part, you initiate the movement by shifting your body and falling out of the Headstand. In the second part, you use the pushing mechanics developed in the Push-up section (page 157) to push away from the ground and start connecting the pushing to the inverted position of the Handstand Push-up.

fall-press

Once you have mastered this two-part Handstand Push-up progression, you can use the Shift-Connect-Flow approach to progress to the next stage of difficulty. Here, you change points of connection by making it a one-part movement and letting your head leave the floor as the shift occurs. That change in points of connection makes the movement more difficult because it requires increased stability and movement control, but it also introduces more flow. By making the movement sequence more fluid, your momentum can facilitate the pushing mechanics as previously discussed.

fall-press 01 Start in a balanced Headstand.

02 Allow yourself to fall off your base of support as you did in the Fall-Pause-Press progression. In this case, you utilize the momentum created by the fall to allow your head to come up off the ground and facilitate the pushing mechanics. Your elbows remain right on top of your hands, and your head is in line with the rest of your body.

03 Without pausing in the transition as you did in the Fall-Pause-Press, where your head ends up on the ground, allow yourself to transition straight into plank position.

fall-olympic

Once you have developed a good foundation of the shift and flow to assist the pushing mechanics from an inverted position, I like to increase the range of motion locally at shoulder level in order to get you closer to the pushing range required to perform a full Handstand Push-up. The main difference in this stage is the finish position, which is an Olympic plank rather than a regular plank. In the Olympic plank, your shoulders must travel farther into flexion or overhead.

In addition to increasing shoulder range of motion, this stage adds speed to the movement that you must control. The increased speed comes with an increased amount of force projected onto your spine during the landing, which is best countered by squeezing your butt and pulling your belly in and up toward your spine for optimal stability. This stability is important from a safety standpoint, but also to develop movement control for the next level of progression.

This progression can be tricky, as the fall toward the ground can generate enough speed to hurt your feet on landing. I recommend that you learn how to make the fall as controlled as possible by tightening up your body, focusing on projecting most of your weight toward your upper body, and potentially placing a mat in the landing position to reduce the impact on your feet.

fall-olympic 01 Start in a balanced Headstand.

02 Allow yourself to fall off your base of support in the direction you can see. As in the previous progression, start pressing away from the ground and allow your head to lose contact with the ground as you transition. In this case, though, instead of finishing in plank position, push a little farther away from the ground.

03 Finish in an extended plank position with your hands in front of you, your shoulders over your head and in line with your ears, and the rest of your body in a globally flexed or hollow body position.

wall handstand push-up

Now that you have developed the foundation for the Handstand Push-up, you can move on to the Wall Handstand Push-up. It's best to think of this progression as a progressive inversion of your body. Specifically, you change your global orientation in space by rotating your body forward and adapting the pushing mechanics to this new orientation in space.

A wall is a useful tool for creating a stable finish position. Changing the angle from which you approach the wall allows for a progressive increase in load and helps you adjust to the orientation in space required to perform a full Handstand Push-up.

The same way you performed the 45-degree-angle Handstand Push-up progression, you can perform the progression with your chest facing a wall. You can inch your way in according to your level of performance until you reach the point where your hands are almost in contact with the wall or your forearms are almost in line with the wall.

wall climb

This progression requires you to learn how to get into the finish position or partial Handstand against a wall. You find this position first by placing your feet against the wall while you are in plank position. From the plank position, you start taking small steps up the wall until you reach the highest point that your feet can reach without moving your hands from the original plank. This partial Handstand should be at about a 45-degree angle. The points of performance for the partial Handstand are the same as those for the Olympic plank, with the exception that the partial Handstand makes you carry more load on your upper body. The act of walking up the wall in this fashion is commonly known as a Wall Climb.

wall climb 01 Start in plank position with your feet against a wall and your hands right under your shoulders.

02 Without moving your hands, begin walking your feet up the wall.

03 As you walk up the wall, your head is neutral, but you are making eye contact with the point where your feet contact the wall, which will be your mark as you perform the Kipping Handstand Push-up.

04 Continue to walk until your feet are as high as you can get them without moving your hands. Your toes are pointed, knees locked out, butt and belly tight, and arms in line with your ears.

Once you have mastered the partial Handstand, you can use the two positions—plank and partial Handstand—to create a start and a finish position for the Wall Handstand Push-up progression. The plank position, with your feet glued to the wall and your hands under your shoulders, establishes the distance from the wall from which you should start your Handstand Push-up. Without moving your hands in the plank setup, you get your body into a Tripod and then into the Headstand or starting position for the Handstand Push-up.

fall-45 and fall-chest to wall

The next step is similar to the floor Handstand Push-up progression. You create movement by shifting your hips to the edge of your base of support and essentially falling forward. After initiating the fall, you can push through the fall as you did in the floor progression. The effort to get your body to meet the 45-degree angle is not much greater than in the Olympic Handstand Push-up progression on the floor, but it requires more upper-body strength.

If you look at photo 2 in the Olympic Handstand Push-up progression on the floor (page 181), you can see that even though my body is at midpress, it is at approximately a 45-degree angle to the wall. In this wall progression, rather than simply allowing your legs to fall to the wall, you have to make an effort to keep your legs as high as possible. Doing so helps you hit full lockout in your arms before your feet reach the wall.

If your global shape changes as you reach the wall, you may not be ready for this stage. The typical causes for this global shape change are:

1. Improper setup for the Headstand—see page 176
2. Missing the shift concept to create movement—see pages 179–180
3. Pushing too late after the shift—see page 180
4. Lack of shoulder pushing mechanics—see page 168

Each potential hole indicates a progression stage that would be beneficial to practice.

The points of performance addressed in the Headstand and Handstand sections of this chapter must carry over to the Handstand Push-up and pushing mechanics. Your global line remains the same, and your pushing mechanics should be efficient, focusing on your elbows in relation to your wrists, even as the Push-up is occurring. A good way to cue the global line is to look at your toes throughout the press, regardless of how vertical you get. Make sure to shift first; looking at your feet may cause you to rotate forward and fall over (see the Forward Roll as exit strategy on page 346).

The beauty of the Wall Handstand Push-up progression is that its continuous nature helps acclimate you to incrementally more inversion. You increase the difficulty simply by setting up the Headstand closer to the wall. You can make it as progressive as you want, from a millimeter at the time to a foot or more, depending on your performance of and experience with the movement.

fall-45 01 Perform a Headstand away from, but facing, a wall.

02 Allow your hips to fall off your base of support in the direction you can see (toward the wall). As you initiate the fall, allow it to facilitate the pressing mechanics away from the floor.

03 Once you reach full elbow extension and lock out in the overhead position, you should have reached the wall and landed with your feet against the wall at a 45-degree angle and your hands on the ground. Keep your head in, and always look at the point where you want to make contact with your feet.

fall-chest to wall 01 Perform a Headstand facing a wall with your hands as close to the wall as possible. In the photo, my toes are in contact with the wall, but you can start with your feet slightly off the wall to give yourself more room to utilize the falling mechanics.

02 Fall toward the wall by slightly shifting your hips over your hands and toward the wall, but without losing balance. Use this shift to initiate the press through your arms away from the ground.

03 Finish in a full Handstand with your head tucked in and looking toward the wall. Both your chest and your toes should be in contact with the wall.

Another important benefit of this progression is that it is a good way to practice the descent to the Headstand position. It's helpful to have the wall as a stopping point at the top of your Handstand because it allows you to refocus on maintaining the proper shoulder mechanics as you descend. The descent, even though it doesn't require as much strength as the ascent, still requires a lot of attention to detail in terms of establishing proper position. The descent is an often overlooked key to stringing together multiple Handstand Push-ups, and this stage is an important time to develop that part of the movement. In addition, working on the descent phase is known as "working negatives," and it's a great way to build up the movement control required for the ascent, or positive phase.

Once you get close enough to the wall, the setup of the Wall Handstand Push-up makes it hard to perform. When your hands are almost at the wall, the rest of your body, especially your legs, do not have enough room to shift your hips in order to start the movement. In addition, getting into the Headstand itself becomes a little awkward. For an easier way to get into the Headstand, see the Straddle Press to Headstand in chapter 8 (page 332).

back-to-wall handstand push-up

Each stage of a progression is typically a continuation of the previous stage. In this case, you're simply flipping your body 180 degrees. Instead of having your chest against the wall, you have your back against the wall.

fall-back to wall

The setup for this stage is simply to get into a Headstand with your back facing a wall. This progression allows you to perform the same mechanics, but without having a wall to support the Handstand position until the very end of the Push-up. As simple as it may seem, this change can be a make-it-or-break-it factor. It also seems to come into play when it's time to move on to higher levels of performance for the Handstand Push-up.

By starting with your back against the wall and not allowing your body to touch the wall at the bottom, you get a sense of freestanding. This is also a gradual introduction to controlling your inverted body position in space for optimal performance. The mechanics in this movement work exactly the same as in the previous stages of the progression, where shifting your center of mass comes first. This may seem counterintuitive with your back facing the wall, as the shift requires you to move away from the wall, but it pays off big as you advance.

Once you initiate the Handstand Push-up and your head leaves the ground, it is very important to start readjusting the path of the Push-up toward the wall. Even though you initiate the shift away from the wall, right before your elbow flexion passes 90 degrees, you must redirect your center of mass toward the wall by driving your heels over your head. If you do it properly, you will finish in slight extension as you lean against the wall.

One of the most important points of performance here is to finish with control, without letting your legs crash into the wall. I like to think of it as kissing the wall with your heels. The kiss must be gentle yet firm.

The optimal descent or negative phase of this stage requires your feet to leave the wall before your arms start bending. This order again follows the Shift-Connect-Flow principle and is an important next step toward the Freestanding Handstand Push-up progression.

fall-back and feet to wall

You can also start this progression in a Headstand with your back and feet touching the wall. This adds stability to the starting position, as you have connection with the wall throughout the full range of motion. Unfortunately, this style can be limited in terms of universality, as it doesn't allow for the important shift to initiate the movement.

fall-back to wall 01 Perform a Headstand with your back really close to a wall, but not in contact with it. Your feet are away from the wall because you are adopting a balanced Headstand position.

02 Initiate the fall or displacement of your center of mass in order to facilitate the pushing mechanics, as seen in the previous progressions. Allow that shift to help you push away from the ground. Once you reach this position, your center of mass must remain on top of your base of support.

03 Drive your heels toward the wall in order to finish in the Handstand position, with only your feet in contact with the wall. To reverse this movement, you have two options: You can slide your legs and body down the wall, reaching the Headstand position seen in photo 1, or you can reverse these steps by separating your feet from the wall and then lowering your center of mass toward the Headstand by dropping your shoulders forward, but under control so as not to crash against the wall.

fall-back and feet to wall 01 Start in a Headstand with your back facing a wall and your feet in contact with the wall.

02 Press yourself away from the ground into a Handstand, sliding your feet up the wall without letting them lose contact.

freestanding handstand push-up

The Freestanding Handstand Push-up requires 100 percent of the movement ability developed in the Handstand Push-up progression. The only added difficulty is the capacity required to perform and balance in the Handstand.

This progression starts in a Headstand, and once again you begin the movement by shifting your center of mass over your hands. As soon as you initiate the Push-up, you must shift your center of mass back over your center of your base of support by directing your feet and legs over your head. You are looking for a sweet spot where you can balance more easily throughout the push. When you find this spot, you keep directing your feet up and over your fingertips.

Once you reach full lockout of your arms, you've reached the top, or Handstand position. In the most universal Handstand position, your neck is neutral to your spine and you are looking in the direction in which your head is oriented. Unfortunately, this position is very

handstand push-up 01 Start in a Headstand in the middle of a room, without a wall near you.

02 Allow yourself to establish the fall of your hips on the back edge of your base of support as you did in the previous progressions.

handstand position

Holding a Handstand with your head tucked in is harder than holding a Handstand while looking at the ground. The experience is similar to standing on one leg. If you try standing on one leg, you will likely be able to balance, but if you close your eyes, you will start to lose balance and begin wobbling in a matter of seconds. This is due to the lack of visual contact, which causes a sense of instability as you lose proprioception (your sixth sense). The same thing occurs in the Handstand position. Having your head in is like closing your eyes while standing on one leg, and looking at the ground is like keeping your eyes open.

difficult to master because you can't see the ground. For better control and balance in the Handstand, I recommend glancing at the ground by slightly extending your neck. A useful cue to keep your head in line with your neutral global position is to keep your ears in line with your shoulders.

The descent from the Handstand is exactly the same as it is in the Back-to-Wall Handstand Push-up progression. You start by shifting your hips over your hands, thus lowering your legs slightly closer to the ground. This shift also preloads your shoulders so that they are ready to support the descent. You engage your shoulders by flexing your elbows and directing your shoulders forward while your head aims for the Tripod in the Headstand position. You should reach this position with enough control and balance that you finish in a resting position.

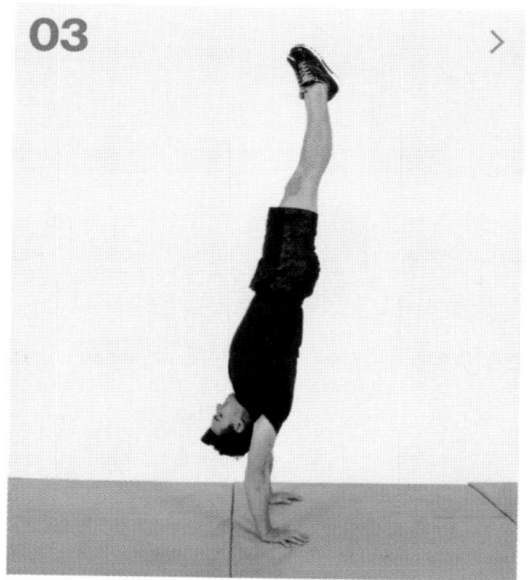

03 Find balance and drive your heels over your head and hands in order to reach a full Handstand position with your head tucked in, your arms locked out, and your body in a neutral global line.

04 It is hard to balance in a Handstand with your head tucked, as you don't have a visual cue to give you a point of reference or feedback loop. You can descend to a Headstand or, if you want to balance for a longer period and with more control, proceed to a Handstand position where you're looking at the ground, as shown here. Your neck is in slight extension, but you remain in a neutral global position, with your shoulders in line with your ears.

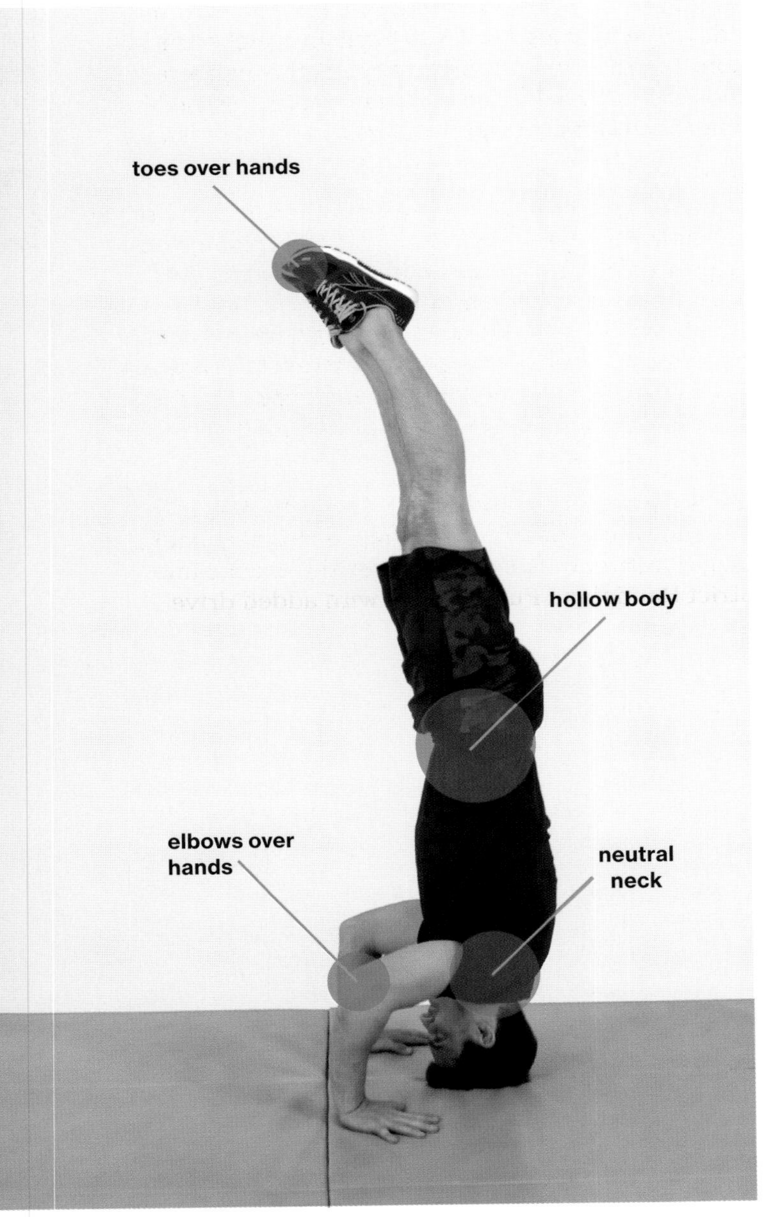
toes over hands
hollow body
elbows over hands
neutral neck

toes pointed
straight legs
hips neutral
arms next to ears
straight arms

K I P
P I N
G H S
P U

The Kipping Handstand Push-up takes the strict Handstand Push-up progression and adds a dynamic leg kick. You begin in a tucked flexed hip and knee position, and the dynamic kick happens through a rapid extension of your hips and knees. The momentum created by the kip facilitates the pushing mechanics required to perform the Handstand Push-up.

The Kipping Handstand progression starts in a Tripod position, with your knees off your elbows and your back flat. From the Tripod, you perform a rapid extension of your hips and knees. This extension creates an upward drive of your center of mass that you can take advantage of in order to perform the Push-up. If you perform the Kipping Handstand Push-up correctly, the pushing strength required is minimal. Keep in mind that the kipping motion adds speed to the movement, so it requires a higher degree of movement control to perform.

As you move into the Kipping Handstand Push-up progression, it is important to bring all the concepts already addressed in this chapter with you. The Kipping Handstand Push-up requires the exact same mechanics as the strict Handstand Push-up, but with added drive from your legs.

teeter

Before moving into the Kipping Handstand Push-up progression, it's important to revisit the Tripod position seen in the Headstand progression (page 173). The most universal style of Kipping Handstand Push-up has your knees off your elbows and your back flat, but you should begin with your knees on your elbows, the most stable starting position.

Similar to the strict Handstand Push-up progression, you start the floor progression with a two-part Handstand Push-up. The main difference here is that you begin with a Teeter from a Tripod position with your knees on your elbows.

teeter 01 Start in a Tripod position with your knees on your elbows and fully flexed, and your heels as close as possible to your hips. Your elbows are on top of your wrists, and your neck is in a neutral position. From here, press your body away from the ground as you shift your hips in the direction you can see.

02 Your head is off the ground, and you're pressing away from the ground without your feet touching the ground.

03 You have reached a full lockout of your elbows, but your knees are still in contact with your elbows, and your neck is in a straight line with your spine.

kick-pause-press 01 Start in a Tripod position with your knees on your elbows and fully flexed, and your elbows on top of your hands.

02 Perform a controlled lift of your knees off your elbows, directing your feet in the direction you can see and extending your legs slowly with your hips falling through.

kick-pause-press

You initiate the Kick-Pause-Press movement by extending your spine into a neutral position, where your hips are over your head and your back is flat. From this position, you perform a slight shift of your center of mass over your hands. Right after this shift, you extend your hips and legs into plank position while leaving your head and hands on the ground. The extension of your hips and knees must be slow and controlled at this stage of the progression.

Once you've reached plank position with your head on the ground, you perform the rest of the movement just like in the strict Handstand Push-up progression. You can use this moment to pause and find stability for the pushing mechanics that come next. Having your head on the ground is also a great strategy for blocking poor shoulder mechanics during the kick-out. Despite this blocking, it is your responsibility to keep lateral (in-and-out) control of your elbow position. Performing a Push-up out of this position is the final step required to complete the progression.

04 Allow your feet to touch the ground, remaining in the locked-out elbow position with your knees in contact with your elbows.

05 You can reverse this movement by picking up your feet and going back into positions 3 and 2.

06 From there, start bending your elbows and dropping your shoulders toward the ground until you reach position 1, a Tripod. This movement requires you to fight hard to keep your elbows right on top of your hands or on top of the center of your base of support. Starting and finishing the movement requires you to control the shift of your center of mass to pivot over your hands.

03 Finish with your feet on the ground and your head in the same position. This is the same position you adopt during the Kick, Fall, Pause, and Fall stage of the Handstand Push-up progression.

04 Press your body away from the ground, finishing in plank position with your elbows locked out and your head in line with your body.

kick-press

Once you have mastered the two-part Kipping Handstand Push-up progression, it's time to add the explosive kick. You perform this kick by extending your hips and knees, adding momentum to the movement that helps lift your center of mass up and slightly to the back and creating an important moment of weightlessness as your head leaves the ground. This moment of weightlessness is the moment you follow through with the Push-up.

You start your Push-up when your hips and knees reach full extension during the kip. This timing guarantees that you are maximizing the power generated from your lower extremities. Furthermore, it follows the principle of primary mover (hips) before secondary mover (shoulders). Despite the dynamic kicking motion, the finish position should be a strong, controlled plank, as in the strict progression.

kick-press 01 Start in a Tripod position.

02 Extend your legs, violently separating your knees from your elbows. As you do, glue your legs together.

03 Aggressively extend your legs, using the momentum of the kick and hip extension to lift your head off the ground and start extending your elbows.

04 Once your feet reach the ground, adopt a strong plank position.

kick-olympic

Now that you can use the kip to facilitate the Push-up into the plank, you can progress the movement to finish in the Olympic-style plank. Just as in the strict Handstand Push-up progression, this finish allows you to adopt a position that is closer to the Handstand and covers a greater range of flexion at shoulder level. Remember that this stage of the progression adds a great deal of speed and can make for an aggressive impact on landing. The stress created by the increased distance between your feet and hands on landing requires you to perform the movement with a higher degree of control over the position of your spine.

kick-olympic 01 Start in a Tripod position.

02 Extend your legs, violently separating your knees from your elbows. As you do, glue your legs together.

03 Fully extend your legs and hips, creating momentum up and forward in the direction you can see, which allows you to push away from the ground.

04 Keep extending your legs and body and pushing away from the ground, reaching with your arms over your head until you finish in the Olympic Push-up position.

wall kipping handstand push-up

Once you have mastered the floor progression, you can start increasing the change of orientation in space of the finish position. This progression uses a wall to help you find a stable finish position. The wall is a great tool for progressively increasing the load that you must handle during the movement. You are also simultaneously adjusting your orientation in space toward the full inversion of the Handstand. You carry out this progression by following the same steps as in the strict Handstand Push-up, but using a kipping motion.

This progression starts at the same 45-degree angle as the strict Handstand Push-up. You need to mark the distance and use a Wall Climb, as described on page 181. Essentially, you need to get into a Tripod that is approximately your body length or plank distance away from the wall. The main difference is that you are not starting from a Headstand. Instead, you start in a Tripod with your legs off your knees and use the kipping motion at a 45-degree angle toward the wall to finish in the same partial Handstand position established previously.

There are three common errors to watch for here:

1. ***Looking at the ground:*** This compromises your neutral global position as you go into extension. The neutral global position is key for generating efficient pushing mechanics.
2. ***Separating your legs as you kip:*** This causes a huge loss of muscular tension and ruins the direction of the kip, which should be like an arrow straight toward your target.
3. ***Exploding the kip right from the knee-on-elbow Tripod:*** It is important to progressively pick your knees up off your elbows until your back reaches the neutral spinal position. Only when you've reached that position, with your hips in the air and your knees off your elbows, do you initiate the kip by slightly shifting your hips forward and then explosively extending your hips and legs toward the wall.

The beauty of this progression is your control of the progressive difficulty. You should always feel comfortable with your performance of the Push-up before you increase the distance and move on to the next level of difficulty.

kick-45 01 Start in a Tripod position.

02 Initiate the movement by lifting your knees off your elbows and flattening your back, keeping your hips directly over your head.

03 Violently extend your legs up and toward the wall, always making eye contact with the point of reference created from the walk up to Handstand into a partial Handstand.

04 Finish in a partial Handstand with your head tucked in, toes pointed, knees straight, butt and belly tight, and arms locked out and pressing into the ground.

first pull

For you Olympic-style weightlifters, I like to compare the progressive lift of the knees off the elbows to the first pull in Olympic weightlifting. It must have a lot of muscular tension and good movement control, and it cannot be a "jolt." It must be smooth. Once your back is flat during the Handstand Push-up, you can perform an explosive kick, which I like to compare to the second pull in Olympic weightlifting, where you must be explosive and fast through the middle to maximize the muscular tension created in the first pull and the position adopted for the optimal bar path, which in the case of the Handstand Push-up is the path of the body.

As you progress through these distances, you eventually get so close to the wall that your chest is touching the wall in the Handstand Push-up. At this point, you may have trouble even getting into the Tripod position. Despite this possibly awkward start, the good news is that if you are successful at hitting the partial Handstand with your hands a foot or even two feet away from the wall, then you are pretty close to vertical already. In fact, at that point you are probably close enough to vertical that you are ready to move on to the next stage of the progression. Also, remember that even if you are comfortable with the ascent, this is a great opportunity to practice the descent.

The descent for the Kipping Handstand Push-up works exactly the same way as the strict version, where you lean your shoulders and direct your head forward toward the Tripod in the Headstand position. It is important to maintain straight legs until your head touches before you come back to the bent-knee and flexed-hip position that is required for the kipping motion.

This stage of the progression is also a great time to play with shortening the range of your kip. You don't have to bring your knees all the way down to your elbows. Ideally, you perform your kip with a flat back, and your knees just pass hip level. Passing hip level is key so that your hips and knees are flexing enough to have the range of motion and hip tension required for optimal kipping mechanics.

kick-chest to wall 01 Perform a Tripod with your feet and body as close as possible to a wall. As you adopt the Tripod position, your hands have to be a little farther away from the wall than in the strict version of this progression, as your feet need some room to perform the Tripod.

02 Adopt a flat-back position with your knees off your elbows. Your back is now in line with the wall, and your shins are completely vertical, with your toes pointing straight up.

03 Perform a violent extension of your legs straight up, directing your head toward the wall almost as if you were reaching your head through the window created by your arms and shoulders. With your head in, you will have more stability in the finish position. Your toes are pointed, legs straight, butt and belly tight, and arms in line with your ears.

Once you have reached the point where your chest finishes as close to the wall as you can get it and you are very close to a vertical Handstand in the finish position, you should try the next part of this progression.

back-to-wall handstand push-up

By now you should be familiar with these stages of the progression, as they are exactly the same as in the strict Handstand Push-up progression. Again, you flip around so that your back is against the wall in order to get closer to the Freestanding Handstand Push-up. This setup enables you to perform the Kipping Handstand Push-up with less external assistance except in the finishing Handstand position. In the finish, your heels should just touch the wall for support and stability. Remember to "kiss" the wall gently yet firmly.

The descent is performed in the same way. Your feet leave the wall first, and then you descend with a straight body until you reach the Headstand position. The moment your head touches the ground, you bring your legs into a tucked position for the kip. Ideally, this kip shouldn't happen before your head touches, or you will lose proper sequencing of the movement. Once you master this movement and you can perform many repetitions at high speeds, you can learn to bring your legs down during the descent from the Handstand to the Headstand. This is a great strategy for increasing the speed and efficiency of the movement.

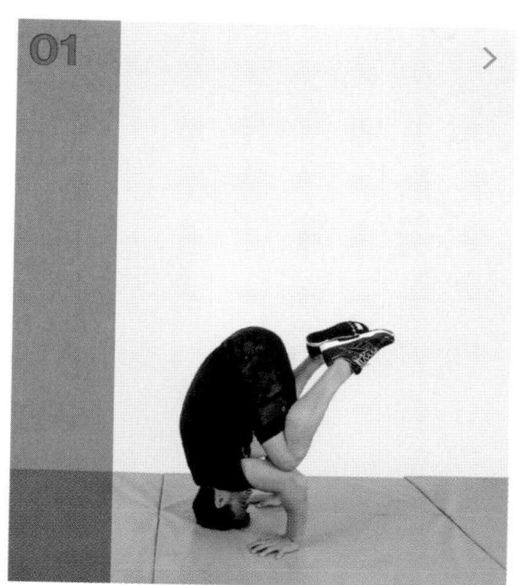

back-to-wall handstand push-up 01 Start in a Tripod position with your back facing a wall, but not in contact with the wall.

02 Lift your knees off your elbows until your back is flat, bringing your back parallel to the wall, with your toes pointing straight up and your shins vertical.

03 Perform an aggressive kick up until you reach the Handstand position, which finishes with your body in slight extension. Your head is through your arms, arms locked out, butt and belly tight, knees straight, and toes pointed. You can reverse this motion by sliding your feet and body down as you perform the descent, the same way you did for the strict Handstand Push-up, or separate your feet from the wall and come down to a Headstand. From the Headstand, simply reverse your knees and bring them down into position 2. You can come all the way down to position 1 with your knees on your elbows, but this is not required.

freestanding kipping handstand push-up

As mentioned in the strict freestanding version of this progression, performing the Kipping Handstand Push-up successfully requires 100 percent of the movement ability of the previous stages.

The Kipping Handstand Push-up starts in a Tripod position with your knees off your elbows and your back flat. From there, you perform the same kipping motion followed by a push to a Handstand. Again, the ideal Handstand position has your head tucked in, but this position is difficult to master. The option that I suggest for most people is to perform the Handstand with your head facing the ground, as long as your ears are in line with your shoulders.

The descent from the Handstand is exactly the same as in the Back-to-Wall Handstand Push-up progression: you shift your hips over your hands and move your legs toward the ground. After the shift, your shoulders are preloaded and ready to initiate the descent, which you do by flexing your elbows and directing your shoulders forward. Your

kipping handstand push-up 01 Start in a Tripod position with your knees on your elbows and in full flexion, with your elbows on top of your hands. Your neck is neutral, in line with your back.

02 Adopt the knees-off-elbows position with your hips and knees in flexion and your back flat. This can be your starting position if you feel really comfortable with your Tripod, but if you don't, put your knees back on your elbows and make sure that you feel stable.

head should aim for the Tripod in the Headstand position. After your head touches the ground, you can flex your hips and knees back into the starting Tripod position.

The Kipping Handstand Push-up is a powerful movement that delivers many benefits in terms of movement ability and skill transfer. This style of Kipping Handstand Push-up develops overhead pushing mechanics for the upper body and pushing from the lower body as you perform the kip. Your body is designed to do these types of complex movement patterns, and learning them with these universal styles prepares you to perform other movements with similar movement patterns and to add different combinations of movement patterns—for example, the leg pull seen during the Full-Range-of-Motion Handstand Push-up progression on the rings, which you will learn in the next section.

03 Perform an aggressive kick straight up to the sky, creating momentum and pressing yourself away from the ground as you separate your head from the ground. There's a slight lean, with your toes going in the direction you can see.

04 Right when your elbows pass 90 degrees of flexion, drive your heels over your head, adopting the Handstand position, with your head through your arms and rest of your body in line with your toes.

05 It's hard to balance in the head-in position unless you've mastered the Handstand. You can adapt it into the more common Handstand position shown here, with your eyes looking at your hands, as long as your ears are in line with your shoulders. Here I'm barely peeking at the floor; the slightest tilt of the head can make a big difference.

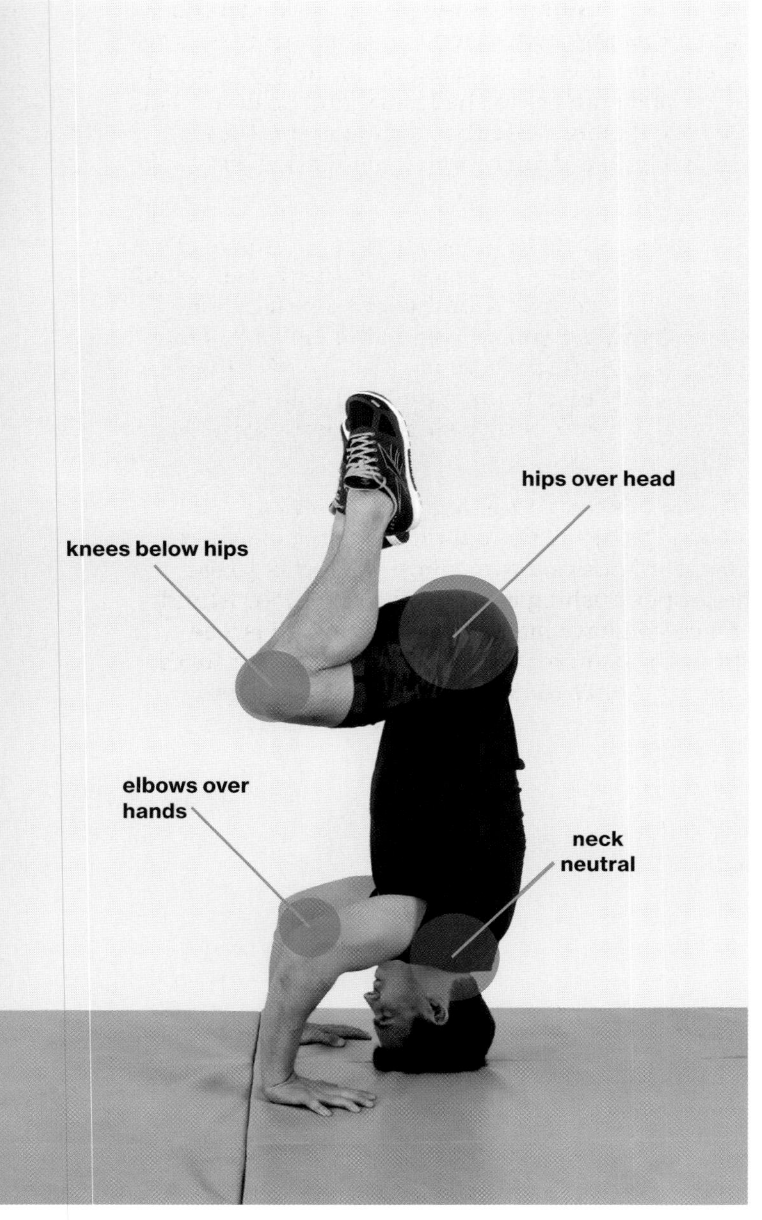
hips over head
knees below hips
elbows over hands
neck neutral

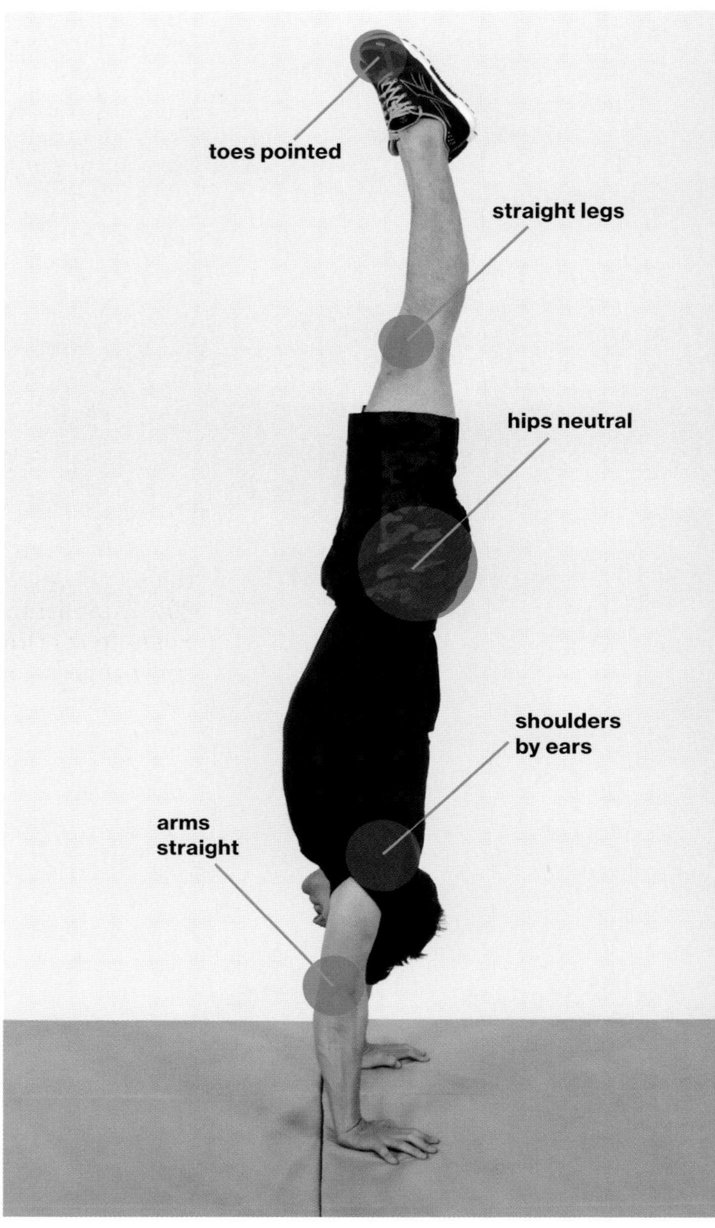
toes pointed
straight legs
hips neutral
shoulders by ears
arms straight

F U L
L R A
N G E
H S
P U

The Full-Range-of-Motion Handstand Push-up, or Ring Handstand Push-up, is a Handstand Push-up performed while balancing on a set of rings. The rings, a common piece of equipment in the gymnastics world, bring an element of instability to the Handstand position. This instability forces you to add more muscular tension around your shoulders in order to maintain a strong enough overhead position to hold your Handstand.

Another benefit of the rings is that they enable you to perform a Full-Range-of-Motion Handstand Push-up. Because the rings are elevated off the ground and you can place your head between them, your head can go below hand level and you can reach full elbow flexion, bringing you closer to anatomical shoulder position. In addition, the rings give you the opportunity to perform a pull with your lower body as you push with your upper body, using your legs to help you perform the movement.

I think it's important to follow the Handstand progressions from the floor before moving to the Ring Handstand Push-up, based on the progression principle of position over range of motion (page 80). Establishing the proper pushing mechanics for the Handstand Push-up is critical. Once you have mastered those positions, the ring progression allows for an increased range of motion and further challenges your positions thanks to the instability of the rings.

parallette handstand push-up

A great way to bridge the gap between the Handstand Push-up progression on the floor and the Handstand Push-up progression on the rings is to learn how to perform a Full-Range-of-Motion Handstand Push-up on a set of parallettes, boxes, or stacked bumper plates. These elevate your hands off the ground so that your head can go past hand level at the bottom of the Handstand Push-up, but they offer more stability than the rings.

parallette handstand push-up 01 Start in a Tripod position as on the floor, but in this case your head is below your hands. Your hips and knees are in flexion, your back is flat, and your elbows are on top of your wrists. Your hands are level with your shoulders, and your ears are below the parallettes or at parallette level.

02 Perform the movement in exactly the same way you would perform a Kipping Handstand Push-up on the floor. The only difference is that here the kip has to be more aggressive, and you need to have better control of the movement in order to find the strength to make your way through the full range of motion and finish in the Handstand position.

The mechanics and technique that you use on the parallettes are exactly the same as those developed in the strict and Kipping Handstand Push-up progressions presented earlier in this chapter (pages 171 and 189, respectively).

03 The Handstand mechanics are exactly the same once you reach the finish.

04 Similar to a Handstand on the floor, you may want to finish with your head tilted down slightly to look at the ground, with your ears in line with your shoulders.

ring handstand

The Ring Handstand Push-up follows the same principles addressed in the Handstand Push-up section of this chapter (page 171). The only difference is that here you are dealing with an unstable base of support. To maximize your performance of the Handstand Push-up on the rings, you must establish a stable shoulder position. The most stable position you can adopt at shoulder level, while in flexion, is external rotation, or simply turning your hands out.

Before you learn how to perform a Ring Handstand Push-up, it's important to understand how to get into a Ring Handstand safely.

jump to handstand from the floor

I highly recommend that anyone who is trying to work on the Handstand Push-up on the rings should master the Press to Handstand mechanics in chapter 8 (page 330), even though the truth is that neither the Press to Handstand nor the roll to shoulder stance is a requirement for learning the Handstand Push-up on the rings.

A good alternative to the Press to Handstand is the Jump to Handstand, a dynamic way of jumping from a standing position into a Handstand position. This jump should be learned on the ground, from the same bent-over position seen in the Old Man Squat in chapter 4 (page 106), where your hands are fairly close to your feet. From this position, you initiate a jump through your legs and allow your hips to roll over your head while you press away from the ground with your arms.

The shape and path of your legs can adopt three different styles:

1. ***Tuck:*** A ball shape for your body, where your hips and knees are in full flexion and your ankles are in plantarflexion or pointed-toe position.
2. ***Straddle:*** A wide-leg position or abduction of your legs, with your hips in full flexion, your knees in extension, and your ankles in plantarflexion or pointed-toe position.
3. ***Pike:*** A narrow-leg position or adduction of your legs, with your hips in full flexion, your knees in extension, and your ankles in plantarflexion or pointed-toe position.

tuck, straddle, pike

The tuck, straddle, and pike positions are the most common gymnastics shapes you should know for any movement that involves manipulating your body weight through space.

The tuck is the most natural position for most people to adopt.

The straddle usually requires the least effort in terms of strength, but it typically takes more practice because it is not the most intuitive position.

The pike is the most advanced shape but is also the simplest in terms of the movement pattern.

tuck-up to handstand 01 Bend over and place your hands flat on the ground in front of your feet.

02 Shift most of your weight over your hands.

03 Jump away from the ground and direct your hips over your head. Adopt a tuck position with your hips and knees flexed and your legs together.

04 Once your hips are over your head, extend your legs and adopt the Handstand position.

straddle-up to handstand 01 Bend over and place your hands flat on the ground in front of your feet.

02 Shift most of your weight over your hands.

03 Jump away from the ground and direct your hips over your head. Adopt a straddle position with your hips flexed and abducted and your legs straight.

04 Once your hips are over your head, extend and adduct your hips to bring your legs together and overhead and adopt the Handstand position.

pike-up to handstand 01 Bend over and place your hands flat on the ground in front of your feet.

02 Shift most of your weight over your hands.

03 Jump away from the ground and direct your hips over your head. Adopt a pike position with your hips flexed and your legs adducted and straight.

04 Once your hips are over your head, extend your hips into the Handstand position.

jump to handstand with wraps from the floor

Once you have mastered the Jump to Handstand on the ground, you can try setting up a pair of straps with no rings, attaching the straps to parallettes. You just need a setup that enables you to practice the Jump to Handstand and the different styles of wraps.

From this setup, you are going to get up to a Handstand and finish by wrapping your legs around the straps. The wraps serve as a balance in the finish position and will serve the same purpose when you learn to wrap on the rings. Here, you will learn the full wrap and then the half wrap.

parallettes wrap progression

01 Attach straps to an anchor directly above the parallettes, with the straps looped around the parallettes. Bend over and grip the parallettes with the straps behind your hands.

02 Perform a straddle-up onto the parallettes until the backs of your legs reach the straps in a straddle position.

03 Bend your knees until your feet are in front of the straps.

04 Perform a full wrap around the straps by wrapping your legs from the outside in.

full wrap

In the full wrap, you wrap your lower legs around the straps with a full revolution. The full wrap requires a slight straddle or abduction of your legs to initiate the wrap from the outside of the straps. The straps should rest on your inner or medial lower legs, as shown in the photos below. You continue to wrap your legs by bringing your toes through the inside of the straps and placing the lateral aspect or side of each foot against the strap. This creates a spiral wrap of the straps around your legs. Finally, you tighten the wrap by extending your knees and dorsiflexing your feet.

half wrap

In the half wrap, you wrap the inner or medial aspect of your legs around the straps in a half revolution. The half wrap requires a slight straddle or abduction of your legs to place the insides of your legs against the outsides of the straps, as shown below. The difference from the full wrap is that your feet don't keep wrapping around the insides of the straps; you simply rest the inner or medial aspect of each foot against the strap.

full wrap 01 Perform a straddle-up toward the straps, where your legs go into abduction. The straps are making contact with the backs of your legs, specifically crossing your knee pits. Your legs are straight, and your feet are out to the side.

02 Once you find support by leaning against the straps, wrap your legs around the straps from the outside in.

03 Flex your feet and allow the straps to make contact with the outsides of your feet. Wrap toward the insides of your legs, again making contact with your knee pits. This creates a spiral wrap around your legs, giving you a lot of stability and tension. You can increase the tightness or strength of the wraps by separating your legs out to the side, flexing your feet, or extending your knees.

half wrap 01 Perform a straddle-up toward the straps, hitting the same straddle position where you're leaning against the straps such that the straps are making contact with your knee pits.

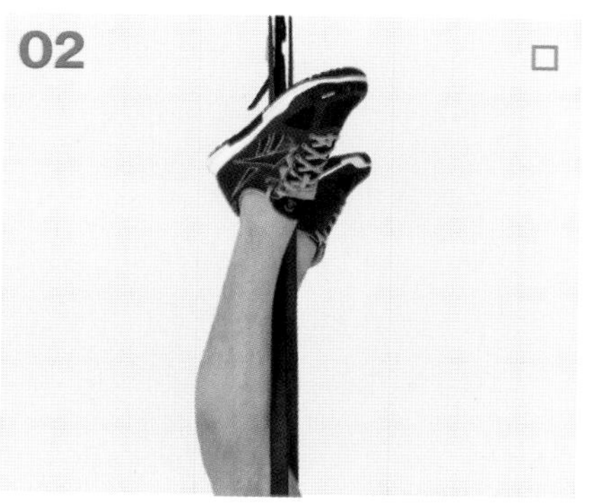

02 Instead of wrapping your legs around the straps, perform an adduction or compression of your legs toward your midline, pressing the insides of your feet against the straps. The best position to adopt here is a pointed-toe position, which guarantees tension throughout your midline.

shoulder stance

You need to learn how to get into the bottom support position on the rings, also known as a shoulder stance. You can use the leg wrapping you just learned to practice three forms of the shoulder stance:

1. Full wrap
2. Half wrap
3. Freestanding

I cover only the freestanding shoulder stance here as it is important to master before you move on to the Handstand on the rings. If you are not ready for the freestanding form, simply incorporate the wraps shown in the previous section for more stability until you are ready to move on.

If I were teaching you proper gymnastics progressions, before teaching you the Handstand on the rings I would teach you a simpler inversion, such as the shoulder stance on the rings. This is a good precursor because it exposes you to balancing while inverted, but with a much more stable base of support due to the tension around your shoulders and the shortened distance between your center of mass and your base of support (see the progression principles section of chapter 3). This exposure to inversion with a more stable connection is exactly why you start with a Headstand before learning to perform a Handstand on the floor.

parallettes shoulder stance
01 Bend over and grip the parallettes.

02 Bend your arms and lower your head until you reach full flexion of your elbows and your head is under your hands.

03 Once you find stability in your hands and shoulders, bend your legs to pick your feet up off the ground.

04 After finding balance with your legs bent, extend your legs up into a similar global angle as seen in a Headstand on the floor.

ring shoulder stance 01 Start in a support position on the rings with your arms locked out and your body in a tuck position.

02 Initiate an elbow bend and allow your body to roll forward.

03 Continue to roll forward until your head is below your hands and your hips are directly above your hands.

04 Once you find your balance, extend your legs into a shoulder stance.

ring handstand

After you feel comfortable using both wraps for support and balance, it's time to dive into how to get into a Handstand on the rings.

The same way you initiated the shoulder stance by rolling forward into the equivalent of a Headstand on the rings from a support position, you can perform a Handstand as well. The difference is that you must perform the Handstand without allowing your arms to bend as much as the shoulder stance as your hips roll up above your head. This limitation makes it a much more demanding strength movement. It is known in the world of gymnastics as a Press to Handstand (page 330).

On low rings, you can get into a Handstand by using the jumps you learned on the floor (page 202). These jumps require less strength than the full Press to Handstand and allow you to focus on the hand-balancing component on the rings.

Start by standing in front of the rings in a bent-over position with the rings at hand level. It is important to get as close as possible to the rings in order to get your starting base of support as close as possible to your final base of support.

To perform a tuck-up or straddle-up to a Handstand, you jump up off the ground and drive your hips over your head as you fold your legs into a tuck or straddle position. After the inversion has occurred and your hips are almost above your head, you start unfolding back up into a Handstand position. A well-timed folding and unfolding of the body facilitates a stable turnover. If you kept your body straight, there would be a big swinging motion up into the Handstand. In addition, because the rings are not static, they are not a good support for the straight-body swinging approach.

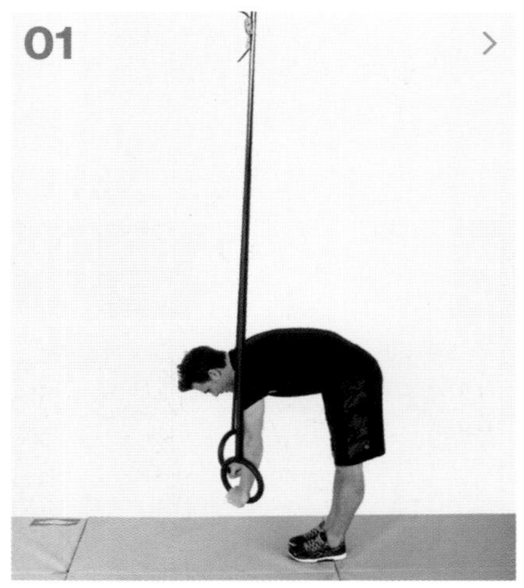

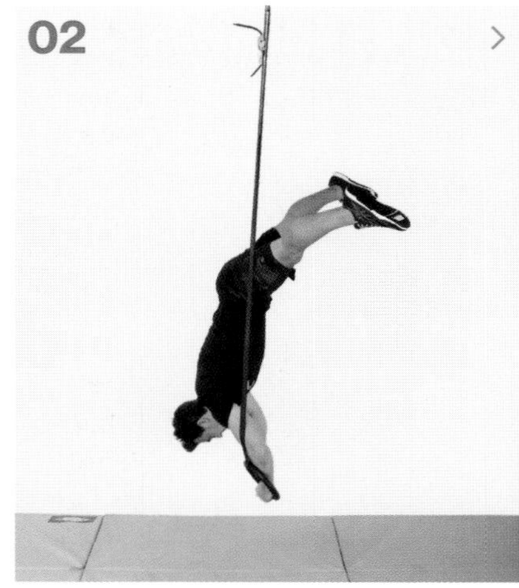

straddle-up to full wrap 01 Bend over and place your hands on the rings with your shoulders directly over your hands.

02 Perform a straddle-up until the backs of your legs reach the straps.

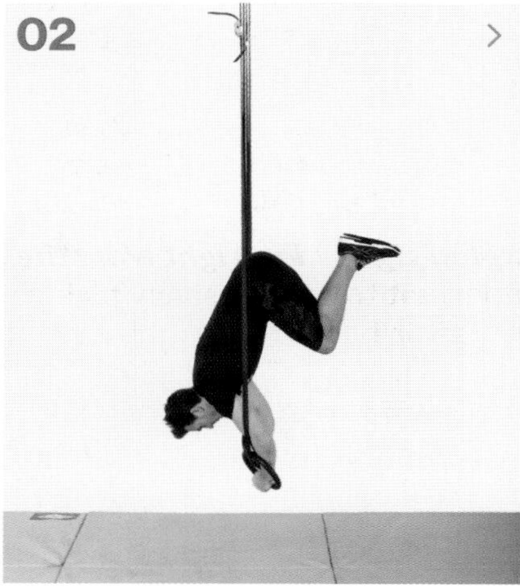

tuck-up to half wrap 01 Bend over and place your hands on the rings with your shoulders directly over your hands.

02 Jump and perform a tuck-up.

bent arm on strap You can kick up to a Handstand on the rings with your hands turned in and your upper arms leaning against the straps. This version is easier for most people to start with, as it provides additional stability.

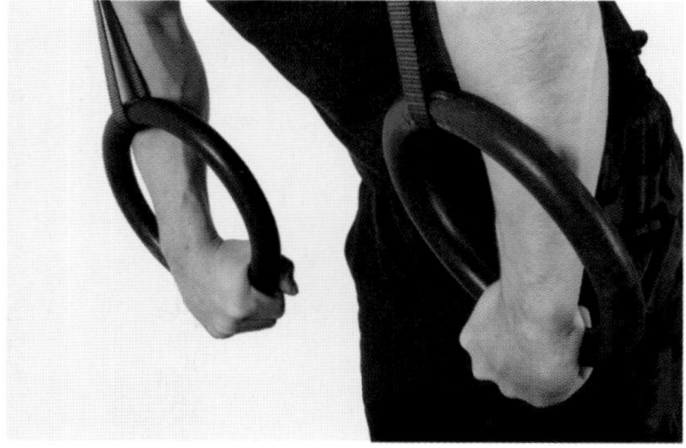

03 Allow your lower legs to reach outside and behind the straps.

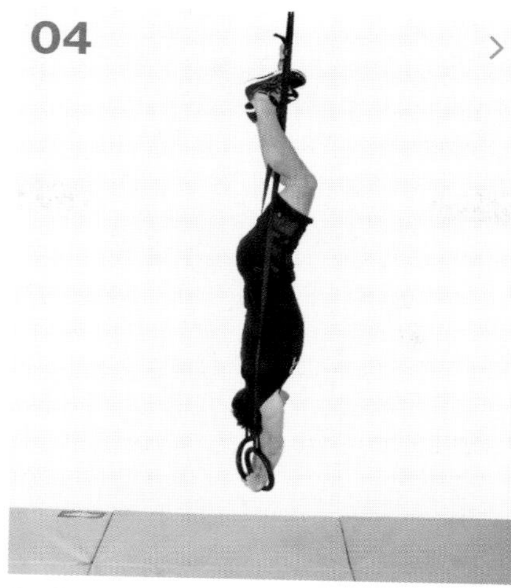

04 Continue to wrap your legs by bending your knees and placing your feet on the insides of the straps.

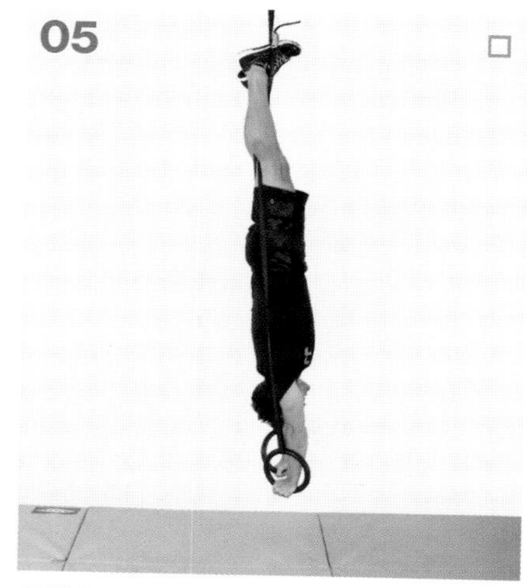

05 With the full wrap, extend your legs to finish in a Handstand.

03 Continue to roll up and unfold until your hips are over your head.

04 Once your feet reach past the straps, perform a slight straddle.

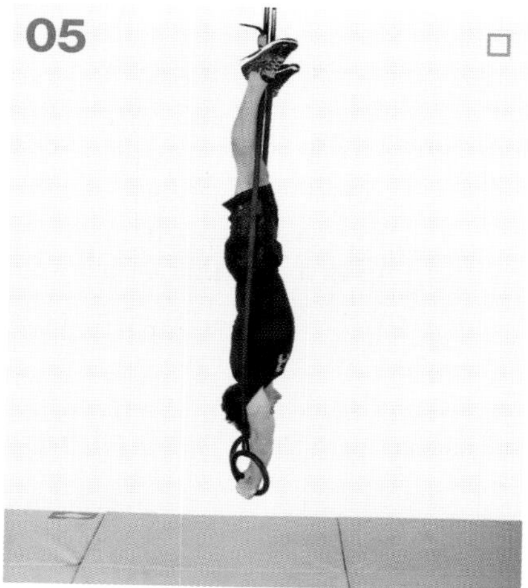

05 Place the insteps of your feet on the outsides of the straps and finish in a Handstand.

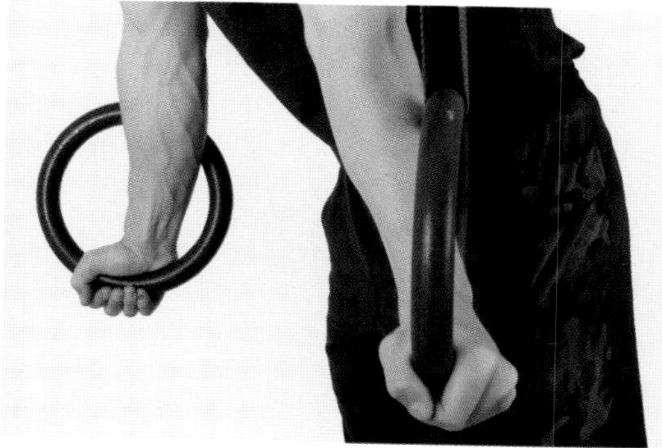

straight arm off strap You can also kick up to a Handstand on the rings with your hands turned out and your arms not in contact with the straps at any point during the movement. This position is preferable because of its transferability to more movement patterns.

Once you reach the Handstand, you can adopt either wrap. The full wrap is safer and stronger, and the half wrap is slightly less stable and more advanced. You should master both wraps in order to progress closer to the universal Handstand Push-up on the rings.

leg handstand push-up

Once you understand the mount or get-up into a Handstand Push-up, you can start addressing the different variations of the Handstand Push-up with wraps. You can start with a Leg Handstand Push-up, using your wrapped legs to pull your body up to a Handstand from a shoulder stance. You can use a full wrap or a half wrap for this style of Handstand Push-up.

full wrap leg handstand push-up

The Full Wrap Leg Handstand Push-up starts with a straddle up to a Handstand followed by a full leg wrap around the ring straps. Once you are in this position, with your legs fully locked out, you start your descent into the shoulder stance by flexing your elbows and allowing your shoulders to extend so that they are closer to anatomical range

full wrap leg handstand push-up
01 Get into the Full Wrap Handstand position (page 205). Make sure to keep your arms fully locked out in a perfect Handstand to initiate the best Handstand Push-up on the rings.

02 Initiate the descent by leaning your shoulders forward and bending your elbows. Keep your forearms in line with the straps (notice how my forearms are parallel with the straps), and control your descent by squeezing your legs more or less tightly against the straps in order to give you more or less assistance.

03 You have reached the bottom position of the Handstand, which is a shoulder stance with the full wrap. Here's where the hard part begins.

of motion. It is important that your legs remain straight during this phase, which gives you more stability and control over the descent and adds a greater pulling range with your legs from the bottom position.

Your legs help initiate the ascent back up to the Handstand from the bottom position. You start pulling your body up by gripping the ring straps with your feet or flexing your feet into dorsiflexion and then flexing your knees and hips. As you flex your knees and hips, your body starts ascending, and your arms must assist the Handstand Push-up by pressing away from the rings. Around mid-pull with your legs, there may be a loss of tension of the wraps. To avoid this loss of tension, you need to push your knees and legs out to the sides. Maintaining tension is important for optimal pulling mechanics.

04 Create tension by bending your legs and flexing your hips as you anchor your feet tightly around the straps to pull yourself up. This pull moves your body away from the rings, which you should assist by extending your elbows and pushing away with your shoulders.

05 By the time you finish your leg pull, you should reach full knee flexion and full elbow extension. Sometimes you don't reach these positions if you start too low in your shoulder stance.

06 To finish, simply extend your legs to get into the full Handstand position with the full wrap.

half wrap leg handstand push-up

Once you have mastered the full wrap, you're ready to move on to the half wrap. The Half Wrap Leg Handstand Push-up is similar to the full wrap variation. The main difference occurs in the straddle-up, where the wrap is now a half wrap.

As you initiate your descent, you can control your speed and stability by pressing your legs into adduction or into the straps for better traction. Once you are in the shoulder stance position, you can ascend by pulling from your legs. This is where the half wrap differs from the full wrap.

Another difference is the direction of your body, or your global motion. Your legs cover less range of motion than in the full wrap because of the inward hip and knee flexion. This range of motion change often requires you to lean away from the ring straps to achieve a full lockout of your arms.

half wrap leg handstand push-up 01 Perform a tuck-up or straddle-up to a half wrap, where your feet finish on the outsides of the straps.

02 Perform the same descent seen in any other Handstand Push-up. The difference here is that you can control your descent by squeezing your legs in toward your midline, pressing against the straps to decelerate the motion. Keep your forearms vertical to the straps and as pointed forward as possible with your thumbs. This guarantees that you're creating a good position at shoulder level, or external rotation.

03 When you reach the bottom position or shoulder stance, your head is below the rings and your elbows are completely vertical.

Once your arms are fully locked out, you can extend your hips and knees into the starting Handstand position.

Even though you need the same dorsiflexion of the ankles to establish a strong grip around the straps, your knee and hip flexion will cause you to use an inward knee bend to create optimal pulling mechanics. This knee-in position is the most effective way to gain traction in the wrap to support pulling your body. It is effective because the wrap starts with your legs on the outsides of the straps.

The wrap in motion can easily cause friction and potential burning of the skin. I recommend that you wear clothing or compression wear around your legs for protection. However, more advanced athletes can usually control the amount of tension around the straps while performing this movement.

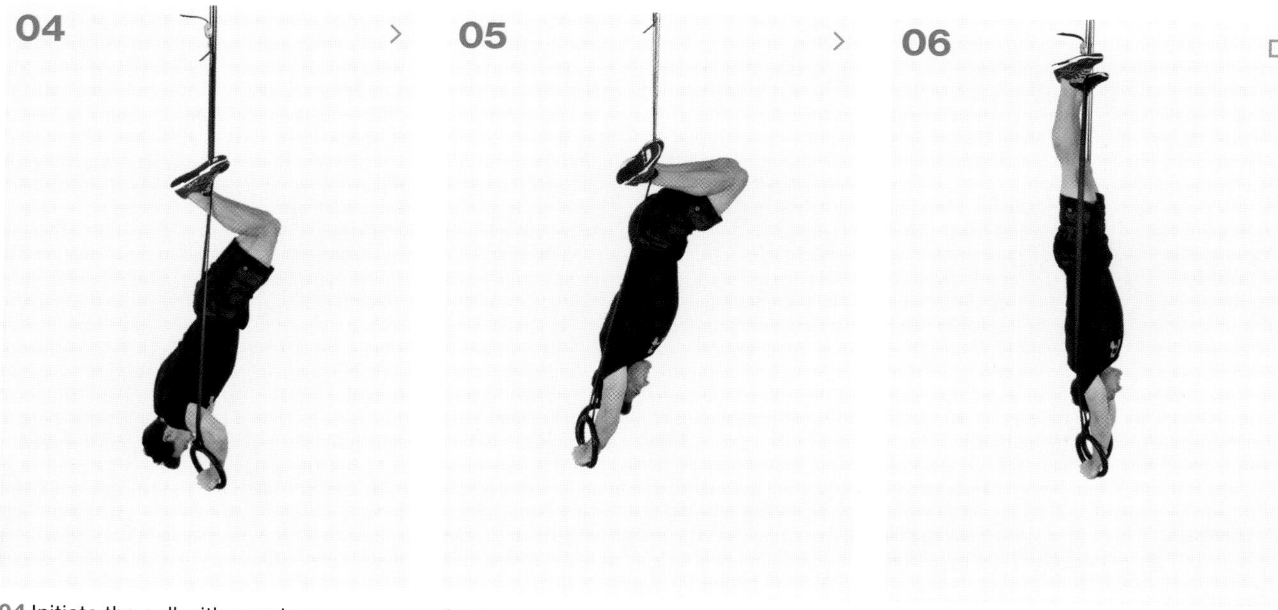

04 Initiate the pull with your legs as you bend your knees and flex your feet to grip the straps. As you do, your knees will cave in; that's the only way to find tension around the straps with your feet.

05 As you start bending your knees and reach full knee flexion, you must create a slight lean, with your body falling at a slight angle in the direction you can see, due to the lack of hip flexion you can utilize because of the wrap. This lean is not a problem since you have a good wrap around the straps.

06 Extend your legs, and the rings will automatically swing under your hips and place you in a full Handstand position.

ring handstand push-up

After developing a solid foundation of the pushing mechanics covered in this chapter and practicing them with the leg wrap support on the rings, you are ready to approach the Freestanding Ring Handstand Push-up. This means removing the leg wrap pull. Your ultimate goal is to progress to a Ring Handstand Push-up without using your legs for pulling or to support the Handstand position.

half wrap with no pull ring handstand push-up

In the strict version of the Ring Handstand Push-up with a half wrap, you perform a Handstand Push-up without using a leg pull to assist. Even though your legs don't pull, they remain in the half wrap throughout the full range of motion covered by your shoulders. The half wrap acts as a support for the Handstand and shoulder stance positions and allows you to develop the strength required to perform the freestanding version.

This movement can be extremely difficult to perform, but beauty of it is that it is extremely simple and elegant if done right.

half wrap ring handstand push-up 01 Tuck up to the Handstand position and perform a half wrap.

02 Initiate your descent by bending your elbows.

03 At the bottom of the Handstand Push-up or shoulder stance, your head is below the rings. Your legs are maintaining the half wrap, with your feet pressing in toward the straps and the straps making contact with the insides of your feet.

You start by performing a straddle-up into a Half Wrap Handstand. Then you perform a controlled descent toward the shoulder stance. Once you reach the bottom, you begin the ascent by pushing away from the rings. During the push, it is important to remain tight around your spine by squeezing your butt and belly. This tightness helps you keep a neutral global position to facilitate the pressing mechanics.

The half wrap should be used simply as a support to keep a neutral global line and therefore should cause the least amount of friction possible. The wrap must be very light for you to reach a full lockout of your arms and finish in the starting Handstand position.

It is important to begin understanding the wrap tension during this movement. Specifically, adding more or less tension during the descent should be easy. You can play with it in order to build the negative or eccentric contraction on the way into the shoulder stance from the Handstand.

Remember that working on the negative phase of a movement is a great way to develop control over the full range of motion and the movement control required to perform the positive/ascent/concentric phase of the movement.

04 Instead of using the straps to get up, use your upper-body strength to push yourself away. In the photo, I'm halfway through the press and still in contact with the straps. It is important to control how much tension you put around the straps to facilitate the movement. If you put a lot of tension toward the straps, you are fighting against a lot of resistance, and the movement will be harder. The less tension you put against the straps, the more unstable you are and the more you need stability and balance rather than pushing mechanics to get yourself up.

05 When your elbows reach full lockout, finish in a full Handstand Push-up position. Notice that my head is tucked in for instructional purposes and to showcase a better midline position.

This is a game of balancing how much tension you put around the straps and how much support you need to maintain stability for optimal pressing mechanics.

freestanding ring handstand push-up

In the Freestanding Ring Handstand Push-up, you perform a Ring Handstand Push-up without assistance from your legs for pulling or support in terms of stability or balance. Fully controlling and performing this stage of the progression requires 100 percent development and understanding of all the previous stages. Developing this style of Handstand Push-up can take several years, but with a mastery of the basics, anything is possible.

You can start the Freestanding Ring Handstand Push-up from any get-up into a Handstand. Unless you are extremely comfortable with the movement, I suggest that you start with a half wrap and slowly adapt it into a freestanding Handstand for optimal control.

You descend from the Handstand in exactly the same way you learned in the Wall Handstand Push-up (page 181). Your hips shift over your hands as your body leans. This lean and shift directs your shoulders forward. Your toes and legs should be pointed in the opposite direction to create a natural lean for balance. The lean is very similar to the lean seen in the Headstand section of this

ring handstand push-up 01 Tuck yourself up into either a half wrap or a freestanding Handstand position. It is up to you to decide what you're capable of. If you are familiar with the Handstand on the rings, feel free to tuck up and hit the Handstand directly.

02 Initiate your descent, where your elbows are bent but your forearms are still in line with the straps. As you transition into this position, your body is at a slight angle, with your shoulders traveling away from the straps.

03 Your body angle has increased, and your elbows have broken 90 degrees and are in full flexion. This angle is required to maintain your center of mass right on top of the rings. Keep a nice straight line from head to toes in order to control the movement. In the photo I am looking at the ground for better balance. If you were performing the most universal movement pattern, you would have your head tucked in or neutral to your body.

chapter (page 176). The main difference is that it requires slightly greater muscular tension to control the movement. Your angle should become more upright as you become more proficient and develop your movement ability.

With a successful shoulder stance, the shift of your hips facilitates your initial push away from the rings. As your arms start to extend and your elbows reach approximately 90 degrees, your hips need to shift back over the rings. Your shift back should be immediately followed by a vertical press with your arms. You continue this press, with this position of your hips, until you reach a full lockout of your arms.

As in the progression on the floor, the optimal Handstand finish is head-in, but this position is difficult to balance in. Glancing at the rings for visual feedback is a great strategy to build your confidence and balance. Remember to keep your ears in line with your shoulders as a cue for maintaining a straight line or neutral global position.

04 Proceed to a shoulder stance, where that angle decreases slightly but is still maintained for balance. Your elbows are still on top of your wrists, and your body is in a nice straight line. To initiate the ascent back up, perform the exact same mechanics seen in the strict Handstand Push-up progression. Allow your hips to fall and press yourself away from the rings.

05 Find balance by driving your heels over your head and over the rings. Once you find balance, you can lock out your elbows and extend your body into a full Handstand position.

ring handstand push-up

points of performance

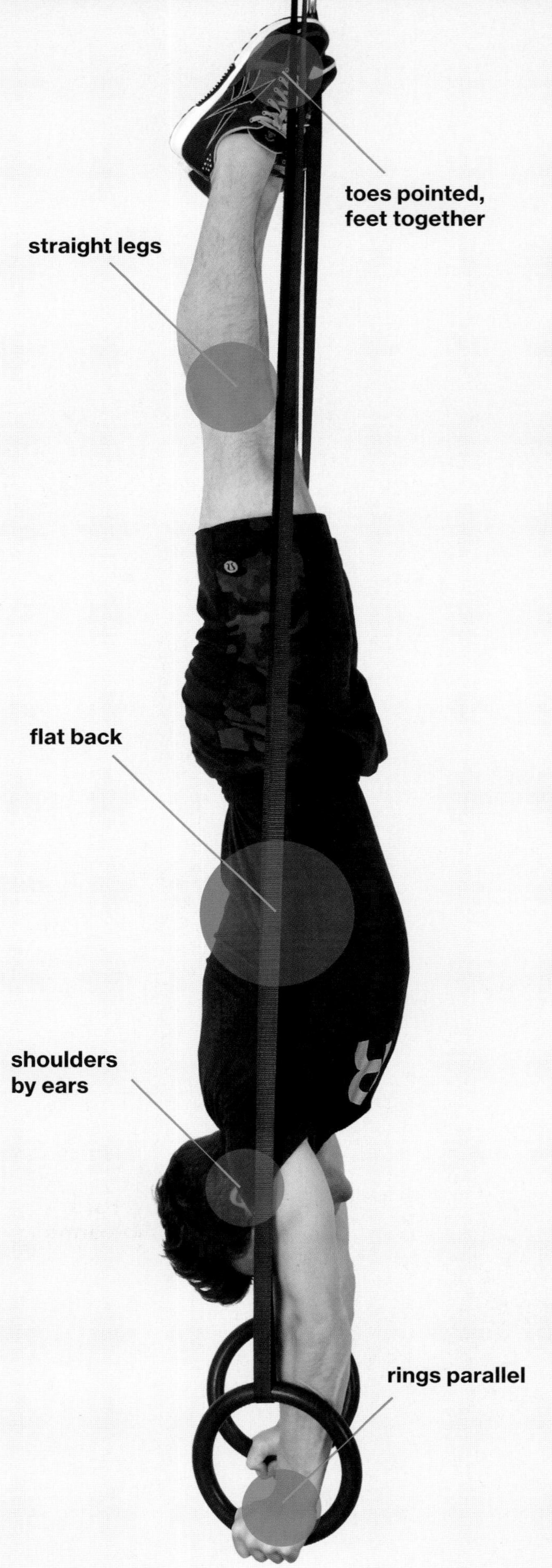

hollow body
shoulders below elbows
vertical forearms

Photo by Paolo Sanchez

the muscle-up

06

I'm not sure where the term "Muscle-up" came from, but it is commonly used in men's artistic gymnastics to describe how a gymnast pulls himself up and over a set of rings. This term is not limited to the sport of gymnastics, however; Muscle-ups are very popular among certain fitness groups, such as CrossFit and the rapidly growing calisthenics movement.

Even though the Muscle-up is most common in niche fields, the functionality that this movement develops is important for everyone. The Muscle-up develops fundamental pulling and pushing mechanics at shoulder and even hip level. It develops these mechanics in a way that I believe is critical for every fully functional human being. Besides developing fundamental pulling and pushing mechanics, the Muscle-up movement itself is a great way to work on the complex ability to get over an obstacle. Whether the obstacle is a set of rings for a gymnast, a bar for a CrossFit athlete, a wall for a soldier in training, or even a pool deck for a swimmer trying to get out of the water, learning the Muscle-up builds and expands movement ability.

The style of Muscle-up varies from one group to another and their purpose for performing it. For example, a gymnast performs a Muscle-up on a set of rings, maintains a straight line from head to toes, and utilizes his upper body for most of the movement, while a calisthenics athlete performs a Muscle-up on a bar and utilizes a slight swing to generate momentum. Finally, a CrossFit athlete performs this movement on either rings or a bar and often uses a big swing that requires full-body mechanics.

In this chapter, I present the kipping-style Muscle-up that is most popular with CrossFit athletes. I believe that this style is the most universal, as it provides the best overall movement ability benefits. That said, most people are not able to start with this movement. In fact, I consider it an advanced movement for the people who train with me. So this chapter breaks down the Muscle-up into its individual components, details a methodical progression to develop each component, and then builds the components back together to form the full movement in all its glory.

The Muscle-up is a combination of pulling and pushing mechanics, and it can easily be defined as the combination of a Pull-up and a Dip. To explain how these two movements combine to create the Muscle-up, I have divided this chapter into four sections:

1. Kipping Pull-up
2. Kipping Dip
3. Muscle-up
4. Kipping Muscle-up

KIPPING PULL-UP

The Kipping Pull-up is a Pull-up performed by using the momentum created by swinging the body back and forth from global extension to flexion. I believe that this Pull-up is one of the best movements for developing pulling strength that transfers to so many other movements.

Interestingly, many coaches and trainers in the strength and conditioning and fitness industries consider the Kipping Pull-up cheating. They call it cheating because the purpose of a Pull-up is to develop pulling strength in the upper body, and the momentum created by the swing contradicts this purpose. Even though there is some truth to this point of view, the strict Pull-up is not the only form of developing upper-body pulling mechanics and pulling strength. This type of thinking is limited because it fails to recognize the value of other types of Pull-ups, even though this added momentum has been shown to be extremely valuable among the most serious heavy weightlifters.

The goal of powerlifters is beautifully simple: lift as much weight as possible for one repetition in the Squat, the Deadlift, and the Bench Press. To accomplish this goal, powerlifters train an infinite variety of styles of those movements, with varied loads, speeds, and combinations with other movements in order to reinforce their desired movement patterns and develop the strength required to perform at the highest level.

One important division of styles frequently discussed in this community is between slow and fast. Powerlifters often use techniques that enable them to rip the bar as fast as possible with lightened loads, which delivers dramatic benefits when it comes to pulling the slowest, heaviest weights. Basically, one movement doesn't necessarily serve just one purpose, and one purpose is not necessarily served by just one movement or style of movement.

In CrossFit, the Kipping Pull-up adds speed and repetitions to the act of pulling in order to express greater power output and increased work capacity. For me, the Kipping Pull-up, beyond the pulling mechanics and strength development that it provides to athletes, is a great way to develop a movement pattern and skill that can be transferred to other sports and aspects of life. These include the snapping motion required for tumbling and gymnastics, the snap of the body required to perform a soccer overhead throw-in, and the dolphin kick that a swimmer performs in the butterfly stroke.

In this section, I explain how to develop the Kipping Pull-up in order to fully understand how the Kipping Muscle-up is performed, and how following these progressions develops an amazing foundation of movement ability for pulling.

This section is divided into three progressions:

1. Row
2. Pull-up
3. Kipping Pull-up

row

The Row is the most basic bodyweight style of Pull-up you can perform. I mention body weight here simply because the rowing motion is seen during a seated Row performed on a gym machine, a bent-over Row performed with a barbell, and even the act of rowing a boat. The bodyweight Row involves pulling yourself up toward a bar, a set of rings, or some other piece of equipment that you can hang from.

The Row is a basic form of pulling mechanics, as it starts at midrange of the shoulders' range of motion, with the elbows in extension and the wrists in a neutral position, and finishes with the shoulders in extension, the elbows in full flexion, and the wrists remaining in a neutral position. If you compare these two positions with the Push-up positions, you will notice that the local and global body shapes are exactly the same. They differ simply in the muscular contraction required to perform the movement. The Row is a pull, and the Push-up is a push.

Before I dig deeper into the Row, I want to address a very important component of this movement (and all other pulling mechanics performed with the upper body). Specifically, before you pull, you must learn how to grip the bar, the rings, or whatever piece of equipment you are using.

grip

Having a good grip on the piece of equipment you are using to develop the Row, the Pull-up, and eventually the Muscle-up is almost more important than how you perform the movements themselves. Learning to grip effectively is like learning to stand before you walk.

The equipment you will use is a bar and a set of rings. The bar and the rings are great for developing the most universal style of grip for hanging purposes, which can easily be transferred to other equipment.

By learning how to address a bar or a set of rings with a proper grip, you can achieve two things:

1. A stronger grip
2. A better shoulder position

hook grip: To me, the most universal gripping style is a full wrap of the hands and fingers around the bar or rings, with the fingers overlapping. This style of grip allows for maximum support with minimum strength and the best positional stability at shoulder level. The overlap of the fingers is known as a hook grip.

The hook grip is a great technique that helps lock the grip down as load and tension are added, acting as a knot that gets tighter as you put more tension around it. But you must develop it in order for it to truly work for you.

You create the hook grip by overlapping your thumbs over your index and middle fingers as you grip the bar or rings. Due to the rotational forces put on your hands as you hang from the bar or rings, your hands tend to slip. You can fight this rotational force by squeezing the bar or rings tighter, but the amount you can squeeze is very limited. The hook grip helps reinforce the squeeze because it acts as a lockdown mechanism, pulling from the opposite side of the bar or rings. It can also be considered a blocked movement because keeping your thumbs wrapped around your fingers guarantees that your hands are in a position that also requires your shoulders to be externally rotated.

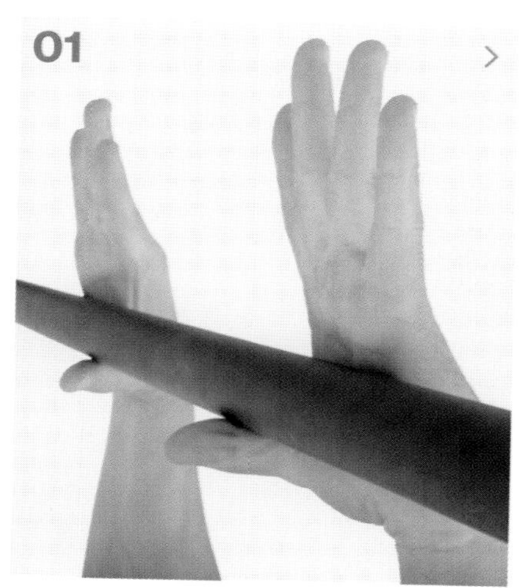

hook grip 01 Open and extend your hands. Place your hands with the bar crossing them at mid-palm, and splay your fingers to create tension.

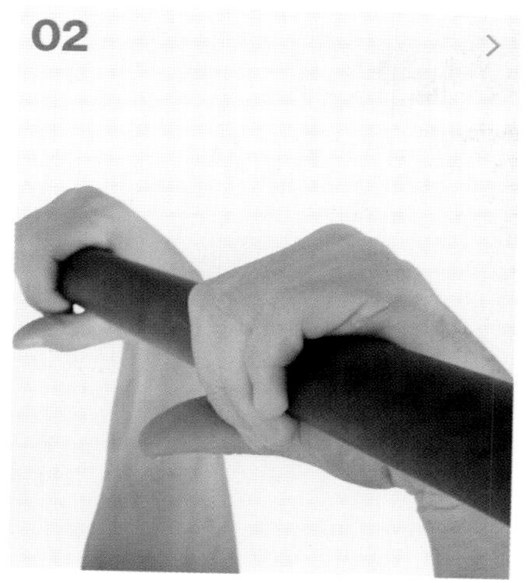

02 Grip the bar by curling your fingers and reaching as far under the bar with your fingers as possible without your thumbs getting in the way.

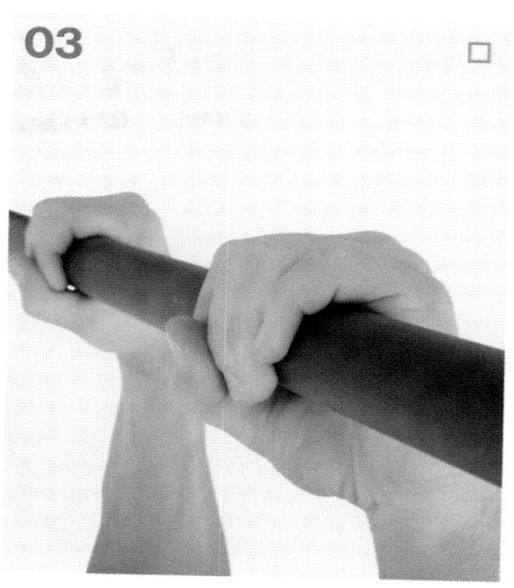

03 Wrap your thumbs over your index and middle fingers.

pinky knuckle over the bar: There is one more detail to keep in mind that heavily influences the position of your shoulders while you hang. Thanks to the architecture of your shoulders and arms, you can use this grip detail to set up your shoulders for success throughout any pulling movement that you see in this chapter. Notice in the photos below that as I grab the bar, I place my pinky knuckle above the bar. That gives me a better chance to find the hook grip and adds a rotational component that projects farther down to my shoulders to establish a better shoulder position.

This works because of the body's architecture. If you measure the distance from your shoulder to your pinky knuckle and compare it with the distance from your shoulder to your middle knuckle, you will notice that the distance to the pinky knuckle is shorter. The difference in lengths creates a rotation in the arms that sets the shoulders in external rotation. This external rotation at shoulder level is what some trainers call an "active shoulder" position. The shoulders can be elevated or depressed, but as long as they are in external rotation, you can consider them active, which simply means that they are optimally set up to perform a movement. The specifics of this active shoulder position vary according to the style, load, speed, and range of motion required to perform the movement.

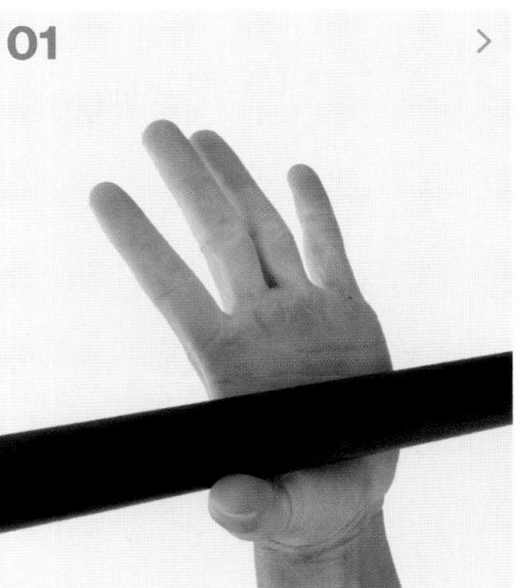

pinky knuckle over bar 01 Reach for the bar with outstretched fingers and a slightly tilted hand so that your pinky is pointing straight up. The distance from your pinky knuckle to your shoulder is less than the distance from your middle knuckle to your shoulder.

02 Your pinky knuckle creates external rotation at shoulder level (an active shoulder position). The pinky knuckle is always over the bar.

supine grip: Another way to achieve the same result is to perform a supine/under/chin-up grip. This style of grip creates near end range of external rotation at shoulder level and therefore blocks the shoulders from adopting poor motor mechanics due to the freedom of movement that the overhand grip gives the shoulders. It is not the most universal grip, however; even though you could use it to perform a movement such as the Muscle-up, it does not create the safest platform as you transition from one movement to another, such as from a Pull-up to a Dip. Furthermore, this underhand grip is not often the most applicable to daily life activities like twisting a doorknob and pulling a door open, steering a bike, driving a car, or even typing on a computer.

prone grip Hang from a bar with your palms facing forward, in the same direction as your body. This prone grip creates less tension around your shoulders, gives you more freedom of motion, and is more universal and applicable to other movements. Your arms are able to hang straighter than in the supine grip. The prone grip around the bar is also easier to hold.

supine grip Hang from a bar with your palms facing behind you. This supine grip creates a lot of tension around your shoulders. Although the tension may feel a little uncomfortable, it is beneficial for movement control during a Pull-up. Your arms are straight overhead, and you're gripping the bar with a hook grip.

scaled ring row

This style of Row is great for a beginner because you can increase or decrease the load simply by changing the angle of your body. The more vertical you are, the easier it gets, and the more horizontal you are, the harder it gets.

You can perform this Row on rings or a bar. The benefit of using rings is their mobility, which allows you to change your orientation easily. This orientation change enables you to adjust the load in addition to changing the setup according to your height.

The angle that your body makes with respect to the straps, especially in the start and finish positions, is a key to progressing this movement. These positions are critical because they are the most relevant indicators of the quality of your shoulder mechanics during the Row.

For example, if you start at a 35-degree angle, the straps should be at a 35-degree angle in the opposite direction, and if you finish at a 45-degree angle, the straps should also be at a 45-degree angle. These angles are eyeball estimates and don't necessarily need to be measured. What is important is that when the angles are way off, the mechanics at shoulder and elbow level are also way off.

Another easy way to see if your shoulder mechanics are close to optimal is to look at your forearms in relation to the rest of your body in the finish position. Your forearms should be perpendicular to your midline and in line with the straps.

reverse steps 3–1

scaled ring row 01 Hang from a pair of rings with your arms fully extended and your elbows locked out. Your body is in a straight or neutral global position. Your shoulder blades are squeezed together, and your neck is in line with the rest of your body and looking straight up. Try to keep your body angle at 45 degrees or less. Anything higher will make the rowing mechanics at shoulder level dysfunctional.

02 Pull yourself up toward the rings by bending your elbows. Keep your forearms as perpendicular to your body as possible. Your legs remain straight, your feet are together, and you are fighting not to change the neutral global position of your body, even though in the photo I am going slightly into global extension. This is fine, as the shoulder mechanics are fully controlled.

03 You have reached the top of the Ring Row when your chest touches the rings. Your forearms are perpendicular to your spine. Your body is in slight global extension, and your neck is in the same position as when you started. Your legs are still straight, and your feet are still together.

Once you have developed the proper mechanics with the scaled version, you can slowly start decreasing the angle of your body until you are horizontal to the ground in the finish position of the Ring Row. The box enables you to adopt the most horizontal finish position possible, optimizing your midrange pulling mechanics.

ring row

Setting up your shoulders is the most important thing to focus on for this movement. Set them up so that they fall behind your chest and low to facilitate a long neck. In addition, I suggest trying to maintain a globally neutral position throughout the entire movement.

If you were to hang from the rings and relax your shoulders, your shoulders would be pulled in front of you, creating a concave shape between your shoulders and chest. This shape is not ideal for establishing a strong shoulder-loaded position that develops skill transfer to other movements.

Depending on your movement ability, you may find it difficult to prevent your shoulders from being pulled forward and creating the concave shape in your chest and a rounded back. To fight this pull, think "Chest up," where up is in the direction you are pulling yourself. In addition, contracting your belly and butt helps you maintain a neutral spine when your shoulders are in motion.

Once you've developed the proper shoulder mechanics for the Ring Row and have the strength to maintain good positions for several repetitions and at different speeds, you can add more complexity to the movement and adapt the Ring Row into a Kipping Ring Row.

ring row 01 Grasp the rings and place your heels on a box that is approximately as high as the rings. Extend your legs and make a straight line from head to toes. Keep your arms straight so that they are in line with the straps, creating the most optimal pathway for the Ring Row.

02 Initiate the pull by bringing your shoulder blades together behind you, squeezing your butt and belly, and bending your elbows straight back.

reverse steps 3–1

03 Continue to bend your elbows until you reach full elbow flexion and your chest is in contact with or even past the rings. Your body has gone into slight global extension, but you are still looking straight up to maintain global uniformity.

kipping ring row

The Kipping Ring Row adds a dynamic snap of the body to the Row. You create the dynamic snap by bowing from global flexion or hollow body position to global extension and utilizing that momentum to facilitate the rowing motion. This style of Row teaches you to add speed to the shoulder pull while maintaining good mechanics and control of the shoulder position. In addition, performing this Kipping Ring Row motion is a great way to learn how to perform the kipping motion in the Kipping Pull-up (page 236).

If you perform the snapping kip correctly, at the top of the hip extension you will experience a moment of weightlessness and a momentary upward drift as if you had been shot up with a slingshot. This is your window of opportunity to perform a very fast pull. The pull should send your chest toward the rings and enable you to reach a strong and stable top position. This position should be stable enough to allow you to pause and pose as if someone were taking your picture.

Even though this movement is straightforward, it is great for developing shoulder strength. It establishes very strong shoulder posture during midrange movement and develops basic pulling mechanics. Its uncomplicated nature is also a benefit in that it makes the movement approachable for athletes across all fitness levels.

kipping ring row 01 Start with your feet on the edge of a box that's approximately the same height as the rings. With your feet on the box and your legs in extension, allow your body to touch the ground, creating a globally flexed or hollow body position. Holding the rings, your arms are in line with the straps, even though they may angle slightly toward your body due to the slack created as you relax against the ground. Your head is off the ground.

02 Without using your arms to pull, initiate a hip drive toward the sky by squeezing your butt, maintaining straight legs. This lifts your body off the ground and initiates the kip.

negatives

Understanding the eccentric or negative phase of a movement is a great way to develop traction or movement control across full range of motion in order to enhance the concentric or positive phase of the movement. This can also be done between different movements. For example, a Pull-up can get you stronger at doing Handstand Push-ups, as the concentric phase of the Pull-up acts like and will help develop the eccentric phase of the Handstand Push-up.

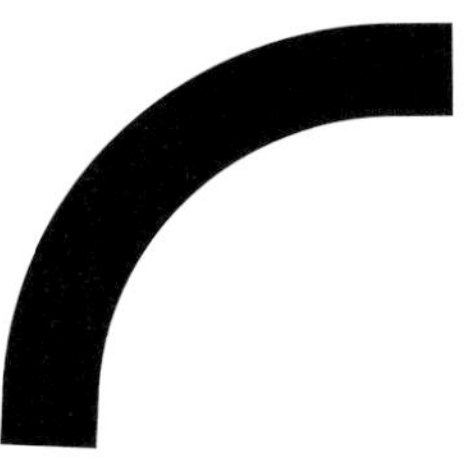

03 Use the momentum created by the hip drive to aggressively pull as you did in the Ring Row. When you reach the rings, your body is in extension, which is a complete inversion of the flexion in the starting position. Your elbows and forearms are still in line with the straps. You are looking straight up, and your body is as tight as possible without losing the leg straightness and toe point.

04 Descend with control until you return to position 2, with your hips up and your elbows locked out. You should be able to arrive at this position without losing stability at shoulder level. In the early stages of development for this progression, make this descent slow and progressively build more speed as you develop the movement.

05 Drop your hips toward the ground and finish in a hollow body or globally flexed position, as in position 1. If you want to perform multiple repetitions of this movement, keep the contraction or muscular tension in your shoulder so that you can recycle it to the next kip.

pull-up

After mastering the pulling mechanics of the Row and developing a good foundation of shoulder strength, you are ready to move on to a higher level of pulling mechanics with your upper body. The Pull-up is more challenging than the Row for three reasons:

1. You are moving a heavier load: your body weight.
2. You have less connection and therefore less stability since your feet are off the ground.
3. The movement starts at close to end range of shoulder flexion.

These three aspects of progression were defined in the progression principles section of chapter 3 (page 72) and can easily be translated to this example of progressing pulling mechanics from the Row to the Pull-up.

what is "strict"?

Many people use the term "strict" to characterize a movement that typically minimizes three characteristic variables:

1. Change in shape at global level
2. Number of moving joints at local level
3. Shift in mover's center of mass in relation to her base of support or anchorage point

Think of a Pistol versus a Rolling Pistol, for example, or a Pull-up versus a Kipping Pull-up.

Globally, your body should be in the most neutral position possible throughout this entire movement. This style of pulling mechanics starts at near end range of shoulder flexion, with your arms straight overhead and your wrists in a neutral position, and finishes with your elbows in full flexion and your shoulders at midrange to slight extension. The amount of extension you have in the finish depends on how high you pull. The shoulder range covered changes from one style of Pull-up to another—for example, Chin-over-Bar or Chest-to-Bar.

pull-up 01 Hang from a bar with your arms locked out and your hands right above your shoulders. Your neck is in a neutral position, looking straight ahead, and the rest of your body is straight or in a slightly flexed position. Your feet are together, toes pointed, knees straight.

02 Pull by bending your elbows as you did during the Row. The only difference here is that you need to retract your shoulders by pulling them back and down, creating a long neck. Your body adopts a slight angle where your shoulders are behind your elbows and your feet are in front of your elbows. This is the natural angle required for proper hanging without losing spinal and global position.

This movement can be performed on a bar or rings, and it is a style of pulling that never gets old, regardless of your level of performance. Being able to perform a Pull-up is more than just a feat of strength. It is also a great expression of overall health at shoulder level for pulling mechanics.

You progressed the Row from a 45-degree angle into a more horizontal position for the finish of the pull. For the Pull-up, you revert to a more upright position. You could take the box setup you used for the Row and simply make the rings higher in order to get yourself into a more upright global position. In this case, breaking the rule of maintaining equal body and strap angles throughout the movement as seen in the Row is appropriate in order to adapt Row mechanics into Pull-up mechanics.

For the 45-degree Row, I introduced a positioning shortcut of maintaining the same angle of straps to the body from start to finish as a way to force your shoulders into a position that offers the best pulling mechanics—that is, the typical Push-up position. As you move into a more vertical body position, you need to think about what underlies this cue, because your shoulders will start to adapt a form more similar to the Headstand position. The key point of overlap among all these movements—the Push-up, Row, Handstand Push-up, and Pull-up—is that your forearms remain perpendicular to the ground or the anchor to maintain the ideal shoulder position; see the Headstand explanation on page 176.

03 Keep pulling yourself up until your chin is over the bar and you can see the wall or whatever is in front of you over the bar. Your body position has not changed from the initial pull: your feet are still together, toes pointed, legs straight, and neck in line with the rest of your body.

04 Initiate your descent by extending your elbows and slowly returning to the starting position. As you go through the 90-degree angle, fight to keep your elbows in and maintain the same hanging angle, where your shoulders are behind your elbows and your feet are in front of your elbows.

05 Return to the starting position, where your shoulders are now in full flexion and glued to your ears, your belly and butt are tight, your feet are together, and your legs are straight. When you reach this position, it's important to maintain contraction and muscular tension around your shoulders in order to repeat the steps and perform another Pull-up.

An additional problem for establishing the ideal shoulder position in the Pull-up is that when your head passes the bar, gravity tends to pull your lower body down, creating a counter-rotation to the upper body. This counter-rotation makes maintaining "vertical" forearms difficult. So, at the top of the Pull-up, think about keeping the bar as close as possible to your chin and chest and allow yourself to lean back. This lean elevates your lower body and creates an angle at the top of the pull that is close to 45 degrees, as seen in the original Row progression and in the Headstand lean (page 177).

In addition to altering the angle of your pull, using either a band or a spotter can help reduce the load demand while helping you maintain a vertical pull. A spotter can assist you by pushing parts of your body up as you pull. You can hook a band to the bar between your hands and reduce the load by standing on it as you pull upward.

You can also opt to perform a negative or eccentric loading Pull-up, where you start at the top and focus on descending to the bottom in a slow and controlled manner. This style develops the physiological connection to create stability (page 81) and optimal application of force during the pulling mechanics for the Pull-up.

band pull-up 01 Hook a band to the bar.

02 Grab the band with two hands and pull it toward your feet. As you pull, make a loop with the band.

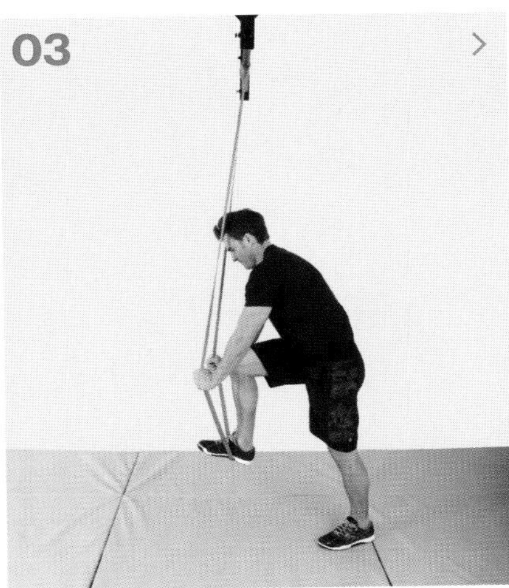

03 Place one foot on the bottom of the loop.

band pull-up

Anytime you are trying to develop your pulling strength with the Pull-up so that you can apply that strength to other aspects of sport and life, it's best to focus on shoulder mechanics before focusing on the number of repetitions, speed, or style.

Here is a basic overview to keep in mind:

1. ***Full range of motion:*** Start from a hanging position with your shoulders by your ears, and finish with your shoulders as far back and down as they will go.
2. ***Midline stability:*** As your perform a Pull-up, multi-angled forces are applied to your spine, causing your global position to want to change. Fight to keep everything in line and keep your butt and belly tight, and try to direct your chest in the direction you are moving, which in this case is up.
3. ***Shoulder mechanics:*** The forces on your spine can cause your shoulders to want to fall off the tracks, meaning that they want to roll in and your elbows want to flare out. The amount of change here depends on your movement ability.

One of the most helpful mental cues I use (and the reason why rowing is a fundamental part of this progression) is to think of the Pull-up as a Row that starts from a full hanging position under the bar or rings.

Once you have developed the proper shoulder mechanics for the Pull-up and have the strength to maintain good positions for several repetitions and at different speeds, you can add complexity to the movement and adapt the Pull-up into a Kipping Pull-up.

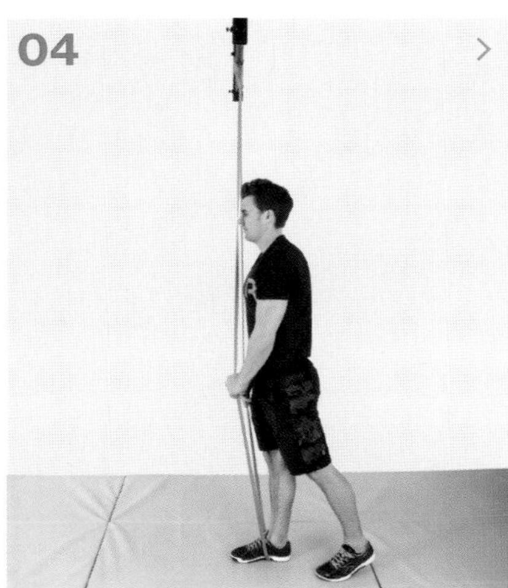

04 Step down firmly until your leg is fully extended.

05 Grab the bar in Pull-up position.

06 Perform a Pull-up.

kipping pull-up

The Kipping Pull-up adds a dynamic swing to the Pull-up. You create the swing by snapping your body from global extension to flexion, which adds momentum in the same way that the Kipping Row adds momentum to the Row. The kipping motion should always be performed while maintaining good mechanics and control at shoulder level during the pull.

kip 01 Start in global flexion with your shoulders in slight flexion, arms straight, feet together, toes pointed, and butt and belly tight.

02 Initiate the swing by going into slight global extension with your shoulders in full flexion, arms straight, feet together, toes pointed, and butt and belly tight.

kipping pull-up 01 Hang from the bar with your arms straight and right above your shoulders. Your body is in a straight line, looking straight ahead, with feet together, knees locked out, toes pointed, and butt and belly tight.

02 Initiate the swing by going into global extension with your arms still straight, but now behind your ears. You are still looking straight ahead, your spine in extension without losing contraction at belly and butt level. Your knees are straight and your toes are pointed. Fight to keep your feet together in this position.

03 Drive your toes forward and kick an imaginary object in front of you, but without losing muscular tension in the rest of your body. Adopt a more hollow body or globally flexed position as you allow your shoulders to swing back in pendulum fashion, creating a slightly shallower angle than in the hanging position, almost mimicking the starting position of the Row. You should feel weightless at the peak of this swing.

The kipping sequence snaps your body from an arched or Superman position to a hollow body position. If performed correctly, there is a moment of weightlessness caused by an upward drive of the momentum at the end of the swing. This is your window of opportunity to perform a very fast pull. If you look closely, it almost looks like a Row, sending your chest toward the bar until you reach a strong and stable top position. Being able to pause at the top as if you were posing for a picture is important to showcase control over the movement. Freeze!

03 Return to global flexion, but with your shoulders in midrange. A moment of weightlessness should occur at the top of this part of swing.

04 Swing back to full global extension, with your shoulders in full flexion.

04 Take advantage of the moment of weightlessness and aggressively drive your elbows toward your back. You are essentially performing a Row and driving your body up toward the bar. Your chin finishes right over the bar, and your elbows are in full flexion. Your body is in a globally neutral position.

05 Reverse the movement by extending your elbows and reaching back to the hollow body position with your shoulders at midrange and your arms straight out in relation to your midline.

06 Flow to the front swing in a continuous motion. You can recycle the kipping momentum for the next Pull-up without losing tension.

kipping pull-up variations

I like to consider three different styles of Kipping Pull-ups. These divisions derive from the range of motion covered by the shoulders and the transition position or top of the Pull-up:

1. ***Chin over Bar:*** Your chin finishes over the bar, and your body remains in a neutral global position. The movement ends when your chin is over the bar and usually matches your elbows reaching full flexion and your upper arms matching the frontal plane. This is the Pull-up seen on the previous page.
2. ***Chest to Bar:*** Your chest finishes in contact with the bar, and your body remains in a neutral global shape. This shape should mimic the bottom of the Push-up position. Your shoulders should be in extension, your elbows in full flexion, and your forearms perpendicular to your body.
3. ***Hips to Bar:*** Your hips finish in contact with the bar, and your body is now in global extension. Your shoulders are in slight extension behind the frontal plane, whereas your elbows remain in slight extension in order to get your hips to meet the bar.

chest-to-bar pull-up 01 Hang from the bar with your arms straight and right above your shoulders. Your body is in a straight line, looking straight ahead, with feet together, knees locked out, and butt and belly tight.

02 Initiate the swing by going into global extension, with your arms still straight, but now behind your ears. You are still looking straight ahead, your spine in extension without losing contraction at belly and butt level. Your knees are straight and your toes are pointed. Fight to keep your feet together in this position.

These three progressions are a great way to get yourself closer to the Kipping Muscle-up, as they address a progressive increase in the range of motion covered locally for your shoulders and globally for your body.

03 Drive your toes forward and kick an imaginary object in front of you, but without losing muscular tension around the rest of your body. Adopt a more hollow body or globally flexed position as you allow your shoulders to swing back in pendulum fashion, creating a slightly shallower angle than seen in the hanging position, almost mimicking the starting position of the Row. You should feel weightless at the peak of this swing phase.

04 The main difference between the Chin over Bar and Chest to Bar variations is this position. Here your chest is in contact with the bar, adopting the same bottom shape seen in a Push-up and the same top shape seen in a Ring Row. This requires a little more strength and control at shoulder and global level, as the swing is bigger and the range of motion covered at shoulder level is greater. Fight to keep your elbows against your body as much as possible.

The Hip-to-Bar Pull-up adds a second kip. This second kip is essential to complete the transition over the bar or rings while performing a Muscle-up. The first kip happens during the first swing, and the second kip assists the pulling mechanics that occur at shoulder level in order to send your hips to the bar.

hip-to-bar pull-up 01 Hang from the bar with your arms straight and right above your shoulders. Your body is in a straight line, looking straight ahead, with feet together, knees locked out, and butt and belly tight.

02 Initiate the swing by going into global extension, with your arms still straight, but now behind your ears. You are still looking straight ahead, your spine in extension without losing contraction at belly and butt level. Your knees are straight and your toes are pointed. Fight to keep your feet together in this position.

03 Your toes are farther in front of you than in the regular Kipping Pull-up, and you are in a position of more global flexion. Your feet are still together, with pointed toes and straight legs. Your arms are in front of you, and you're looking straight ahead, not up toward the bar.

04 Thrust your hips up toward the bar and press your hands down toward your hips. Allow your elbows to bend slightly, but keep your shoulders back and down. Continue looking straight ahead and allow the rest of your body to go into global extension. Your feet are still together, toes pointed, and legs straight.

05 Reverse the movement as you would for any kip. Slowly extend your arms or allow your shoulders to go into flexion while you adopt a hollow body position. This is performed with control, but without losing momentum so that you can transfer it into the next kip.

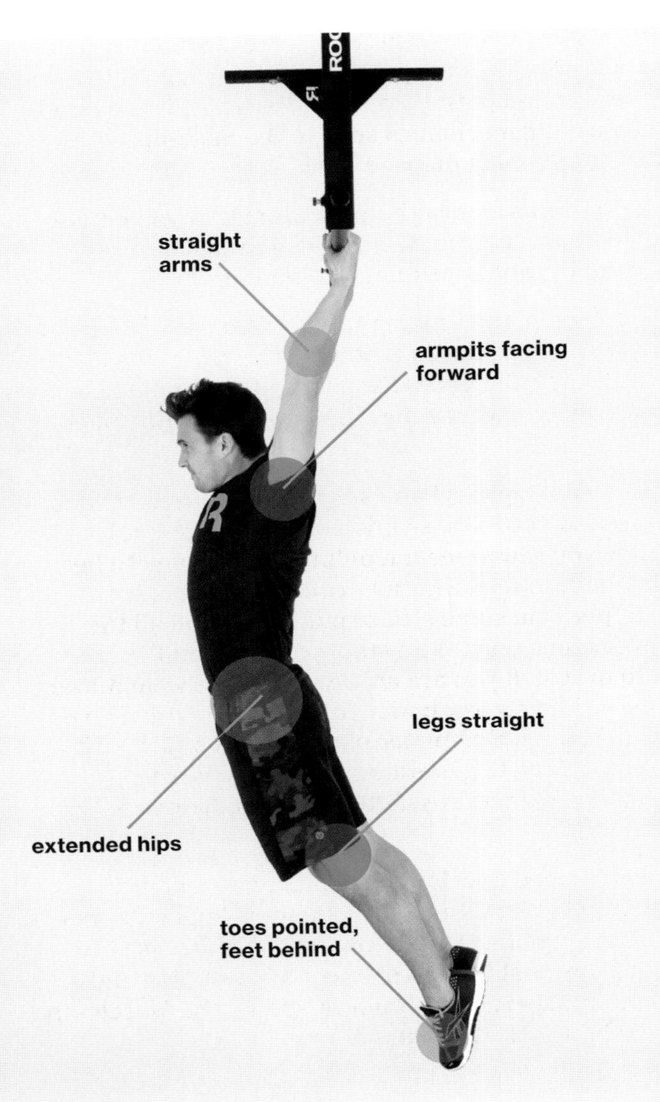
straight arms
armpits facing forward
legs straight
extended hips
toes pointed, feet behind

neutral neck
straight body
forearms perpendicular to midline
legs straight

KIPPING DIP

Now that you understand how to develop the pulling mechanics and kipping style required for the Muscle-up, it is time to transition into the second part of the Muscle-up: the Dip. The Dip can be considered a continuation of the pushing mechanics seen in the Push-up, described in chapter 5 (beginning on page 157).

The Kipping Dip is a Dip performed with momentum that you create by flexing and extending your hips and knees. It allows you to add speed and repetitions to the act of pushing at shoulder level.

Similar to the Kipping Pull-up, the Kipping Dip is extremely beneficial for developing the shoulder mechanics that have the greatest skill transfer. Unlike the Kipping Pull-up, the Kipping Dip develops the combination of the shoulders pushing and the lower body pulling for the kip.

The opportunity to train pulling mechanics for the lower extremities doesn't occur very often in most fitness practices. Think about it: When was the last time you saw someone pulling an object with her lower body? Probably not too recently. But at the same time, you know that you have to perform some sort of pulling motion all the time. For example, every time you take a step, you must pull your foot up in order not to drag it. If you are an Olympic-style weightlifter, you pull from your lower body to get under the bar. If you are a diver performing a Triple Backflip off a 10-meter platform, you must pull your legs into the tuck position to generate the rotation needed to perform the dive. And if you are a CrossFitter performing toes to bar, you must pull your legs up.

In this section, I explain how to develop these pulling mechanics with the Dip and the Kipping Dip. This development is important not only because the Dip is part of the Muscle-up, but also because the kipping mechanics and the combination of lower-body pulling and upper-body pushing are fundamental to understanding the Muscle-up and getting the most skill transfer from it.

dip

In the Handstand Push-up chapter, I reviewed the foundation of pushing mechanics for the upper body by talking about the Push-up and the basic mechanics required to perform it. Just like the Row is the foundation of pulling mechanics for the Pull-up, the Push-up is the foundation for the Handstand Push-up and the Dip. So the pushing mechanics in the Push-up can be considered a prerequisite for developing a good foundation of upper-body pushing strength for the Dip.

The key difference in pushing mechanics between the Dip and the Handstand Push-up is that the Dip starts with the shoulders in the anatomical position and transitions into a position that is at near end range of motion of shoulder extension.

I consider the Dip to be a higher-level movement than the Push-up because of four factors:

1. Increased load on your shoulders due to supporting the weight of your entire body
2. Less stability because your feet are not connected to the ground
3. Further connection complexity when performed on the rings
4. Greater shoulder range of motion

Although I show the progression on the rings because our goal in this chapter is to perform a Muscle-up, the Dip is best learned on a set of parallel bars. The bars allow you to hold a support position with your arms locked out and your legs straight below the bars without having to stabilize the base of support (the rings). You should have enough room beneath the bars that you can perform a deep Dip where your shoulders reach near end of extension and your elbows reach full flexion without your feet touching the ground.

dip 01 Start in a support position with your body in a straight line.

02 Initiate the Dip by slowly bending your elbows, controlling your descent and allowing the natural angle that shoulder mechanics require to facilitate your descent.

This style of pushing mechanics starts at midrange of shoulder range of motion. Specifically, it starts in the anatomical position with your arms locked out and your wrists in flexion, allowing your hands to create a flat base of support for your arms and body to rest on. The finish position is at near full shoulder extension with full elbow flexion and the same wrist flexion. Globally, your body remains neutral throughout the full range of motion. Note the slight angle of the hang. This is the natural balanced state for the bottom of the Dip.

The Dip is a not just a feat of strength; it can also be considered a test of overall health at shoulder level for pushing mechanics. Pushing mechanics overhead are extremely beneficial and in my opinion more valuable in terms of functional application and utility. That said, being able to push from a position of full extension requires you to be close to the top of your game when it comes to movement control at shoulder level. In addition to improving your shoulder pushing mechanics, training the Dip has a huge number of mobility benefits (see the MobilityWOD website for more information).

In chapter 5, you progressed the Push-up from a 45-degree angle down to horizontal. Having developed horizontal pushing, you can reverse that progression to work the angle back up to a vertical body position. As you reach a more upright position, you can assist the pushing mechanics by adding a band to your Dip station, bars, or rings. You can even perform a Dip on a box or set of boxes.

03 Reaching the bottom of the Dip, keep your shoulders in front of your hands, your forearms vertical, and the rest of your body straight. Your feet are together, knees straight, belly and butt tight, and you are looking down. Looking up is OK as long as your neck is neutral and in line with your spine.

04 Initiate your ascent by starting to lock out your elbows while maintaining the same global position. Lift your chin up, allowing your body to get into a more vertical position to prepare for the support and the finish.

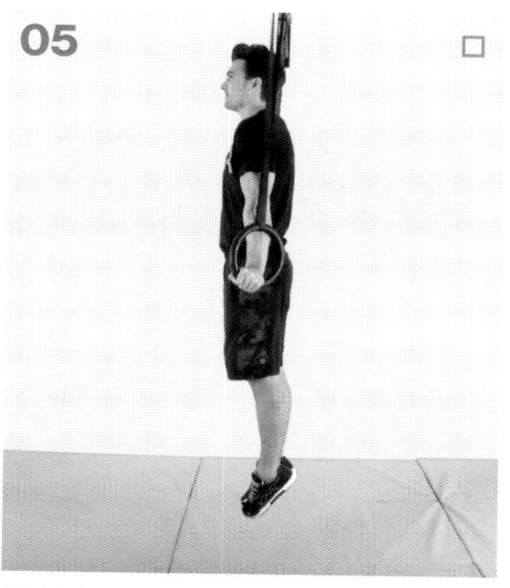

05 Finish in full lockout, making sure to turn your thumbs up for better stability and shoulder position and align your body with the straps (the same as the starting support position).

The same points of performance seen in the Push-up, such as maintaining a neutral global position, externally rotating your shoulders by keeping your arms close to your body, and keeping your forearms vertical, apply equally to the Dip. These points of performance are especially crucial when performing a Dip on the rings, where the surface is not as stable. It can be more difficult to see whether the forearms are vertical because of the angle that the body must adopt during the Dip. A good way to check if your forearms are vertical is to match your forearms to the ring straps. If they are parallel, your forearms are vertical.

scaling the dip with a band

You can scale the Dip by placing a band around the rings, placing your feet on the band, and using the tension created by the band to assist the movement. For less assistance, you can perform the same drill with your knees on the band, which creates additional slack in the system and allows you to take up more of the effort as you perform the movement. You can also scale the Dip by sitting on the band, which is similar to the knee version but takes further tension off the band. This last version can be difficult if you're trying to maintain the correct angle as you descend into the Dip, so treat it as just another alternative.

Besides getting weight assistance from a band, you can also progress the Dip by focusing on the negative or eccentric loading part of the movement. Starting from the support or top position, you lower yourself down as slowly as possible. This helps you develop the muscular contraction required throughout the full range of motion.

Anytime you are trying to develop pushing strength and you want to be able to apply it to other aspects of sport and life, the mechanics take priority over the number of repetitions, speed, and load.

band dip 01 With the band hooked around both rings, place your foot on top of the band.

02 Push down against the band until your leg is fully extended.

Here are three points of performance for the Dip:

1. ***Full range of motion:*** Start from a support position with your shoulders back and down, creating a long neck. Your arms are close to your sides, with your elbows fully locked out and your hands turned out for better movement control at shoulder level.
2. ***Midline stability:*** As you perform the Dip, multi-angled forces are applied to your spine, causing your global position to want to change. Fight to keep everything in line, with your butt and belly tight. Try to direct your chest in the direction you are moving, which is down during the descent.
3. ***Shoulder mechanics:*** The forces seen on your spine also affect your shoulders and can cause your shoulders to want to fall off the tracks, meaning that they want to roll in and your elbows want to flare out. How much they move depends on your experience with the movement, your strength, and your mobility. Fighting these forces guarantees that things are at least moving in the same direction.

A good mental cue that I often use is to think of the Dip as a Push-up that starts from a support position over the bars or rings. As you get closer to the bottom of the Dip (the transition), you can adopt a more horizontal position and mimic a pseudo-Push-up position. Maintaining a more upright position might be useful for the more advanced Dip styles, especially the Bulgarian Dip (wide grip) and the Korean Dip (behind the back).

Once you've developed the proper shoulder mechanics for the Dip and have the strength to maintain good positions for several repetitions and at different speeds, you can start adding more complexity to the movement and adapt the Dip into a Kipping Dip.

03 Place your other foot on the band and get into the shape of the bottom of the Dip.

04 With your legs straight, use the assistance provided by the band to press out of the Dip.

05 Continue to press away until you are in a support position.

kipping dip

The Kipping Dip is a Dip with a dynamic kick created by rapidly tucking your legs into flexion from an extended position at the bottom of the Dip, as seen in the photos below. This kip creates momentum that has similar utility to the Kipping Pull-up, but instead of being a pendular or curvilinear motion, the Kipping Dip is a rectilinear motion—in other words, the direction of the kip is in line with the direction you want your center of mass to travel. As with any kip, it's important not to alter the shoulder mechanics during the kip.

You start with a kicking motion, pulling your legs up into a tuck position by flexing your hips and knees aggressively up and forward. The moment your hips pass 90 degrees, the momentum from the kick starts propelling your center of mass upward and causes a sense of weightlessness, as seen in the Kipping Pull-up. This moment of weightlessness is your window of opportunity to perform a quick push away from the bars or rings. As your legs reach full flexion during the kip and your arms start to lock out, a quick extension of your legs back to a neutral position helps facilitate the last bit of the kip and finishes the Dip in a full support position.

If you perform the Kipping Dip correctly, the pushing mechanics seem to disappear, and your upper body seems to be mostly an elbow lockout—that is, enough momentum is generated that you simply need to straighten your arms under little or no load.

kipping utility

Some coaches think of the weightlessness created by the kip as proof that kipping movements are cheating, but I like to compare kipping movements to the utility of movements seen in Olympic-style weightlifting. In Olympic weightlifting, you can press a barbell overhead strictly, but in order to get more weight overhead, every Olympic weightlifter performs a Jerk. These more dynamic movements are the most efficient ways to get the most weight overhead. This relates to my concept of functional movement in that I prefer to spend most of my time focusing on developing the movements that last the longest.

Dip = Press

Kipping Dip with no leg extension = Push-Press

Kipping Dip with leg extension = Push-Jerk

kipping dip 01 Start in a support position with your hands wrapped around the rings and your palms facing down. Your elbows are locked out, your shoulder blades are back and down, and you're looking straight ahead. You're in a globally neutral position with your butt and belly tight, legs straight, feet together, and toes pointed.

02 Initiate the descent by bending your elbows, fighting to keep your forearms in line with the straps. Create a slight angle with your body as your shoulders travel forward in front of the rings to maintain proper shoulder mechanics. Look down toward the ground, preparing for the bottom position of the Dip.

03 When you reach the bottom of the Dip, your shoulders are in full extension or close to end range of extension. Your forearms are vertical, and your hands remain in the same position. You have an exaggerated global angle. As you look down, try to create the straightest line possible from head to toes. The position of your neck depends on your shoulder mobility. I have stiff shoulders, so my neck tends to flex a little more, and I look down slightly.

With this type of dynamic movement, it's important to be able to mark the Start-Transition-Finish position at any time as if you were posing for a picture. Especially in the Dip, the bottom position should be sustainable for long periods if trained, just like a Squat, as described in chapter 4 (page 105).

By combining advanced upper-body pushing mechanics with lower-body pulling mechanics, the Kipping Dip gives you an opportunity to train crucial movement ability. Specifically, you are training the timing of combining pushing and pulling that is the key to the Muscle-up transition, Olympic weightlifting, running, and so many other movements; see the Simple-Complex-Simple progression method in chapter 3 (page 91).

dip vs. handstand push-up

When comparing the amount of effort required to perform a Dip versus a Handstand Push-up, most people have a harder time with the Handstand Push-up. This is interesting because in both movements you are supporting and pushing your entire body weight using your shoulders as the prime mover. In both movements, your shoulder goes to end range of motion. We can get a better idea of why this difference in effort exists by using the progression principles.

First, the progression principle of orientation suggests that the upright position of the Dip would be easier to perform than the inverted position of the Handstand Push-up. Second, the Dip starts in an anatomical position (low muscular tension) and transitions through an end range position (high muscular tension). The Handstand Push-up starts at end range of motion (high muscular tension) and transitions through midrange of motion (low muscular tension). Combining the principles of stability with Start-Transition-Finish and Shift-Connect-Flow, we can theorize that the additional muscular tension in the bottom position of the Dip adds stability due to the physiological connection in the critical transition position.

Handstand Push-up: start (high tension)–transition (low tension)–finish (high tension)

Dip: start (low tension)–transition (high tension)–finish (high-low tension)

04 Perform an aggressive tuck by driving your knees straight up toward your face, but without letting your feet come in front of you. Drive your heels toward your butt, initiating a forward and upward motion.

05 Take advantage of the momentum created by the knee drive and start extending your elbows. This allows you to reach the top of the Dip. This rise should happen very quickly and feel almost weightless. Your knees are still bent as you're about to reach full lockout.

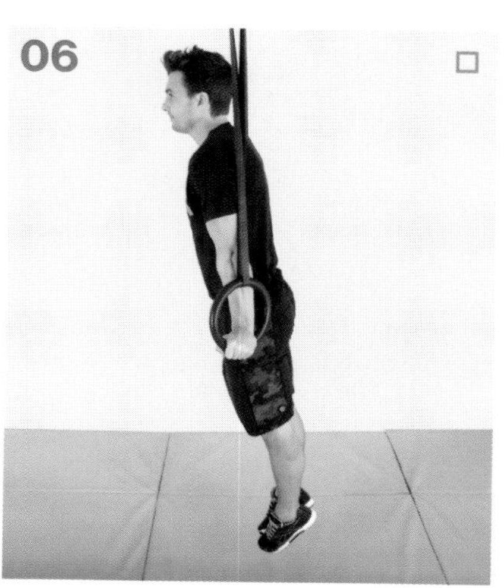

06 Finish in the same support position seen in position 1, with your arms locked out, your thumbs turned out, and looking straight ahead.

shoulders below elbows
vertical forearms
hollow body

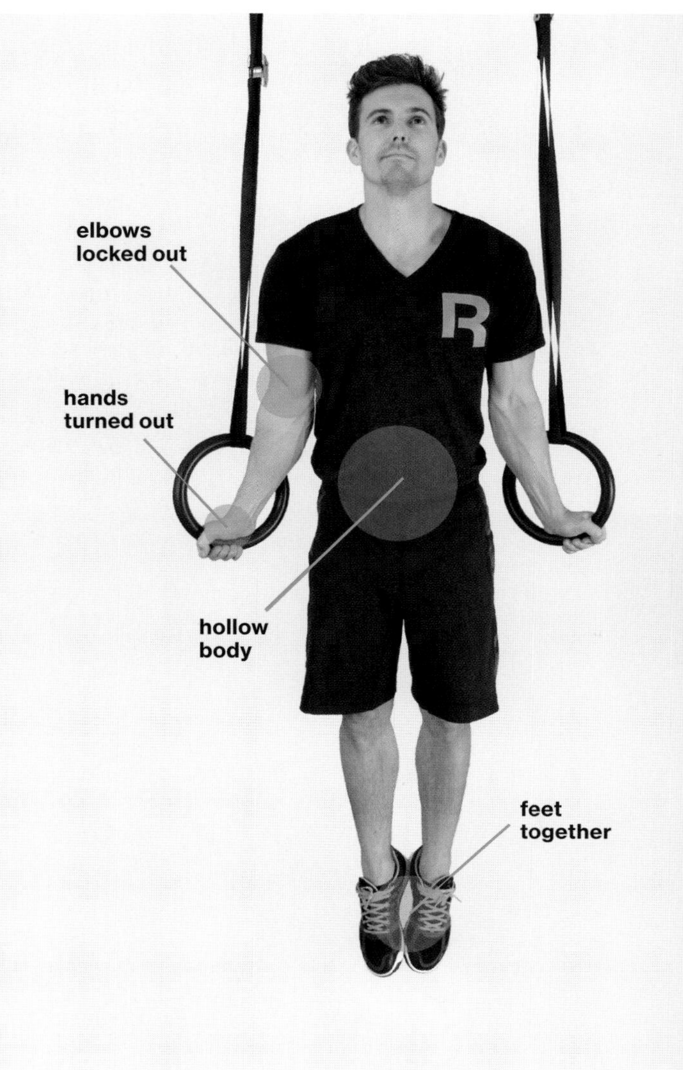
elbows locked out
hands turned out
hollow body
feet together

MUSCLE UP

Now that you have developed a good foundation of pulling and pushing strength from the Pull-up and the Dip, it is time to connect both pieces of the Muscle-up puzzle to create the final product.

One fascinating aspect of the Muscle-up is that it requires a full-range-of-motion pull that starts at near end range of flexion at shoulder level, as seen in the bottom of a Pull-up, and ends all the way at near end range of extension at shoulder level, as seen in a Dip. Another way to describe the complexity of this movement is to compare it with the "full" Clean or Snatch movement in Olympic-style weightlifting. In a full Clean, the hip pulls from full extension during the second pull of the lift or transition and into full flexion, as seen in the Squat or receiving position. Both are beautiful movements for covering the full range of joint motion and offer tremendous opportunities for skill transfer.

grips

Before we get into the Muscle-up progression, it's important to know about two common grips: false and normal. The normal grip (or hook grip) was described earlier in reference to the Pull-up (page 224). The only difference here is that you're hanging on the rings instead of a bar.

The false grip exaggerates the hand position described in the previous grip section. The concept behind it is to create a hinge in your wrist, which allows you to place the medial side of your wrist,

false grip 01 Extend your hand, splay your fingers, stick your hand through the ring, and place the inside of your wrist or bottom of your hand on top of the bottom or lowest point of the ring.

02 Flex your wrist, dropping your palm toward the ground. Thread your thumb around and behind the opposite side of the ring.

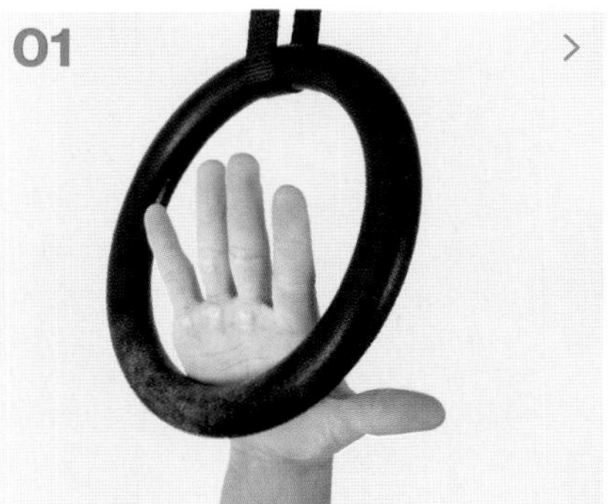

normal grip 01 Extend your hand, splay your fingers, and place the the ring across the middle of your palm. Make sure that your pinky knuckle is above the lowest part of the ring.

02 Close your hand, wrap your fingers around the ring, and keep your thumb splayed out to the side.

or the side opposite your thumb, above the rings. This starts your hand in a position much closer to the one in which it will finish once you make it above the rings after the pull. This style of grip is great if you are desperate to get your first Muscle-up or you want to use it as a progression step to improve your transition. But do not make it your default position, as it is limited to this movement and does not translate across the spectrum of life and sport.

03 Close your fingers, wrapping them around the ring.

04 Place your thumb overlapping your index and middle fingers to create a hook grip.

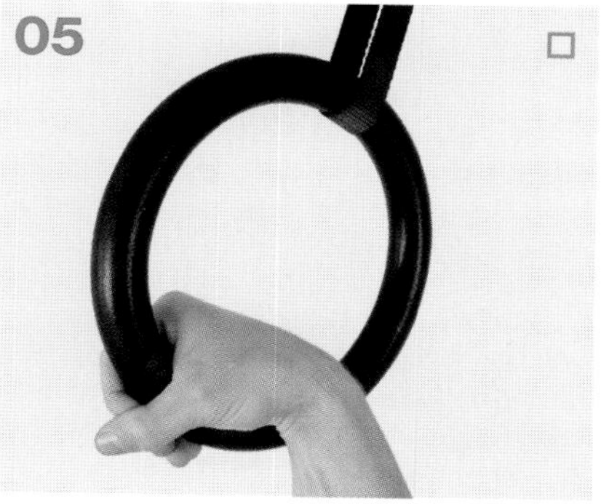

05 Your wrist should remain in a flexed hook grip position.

03 Wrap your thumb around and place it over your index and middle fingers, creating a hook grip.

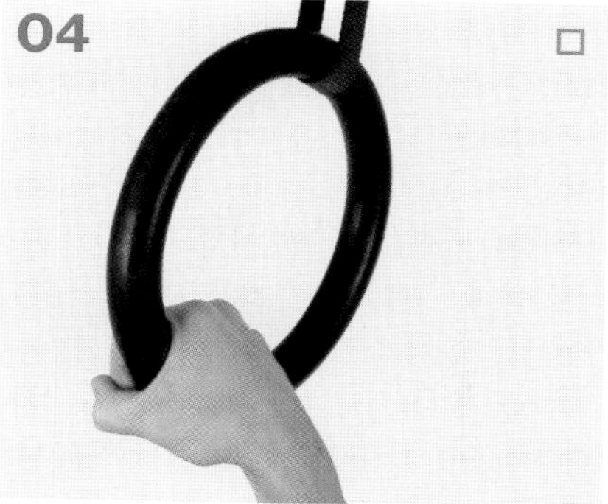

04 Your wrist is in a more neutral position than in the false grip, creating a more normal position in which to work. This grip is more universal and is highly recommended for both beginners and advanced athletes.

muscle-up

The Muscle-up typically requires either a Pull-up bar or rings. I explain the Muscle-up on the rings, because the rings allow you to cover a true, full range of motion at shoulder level. A bar offers only a partial range of motion for the shoulders, because it blocks your body from moving through a position that would cover that shoulder range.

This movement is often considered tricky because of the slightly counterintuitive transition position, where your shoulders move from below the rings to above. While many athletes focus on acquiring the pulling mechanics, discussed in the Kipping Pull-up section (page 223), and the pushing mechanics, discussed in the Dip section

muscle-up transition

The hard part of the Muscle-up is the transition. Most people see the Pull-up as a vertical pulling motion and end up getting stuck in the transition. But if you think of the Pull-up as a Ring Row and keep your body stiff in a neutral global position, you will naturally adopt a slight angle or backward lean. Once you reach the top of the Pull-up, the lean can't continue unless you get out of its way, which you can do on the rings by allowing your body to rotate forward as the pull continues to take you over the rings and into a Dip.

muscle-up band progression 01 Set up on the band in a scaled Row position.

02 Perform a Row while maintaining the natural hang angle with your body.

muscle-up 01 Hang from the rings with your arms straight overhead. In the photo, my hands are slightly turned out to showcase full lockout at the elbows. Your shoulders are in full flexion, your body is straight, and you're looking straight ahead. You can also opt to look down. Your feet are together, toes pointed, legs straight.

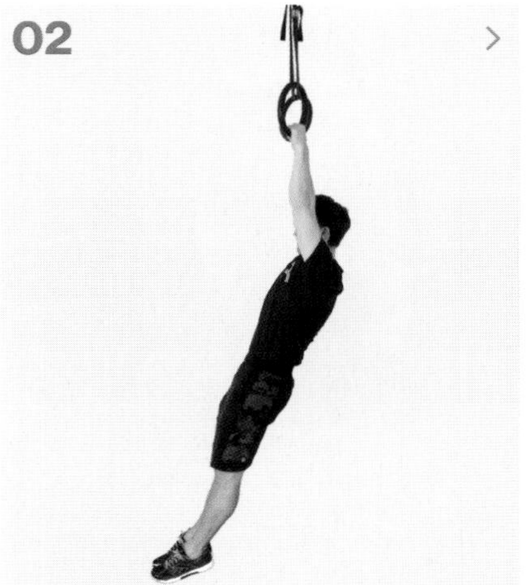

02 Initiate the pull the same way you would in a Pull-up, but allow for a greater angle as your toes come up in front of you and your body rocks backward.

03 Keep pulling your elbows behind your back.

(page 245), they often miss the subtle movement required during the transition.

Without completely ruining the surprise for you, during the transition you need to master using the rings as a pivot point for your body to change orientation in space, from a supine position during the Pull-up to a Push-up position in the Dip. However, if you have developed the proper pulling mechanics, especially as demonstrated in the Row (page 224), you will be that annoying person who gets on the rings for the first time and performs a Muscle-up without really knowing "how" to do it.

03 Pull until your chest reaches the rings.

04 As you continue to pull and slightly drop your legs, your body rotates over and around the rings.

05 Continue to pivot over the rings until you reach the bottom of the Dip position.

04 When you see the tops of the rings, try to drive your shoulders through the straps and over the rings as you drop your feet down toward the ground, creating a rocking motion that facilitates your transition. This is still part of the pulling phase for the Muscle-up.

05 Having pulled your arms all the way into extension, you are at the bottom of the Dip, with your elbows right on top of your hands, your forearms in line with the straps, your body straight, and looking slightly down, as in the Dip.

06 Initiate the ascent by extending your elbows, pressing away from the rings without losing position and fighting to keep your elbows in and thumbs slightly turned out for better shoulder position. Finish in a support position, looking straight ahead, elbows locked out, and thumbs turned out, maintaining the exact same global position defined in the Dip.

eyes over rings
lean back, driving hips up
forearms as vertical as possible
straight legs

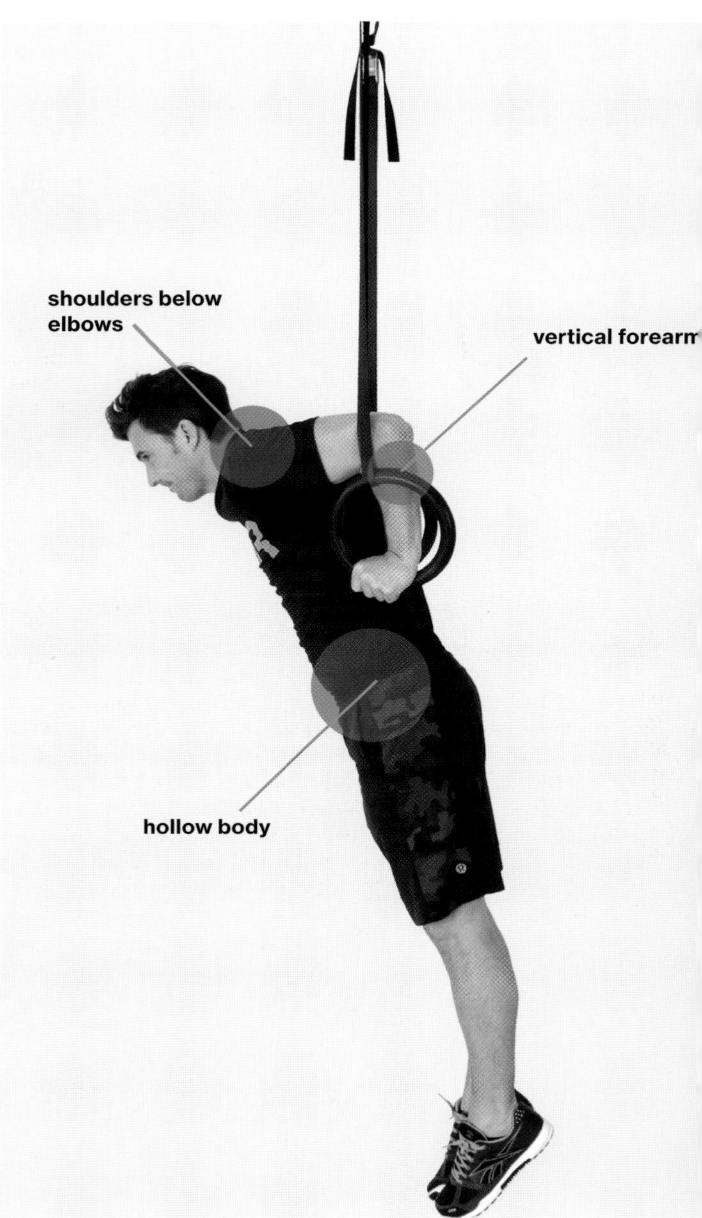
shoulders below elbows
vertical forearm
hollow body

KIPPING MUSCLE UP

The Kipping Muscle-up is a Muscle-up performed with the momentum created by swinging your body back and forth from global extension to flexion. This style of Muscle-up is best learned on a set of rings but can also be performed on a bar. Even though the bar may limit your range of motion at shoulder level by getting in the way of the transition, it can be safer to practice on at first. The safety comes from the added stability of anchoring to a bar rather than to independently moving suspended rings.

As I mentioned in the introduction to this chapter, the style of Muscle-up that I present in this chapter is part of the natural progression and adaptation forged by practicing the Muscle-up at high speeds, at high repetitions, for long periods, and with heavy loads. I consider this movement "complete" because it includes pushing and pulling for the upper and lower body, change of orientation in space, and full global flexion and extension.

In the strict Muscle-up section (page 254), I focused on progressing the transition position. This section follows the same principle, but with a more detailed five-step progression due to the complexity of this transition position. This five-step progression will help you master the transition by connecting to the process of learning the Kipping Pull-up and the Kipping Dip (pages 223 and 243, respectively).

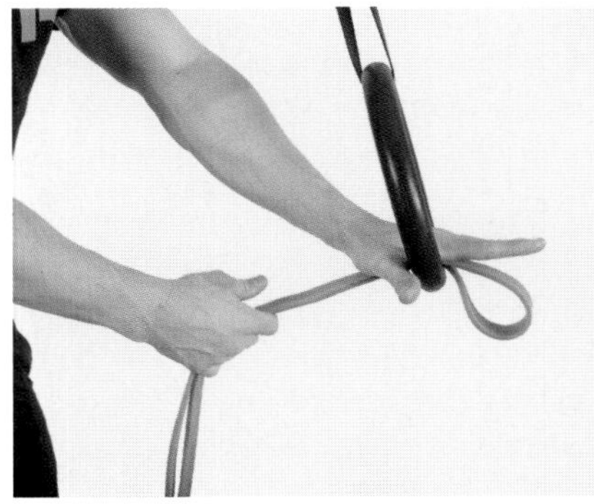

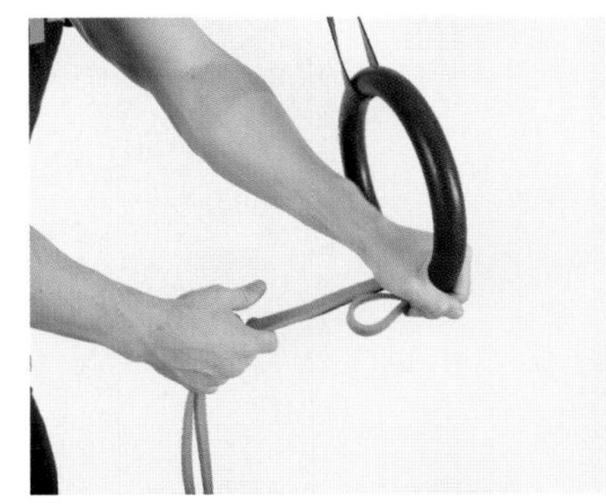

band setup 01 Thread the band through the ring, placing it at the bottom or lowest point of the ring.

02 Place one hand on top of the band with your fingers splayed, making sure that the band is not wrapped around any of your fingers.

03 Squeeze the band around the ring by wrapping your fingers around it and placing your thumb over your index and middle fingers, creating a hook grip. The band is threaded in a way that does not have any wrinkles or overlap with your fingers.

band kipping muscle-up

The Band Muscle-up is a simple drill that anyone can do to achieve the proper mechanics required to perform this high-level movement pattern. Thanks to the band, most athletes can safely practice the specifics of this movement even if they have yet to acquire the full ability to perform Kipping Pull-ups and Dips. ***Note:*** It is ideal to progress this drill in coordination with the Pull-up and Dip progressions discussed earlier in this chapter.

hip drive

While sitting on the band in a hollow body position with your hips approximately a foot under the rings, perform a slow and controlled hip extension. Once you have mastered this maneuver, perform the fastest hip extension possible. Make sure not to pull with your arms.

04 Grab both rings, completely wrapping your hands around the band and making sure that it's tight inside your grip. Place the band behind your back. Allow the slack of the band to sit underneath your hips, creating a hammock that you can sit in.

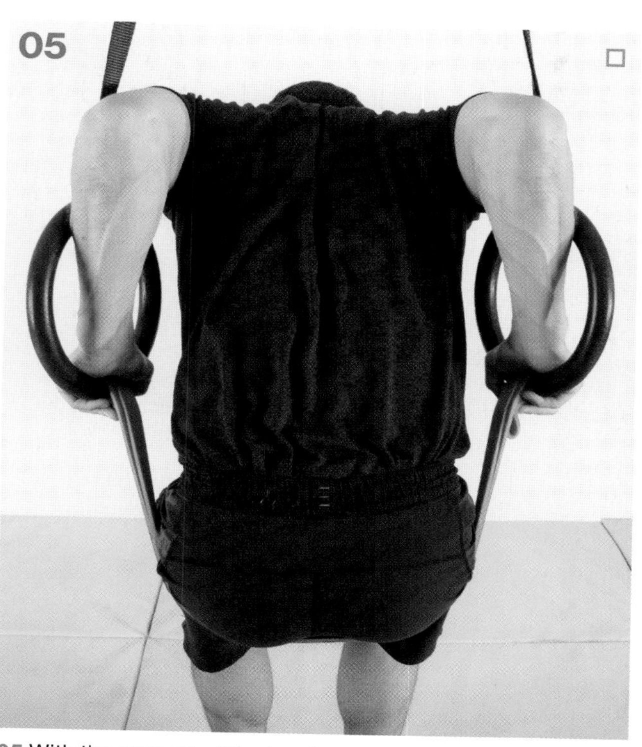

05 With the support of the band, you can perform a deep Dip where there's tension around your hips and no overlap between the band and your fingers. The band is also far enough down behind your legs that it won't slip upward and hit you in the back.

hip drive 01 Start in a hollow body position, with your toes just below eye level.

02 Without pulling with your arms, extend your hips by driving your feet and shoulders toward the ground. Perform this movement slowly to get the feel of driving your hips without an arm pull.

03 Once you are comfortable with the slow hip drive, practice with a more aggressive snap, which drives your center of mass until your hips reach the rings. Facilitate the hip drive by bending your arms, getting them out of the way but never pulling with your arms.

band sit-up 01 Start in an extended body position, with your hips as close as possible to the rings. The band is tight and supporting most of your weight.

02 Trying to keep your feet in the same position, drop your hips or press them into the band to initiate a Sit-up.

03 Flex your hips to continue the Sit-up and initiate the rotation of your upper body over the rings. Your arms are bent but are not pulling you to the rings.

knee bend sit-up 01 Start in an extended body position with your hips as close as possible to the rings. The band is tight and supporting most of your weight.

02 Aggressively bend your knees, driving your heels behind you while maintaining hip extension.

band sit-up

Sit on the band in an extended body position. Your hips should be as close as possible to the rings, as if you had paused at the top of step 1 of the hip drive. The ideal way to get into this position is to have someone hold your legs or to hook your legs into something. Once you are set up, perform a Sit-up.

knee bend sit-up

Because the Band Sit-up does not translate to the reality of the Muscle-up, you have to add a movement that maximizes anterior hip tension and facilitates orientation or rotation in space. While sitting on the band in the same fashion, perform a knee bend followed by a Sit-up, and finish in a Dip position.

04 To continue the rotation, allow your feet to drop to the ground.

05 Finish in the Dip position, with your hips remaining in flexion.

03 Use the tension created by the knee bend to perform a Sit-up with rapid hip flexion.

04 The aggressive knee bend and hip flexion slingshot you around the rings.

05 Continue the rotation until you reach the Dip position.

muscle-up floor drill

This drill is designed to help you perform the transition for the Muscle-up with only your hips and without the use of your arms.

muscle-up floor drill 01 Start in a bridge position, with your hips off the ground and your body in global extension.

02 Drop your hips to ground, bend your elbows, and place your hands in front of you. This mimics the setup transition on the rings.

03 Continue to flex your hips until you reach full flexion and your arms mimic the Dip position on the rings, with your forearms as perpendicular to ground as possible.

dip balance

The Dip Balance is a key component of this progression. It is designed to teach you how to keep your center of mass at ring level in order to facilitate the rotation and improve your receiving position. This progression starts from a support position and finishes in a deep Dip with your legs tucked into a ball. The goal is to learn how to pull yourself into this tuck position as fast you can, ending in the most silent and stable position possible.

dip balance 01 Start in a Dip support position with the band below your butt.

02 Pull yourself into a tuck position without allowing your center of mass to change position.

toe-hip-knee-sit-balance 01 Sit on the ground with the band underneath your butt and your arms relaxed. You are in a hollow body position with your legs and feet on the ground as you look to the horizon.

02 Elevate your legs, but without letting your hips leave the ground, adopting a more aggressive hollow body position. You should always be able to see the rings and the wall in front of you.

03 Drive your hips aggressively up toward the rings by snapping your hips into extension. Your hips being off the ground gives you a little hang time. Your body is in extension, and you're still looking straight at the horizon.

toe-hip-knee-sit-balance

The fifth and final stage of the progression is designed to put the previous four stages together.

Sit on a band, but with little tension in the band so that your body rests on the ground. The goal is to create a sequence of movements that acts as a wave. This wave creates a whipping motion that starts from your toes and goes all the way up to your shoulders.

The first move is to drive your toes up, followed by an aggressive hip thrust. Make sure to keep your feet below eye level. This hip thrust creates a moment of weightlessness. That moment is your opportunity to initiate the transition by quickly bending your knees, followed by a quick Sit-up performed by flexing at the hips. Once your knees and hips have bent, your arms follow and assist the transition by pulling your body over the rings, finally finishing in a tucked bottom Dip position.

In photo 4, my feet remain together even though my knees have come slightly apart. Anytime your hips are in extension, your legs will want to abduct, which is OK as long you fight to create tension by gluing your toes together. Also notice that the rings are in a neutral position, and I am gripping the rings the same way I would grip a bar. As I move into the bottom position of the Dip, the rings rotate 90 degrees.

Once you have developed the Muscle-up transition, it's time to connect all the pieces described in this chapter: the hip-to-ring Kipping Pull-up + the Band Muscle-up transition + the Kipping Dip.

Remember that the Kipping Muscle-up, as complex as it may seem, is composed of simpler movements. Anytime you are learning a complex movement, it is important to return to the basics, especially since the simpler fundamental movements that comprise a complex movement always contain the keys to why you are or are not performing the movement effectively!

04 Bend your heels aggressively, driving them behind you and fighting to keep that extended body position. Your face is still directed toward the rings and the wall in front of you.

05 Perform an aggressive Sit-up, creating the transition by flexing your hips and fighting to maintain a tucked position.

06 Maintain the tucked position until you land in the bottom of the Dip. Your thighs are close to your chest, your heels are close to your butt, your forearms are vertical, and you are looking straight down.

kipping muscle-up

The swinging phase of the Kipping Muscle-up takes your body between global extension and flexion. At the moment your body hits the hollow body position in the front swing, the second kip, as seen in the Hip-to-Bar Pull-up (page 240), takes your body into global extension and initiates the pull at shoulder level. The pulling occurs during the moment of weightlessness discussed in the Kipping Row, Pull-up, and Dip sections. But in the case of the Muscle-up, it occurs specifically in the transition from under the rings to over the rings.

At this moment, your knees initiate a bend by driving your heels down and back, starting a chain reaction, which involves a forward rotation of your body plus muscular tension in the anterior aspect

kipping muscle-up 01 Hang from the rings with your arms straight overhead. Your belly and butt are tight, legs straight, and toes pointed, and you're looking straight ahead.

02 Initiate the swing by kicking your toes forward, getting into a hollow body position. Make sure that your body is as tight as possible in preparation for the next swing.

03 Drive your heels behind you and allow your body to go into extension. You're still looking straight ahead and adopting a globally extended position, with your arms still straight in full flexion and your hands turned out slightly for better tension on the rings.

07 Initiate the transition by performing a Sit-up without losing that knee bend or heel drive behind you.

08 Continue to drive through as your elbows reach full flexion. It's all about maintaining that tuck position to facilitate the movement, so fight to stay tucked.

09 You are now in the bottom of a Dip. Your legs are bent and you're in a tuck position, with your heels close to your butt and your thighs close to your chest. You are looking straight down, and your forearms are vertical, in line with the straps.

of your hips. This knee bend is followed by a quick Sit-up that you perform by flexing your hips, further accelerating the forward rotation over the rings. Finally, your arms go to work, with your elbows driving backward, which pulls your shoulders forward into extension. These steps provide a point of rotation around your hands, and therefore the rings, allowing your body to reach the bottom of the Dip. From there, your legs extend down and can now proceed to perform the Kipping Dip to finish off the Muscle-up. By pulling your legs up and facilitating the extension of your elbows into the support as your legs kick back out into extension, your arms finally reach full lockout in the support position.

04 Snap your body into flexion and elevate your toes, but do not allow your toes to swing above eye level. You should always be able to see the horizon in front of you. You are in a globally flexed or hollow body position.

05 Snap your hips to the rings, pulling slightly with your arms and bending your elbows, but always thinking about directing your hips toward the bottom of the rings. Your feet are together. Your body is in extension, and you're still looking straight toward the horizon.

06 Drive your heels aggressively toward your butt, but without letting your knees come up above your shoulders or above eye level. Keep pulling with your arms and fighting to maintain global extension.

10 Extend your legs without losing the shoulder extension seen at the bottom of the Dip.

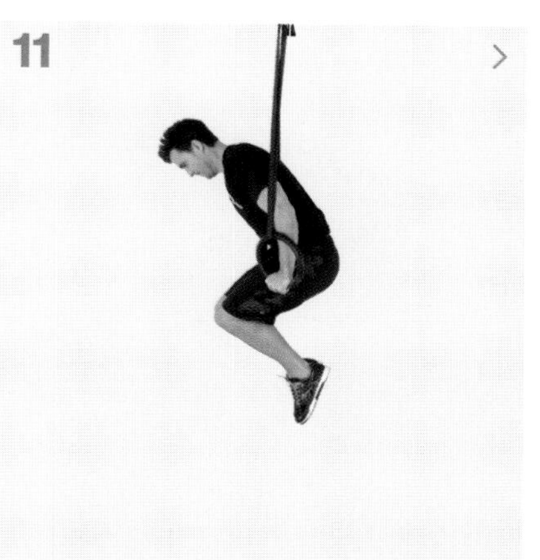

11 You can now perform an aggressive knee drive up and forward, bringing your thighs toward your chest and your heels toward your butt, creating momentum that picks you up and lifts you away from the rings.

12 Finish in a support position with your elbows locked out, your thumbs turned out, and your body extended, looking straight ahead. To reverse this movement, perform a Dip without bending your legs, and then perform the same swing back. Going down is a reversal of the movement seen in a strict Muscle-up, which allows you to go straight into the kipping motion and the next repetition.

candlestick transition drill

The Candlestick Roll mimics the Kipping Muscle-up transition. The Candlestick Transition Drill is important because it teaches you the forward rotation required to get over the rings. Adding the arm movement seen in the Muscle-up is a great way to start understanding how to move your arms into the positions required for the Muscle-up without having to pull or having something to pull from. The Candlestick Roll also helps you perform the hip movement required to create the transition for the Muscle-up on the rings.

candlestick transition drill 01 Start in a shoulder stance with your arms flat on the ground over your head. This mimics the front swing on the rings. From here, initiate the descent or forward rotation of the Candlestick Roll as explained in chapter 4 (page 142). Once you initiate that roll, the heel drive and hip flexion required to finish the roll mimic the act of transitioning on the rings.

02 Finish the heel drive with your feet on the ground, your heels close to your butt, and your hips in full flexion. Your arms are starting to initiate a pull, as seen on the rings.

03 You're in a partial Squat with your hips flexed, knees bent, and shoulders in extension. Even though your forearms are not vertical, they are mimicking the bottom of the Dip.

04 Stand up to mimic the act of pressing away from the rings.

bar muscle-up floor drill

The Bar Muscle-up involves the exact same mechanics as the Ring Muscle-up. The Bar Muscle-up can be difficult, as it requires a bigger pulling phase in order to clear the bar due to the lack of space that your shoulders have to move as you perform the transition.

The Bar Muscle-up is essentially a Hip=to-Bar Pull-up plus a fast Sit-up over the bar. Your feet always remain bellow eye level, and you can see the horizon. You use the falling weight of your legs to facilitate the transition. As you finish, remember to focus on a Push-up shape, not a support. The Push-up shape allows you to rest your belly on the bar and use the bar for support before you finish the movement and lock out your arms into a support.

I like to perform a simple drill on the floor that most of the time is the missing link that enables people to transfer the movement ability acquired in the Kipping Muscle-up to the Bar Muscle-up. Practice this drill in slow motion to get the movement pattern down, and then progressively add speed until you are ready to try the movement on a high bar. When performing it on a high bar, the Sit-up is the key to a successful transition. If you have developed adequate movement strength in your pulling mechanics, the Bar Muscle-up will feel even more stable and less technical than the Kipping Muscle-up.

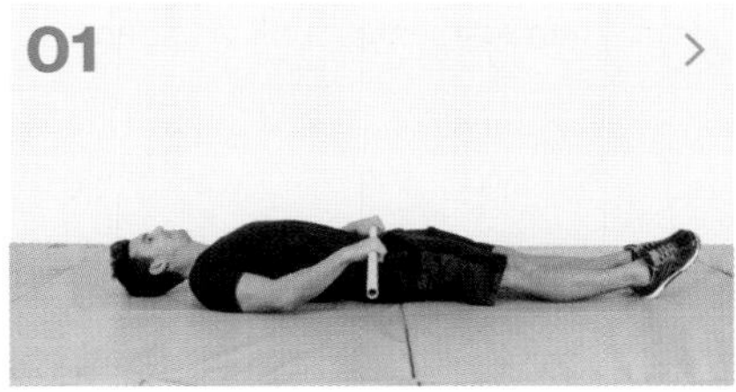

bar muscle-up floor drill 01 Lie down in a supine position with a PVC pipe, bar, or stick in your hands and placed across your hips.

02 Lift up your hips, allowing your body to bridge into an extended position.

03 Drop your hips back down and, without letting your legs come up off the ground, start performing a Sit-up by hinging in your hips and rotating your upper body around the bar.

04 Finish the Sit-up with your shoulders past the bar and your elbows directly above the bar.

muscle-up

points of performance

Once you have mastered all styles of Muscle-ups, clearing an obstacle will never be a problem again. Not only that, but adding a movement after the Muscle-up will be a cakewalk—Muscle-up to Ring Handstand Push-up, for example!

neutral neck
fastest sit-up
you've ever done
vertical
forearms
full tuck

10
15

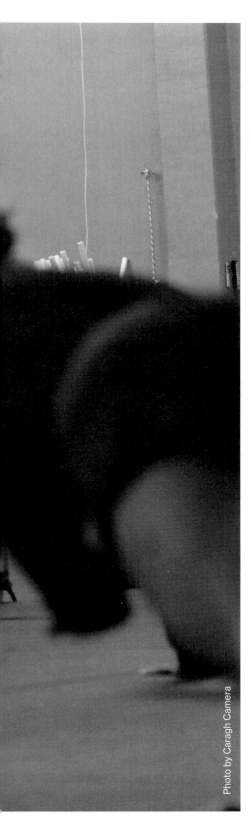
Photo by Caragh Camera

the burpee

07

Standards must be set to control the game, but must be broken to change the game.

A Burpee is simply the act of lowering your body to the ground in a prone or facedown position and then standing up again. Often people add a jump as they stand up.

Of the Freestyle Four movements that I present in this book, the Burpee is hands-down the most complete. I like to joke that understanding the Burpee is like understanding the meaning of life. It's funny how such a simple movement (which I used to look down on, actually) contains so much valuable information. I firmly believe that everyone who cares about human movement should study the Burpee.

In the middle of a seminar I taught in London, a young athlete asked me why I didn't talk about the Burpee. My first thought was, "Because anyone can do a Burpee; it's too simple."

Well, I guess she made an impression on me. I started seeing the Burpee everywhere—in the kids I was coaching, in the gymnasts I was coaching, in my private clients, in surfers standing up off the board. But it wasn't until I saw my beautiful fiancée doing Burpees during a workout that I saw the light.

I can't say exactly whether I was struck by love or a moment of sheer clarity, but I realized that everything I knew about human performance from a movement perspective could be explained with the Burpee.

This realization only burdened me with more questions. Why do coaches love prescribing the Burpee? Why do athletes dread performing this movement? Why does a Burpee look the way it does? Why do coaches teach it the way they do? Is there one technique that is better than others?

I had yet to put my finger on it. All I knew was that the Burpee is everywhere, and the function it serves is to get up and down. But most people can do that, so who cares?

I couldn't stop thinking about it. I thought about it when I got up in the morning, I thought about it at work, and I thought about it when I got back in bed at night. This obsession led me to start playing with variations of this movement. My experiments led me to discover some very basic progressions for performing the Burpee, and they are what I present in this chapter. Because the Burpee is a form of getting down and back up off the ground, I think it's important to study it from that more general viewpoint. So this chapter shows you two formal approaches for getting down and then up that are heavily used in strength and conditioning and fitness: the Get-up and the Burpee.

GET UP

The Get-up is the act of getting up off the ground from a supine or faceup position until you are standing and then returning to the same starting position. It is usually performed with a weight in hand.

In the most common variety, you hold the weight in one hand. That arm is projected straight out away from your body. When you are lying down, you hold the weight above your shoulder or have your arm perpendicular to the ground. When you are standing, you hold the weight overhead.

The Get-up is a great way to challenge many different aspects of your movement ability because:

1. It is similar to a weighted Sit-up.
2. It adds unilateral loading, and thus rotation, to the Sit-up.
3. It changes your orientation in space.
4. It adds a unilateral leg sweep as you move into the Lunge position.
5. It challenges balance with the arm and weight overhead.
6. It requires you to balance on opposing limbs while changing your body shape.
7. It requires you to perform the unilateral squatting mechanics seen in the Lunge (page 119) in order to stand up.
8. It develops your ability to reverse all those movements with precision.

The Get-up is clearly a bomb of information for a movement geek, and I hope that the basic principles for observing and describing movement can help you study, appreciate, and adapt it to the tasks you care about.

In this section, I present a Get-up without weight, but the same positions and development of the movement are useful for weighted varieties as well.

You start the Get-up lying on the ground in a supine or faceup position. Your arms should be slightly out to your sides, almost at a 45-degree angle of abduction away from your midline, with your palms facing down. Starting with your arms in this position helps you establish a strong base of support and set up the proper shoulder mechanics.

Select one leg to be your posting leg. (If you are carrying a weight, this leg is on the same side as the arm holding the weight.) Slide your posting foot flat on the ground and next to your butt by flexing your hip and knee, as seen in photo 2 below. Now you are in the starting position for the Get-up and are ready to move.

You initiate the Get-up movement with a Sit-up, but not just any Sit-up. Specifically, you perform a Lateral Sit-up. Sit up away from your bent or posting leg and into your posting arm, or the arm opposite your posting leg. When you perform this Lateral Sit-up, there is slight flexion and rotation in that direction. Continue sitting up until your upper body reaches a point where it feels balanced over your posting arm.

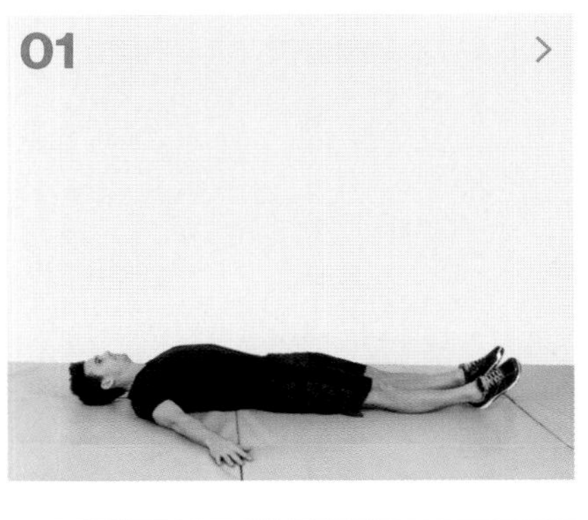

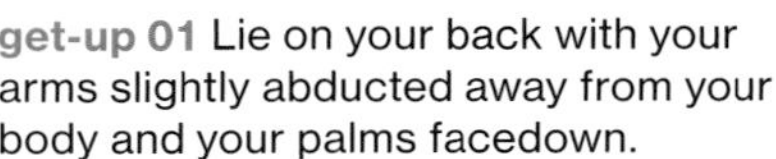

get-up 01 Lie on your back with your arms slightly abducted away from your body and your palms facedown.

02 Bend your left knee, planting your bent-leg foot on the ground.

Your posting arm is bent at the elbow, with your forearm resting on the ground to create a big base of support. You increase the size of that base by spreading out your fingers and even gripping the ground, as seen in the Handstand (page 339). Because of the stability, you can use this position to pause, rest, and find balance before moving on to the next step.

In the next movement, you sit up farther by pressing up with your posting arm. You continue to press up until you reach a full seated position and your body weight is evenly distributed across your posting leg, hip, and posting arm. The key to this step is to synchronize the Sit-up with the pushing mechanics performed mostly from the extension of your elbows.

This position is another moment of stability that you can use to rest and reclaim your balance if needed before taking the next step. The following step requires a fair amount of balance as you perform a slight change in orientation in space. You go from a close relative supine position, or Sit-up, to a relative prone position, or bent-over Lunge.

continues on next page

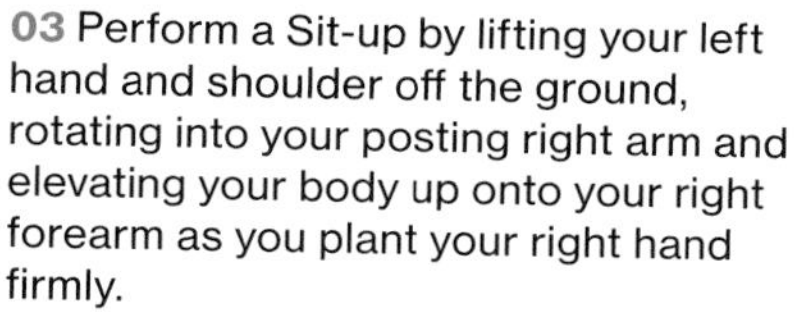

03 Perform a Sit-up by lifting your left hand and shoulder off the ground, rotating into your posting right arm and elevating your body up onto your right forearm as you plant your right hand firmly.

04 Perform an elbow extension with your planted hand, which allows you to get your chest closer to your thigh.

05 Lift your hips by pressing away from your planted left leg and planted right arm, keeping your right leg straight out in front of you.

You perform this step by lifting your hips and pressing your posting leg and arm into the ground. Your lifted hips create a window formed by the space between your posting arm, posting leg, hips, and the floor. You use this window to pull your extended leg and sweep it underneath you. You perform the sweep by bending your knee and hip and sliding it behind your body. Continue the sweep until you reach a position where your knee and lower leg can post on the ground behind you. This puts you in a lunging shape with your legs, with your posting arm still in contact with the ground.

The leg pull for the sweep is very similar to the leg pull required to perform the Muscle-up transition, as seen in the Muscle-up (page 251).

Once in the Lunge, you have another opportunity to regain balance. Your next goal is to get from the Lunge with your arm on the ground to a standard Lunge position by laterally lifting your body up and away from the ground. This lift is a great expression of unilateral loading and having to resist rotation because you perform it with square hips while your legs are in a Lunge.

Once you have pressed yourself up to a full Lunge, you should feel at home with the mechanics you learned in chapter 4. To stand up, you simply hinge in your hips and post over your front leg until you can press to standing with both legs underneath your hips.

get-up (continued) 06 Sweep your right leg under your hip, bringing it back into a Lunge position.

07 Place your right foot and knee on the ground as you keep your posting hand flat on the ground with your arms straight. Your elevated arm remains the same, and your opposite leg (the planting leg that you originally bent) is still flat on the ground with your shin vertical.

08 Lift your chest and bring yourself into a regular Lunge position.

It is important to learn how to reverse the Get-up. You do it by accurately reversing the individual steps and the movements between the steps. In short, you should be able to:

1. Step back into a Lunge.
2. Drop your posting hand laterally.
3. Sweep your back leg in front of your body.
4. Take a seat.
5. Reverse your Sit-up by bending the elbow of your posting arm.
6. Roll back to a supine position on the ground.

If you look back at the mechanics of the Rolling Lunge (page 146), you will see that they are exactly the same, but include the momentum of the roll. In other words, the Get-up can be seen as a segmented version of the Rolling Lunge.

Your body is designed for movement, efficient movement! The Get-up simply formalizes a style of getting your body up off the ground and back down to the ground starting from your back. This approach involves taking the natural act of getting up and breaking it into discrete steps, each of which develops an important component of the overall movement ability.

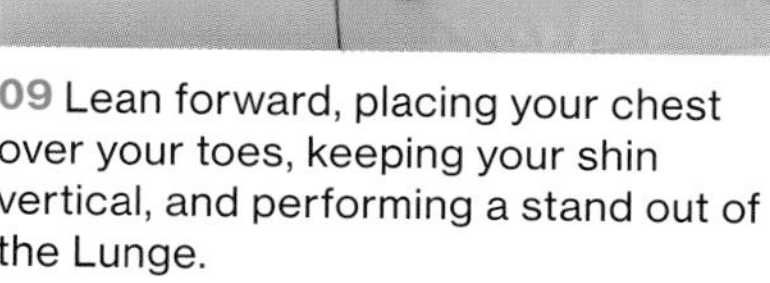

09 Lean forward, placing your chest over your toes, keeping your shin vertical, and performing a stand out of the Lunge.

10 Finish with your feet together and facing forward.

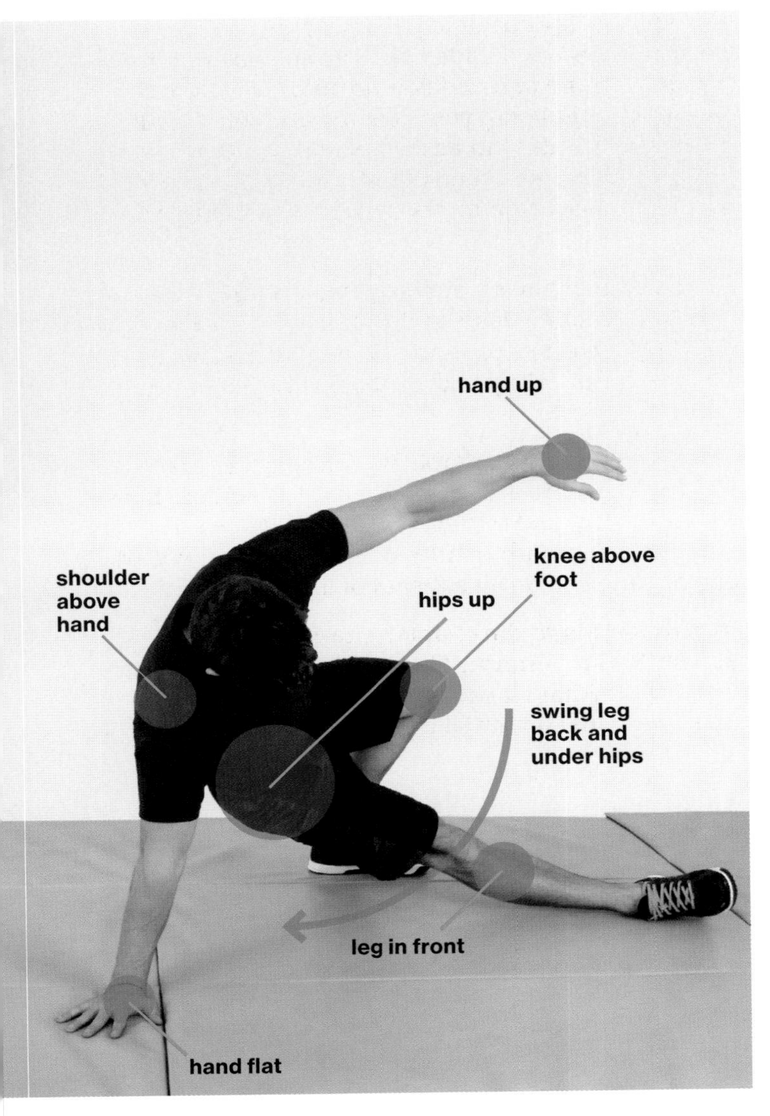
hand up
shoulder above hand
hips up
knee above foot
swing leg back and under hips
leg in front
hand flat

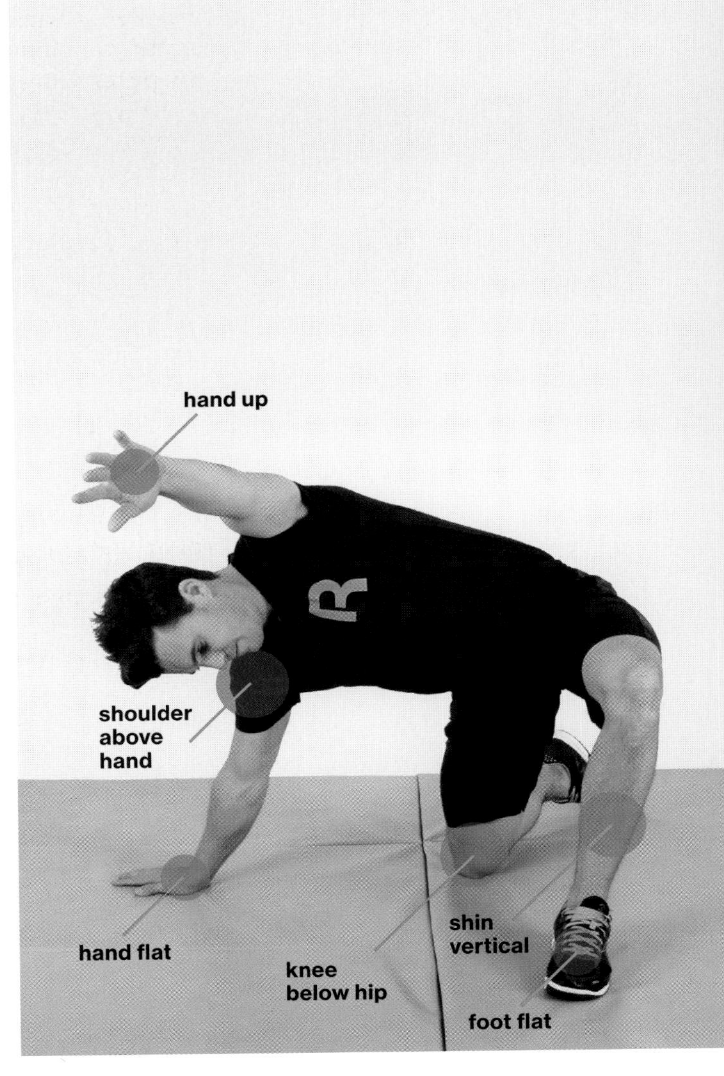
hand up
shoulder above hand
hand flat
knee below hip
shin vertical
foot flat

B U R P E E

Whereas the Get-up is a formal approach to getting up off the ground from your back, the Burpee can be considered a formal approach to getting up and down from a prone or facedown position. You do so by performing a Push-up while jumping your feet toward your hands. Once your feet are near your hands, you adopt a Squat position. From the Squat, you stand, or you jump and then stand. You then reverse the movement until you are once again on the ground in a prone or facedown position.

This movement is found in almost every fitness gym, strength and conditioning room, military training base, and physical education class. I am fond of the Burpee's other common name, the up-down, because that is the essence of it: get up and get back down. So simple, yet able to make any grown man cry.

The beauty of this movement lies in its simplicity. Through a very basic progression and variations on that progression, I intend to show you the abundance of movement ability that the Burpee develops. I also hope to show you the importance of fully understanding the kind of impact this movement can make in all aspects of life and sport.

As mentioned in the introduction to the chapter, the Burpee is a movement that most people can perform. The problem is that not everyone can perform it well. What I mean is that most people struggle to tap into the functional potential and application that this movement has.

box burpee

You can start the Burpee either standing or lying facedown on the ground. I like to begin this progression from a standing position with a box in front of you to limit your range of motion and ensure that you can first establish the best positions.

Most people can get close to achieving the positions showcased in this progression, but some lack the necessary movement ability. This shortfall typically comes from a lack of experience, a lack of strength, or a lack of mobility, the latter being by far the most common. Most people can bend over and touch the ground with their knees bent without their feet coming apart or turning out or their heels lifting, but some lack the mobility to do so.

Some people who are able to adopt the desired bent-over position struggle to return to that position from the plank. This is often due to the amount of muscular tension they must work against in order to get back into that bent-over body shape.

Placing a box directly in front of you and placing your hands on the box instead of the ground should make it much easier to perform the key Burpee mechanics without sacrificing the ideal body positions. You can then slowly increase your range of motion by using a shorter box as your mobility increases. The beauty of these dynamic movements is that when you perform them with the blocking method, they increase your movement capacity and your mobility.

box burpee 01 Stand with a box directly in front of you with your toes up against it: feet together, legs straight, hips in extension or neutral, back flat.

02 Hinge forward and place your hands flat on the box. Your hips always remain on top of or higher than your knees. Your arms are straight, ready for the next movement.

06 Extend your arms, lift your chest, and go into global extension.

07 Snap your hips up aggressively, allowing your feet to come up off the ground and start the return toward the box. Aim your toes toward the box to guarantee that you can return to your feet in a good position.

08 Make sure that your feet land flat on the ground right in front of the box, with your toes almost touching the box.

When people are unable to adopt the necessary positions for the Burpee, I typically examine the movement with respect to the progression principles of position over range of motion and blocking. As shown in the first variation of the Old Man Squat (see page 106), when you place your feet together you are able to block the movement of your legs as you bend over so that your hip position is desirable. You can use the same blocking technique to establish the hip positions required for proper mechanics during the Burpee.

In addition to blocking the leg motion by keeping your feet together, you can use a box to limit your hips' range of motion during the movement. Limiting range of motion is especially useful when you lack the necessary mobility. As an added bonus, the box also blocks the movement by providing a distance standard as you return your feet to the front edge of the box.

03 Jump your feet out and keep all your weight on your hands, allowing you to find balance throughout the motion and while your feet are not in contact with the ground.

04 Land in plank position with your shoulders remaining on top of your hands. Your body is straight, but there is a slight angle. This angle makes the movement a little easier for beginners to hold.

05 Perform a Push-up, dropping your chest down to the box and keeping your elbows right on top of your wrists and your forearms perpendicular to your body. Maintain a neutral global position with your belly and butt tight, keeping your knees locked out and your feet in dorsiflexion, allowing you to keep support on the balls of your feet.

09 Lift your chest as you pick your hands up off the box.

10 Finish with your chest completely upright and your arms and legs positioned to be able to either perform a jump or stand up tall if you are calling it a day.

burpee

In the first part of this progression, you set up in an ideal standing position or anatomical stance. Your feet are together, and your arms are down by your sides.

You initiate the movement by bending over and reaching for the ground. The movement in the first three pictures is the same as the first Old Man Squat progression (page 106). From this bent-over position, you jump out into plank position. When you jump, there is a moment when your upper body is supporting all your weight, almost mimicking a Handstand or Tuck-up position.

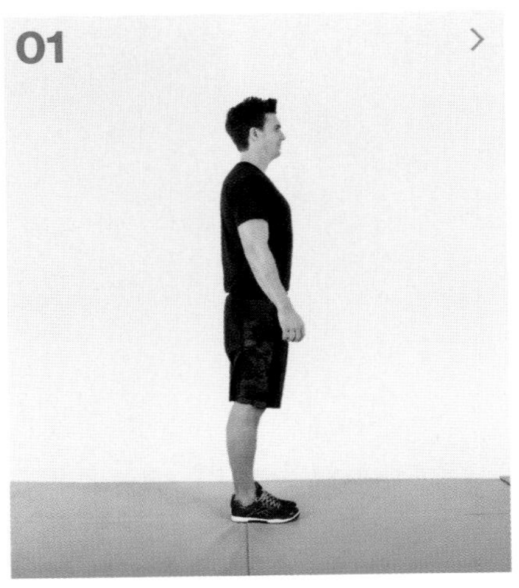

burpee 01 Stand tall, looking straight ahead, with your feet together, knees locked out, hips engaged by squeezing your butt, belly tight, arms by your sides, and back flat.

02 Bend over by hinging in your hips. As you push your hips back, keep your shins as vertical as possible and your feet flat on the ground. Make sure to keep a nice straight line from your hips all the way up to your head, with your neck in a neutral position. Keep your hands and arms close to your body, almost as if you were reaching down for your knees.

03 Touch your hands to the ground right in front of your toes, making full contact with the ground. Your hands should be shoulder width apart. Your feet remain flat on the ground. Your arms are straight. Your knees are slightly bent, and your hips are above your knees. Your spine is in slight flexion, and your neck is neutral with your spine as you look between your legs.

Once you reach plank position, you perform the negative phase of a Push-up until your body reaches the ground. You can reach the bottom position with maximum muscular tension, or you can use it as a momentary resting position.

catch your breath

It's hard to catch your breath in the bottom position of the Burpee, as the compression of your chest against the ground doesn't allow your ribcage to expand. This is important to keep in mind if you are performing many repetitions of the movement for long periods and/or at high speed or intensity.

continues on next page

04 Jump your feet out toward plank position, keeping all your weight on your hands. Your shoulders are slightly in front of your hands or on top of your knuckles. Your chin is tucked in, and you're looking at your toes the whole time, keeping your hips high and your belly engaged.

05 Land in plank position with your shoulders right above your knuckles, your elbows locked out, and your neck in a neutral position. Your legs are straight, and your feet are in dorsiflexion, allowing you to land on the balls of your feet.

06 Drop to the bottom of your Push-up, where you complete the same points of performance seen in a regular Push-up, with your elbows right on top of your wrists, your forearms vertical and perpendicular to your body, your chin tucked in, and your neck in line with the rest of your body. Allow your thighs, hips, and belly to touch the ground as you keep your knees straight and your feet flexed.

From the bottom position, you can perform a strict Push-up to the top of the plank, but I prefer that you bow your body into an arched position, as seen in the Push-up progression in chapter 5 (page 166). I teach the bowing version because it is a more universal form for performing the Push-up.

From the bow or globally extended position, you create a dynamic snap or kip to help get your feet to the ground. By maintaining control over your spine, with your butt and belly engaged, you use the tension in the bow position to perform a dynamic snap. This snap sends your hips up and forward to return you to the bent-over position, as seen in the beginning of the Burpee (page 282).

From here, all you have to do is stand up, although many people add a vertical jump at this point. When performing the jump, you assume a relatively neutral global position, with the exception of your arms and upper body, which adopt a slight hollow body position.

burpee (continued) 07 Lift your chest into an Upward Dog pose as seen in yoga, where you lock your elbows out but keep your hips low, allowing your body to go into global extension. Fight to keep your knees straight.

08 Snap your hips straight up to the sky, allowing your toes and legs to initiate their return toward your hands. Lean your shoulders forward so that they go to the front of the base of support created by your hands and allow you to balance.

09 Allow your feet to land right by your hands, but without passing them, making sure that your feet are together and your heels are in contact with the ground. Bend your knees, keeping your hips above knee level. Allow your back to round, and keep your neck in line with your spine by looking at your toes.

When it comes to landing the jump, I slightly prefer to teach a narrow stance. The narrow-stance landing is not necessarily the most stable, but when performed with a smaller jump, it has less impact and stress on the body and can be maintained even when performing several Burpees in a row.

This approach to the Burpee doesn't necessarily require the arch of the body and the snap back in. A less dynamic Burpee style is certainly valid if you want to focus on developing strength. In other words, less bowing or extending of your body allows you to focus on strength, whereas more bowing allows you to focus on skill. In my opinion, the bowing version fits the principles of functional movement (page 40) better and therefore is my preferred style.

The hollow body position is very common for gymnasts, trampolinists, and divers, as it makes for a more streamlined and balanced position in the air.

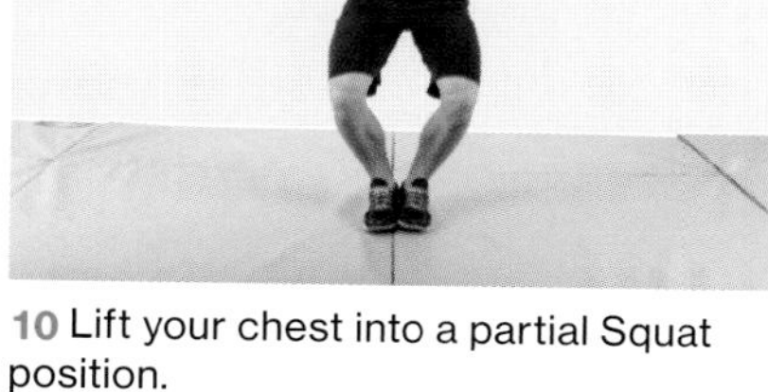

10 Lift your chest into a partial Squat position.

11 Jump as high as you can, keeping your body straight and your arms overhead and reaching slightly in front of you, creating a hollow body position but allowing you to balance. It's almost like you're trying to reach forward.

12 Finish in a partial Squat, landing with your feet flat, taking the impact through your legs in order to slow down the descent and allow for a better landing. Your back is flat, and you create a straight line from your head to your butt. Your arms are in front of you to create tension and better direction and balance.

burpee efficiency

When examining a movement, it is important to ask which style of the movement you would perform if you had to do an unlimited number of repetitions. For each repetition, the load and time requirement could vary. Which style would enable you to last the longest under such conditions? This thought process led me to the way I describe the Burpee in this progression. As with any performance pursuit, tweaks can make a movement more functional. I encourage you to consciously look and think in this manner to find what is useful about my teaching and tweak it to fit your purpose.

Generalities aside, let me show you how to take advantage of muscular tension to facilitate the mechanics of the Burpee. For example, when you bend over by hinging at your hips, you can use the muscular tension created as a slingshot to shoot your feet out into plank position. You use the elastic properties of your muscles to "bounce" out of the bent-over position. This bounce helps you kick your legs out.

descent 01 Bend over, performing a Burpee.

02 Right before your hands touch the ground, jump your feet out and direct them to where they would be if you were doing a Push-up.

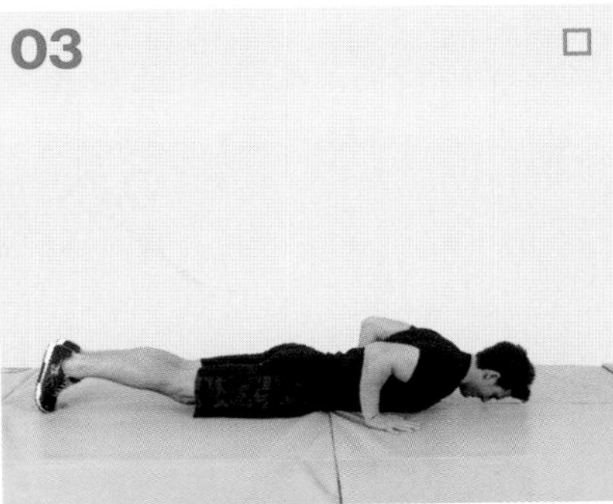

03 Your hands and feet reach the ground simultaneously. Decelerate your body by performing a Push-up descent and smoothly rest your hips and chest on the ground.

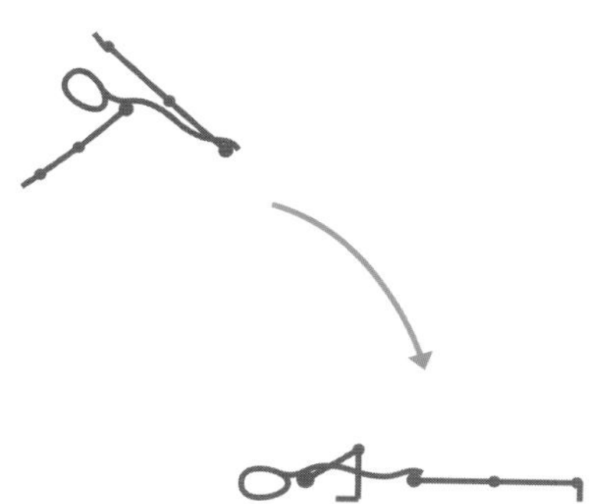

Elena Shushunova, a Russian gymnast who held the world, European, and Olympic champion titles, was well known for her dynamic vaulting and tumbling skills as well as her longevity and exceptional consistency. She was the first person to perform several unique and difficult skills, including her signature Shushunova—a straddle jump to land in a front lying support—in the floor exercise.

When performing the descent in the Burpee, you can utilize a very scaled-down version of the Shushunova where, as your upper body reaches for the ground, you transition through a position where your body is no longer in contact with the ground while you kick your legs out behind you. This makes the transition from the standing position to the bottom of the Push-up much more efficient.

When getting up from the ground, the same elastic properties are important for efficiency. You can use the arch or global extension in the bottom position to snap and, during a moment of near-weightlessness, pull your legs in. This elastic bounce should feel very similar to the bounce on the way down. As simple as this concept seems, it takes many repetitions before most people can master it.

On the opposite end of the spectrum, you could be performing a movement pattern that requires you to move against your muscular tension. The tension creates resistance, which slows you down or, worse, breaks down the movement or compromises your positions, forcing you into non-optimal movement patterns.

Often a good way to tackle this problem is to change your points of connection. As discussed in the progression principles section of chapter 3, you can use points of connection to add stability and useful muscular tension to a movement, but you can also use this principle when you need to remove muscular tension. Changing your points of contact often reduces the physiological tension and allows the movement to flow freely rather than against the tension.

Let's reexamine the bent-over position in the Burpee. I've already explained that you can use the muscular tension of the bend as a spring to help you kick your legs out to the plank, but that same muscular tension creates resistance as you bend over to place your hands on the ground. So is muscular tension good or bad? The key to efficiency is to find the point where you have enough tension to facilitate the leg kick, but not so much that you compromise your hand-reaching position. More specifically, you should kick your legs out just before your hands reach the ground as you bend over.

snap-down

The Snap-down in gymnastics is a technique used to develop tumbling mechanics, and it is the foundation of many high-level gymnastics movements. The Snap-down is the act of performing a Handstand and, from that position, bowing the body into extension and then quickly snapping the feet down and the body into flexion in order to change orientation in space 180 degrees. This style of changing the body's orientation in space is used to connect one acrobatic tumbling movement to the next; the snap of the body plus the release of the hands helps a gymnast perform the most efficient change in orientation possible while tumbling. The snap used to get off the ground into the standing position in the Burpee is a scaled-down version of the Snap-down that takes advantage of the same mechanics and efficiency properties. Instead of performing a 180-degree revolution, in the Burpee you perform a 90-degree revolution.

ascent 01 Bow into extension as if you were performing a Burpee.

02 Aggressively snap your hips up and direct your toes toward your hands.

When you perform this movement correctly, you have enough tension to propel your legs outward and fewer points of connection, as your hands and feet are not simultaneously on the ground when you are bent over.

When performing the movement this way, you may find the plank landing a bit stiff due to the straight-arm position. You need to add some sort of decelerator. You could use your hips dropping while you bow your body into extension as a decelerator, but I think the best style is to drop into the bottom of your Push-up position. You can use this drop as a way to progressively decelerate your body.

You can also find a tension sweet spot in the Burpee ascent. From the bowed position on the ground, snap your hips up and forward to bring your feet to your hands. If you do so aggressively, your body will want to rotate backward. This comes from the rotational force created by your legs coming in and pivoting around your hips.

You should take advantage of this rotational force when lifting out of the bent-over position since it is in the same direction. The most efficient way to do so is to allow your chest, shoulders, and arms to follow the momentum of your body's rotation. This causes you to pick your hands up off the ground just before your feet reach them. The sweet spot here is using the muscular tension to create a useful backward rotational force, but not so much that it compromises your bent-over position or slows your legs' return to the ground.

I hope you have experienced some of the excitement I have for the Burpee, whose essence contains all the principles of pushing, squatting, and kipping mechanics that we have studied in the other Freestyle Four movements. The fact that there are so many variations of the Burpee to which these same mechanics can be applied makes it even better.

03 The momentum generated by the aggressive snap creates a backward rotation of your body that lifts your hands off the ground.

04 Use the backward rotation to facilitate bringing your back upright as you stand.

burpee variations

In this section, I cover three Burpee styles and the demands that may motivate them. Each of these styles has unique features that can help you understand why you should perform the universal style and how it can be applied to different tasks.

The three styles that I present in this section are:

1. Wide-Stance Burpee
2. One-Leg Burpee
3. One-Arm Burpee

As mentioned earlier, the Burpee can be performed in an infinite number of ways, but most people don't really think about these variations and why it may be useful to develop them. I like to use a story to explain how different demands naturally affect the way our bodies adapt to perform a movement and how those natural adaptations give us an idea of the variations we may need to train to handle the various demands that we face.

Imagine you are walking down the street and you see a small puddle. If you can step over it, you do, but if the puddle is a little bigger, you might leap over it by taking off and landing with one leg. If the puddle was so big that you had to get a running start, you would automatically start landing with two feet. Think of how a long jumper in track and field takes off with one leg after a running start and lands with two feet simultaneously. The two-foot landing is a natural adaptation for a more stable landing position. Now let's say that you don't have the option of getting a running start to jump over the puddle. For optimal performance in this case, you would naturally adapt to a two-foot start, the same way you would perform a standing broad jump.

This story explains how different environmental demands motivate different styles of movement. So, based on the task at hand, you may naturally prefer or even perform a certain style.

Specifically, this story demonstrates that having to cover more distance in your jump naturally:

1. Creates a greater range of motion locally
2. Requires you to add speed to increase the distance that your center of mass can cover
3. Makes you adopt a stance that creates more stability at higher speeds
4. Requires you to use a two-foot jump to generate the most acceleration from a static position

The Wide-Stance Squat mimics lateral displacement of the body, such as changing direction simply by lifting one foot.

wide-stance burpee

The Wide-Stance Burpee is simply a Burpee performed with your feet in a wider stance. The distance between your feet can range from slight to as wide as possible.

The points of performance of the Wide-Stance Burpee are mostly the same as those of the universal-style Burpee discussed earlier. The main difference is the position of your feet in relation to your hips.

Separating your feet, which eliminates the movement block for your hips, adds degrees of freedom for movement at hip level. This additional freedom requires you to perform the movement with a greater amount of movement control, and in my experience most people have a hard time with these points of performance.

Specifically, you need to maintain external rotation at hip level to maximize the stability of your hips. Hip stability is important for optimal performance because:

1. The stability of the prime mover is critical.
2. Your hips position your pelvis, which is key for establishing spinal position for overall movement control.

One simplification of the Wide-Stance Burpee is that it lessens the distance that your center of mass must cover to complete a full-range-of-motion Burpee. When a coach asks an athlete to perform many repetitions or at high speed, athletes often have a way of finding this style naturally. In addition, the extra degrees of freedom at hip level impart a sense of efficiency.

Another benefit of the wide-stance style is the acquisition of movement ability, including the mechanics for most types of jumping and landing. This ability can be applied directly to important aspects of sport, such as changing direction laterally.

Note that anything between a wide stance and a narrow stance is considered a normal or neutral stance or, in this book, the universal style.

The key to the narrow stance is the blocking of the hip motion, while the key to the wide stance is the shorter distance between the center of mass and the ground, which reduces the workload. This comparison is important whenever you need to decide which style of Burpee fits your purpose. For example, if you are trying to improve your Burpee mechanics, you should work on the narrow stance. On the other hand, if you are preparing for a competition and want to accumulate as many Burpees as possible in a fixed amount of time, the wide stance may be a better choice. If there is an additional restriction and you need to jump to touch a target during the Burpee, adjust your stance to be closer to narrow or perhaps directly under your hips. Know the purpose of each style.

wide-stance burpee 01 Stand with your feet wider than shoulder width apart. Even though your feet are flat, they are turned out slightly. This turn-out is normal, because anytime you go into abduction of the hips, external rotation at hip level is a natural pattern. This is OK as long as your big toes are pushing into the ground.

02 Hinge in your hips the same way you did in the strict Burpee. The only difference is that you need to fight way harder to keep your shins vertical as you press your knees out. Allowing your knees to cave in is not a good idea for knee safety, and it also destabilizes the hip position, especially when under load or moving at high speeds, and especially for beginners.

03 Touch your hands to the ground, still fighting to keep your knees out and your shins vertical. In the photo, notice how my right knee is caving in slightly more than my left. This is because my right hip is a little messed up from a previous injury.

07 Drive your chest up by extending your elbows.

08 Snap your hips up. As your feet come off the ground, your toes turn in slightly, trying to find tension and stability at hip level. As you're coming out of the jump, you want to get ready to receive in a strong position when your feet touch the ground.

09 Your feet are flat on the ground. Your knees are out, and your hips are slightly lower than in position 3. Once again, this is due to the higher amount of tension and speed added into the return from Push-up position to squatting position. It's like working against something with resistance.

The Wide-Stance Burpee requires you to perform the movement with a greater amount of movement control.

04 Jump your feet back, keeping your hips above your head.

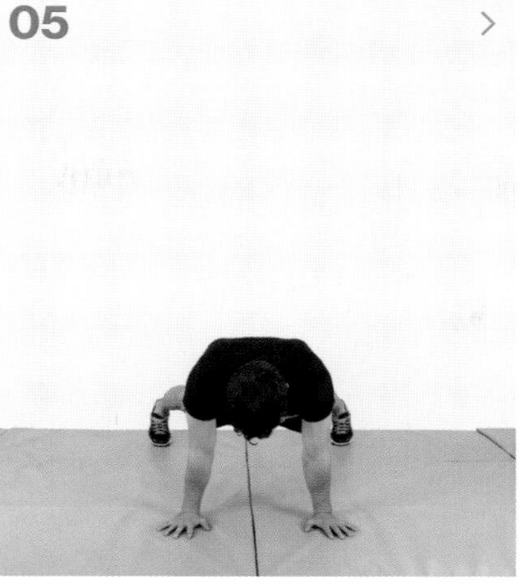

05 Receive in plank position, making sure to maintain a wide stance. The reason you're practicing a wide stance is to learn how to control global positions with different local positions, in this case local position at hip level.

06 Drop down to the bottom of your Push-up, where your elbows remain on top of your hands but your stance has not changed.

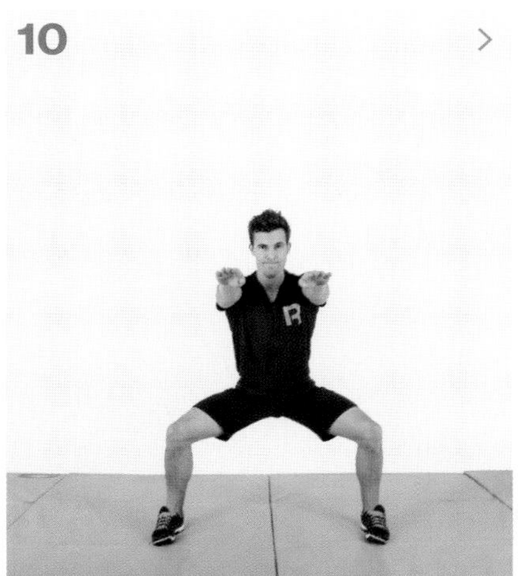

10 Stand tall and adopt a Sumo Squat, in this case a partial Squat because your hips are not below your knees.

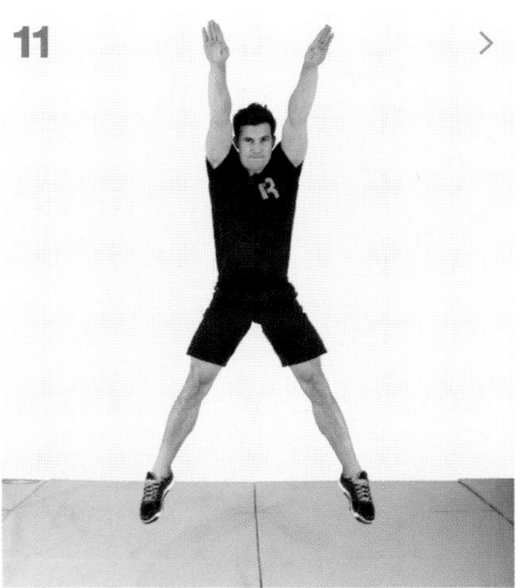

11 Do a high jump with your arms overhead and your legs in a straddle position. Being able to perform a straddle position in the air is good practice for learning how to create better hip stability when you are not in contact with equipment or when your feet are not touching the ground.

12 Land in the same Sumo Squat seen in position 10. The only difference you may see is that your feet may be a little narrower; this is because you have less stability as your feet go wide, and the narrower your feet, the more stable you are. This just happened to be my landing position for this particular progression.

one-leg burpee

The One-Leg Burpee is a Burpee performed with one leg acting as a posting leg and the other leg elevated. This style of Burpee adds a component of unilateral loading on your lower body. Because of the resulting rotational forces, the ideal placement of your posting foot is

one-leg burpee 01 Stand on one foot, with your opposite leg in front of you and elevated slightly off the ground, your arms at your sides, and looking straight ahead.

02 Bend over by hinging in your hips, keeping your posting foot flat on the ground and reaching back with your elevated leg. As you reach forward, look down at the ground, trying to keep your back as flat as possible.

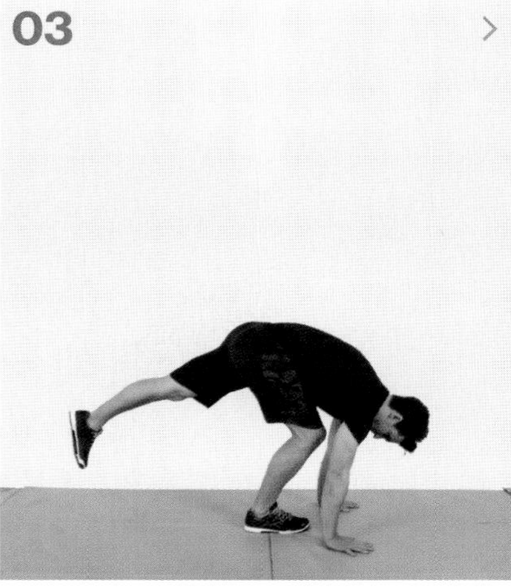

03 Bend your posting leg until your hands touch the ground, keeping your hands in front of your toes and fighting to keep your posting foot flat to the ground. The opposite leg stays extended behind you to facilitate a better position. Look through your arms and try to keep a neutral neck in relation to your spine.

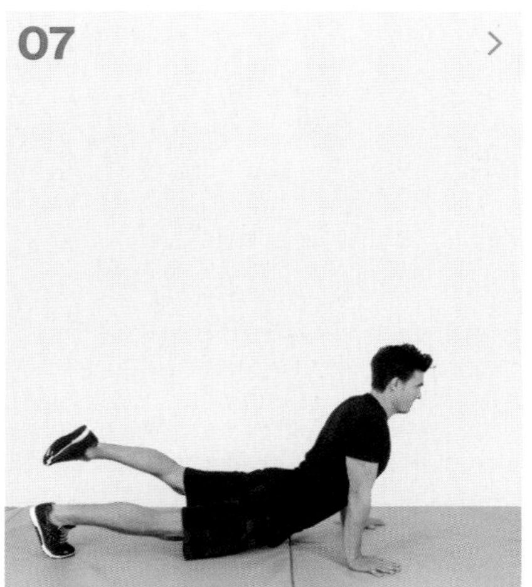

07 Extend your arms, lift your chest, and bow at the hips as you keep your elevated leg off the ground and your posting leg in plantarflexion, fighting to keep your posting leg as straight as possible.

08 Snap your hips up, allowing your posting leg to return to the original bent position as you kick your elevated leg up to the sky. If that back leg were not working, you could keep it dragging down by your side, but the kick makes for a more efficient Burpee.

09 Land on your posting foot with your foot as close as possible to your hands, keeping your back leg elevated. Your spine is slightly rounded or in flexion, but your neck is in line with your spine.

directly under your hips, as if you were performing a universal-style or narrow-stance Burpee. The hip mechanics that you develop by training this style apply directly to the mechanics required for the Pistol and therefore to all the applications of the Pistol as well.

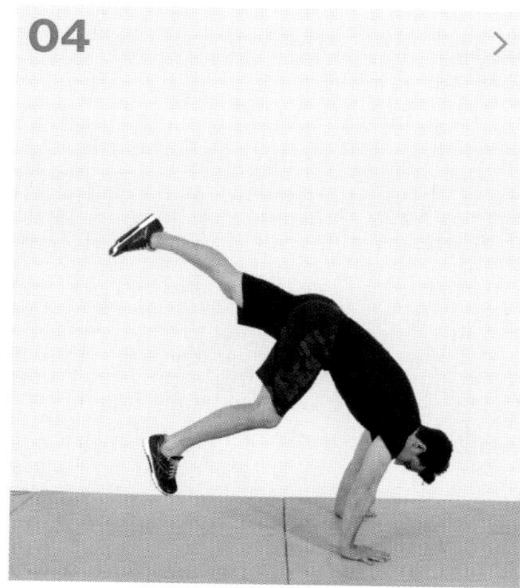

04 Jump off your posting leg, reaching it back behind you as you lean forward slightly with your shoulders, keeping your center of mass as balanced as possible. Your elevated leg is higher in the sky to provide stability and support.

05 Land in plank position with your foot in dorsiflexion, allowing the ball of your foot to take the impact. Make a straight line from your heel all the way up into your head, and keep your elevated leg as high as possible for training purposes. Your arms are straight as in the plank position.

06 Drop down to the bottom of a Push-up, completing the same points of performance demonstrated in the Push-up in the universal-style Burpee progression. Your back leg is off the ground to showcase the one-leg stance for training purposes.

10 Lift your chest, keeping your back leg elevated.

11 Perform a straight jump, extending your posting leg and pressing your weight from the ground as you reach up with your arms. Counterbalance your elevated back leg by reaching slightly in front of you for better stability in the air.

12 Land with your posting foot flat on the ground, your back leg behind you, and your arms in front of you.

one-arm burpee

The One-Arm Burpee is simply a Burpee performed with only one arm. The key purpose of performing this Burpee style is to develop mechanics for dealing with unilateral loading on the upper body. This is the first movement in this part of the book that involves unilateral loading, even though the Pistol resistance of rotation comes from the upper body.

one-arm burpee 01 Start with your feet in a wide stance. This is the easiest and most stable position for performing a One-Arm Burpee or even a One-Arm Push-up.

02 Hinge over as in a regular Burpee. The only difference is that your elevated arm is out to the side, creating a 90-degree angle with the arm that's reaching down. This gives you stability and support as you try to resist the rotation that the unilateral loading is causing.

03 Place your hand flat on the ground, and keep your elbow as locked out as possible. Your shoulder is on top and slightly to the outside edge of your hand, or over the blade of your hand. Your feet are still flat on the ground, and you're fighting to keep your shins vertical and your knees out as you extend your other arm out to the side.

07 Lift your chest by extending your posting arm. Your hand is in front of your belly, almost in the center of your chest, and your opposite arm remains out to the side.

08 Drive your hips up as you would in a regular Burpee, snapping from extension into flexion. Because of your original position with rotation from your upper body, your lower body remains stable and balanced as you perform this snap.

09 Land with your feet flat on the ground, with your toes driving into the ground and your knees out as much as possible. Your elevated arm returns to an almost 90-degree position with respect to your posted arm, as seen in the starting position.

The pushing mechanics involved in the Burpee mimic the points of performance seen in the Push-up. For a better understanding of how to maximize unilateral loading for upper-body pushing mechanics, see chapter 8 (pages 307, 320, and 321).

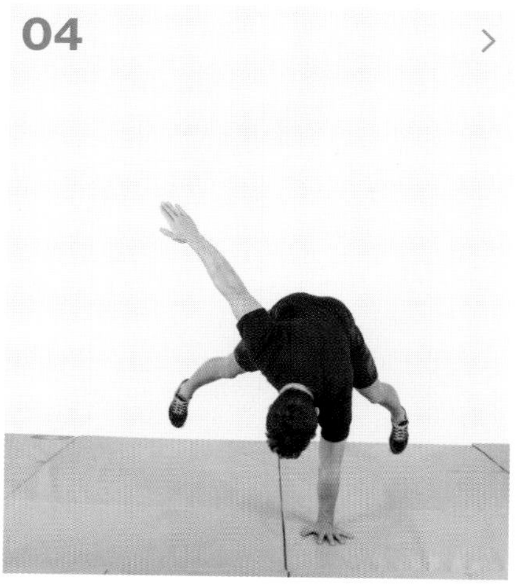

04 Perform a jump to propel your hips over your head. Note that in the photo there is a slight tilt in my hips. This tilt is caused by the rotation required to perform unilateral loading or unilateral movements as my elevated arm reaches up toward the sky, resisting that rotation.

05 As your feet touch the ground, maintain a wide-stance plank position for better stability and support. Your elevated arm has dropped down and made the same 90-degree angle seen in the starting position. Your hand is under your shoulder, but slightly rotating your upper body, so it's placed under your chest.

06 Drop down to the bottom of a One-Arm Push-up. During the descent, your body is slightly off to the side. This angle is normal and can be addressed simply by thinking about the position of your forearm. If your forearm is vertical (elbow on top of wrist) and your body is tight, you'll be able to generate a better position for the efficient application of force required for the Burpee.

10 Lift your chest into a Sumo Squat and, just for instructional purposes, maintain your elevated arm out to the side.

11 Perform a straight jump, reaching up with your posting arm and keeping your opposite arm out for instructional purposes. Notice that my legs are in a wide stance in order to maintain the same general shape throughout the movement. You can close yours for better stability.

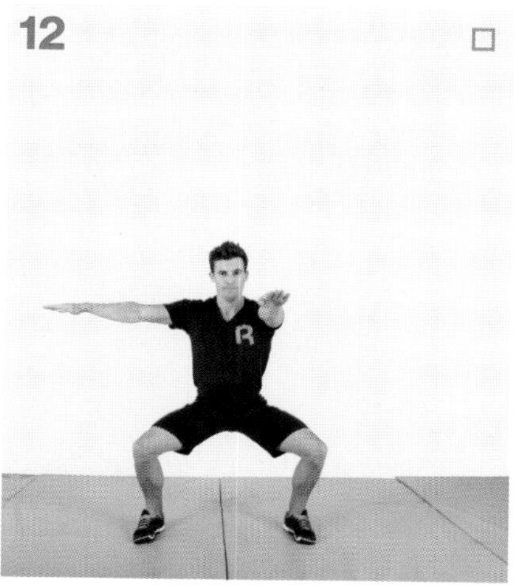

12 Land in a Sumo Squat with your knees out, shins vertical, and chest and hands up, looking straight ahead. Your elevated arm remains in the same position.

burpee

points of performance

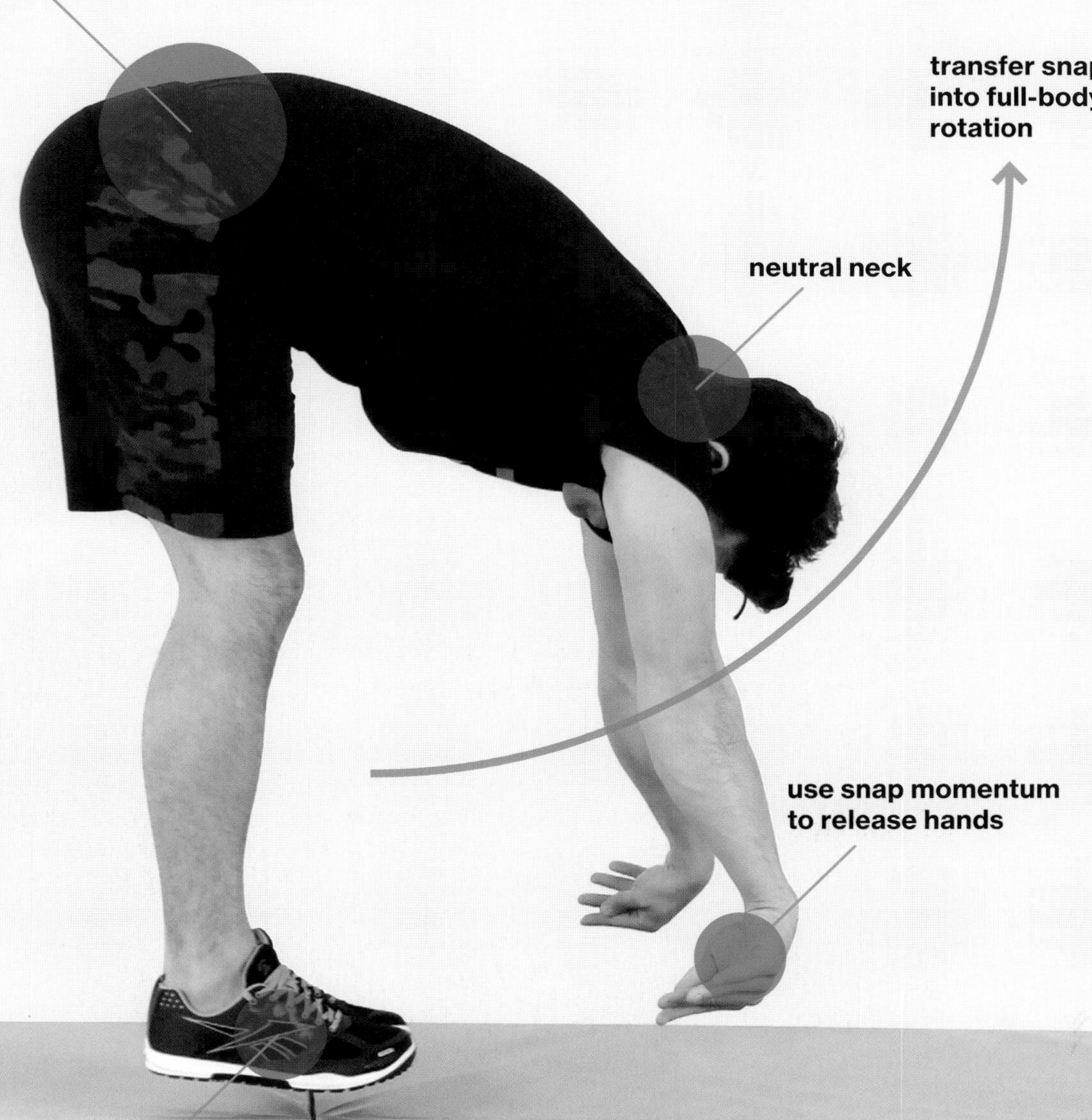
hips snap into
flexion
transfer snap
into full-body
rotation
neutral neck
use snap momentum
to release hands
return feet to
standing position

the burpee & the meaning of life

The variations of the Burpee presented in this chapter are simple examples of how the Burpee can be optimized and later adapted to different styles. When trained, these adaptations can provide different benefits to movement ability. Including the Get-up, I've detailed five different styles for getting up from the ground and back down.

But you still may be wondering, "Why should I care so much about getting up and down?" At my seminars, I like to play a game to answer this question. I call it the Imagine Game.

The first thing I do is ask the attendees to lie facedown on the ground. Then I tell them, "Imagine you were walking down the street and fell down. Now get up." Most of the time, if they aren't too caught up in the techniques they know so well, they start by lifting their chests off the ground. Next, they put their knees on the ground and step into a Lunge or staggered stance and stand up.

Then I ask them to lie down again, and this time I tell them, "Imagine you were being chased and fell down on your stomach. From that position, you have to get back up as fast as possible to escape the danger." They typically perform the same movement as in the first test, but move their feet faster and naturally bring them closer together.

What these two scenarios showcase is that speed affects the strategy used to perform a movement.

I continue by saying, "Imagine you had an accident and broke your leg while you were alone. To get to a hospital, you have to get up off the ground and skip your way there." When they try to get up off the ground with one leg while facedown, they automatically perform something that resembles a One-Leg Burpee. As addressed in the One-Leg Burpee progression, the foot lands right under the hip, exactly the same way the feet land in a feet-together Burpee. This realization usually gets my seminar attendees to realize that the standards I teach are not made up, but are natural strategies created by the body and the demands put on it.

Next I say, "Now imagine you broke an arm, but you were so obsessed with training that you had to go to the gym and do Burpees." Most people try to perform a One-Arm Push-up but quickly realize that the strength required to do so makes it extremely difficult, and automatically default to bowing or arching their bodies in order to make the lift happen. There is not only a bow globally, but also an automatic separation of the legs to create a more stable position from which to perform the One-Arm Push-up, almost creating a Tripod for maximum stability.

The problem with the wide stance is that people who lack experience with formal squatting mechanics tend to lose control of the leg in the landing position and violate the points of performance for squatting, discussed in the Wide-Stance Burpee (page 291) and in the Squat section (page 105). For one repetition, this would not be a problem, but over thousands of repetitions, it would add up and could cause stress or injury.

I continue to beat up their bodies and say, "Imagine you fell facedown and broke both your arms. Try getting up from that position." After a momentary pause, they realize that they have to turn around and face up. From this supine position, most of them automatically sit up and start to get into positions that resemble the beginning of a Get-up, but without the hands. The interesting thing is that if you did have the use of your hands and you were doing a Get-up, but had someone to help you up, you would use the other person to pull yourself up as you simultaneously performed a Get-up.

We are running out of body parts to lose or break, but just once more: "Imagine you fell down and broke both arms and one leg. Try getting up from a facedown position." They have learned by now that they first need to turn over onto their backs. As they have no functioning arms and only one functioning leg, they automatically adapt into a Pistol version of the Get-up. If they have the strength and mobility, they usually perform a Pistol, and if they don't, they naturally adapt into a variation of the Rolling Pistol.

The Imagine Game demonstrates that different demands on the body showcase different movement expressions or styles that best accomplish the task, and that these styles can usually be selected intuitively. My progression principles (see chapter 3) happen to stem from this selection process, and I love using this game to give people a feel for them. These principles are embedded in our DNA.

The get-ups shown in this chapter contain aspects of each of the previous three movements you learned in this part of the book: squatting for standing/jumping mechanics as seen in the Pistol chapter, the pushing mechanics seen in the Handstand Push-up chapter, and changing orientation in space and pulling with the upper and lower body seen in the Muscle-up chapter.

The Freestyle Four movements—Pistol, Handstand Push-up, Muscle-up, and Burpee—are not just a great foundation for human performance, but also a blueprint for learning how to transfer the formal approach to movement seen in the strength and conditioning world to all aspects of life and sport. The ability to train and master a movement in order to maximize its application to other movements is what learning the foundation of human performance is all about: skill transfer (page 63).

freestyle application

If you are square, you can't roll.

The first two parts of this book gave you my framework for observing, describing, and progressing human movement, as well as details on how to do so in order to master the basics of movement along the way to learning the Freestyle Four—which I consider to be the most universal bodyweight movements. This part of the book is about using that basic foundation of movement to maximize your performance in your particular sport and in life.

Chapter 8, Assistance, outlines movements that will assist you in bridging the movement ability you developed with the Freestyle Four to many other movements seen in life and sport. Chapter 9, Programming, presents theories and practical examples for creating a strategic plan to develop your movement ability and your body to handle movement progression within the time frame of your goals. A simple definition of programming is to schedule your training so that you reach whatever movement goals you have in the time frame you desire. However, there is a lot of subtlety to the art of programming, which I think is about balancing the development of a wide base of movement ability with advancement toward specific goals. Finally, in Chapter 10, Lifestyle, I show you how I see movement in the real world and how it relates to everything you have learned from this book.

Photo by Paolo Sanchez

assistance

08

This chapter outlines movements that will assist you in bridging the movement ability progress you develop with the Freestyle Four to many other movements seen in life and sport. It is divided into four sections:

1. Challenging Basic Shapes
2. Feats of Strength
3. Basic Tumbling
4. Accessory Work

This chapter by no means contains all the information that I believe an athlete or any individual who cares about performance should have, but these assistance movements are styles that closely resemble the Freestyle Four, so they also serve to reinforce your ability on the Freestyle Four. They range from beginner to advanced level, and some of them are just for fun or to show you the potential of learning how to move your body through space.

Similar to the challenges to the anatomical or neutral global position that I presented in chapter 2 (page 57), the techniques in this section give you more variations to reinforce form. First, I present the basic shapes that will help you with the Freestyle Four movements. Next, I take you back to variations of the plank and hollow body positions. Finally, I describe movements that challenge global and local positions.

end range positions

Here are several shapes, seen mostly in gymnastics, that help with the desired hip and shoulder mobility that are beneficial for most movements. I consider these end range positions because at a global level you reach end range of flexion and extension, and at a local level you reach end ranges of flexion, extension, external rotation, internal rotation, adduction, and abduction.

side split Position one leg in full extension behind you and the other in full flexion in front of you. Both legs should be straight, with your back upright and flat. Your hips should be square to your shoulders, with your shoulders and hips aligned in the frontal plane and your front and back leg lying within the sagittal plane.

middle split Sit upright with your back flat, your hands in front of you, and your legs as wide out to the sides as possible, ideally hitting the frontal plane.

pancake split From the middle split position, bend forward and take your hips into full flexion. This split can be performed without reaching a full straddle (where your legs are fully abducted and brought to the frontal plane). Your chest should touch the ground, with your arms straight and your spine neutral.

pike Sitting with your legs together and straight out in front of you, flex your hips until your chest reaches your thighs. Keep your back as flat as possible and your toes pointed. You can grab your ankles in order to press your chest toward your thighs.

bridge Support yourself with your arms overhead and in flexion and your legs and feet together in a fully extended global position. Your legs should be straight, and your shoulders directly above your hands. You can use your legs to push away from the ground help you reach further shoulder flexion.

german hang Hang from a set of rings or a bar, with your arms behind you in full extension and in a hollow body position. Your arms should be past 90 degrees of extension at shoulder level.

plank position

Varying the plank position is a great way to develop the ability to resist rotational forces placed on your spine, such as those created by unilateral loading as seen in chapter 4. The added value of these variations is that because you are in a prone position, your lumbar spine must pull away from the ground to stabilize itself as it resists the rotational forces, rather than pushing down into the ground as it does while adopting the Superman position.

plank position 01 Start in plank position with your hands right under your shoulders as if you were about to do a Push-up. Keep your head in a neutral position and your body in line with your neck, creating a neutral spine and global alignment.

02 Pick up one leg, keeping both hands and the other foot on the ground. This position is easy to adopt, but it creates slight rotation at hip and spine level that you must learn to resist. Keep your hips square to the ground.

03 With both feet on the ground, pick up one arm and flex your shoulder until your arm is next to your ear. As you do, your chest will want to lift up and create rotation of the spine. Fight this rotation in order to enhance the skill transfer of this movement to movements involving unilateral loading and locomotion.

04 Keeping your arm up, pick up your opposite leg. The forces now placed on your body will want to send you into a full spin, but you can maintain your balance by reaching forward with your elevated arm and reaching back with your elevated leg by pointing your toes. Being able to fight those forces in order to create contralateral (opposite-side) loading is important for any activity related to locomotion.

The difference between men and women for the middle split is that due to the shape of the femur, hip socket, and pelvis, a woman usually has a harder time getting to a full straddle without having to arch or overextend her lower back. Men have an easier time adopting this shape. Notice how the model's toes are pointed; if she were wearing shoes, the laces would be facing up.

rollover

The hollow body and Superman positions, which I first presented in chapter 2 (pages 54 and 59, respectively), are great for developing muscular strength and especially stamina around your midsection in order to maintain a better spinal position while in a global flexed or extended position.

The movement I present here is the act of rolling over from hollow body to Superman and back to hollow body. This Rollover is ideal for developing the ability to change your global shape without losing control over your spinal position. In addition, it is the most basic way to experience rotational forces at spinal level while learning how to change global shapes.

Starting in a hollow body position with your feet and shoulders off the ground, you simply roll over to the Superman position without letting your shoulders and legs touch the ground. This simple movement creates rotation that starts in the upper body, spirals down to the lower extremities, and carries the lower body over. As the transition happens, the body bows laterally and challenges the spine in a completely different way than the hollow body and Superman positions do when practiced on their own. Once you pass the point of being completely lateral or sideways to the ground, you need to start decelerating the rotation to arrive at the final position with control and adequate form.

As simple as the Rollover may seem, the movement ability that it develops is where people usually run into trouble in life and sport. In fact, one day, Nick D'Amico, one of the designers of this book, told me, "I messed up my back." I asked him how, and he said, "Bowling."

rollover 01 Lie on your back in the hollow body position with your shoulders, arms, head, and feet off the ground.

02 Initiate rotation toward your right side with your upper body. (You could rotate to the left as well.) As you initiate the rotation, make sure to keep your arms, shoulders, and legs off the ground.

03 Continue to rotate with your arms and legs remaining off the ground by getting into slight lateral flexion, especially in your upper body. Squeeze your legs together for better control of the movement.

Yes, bowling can be a pretty dynamic sport, but it doesn't seem so aggressive that it could knock you out to the point where you can't walk or even sleep. Well, this injury is a simple example of someone adding a rotational force through the spine while it is unilaterally loaded and "throwing his back out" due to a lack of movement control at spinal level.

It takes only a little rotational force to damage our strong bodies, and rotational forces can cause much more damage to performance than linear forces. A great practical example that I like to show my students is to have a very strong person grab a lightweight bar or stick with one hand. I stand right in front of him, grab the bar on either side of his hand, and pull straight away from him as hard as I can. It's very difficult for me to rip that bar out of his hand when I pull straight away from him. But things change when I start gently spinning the bar clockwise or counterclockwise—it doesn't matter which direction. Without much effort on my part, the student's hand, wrist, arm, shoulder, and body eventually start contorting in a twisting motion. It almost looks like he is melting right in front of me. And that's when the bar slips out of his hand.

Powerful rotational forces are placed on your body all the time—every time you walk, run, change direction, carry something with one hand, or even shift gears while driving. It's important not just to train and prepare your body to be able to handle these forces, but also to have a strategy for maximizing your performance in their presence. It doesn't get much simpler than this, but working on the Rollover will challenge athletes at all levels.

04 As your chest starts to touch the ground, exaggerate lifting your arms behind your ears. You can facilitate this movement by spreading your arms a little wider away from your ears or simply accelerating the movement. Start extending your body to adopt the Superman shape.

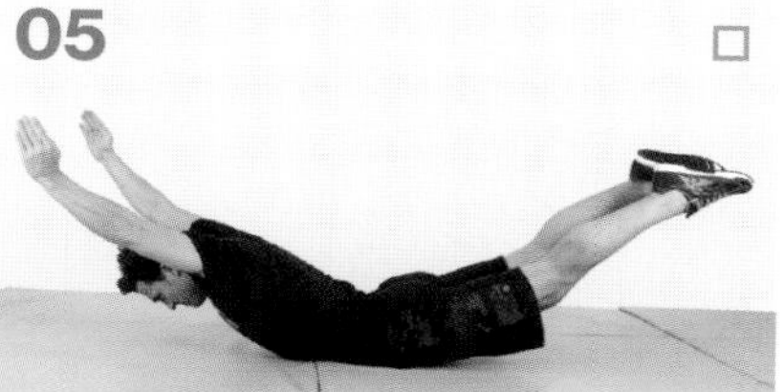

05 Finish in the Superman position with your arms in a straight line above your head, your body in extension, your belly and hips tight, and your legs straight and as high as possible.

sit-ups

The Sit-up is one of the most popular movements out there, and it's powerful in so many ways. Unfortunately, it has lost credibility over the last two decades, being marketed as a movement that will give you shredded abs in two minutes a day, resolve all back pain, and potentially cure cancer. The truth is that, yes, the Sit-up can assist with some of those things, but it also serves essential functions such as helping you get out of bed in the morning. You may roll over (shown above, ironically), drop your legs over the edge of the bed, and perform some sort of half-ass Sit-up, but it is still a Sit-up, and I promise that you would be very sad without it.

If you go back to chapter 7, you will see how the Sit-up and the rotation that occurs in the Rollover are essential parts of performing a Get-up. So, yes, you can use the Sit-up for ab shredding or to help build muscular structure around your spine and promote hip mobility, but its power lies deeper within our need for basic movements for life.

sit-up to pike 01 Start in a supine position with your legs straight, your toes pointed, and your arms glued to your ears. Initiate the Sit-up by lifting your arms and shoulders off the ground and following with your head, making sure to start flexing your spine.

02 As you reach the end of your spinal flexion, start to focus on flexing your hips, with your arms starting to reach up over your head.

sit-up to reach 01 Start in a supine position with your legs straight, your toes pointed, and your arms glued to your ears. Initiate the Sit-up by lifting your arms and shoulders off the ground and following with your head, making sure to start flexing your spine.

02 Keep curling into global flexion, using your arms to reach straight out in front of you. Keep your feet glued to the ground and your legs straight and together with your toes pointed.

The two Sit-ups that I like the most are the Sit-up to Pike and the Sit-up to Reach.

sit-up to pike

The Sit-up to Pike is a way of developing full range of motion for the hips into flexion and spinal flexion. This movement can be performed into a straddle or tuck as well. Think about how this Sit-up can be applied to more difficult and technical movements, such as the Rolling Pistol and the transition on the Muscle-up.

sit-up to reach

The Sit-up to Reach variation teaches you to flex your spine and hips simultaneously. I think it is a great bridge movement between global- and local-focused movements. This style of Sit-up also works great with a weight in hand because it helps you develop a better overhead position.

03 When you reach 90-degree flexion in your hips, your arms are still in front of you and getting ready to reach over your head.

04 Finish with your arms straight overhead, perpendicular to the ground, with your legs straight and together and your toes pointed.

03 Continue to flex your spine, initiating flexion in your hips as you keep reaching your hands toward your toes.

04 Reach past your toes and go into peak flexion at hip level, fighting to keep your legs straight and your toes pointed. Even though your back is rounded, your neck is in line with your spine, and you're not looking at your toes. In the photo, I am a little stiff, and that's why I can't achieve a full pike position. If you have the mobility, you should look exactly like a jackknife.

leg lift

The Leg Lift is a common fitness and gymnastics movement. From a perspective of functionality and application to life and sport, it is important due to its pulling properties from the lower extremities. If you remember the Hollow Rock from chapter 2 (page 57), it is not the forward rock that is difficult to perform (that forward motion or Sit-up is an expression of pushing), but the backward rock, or pull from the lower body.

Pulling from the lower body is something you do all the time as you pick up your feet to walk or run. Even though you do it so frequently, it is common to lose spinal stability, as the pull often takes your lumbar spine into extension. Training and practicing the pull from your lower body is an easy way to educate your body to adopt better strategies to maintain a stable spine while performing lower-body pulling mechanics. One of my favorite movements for this training is the Leg Lift.

This movement, which starts in a supine position with your arms at your sides, requires you to lift your legs off the ground without

leg lift 01 Start in a supine position, with your arms at your sides and your palms facedown for assistance. You can keep your arms close to your body or slightly away if you prefer, with your legs straight, feet together, and toes pointed.

02 Initiate the lift of your legs with your belly tucked in. Think about pushing your lower back into the ground. As you do, your neck tends to want to go into extension, where your chin starts lifting. Fight that tendency in order to maintain a neutral position at spinal level.

leg circle 01 Start in a hollow body position with your palms on the ground near your hips.

02 Swing your legs to one side while keeping the rest of your body as static as possible.

03 Continue to swing your legs around, assisting this swing by flexing your hips.

04 Continue to flex your hips and point your toes over and behind your head as you facilitate the movement by pressing down with your hands and lifting your hips.

allowing your lower back to separate from the ground. Once you reach 90 degrees of flexion, you "rocket" your hips up to the sky and forward, extending them to create a body angle similar to the one seen in the Candlestick Roll (page 142). Accelerating and decelerating your legs with control requires a significant amount of muscular tension, as your legs are off the front edge of your base of support.

For the Leg Lift, think about the transition in the Burpee from the bottom or even the plank position to the standing position for the jump. The leg pull from plank position to the standing position in the Burpee is similar to the lift of your legs in the Leg Lift, and the jump in the Burpee is similar to the extension of your hips in the Leg Lift. Simple, yet really effective.

The Leg Circle is a nice stage of progression from the Leg Lift, as it introduces a simple rotational component that is seen in unilaterally loaded movements or movements that require you to control rotational forces around the transverse plane.

03 When you reach 90-degree flexion at hip level and your legs are pointing straight up to the sky, mentally prepare for the explosion of the final step.

04 Extend your hips explosively, going into a shoulder stance but keeping your toes in front of your eyes, never on top of them. It is important to maintain the slight angle seen here in order to achieve the desired muscular tension, especially for skill transfer into movements such as the Candlestick Roll and the Hollow Rock.

05 Transition the swing to the other side of your body.

06 As you approach the original hollow body position, extend your hips and control the deceleration of your legs.

07 Finish in the hollow body position.

tuck-up/straddle-up/pike-up

These movements are the most popular after the Hollow Rock in the world of gymnastics. They are a great combination of the Sit-up and the Leg Lift and, in addition to developing pushing mechanics from the upper body and pulling mechanics from the lower body, are effective ways to learn how to change shape without losing balance.

I prefer these movements to start in the hollow body position, with the spine under tension, and snap quickly into one of the three shapes:

1. Tuck
2. Straddle
3. Pike

The most valuable aspect of these movements is that they teach you how to keep your balance as your upper and lower body move at the same time. This is important because people tend to move the lower body more than the upper body. In this movement, giving in to this tendency causes a funky, inefficient backward rocking motion. The lack of coordinating upper- and lower-body movements becomes apparent during other useful movements, such as the Dip Balance seen in chapter 6 (page 262).

These movements may look simple, but it takes a long time to develop the technique as well as the capacity to sustain them for repetitions, loads, and time. They never get old, and everyone can benefit from them.

tuck-up 01 Lie on your back in the hollow body position with your shoulders, arms, head, and feet off the ground.

02 Start flexing your hips. As you bend your legs, perform a Sit-up with your upper body as you reach your arms forward.

03 Finish in full compression with your hips flexed, knees bent, and arms in front of you, looking straight ahead in order to maintain balance. You're balanced on your hips, not your lower back.

straddle-up 01 Adopt the hollow body position.

02 Flex your hips and perform a straddle with your legs out to the sides. Your arms and legs should practically align as you aim to touch your toes with your hands.

pike-up 01 Adopt the hollow body position.

02 The only difference from the Tuck-up and Straddle-up is that here your legs stay straight and feet together as you perform the full flexion of your hips. It looks very similar to the Straddle-up, but with your legs together instead of out to the sides. Aim for your toes with your hands and keep the moment of your toes and hands touching right above your hips or slightly in front of them. Balance on your hips, not on your lower back.

l-sit

The L-Sit is one of the most elemental positions a gymnast must learn, and anyone can benefit from it. It is a beautiful yet simple and powerful expression of strength, as it hits every fiber in your body.

You can perform this progression in many different leg positions to progressively increase the load, but the main benefit is that it allows your upper body to support your entire body weight in an anatomical position with your arms at your sides in a support. The L-shape of your body adds a component of stability at the hips as it engages your trunk and pelvis and locks them into a neutral shape under some serious load created by the weight of your legs.

For movement control development and universal application to life and sport, I put my money on the L-Sit.

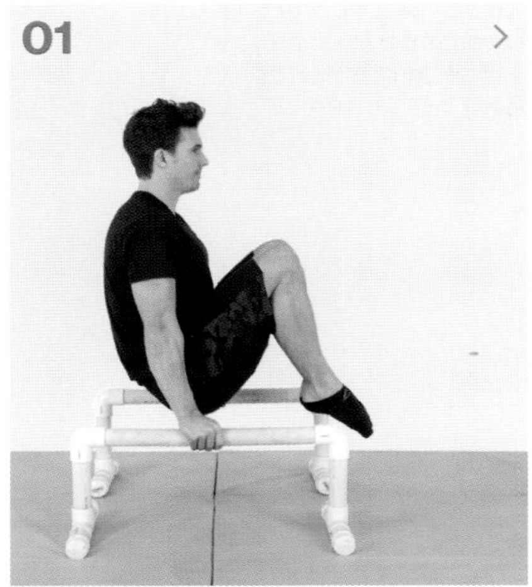

l-sit 01 Start in a tuck position, with your arms straight, hips and knees flexed, knees above your hips, and toes pointed, looking straight ahead. Practice until this position is fairly easy to hold for a few seconds, then move on to the next position.

02 Extend one leg, keeping the opposite leg bent.

03 Extend both legs, making sure that your arms remain straight with your elbows locked out. Look straight ahead, with your spine as straight as possible for better position and balance. Keep your legs straight, with your toes pointed and ideally above hip level.

There are variations of this movement, of course. One of them is the Stalder, a straddle variation of the L-Sit. It is slightly more difficult to perform due to the hip mobility required. You also have to control the degree of freedom provided to your hips by having your legs in abduction (away from your midline).

Josef Stalder was a Swiss Olympic champion gymnast who competed in the 1948 and 1952 Olympic Games. He was known for Stalder circles, a now-common skill that all gymnasts perform on the high and uneven bars.

You can easily cheat this movement by resting your legs on your arms. I am doing it in the photo!

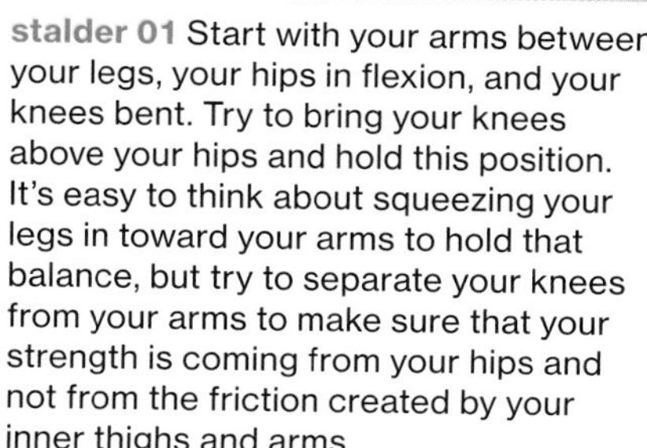

stalder 01 Start with your arms between your legs, your hips in flexion, and your knees bent. Try to bring your knees above your hips and hold this position. It's easy to think about squeezing your legs in toward your arms to hold that balance, but try to separate your knees from your arms to make sure that your strength is coming from your hips and not from the friction created by your inner thighs and arms.

02 Extend your legs, now supporting yourself only on your arms. Make sure that your hips are flexed and your legs are projected out to the sides to create the Stalder shape. Lift your head without allowing your neck to overextend in order to find better balance and proper form for application to other techniques, such as the Press to Handstand.

This section demonstrates how to progress complex movement patterns, as seen in the Freestyle Four, into more challenging simple patterns. These movements adopt body shapes and mechanics that are similar to those required for performing any of the Freestyle Four movements.

This section is dedicated mostly to further developing upper-body mechanics. Because the upper body is designed to perform finer movement patterns, however, the opportunity to develop strength and the capacity to move can be limited in popular sports and usually requires a little more assistance work in the gym. You can use the material in this section as the assistance work for that development.

push-up variations

wide push-up

The Wide Push-up variation requires a progressive abduction of the arms to enhance pushing mechanics. In this progression, the hands go from shoulder width apart to a wider position and then to as wide as you can go and still be able to descend and ascend.

The strict Push-up addressed in chapter 5 (page 168) is a great place to start and make sure that you develop the proper mechanics and principles for pushing from the upper body. As your hands go wider, the principles remain the same, but the Wide Push-up requires a higher level of movement control, as the freedom or physiological connection at shoulder level is less than in the strict style. Eventually, when your hands reach past the point of being able to maintain standards such as elbows on top of wrists and vertical forearms, as seen in the Fly Push-up, the requirements for proper pushing mechanics change as well. For example, the shoulder (primary mover) covers less range of motion than the elbow (secondary mover).

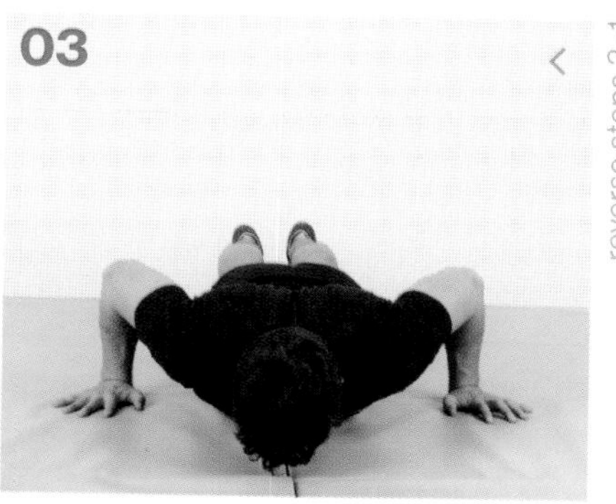

wide push-up 01 Start in plank position with your hands slightly outside your shoulders and your fingers facing forward and slightly separated. Your elbows are locked out. Your feet are together, your body straight, and your head in line with your spine.

02 As you descend, fight to keep your elbows on top of your wrists. They will want to flare out or in, depending on your shoulder mobility and strength.

03 In the bottom position, your elbows remain on top of your wrists as they do when you perform a strict Push-up.

fly push-up

The Fly Push-up is a great way to learn how to transfer the foundation of pushing mechanics to angles that may not get targeted on a daily basis, but do appear in sports such as Olympic weightlifting. During the Snatch, an athlete must lock out his elbows overhead as he transitions under the bar. The angle of the push against the bar is similar to the angle seen in the Fly Push-up. The Fly Push-up requires strong midline stability and a good understanding of movement control at shoulder level. The elbows become the primary mover and the focus of the press.

The Fly Push-up angle also appears in certain throwing sports, such as javelin, baseball, and football, where the arm transitions through full abduction of the shoulder as it pushes the ball forward.

fly push-up 01 Start in plank position with your hands as far out as they can go without allowing your chest to touch the ground. Your elbows are locked out, and your hands turn out due to the architecture of the body. There is a slight arch in your hands because you have to grip the ground more aggressively due to the off-axis loading produced by the angle of your arms.

02 As you descend, your elbows remain inside your hands because your upper arms can't reach the tops of your hands. This makes it harder at shoulder level because of the tension created and makes your elbows the primary mover instead of your shoulders.

03 As you press away from the ground, fight to keep a nice straight line from head to toes and focus on locking out your elbows rather than pushing away from the ground with your shoulders.

narrow push-up

The One-Arm Push-up is a variation of the pushing mechanics above. Here, you develop the unilateral loading by narrowing your hands into adduction instead of widening them into abduction.

Before attempting a full One-arm Push-up, you can start by progressing the strict Push-up into a Narrow Push-up by adducting your shoulders. This Narrow Push-up is also known as a Diamond Push-up or a "Tricep Blaster" in certain fitness communities.

one-arm push-up 01 Start in plank position with one hand planted flat on the ground and that arm straight. Widen your stance slightly to create a tripod-shaped base of support for better balance and stability. Lift the opposite arm (the arm not performing the Push-up) and extend it to the side. You can also perform this Push-up with your hand behind your back.

02 As you descend, the elbow of your pushing arm will want to flare out. Fight to keep your elbow as close to your body as possible. Here, the rotational forces from the unilateral loading will cause problems at spinal level. Resist the rotation and keep your hips square to the ground.

reverse steps 3–1

03 As you reach the bottom of the Push-up, keep your elevated arm off the ground with as much tension as possible and rest your weight on the other hand.

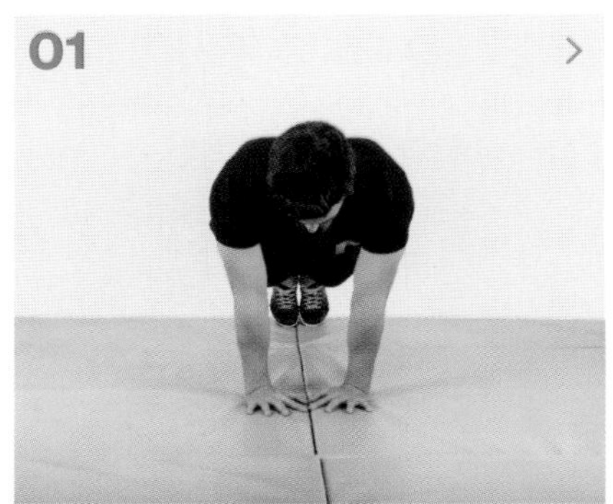

narrow push-up 01 Start in plank position with your arms locked out and your hands right next to each other, with your hands almost forming a diamond (or heart) shape.

02 As you descend, your elbows will want to flare out. Fight to keep your elbows in, even creating a little tension at wrist and hand level.

reverse steps 3–1

03 As you reach the bottom position, your elbows will flare out simply because they need to clear your chest and ribcage.

The Lateral Push-up resembles a One-Arm Push-up but enables you to develop single-joint movements with straight lines, such as Press-outs, V-outs, and other exercises that you may see in gymnastics, such as the Iron Cross.

Again, one-arm pushing is an extremely valuable function to develop for any type of locomotion, such as walking and running, and more specifically for the upper-body pushing required to open a door or perform any kind of throwing mechanics (which, of all the mammals in the animal kingdom, the human being happens to be the most skilled at).

lateral push-up 01 Start in plank position with a wide grip, with your elbows locked out and your hands turned out.

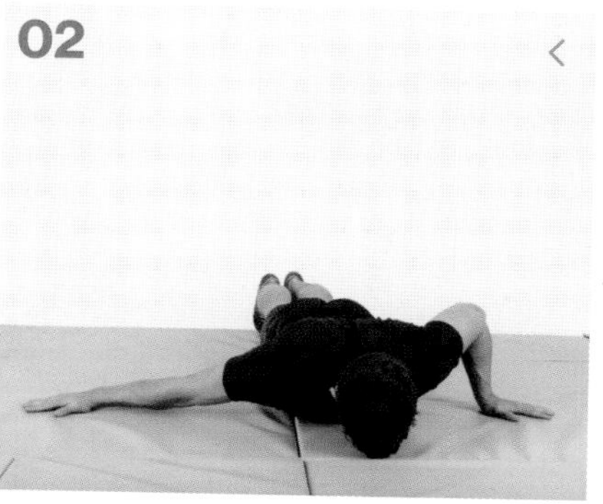

02 Descend to the bottom of the Push-up by bending one arm and shoulder. Your opposite arm (the arm that is not doing the pushing) must remain straight in order to maintain balance and help create stability at shoulder level.

push back to plank and perform on the other side

overhead push-up

The reach of the arms overhead is part of the progression to build up to the Handstand Push-up, but when progressed while you remain in plank position, it gives you some pretty cool movements to develop more specific strength.

The most common expression of pushing with the shoulders in more flexion than is normally seen in plank position is the Elbow Push-up. You see this Push-up in certain fitness competitions, and many bodybuilders perform it to build massive arms. It is the "skull-crusher" version for bodyweight training.

Locking out your elbows is a great way to reinforce their ability to assist pushing mechanics and prepare them to perform serious work if needed. Think about the Get-up and its requirement of locking out your elbows while your shoulders remain almost neutral as you transition from the Elbow Sit-up to the full Sit-up position. Now think about performing a Get-up while wearing a weighted vest or carrying a heavy dumbbell or kettlebell.

The progressive reach overhead eventually leads to a point where there isn't much space left for the elbows to bend. It becomes a movement control exercise for the shoulders and requires more movement strength driven from a global perspective. This movement is called the Olympic Push-up; some people call it after legendary fitness guru Jack Lalanne.

The difference between the Elbow Push-up and the Olympic Push-up is that the Elbow Push-up requires an elbow bend at the bottom position, and your upper arms are perpendicular to the ground. In the Olympic Push-up, there is no elbow or wrist bend. There is only global movement: flexion to extension.

reverse steps 3–1

elbow push-up 01 Start in plank position, but with your hands directly in front of your shoulders and your eyes gazing between your hands. Maintain a hollow body position from head to toes with your feet flexed and your legs nice and straight.

02 Descend to the bottom of the Push-up by bending your elbows and placing them on the ground as your forearms support you.

03 In the bottom position, you need to maintain global flexion (the hollow body shape). Then press back up to the starting position by extending your elbows and pulling up through your belly.

olympic push-up 01 Start in a very open hollow body position with your hands as far in front of you as you can get them without losing global flexion. Keep your arms straight and your feet together.

02 Descend by taking the global flexed-body position into a neutral global position, allowing your hips, thighs, belly, and chest to touch the ground but without losing the straight-leg position. As you do, let your feet go into slight dorsiflexion, allowing you to extend your body and giving you some room and especially support.

03 Instead of pressing down into the ground with your arms and legs, squeeze your belly tight and drive your hips up, returning to the original hollow body position.

underhead push-up

In the same way that you can progress the Push-up into an overhead position, you can progress it into an underhead position, or extension.

As your hands move back toward your hips or toward a more anatomical position, you start to notice a couple of things:

1. Your shoulders take more load and muscular tension.
2. Your hands have to start turning around.

This exaggerated lean on the Push-up is known in gymnastics and calisthenics as the Planche Push-up. This more advanced style makes the pushing mechanics at shoulder level much more difficult and creates more stress at wrist level.

The Blocked Planche Push-up rotates your shoulders even more, giving you more room to perform the pushing mechanics and putting you in a more anatomical position. The difference between the Planche and Blocked Planche Push-ups is that the elbows at the bottom of the Planche Push-up do not remain on top of the wrists, making the pushing mechanics more difficult.

If your hands eventually move so far back that they can't go any farther, it is common, especially in gymnastics, to start adapting the pushing strength into a more demanding position known as the Planche.

planche push-up 01 Start in plank position with your fingers facing forward, your arms straight, and your shoulders in front of your hands. Lean as far forward as you can, or until your wrist flexibility limits you. Keep your body in a straight line from head to toes.

02 Descend by bending your elbows, lowering your body without losing global position.

reverse steps 3–1

03 As you reach the bottom position, your elbows are no longer on top of your wrists but on top of your knuckles or fingers.

blocked planche push-up 01 Start in plank position with your shoulders in front of your hands with your fingers pointed toward your toes, placing your shoulders in external rotation.

02 Descend by bending your elbows.

reverse steps 3–1

03 Reach the bottom position with your shoulders as far forward as possible without losing control.

planche

The Planche is an advanced gymnastics position that is used to demonstrate strength and movement control. It is definitely not a position that I would push my mom to learn, but for younger athletes, it is fun and looks impressive in addition to building superhuman strength.

You can start the Planche progression from the Tripod position that you developed as the base of the Handstand Push-up progression (page 173). From the Tripod position, you can establish a basic understanding of the balance, strength, and locked-out arm position required for the Planche by using the Teeter (page 190). You progress these elements by holding the transition of the Teeter, also known as Crow Pose. Balancing in Crow Pose gives you great exposure to the shoulder position of the Planche while reducing the demands of load and stability because you are resting your knees on your arms.

You can now develop the Tuck Planche as a variation of Crow Pose. With this movement, you can progress toward the Planche and increase the demands on load and stability in your shoulders by supporting your body weight without your knees making contact with your elbows. You start by picking up one knee off of one elbow and progress to picking up both knees—this movement is simple, but developing the strength to perform it takes some work.

01 >

02 □

crow pose 01 Start in plank position, but with your knees bent and resting on the backs of your upper arms. Keep your feet on the ground for balance and support.

02 Pick one foot or both feet off the ground and try to balance on your hands. You have to keep your hips as far over your hands as possible for balance.

tuck planche 01 Start in Crow Pose with your feet off the ground.

02 Pick one knee off of one elbow and place that knee inside your arm, with your other knee still resting on the back of your upper arm. You can opt to rest your back foot on the ground in order to focus on one side of your body holding your body weight. As you get more comfortable, you can pick up the foot that has the knee resting on the upper arm so that half your body is performing a Crow Pose and the other half is performing a Tuck Planche.

03 As you get better, bring both knees between your arms and practice holding this position until you feel strong enough to progress to the next level.

Once you become comfortable with having both knees off your arms in the Tuck Planche position, you can move through the Planche progression:

1. Flat-Back Tuck
2. Bent-Leg Tuck
3. Straddle
4. Full

While moving through this progression, it is helpful to use a band for assistance. You place a band around your waist as you did when progressing the Handstand Push-up in chapter 5 (pages 163 and 175). You hook the band onto a bar or set of rings above your head and around your waist like a harness. You can choose any thickness of band to allow for more or less assistance, but I highly recommend following the order presented in this progression.

flat-back tuck planche Start in Crow Pose and bring your knees off your elbows and between your arms, adopting a Tuck Planche position with a flat back. Pick up your hips, flattening your back and separating your thighs from your chest enough that you're forced into a more neutral global position. This requires a lot of strength and balance.

bent-leg tuck planche Extend your hips from the Flat-Back Tuck Planche, passing 90 degrees. Your heels are higher than your butt, which requires you to lean farther forward with your shoulders. Your goal is to keep your hips over your hands as much as possible to find balance and use the least strength.

straddle planche Extend your legs out to the sides with pointed toes. Keep a nice straight line from head to toes. The straddle makes your body shorter. This is the same way you use a straddle or wide stance to progress a Push-up, as seen in chapter 5.

full planche Bring your legs together until your body is completely straight from head to toes, with your legs and feet together and your toes pointed. Your shoulders shift farther in front of your hands. Keep your hands flat and your elbows locked out.

The Planche could be considered an example of advanced hand-balancing, even though there are people who have developed the strength to perform the Planche but cannot balance on their hands while in a full inversion. So the next movements I'm going to show you are ways of getting into a Headstand and Handstand.

press to headstand

A Press to Headstand or Handstand is the act of getting into a Headstand or Handstand position without jumping or kicking up, but rather by performing a controlled press away from the ground while balancing on your hands and changing the shape of your body until it adopts the desired position. It is a relatively basic movement in the gymnastics world, but it requires a great deal of strength and skill to perform. It's not impossible, but it takes some practice.

The best way to start learning how to perform the mechanics of the Press to Handstand is to learn the Press to Headstand. You perform the Press to Headstand by getting up into a Headstand following a basic progression.

I prefer three styles for performing this press:

1. Tuck
2. Straddle
3. Pike

They are all equal in terms of the purpose for performing them, but each one requires slightly different movement ability.

The tuck is the most natural shape a person who has little to no experience performing a press would adopt, but it is technically more difficult than the straddle. This added difficulty is a result of the change in body mass distribution in relation to the base of support throughout the transition.

The straddle is the easiest of the three shapes in terms of strength, as it allows for the least amount of body mass displacement, but it requires a higher level of movement ability due to the straddle position (especially with straight legs), which, as seen earlier, makes it more difficult to find tension at hip level. It is common to hear someone trying it for the first time say, "I can't even start moving—I don't know where to push to create tension."

The difference between the Tuck Press to Headstand and the Straddle Press to Headstand is that even though your thighs come to your chest in the tuck, they come directly toward your chest with your legs together, and in the straddle they approach your chest toward what is considered the frontal plane. This compression or hip flexion allows you to fold into the narrowest shape possible before you unfold in order to get into the inverted Headstand position.

The pike, even though it is the simplest in terms of moving parts, is the most difficult shape due to the greater distribution of body mass during the transition.

The Press to Headstand is a great way not just to progress toward the Press to Handstand or even the Handstand, but also to learn how to control the Tripod position as your legs are moving. It directly relates to the Handstand Push-up setup (page 171) and is an effective drill for improving the Handstand Push-up in a fun and cool way.

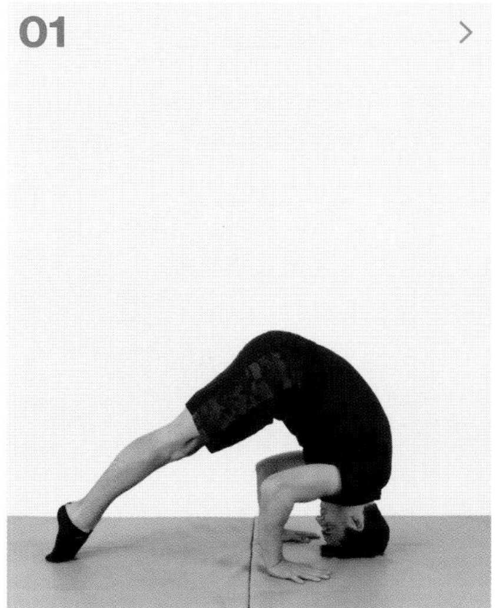

tuck press to headstand 01 Start in a Tripod position with your feet on the ground, your legs straight, and your hips in flexion. Your hands are where you can see them in relation to your head. Your hips are above your head, but your spine is in slight flexion.

02 Pull your thighs to your chest by bending your knees. As you do, you're compressing yourself into a narrow position that facilitates the next movement.

straddle press to headstand 01 Start in a Tripod position with your feet on the ground, legs straight, and hips overhead.

02 Initiate the movement by pulling your thighs toward your chest or toward the frontal plane, straddling or widening your legs out to the sides without bending them. Pull your legs toward you until you can go no farther due to mobility or you reach end range of motion in hip flexion and external rotation.

Note: The Pike Press to Headstand is performed in exactly the same way as the straddle, with the exception of keeping the legs together.

03 Once your thighs are touching your chest, allow your feet to come up off the ground. As you do, shift your weight over your head so that it is above the base of support created by your hands and head.

04 Flatten out your back by lifting your hips. Continue to lift your hips until they are directly overhead.

05 Extend your legs fully with your toes above your hands.

03 Flatten out your back, allowing your hips to come directly over your head and subsequently lifting your feet off the ground.

04 Begin closing your legs over your head slowly with balance.

05 Finish in a full Headstand.

press to handstand

The Handstand has a lot of history, and it is the king position for anyone interested in learning gymnastics. Its importance for life and sport was introduced in chapter 5. There are many ways to get into a Handstand. The Press to Handstand is an important method for bridging the skills developed in the Planche to getting into the Handstand. It's also actually easier to do than the Full Planche.

The Press to Handstand is much more difficult than the Handstand Push-up, but is an evolution from it. There are many ways to learn this movement:

1. Put your head on a higher surface than the floor and start mimicking a straighter arm position.
2. Have someone spot your hips and assist the movement.

tuck press to handstand 01 Place your hands on the ground in a place where you can see them, with your arms straight. Keep your feet as close to your hands as possible, with your knees bent and your hips above your knees.

02 Lean forward with your shoulders, allowing your hips to come closer to your future base of support, your hands. As you do, compress your thighs as far into your chest as possible, as you did in the Tuck Press to Headstand. You should start getting a sense of balance of your hips over your hands.

03 The compression should naturally cause your feet to slowly come up off the ground and initiate the Press to Handstand. If you aren't strong enough to do two legs at once, you can practice with one foot and then the other, but eventually you want to move both feet at the same time.

3. Perform the movement as a Press to Headstand, but fight hard to keep as little weight as possible on your head as the press is happening and, once inverted, perform a Handstand Push-up.
4. Perform the movement with bent arms.
5. Use a band for assistance, which allows you to perform the movement with the band rather than another person assisting.

There is no one right way to learn the Press to Handstand; it is a matter of practicing consistently and making sure that the foundation and principles of all the movements presented in this book are present. This movement will help you get up into a Handstand on the rings as well.

04 Flatten out your back, fighting to keep your thighs compressed to your chest and your hips above your hands and head.

05 Keeping your hips over your shoulders and hands, start extending your legs over your head. Make sure to reach up to the sky and not forward or backward in order to maintain balance.

06 Finish in a full Handstand, with your feet, knees, hips, shoulders, elbows, and wrists in a straight line.

straddle press to handstand 01 Start in a wide stance with your feet flat on the ground and your legs straight. Keep your hands flat on the ground in front of you, with your arms straight and your shoulders right above your hands.

02 Initiate the press by rocking forward or shifting your weight on top of your hands. As you do, focus on compressing your thighs to your chest as much as possible, and try to point your toes to start elevating your hips.

03 When you have leaned so far forward that you're able to balance your center of mass over your base of support, you can start performing the Press to Handstand by widening your legs out to the sides, going further into a straddle. This brings your legs closer to the frontal plane or against your chest, as seen in the Tuck Press or Tuck Press to Headstand.

pike press to handstand 01 With your feet together and your legs straight, bend over and place your hands flat on the ground in front of you.

02 Initiate the press by leaning your shoulders forward and shifting your weight on top of your hands, which will be your future base of support. Compress your thighs to your chest by exaggerating the pike position. In the photo, I'm fighting to keep my legs straight because I'm lacking some flexibility.

04 As your hips come over your head, keep straddling and extending your legs. This is the make-it-or-break-it point: if you don't maintain your hips over your head, you will lose strength and balance and fall toward the ground. Focus on pressing away from the ground with your arms and keeping your hips over your head.

05 Keep straddling your legs and start reaching your legs overhead.

06 Finish in a full Handstand, with your feet together, legs straight, and toes pointed. Make a straight line from head to toes.

03 When you can no longer compress your thighs to your chest, start flattening out your back by driving your hips over your head. Fight to keep a nice controlled lockout in your elbows as you push away from the ground.

04 Slowly start extending your hips as you adopt a more inverted position, getting closer to the Handstand. Really fight to keep your hips over your head, and focus solely on maintaining balance as you extend your hips. Passing the 90-degree angle is the make-it-or-break-it point for any Press to Handstand.

05 After you pass 90 degrees, it's no longer a strength movement; now it's about balance and control. Continue to press until you reach a full Handstand.

band press to handstand

You can perform any variation of the Press to Handstand—tuck, straddle, or pike—with assistance. If you don't have the strength to perform this movement, you can enlist the help of a spotter to get your hips over your head, or you can hook up an elastic band to a bar or set of rings above you and use it as a harness to facilitate the movement.

After you hook up the band and put it around your waist, bend over and place your hands on the ground. It's important that your hips are not under the bar or anchorage point as seen in the other band-assisted movements, such as the Push-up and Handstand Push-up. You must push yourself away from the bar or anchorage point to create an angle that facilitates the shift of your hips over your head.

band press to handstand 01 Adopt a straddle position, with your hands flat on the ground and the band at an angle that assists you in pressing your hips up and toward your hands.

02 Compress your thighs to your chest as much as possible, shifting your weight over your hands.

03 Still in a straddle position, start to elevate your legs and flatten your back.

Notice that the force of the band creates a slight angle in this version of the Handstand. If you went into a full Handstand completely perpendicular to the ground, you would likely fall over. So the slight angle you see in the photo is simply me leaning against the band in order to feel supported as I perform this movement. The thinner the band (that is, the less support you have), the closer you can get to a vertical Handstand position.

04 Continue to bring your hips directly over your head, and start to bring your legs together.

05 Finish bringing your legs together and reach a full Handstand.

rocking handstand push-up

Combining the Planche, Handstand Push-up, and Superman Rock creates another fun variation for getting into a Handstand: the Rocking Handstand Push-up. I like this one, especially because of the Imagine Game presented in chapter 7 (page 300).

The Rocking Handstand Push-up is the act of rocking from an extended body position to a Handstand position. The rock starts from an arched plank position, as described in chapter 7 (page 284). Without changing that shape, you perform a smooth rock forward. By driving your legs toward the sky and pushing away from the ground as if you were doing a Push-up, your chest comes up off the ground and gives you a chance to use the clearance created by the push to place your head on the ground, finish in a Headstand, and then perform a Handstand Push-up.

rock to headstand 01 Get into a fully extended or arched Push-up position with your body in global extension. Keep your arms straight and your hands right under your shoulders, and look straight ahead.

02 Rock forward without losing the globally extended shape, lifting your legs behind you while keeping your feet together and your toes pointed.

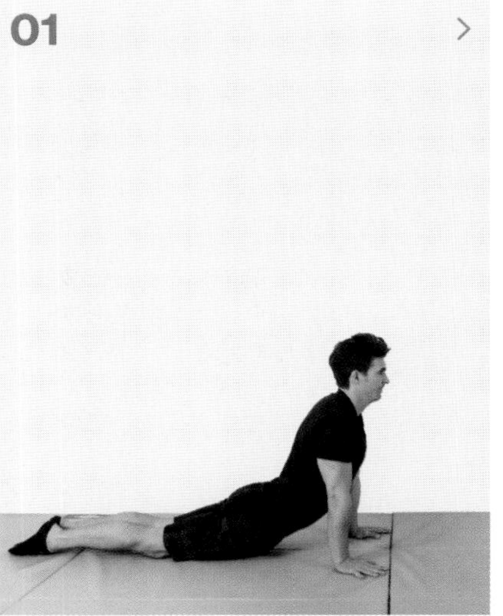

rock to handstand 01 Start in the same position you adopted for the Rock to Headstand above.

02 Perform the same rock forward.

Making it a two-part movement is a great way to progress into the Rocking Handstand Push-up. Eventually, you connect this two-parter into one and flow naturally from the rock straight into the Handstand position, as seen in the progression.

This is a great movement for building pushing strength and a handy accessory movement to have up your sleeve for any work that requires inversion on the rings, such as the Ring Handstand Push-up.

Once again, these positions can hardly be performed without understanding the movement ability developed by the Freestyle Four and mastering a few other positions, such as the Handstand.

03 As you rock forward, drive your heels up toward the sky and start pressing away from the ground with your arms, allowing your chest to come up off the ground. Keep your forearms vertical, with your elbows on top of your wrists. Maintain a neutral neck position with your chin in toward your chest.

04 Reverse the globally extended position into a more neutral global position and finish by sliding your head into the Headstand position.

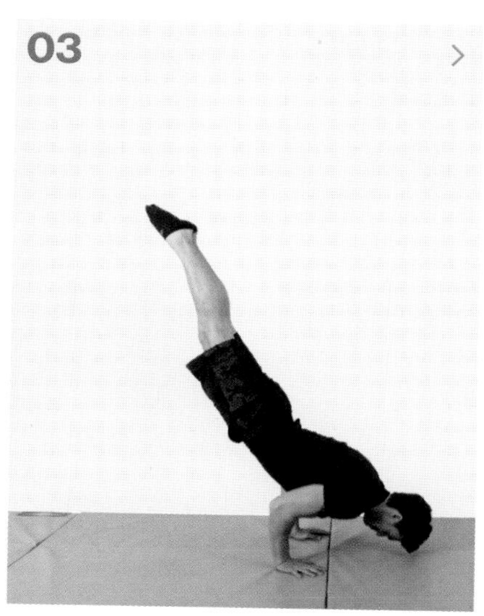

03 Instead of tucking in your chin to perform a Headstand, keep pushing through.

04 Continue to push away from the ground as if you were performing a Handstand Push-up. Fight to adopt a hollow body position for better movement control.

05 Finish in the Handstand position.

handstand

The Handstand is one of those positions that you need to practice. Besides being fun to learn, it can help you build amazing movement control. This book is not about the Handstand per se, but about the movement principles that apply to the Handstand and how the Handstand can affect other aspects of life and sport.

You can use the Handstand Push-up progression to start your journey toward mastering the Handstand, but if you fear getting inverted, I highly recommend that you seek out a coach, and when you feel ready, come back to working on everything I have tried to teach you.

I like to think of the Handstand as an anatomical position with your arms up. When I look at it this way, from bottom to top, I consider the hands the feet, the elbows the knees, the shoulders the hips, the hips the shoulders, the knees the elbows, and the feet the hands. I want there to be a straight line from the hands up, with the arms locked out and the hands gripping the ground. Having a soft hand position is like standing on your heels and not using the balls and toes of your feet for balance. When you are standing, you constantly play with your toes to find balance. You must do the same in the Handstand.

kick up to handstand 01 Start with your arms straight overhead, your butt and belly tight, and both legs straight. Lift one leg up in front of you.

02 Drop into a deep Lunge with your raised leg, making sure that your back leg remains straight.

03 Pivot over your front leg, keeping the shin of your posting leg vertical. Keep the line from your hands all the way to your elevated foot as straight as possible.

04 Continue pivoting over your posting leg until your hands reach the ground in a Handstand position.

05 Push away from the ground with your posting leg while still in a split-leg position. Maintaining the split-leg position makes it easier to balance. When you find your balance, finish by bringing your legs together in a Handstand.

The most universal way to get up into a Handstand is to perform a kick up to Handstand. If you pay attention to the progression, you may notice that kicking up to a Handstand is simply changing your orientation in space 180 degrees by performing a Lunge and pivoting over your posting leg. If you perform it correctly, it enables you to adopt the Handstand position before even you start the movement. Notice how, before starting the Lunge, I have positioned my body in the Handstand position, and as I kick up through the Lunge, I fight to maintain that same position until I reach the ground with my hands. This is a fantastic way to learn how to maintain a neutral global shape while changing your orientation in space and resisting the rotational forces created by the single-leg movement.

When you kick up to a Handstand, it's important to have a distance measured out. That distance should be a body length plus an arm overhead reach, as seen in the photos. To measure this distance, lie down with your arms overhead and your body as straight as possible. This is where you aim to place your hands in the kick up to Handstand.

handstand points of performance

The most important point of performance is to create the strongest and straightest line possible from head to toes, where your hands are your base of support, your elbows are locked out, you're pressing your shoulders up into your ears, and you're keeping your spine neutral, legs straight, and feet together. Keep your toes as pointed as they can be. Pointing your toes creates more tension for better control and balance.

Also focus on your hands, which are your base of support. When you perform a Handstand, it is important that you don't just place your hands flat on the ground, but grip the ground. You want to splay your fingers, keeping your index fingers parallel, and press your fingertips down into the floor. Notice how the pressure creates a change in knuckle color. This pressure allows you to control your Handstand a little better and have more control from bottom to top.

walking handstand

Most people trying to learn how to stand on their hands have a hard time holding the position; either they fall out of it or they end up performing a Handstand Walk until they eventually find balance. The Handstand Walk, though easier than the static Handstand for a beginner to hold, comes with an entirely different set of challenges presented by the constantly changing base of support of the moving hands and the rotational forces caused by the unilateral loading. The most common problems that beginners run into are:

1. Not knowing how to kick up to a Handstand
2. Not being able to walk forward

A good way to learn the kick up to a Handstand and how that skill transfers to the Walking Handstand is to start by kicking up to a Handstand against a wall. The wall acts as a spotter, but you must kick up with control. The moment your first foot touches the wall should be slow and controlled; having full control over the speed is a huge benefit not just for kicking up to your hands to walk, but also for basic Handstand holding.

The other key problem that most people encounter while trying to walk on their hands is being unable to walk forward. This typically occurs because:

1. We like to move in the direction we can see, and in a Handstand you are looking in the opposite direction, which puts you in a momentary short circuit.
2. You try to lead the walk with your hands rather than your legs in order to get your center of mass to shift over the base of support created by your hands.

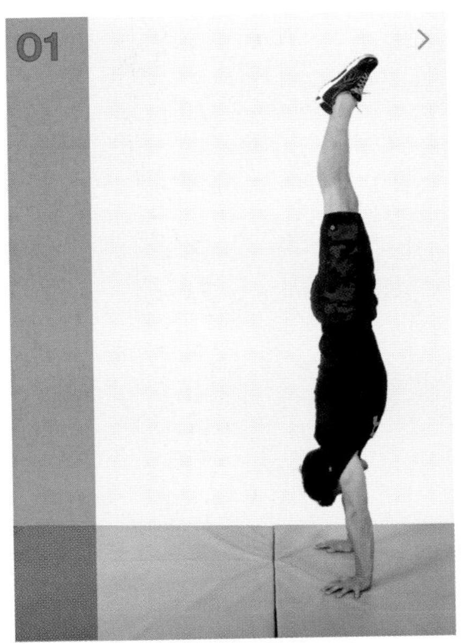

walking handstand against wall 01 Kick up to a Handstand with your back facing a wall that is a few feet away, with your balance shifted toward the wall.

02 As you fall toward the wall with control, take steps with your arms to get you closer to the wall.

03 When you finish in the Handstand, you should be leaning toward the wall with your elbows and arms locked out, toes pointed, and belly tight. The tighter you keep your body, the easier this maneuver is.

Once you can kick up comfortably without your feet crashing into the wall, you can begin to progressively move away from the wall. Start with a few inches and progress until you are far enough away to take a few steps with your hands before falling toward the wall with your feet. The wall gives you an access strategy and not just comfort but also something to aim for in order to progress the Handstand walk.

Now kick up to a Handstand, allowing yourself to fall toward the wall. Instead of allowing yourself to fall back, simply take a step to get to the wall and allow yourself to meet the wall in the Handstand position. You can widen this gap more and more until you feel like you can walk a couple of steps before you meet the wall.

After mastering the Walking Handstand against a wall, you can progress to the Freestanding Walking Handstand. The key to maintaining balance is to initiate the walk with a controlled shift of your center of mass by reaching with your feet over your head. When reaching, you need to maintain a nice straight global line, as seen in the basic Handstand position. The reach of your feet over your head allows you to fall over your hands and take your first steps.

Notice in the photos that even though my hands are lifted slightly, the movement is more of a shuffle.

By using the wall progression outlined in this section, you can progressively increase the distance covered and always have the wall as a target to mark the finish position.

freestanding walking handstand 01 Start in a Handstand with both hands directly under your shoulders.

02 Perform a slight shift of your hips and legs over your head, allowing you to displace your center of mass in relation to the base of support created by your hands. This allows you to take a step with one hand.

03 Continue to shift your hips over your head and alternate picking up your hands to keep you with your shifted weight. At your end mark, finish with a Handstand hold to showcase control.

one-arm handstand

Once you have mastered the walking and static versions of the Handstand, a One-Arm Handstand is a great way to progress your ability to resist the rotational forces created by the demands of unilateral loading while maintaining a strong overhead position.

The two positions shown here are the One-Arm Handstand in a straddle position and the One-Arm Handstand.

You can perform this same One-Arm Handstand by keeping your legs together and directing your toes laterally to the side you want to balance on.

straddle one-arm handstand 01 Start in a Handstand with your legs in a straddle position.

02 Shift your hips over one hand. Keep a straight line from your head to your hips by allowing the leg closer to your posted arm to drop slightly toward the ground. Your opposite hand should start lifting off the ground slightly, but you can use your fingers to help maintain balance.

03 Once all your weight has shifted to your posted arm, you can lift the opposite arm completely off the ground and hope for the best!

one-arm handstand 01 Start in a Handstand.

02 Shift your hips over one hand. Maintain a straight line from head to toes by directing your feet off to the posted arm side as much as possible without losing balance. Your opposite hand should start lifting off the ground slightly, but you can use your fingers to help maintain balance.

03 Once all your weight has shifted to your posted arm, you can lift your opposite arm completely off the ground and leave it out to the side for balance or place it on your hip for style. Now you really have to hope for the best!

levers

The Back Lever can be considered the position halfway between the bottom of the Skin the Cat (German Hang) and the middle of the Skin the Cat (Inverted Hang). Instead of a bent body position, your body is fully extended in a neutral global position parallel to the ground. In addition, this is a static hold. The key to holding this position is understanding the shoulder pushing mechanics developed in the second half of the Skin the Cat.

The Front Lever can be considered the position halfway between the starting hang of the Skin the Cat and the middle of the Skin the Cat (Inverted Hang). Instead of a bent body position, your body is fully extended in a neutral global position parallel to the ground. This is also a static hold. The key to holding this position is understanding the pulling shoulder mechanics developed in the first half of the Skin the Cat.

back lever Your body is horizontal to the ground, facedown. Your shoulders are in extension with your arms pushing down.

front lever Your body is horizontal to the ground, faceup. Your shoulders are in flexion with your arms pulling down.

skin the cat

Skin the Cat combines the challenges to the hollow body position you learned in the Tuck-up, Straddle-up, and Pike-up with shoulder pulling and pushing mechanics with straight arms. The first half of the movement is dominated by pulling the shoulders from full flexion into full extension. The second half is dominated by pushing the shoulders from full extension back into full flexion. The body also goes through a 360-degree change of orientation in space.

skin the cat 01 Hang from the rings.

02 Bring your legs up by flexing your hips, keeping your legs straight.

03 Continue to flex your hips and pull them away from the ground.

04 Initiate a backward rotation of your body by directing your toes over and behind your head.

05 With your hips in full flexion and your body inverted, direct your toes toward the ground.

06 Once your hips pass your arms, progressively extend your hips, directing your toes toward the ground.

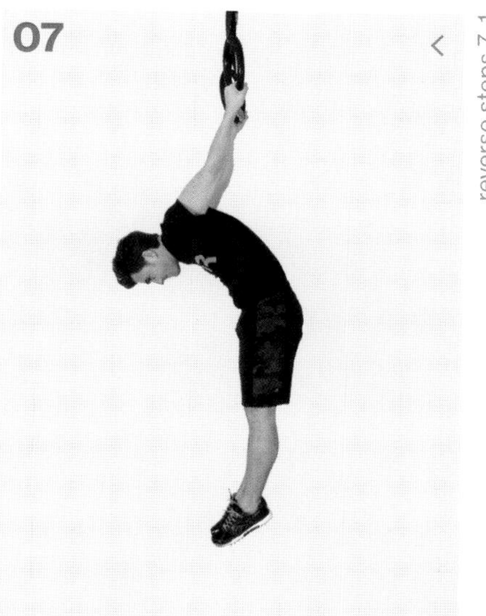

reverse steps 7–1

07 Fully extend your hips in the bottom position. Adopt a hollow body position with your shoulders in full extension. To reverse the movement, tuck your head in and drive your hips up as you bring your thighs to your chest.

This section teaches you some basic tumbling movements. Tumbling is important because it gives you techniques for controlling falls or exiting from movements that involve changes in orientation. It's great for safety and for improving your confidence.

forward roll

In the previous section, the Walking Handstand wall progression was shown to be a great way to increase your walking range on your hands. Unfortunately, when you remove the wall, you usually freeze because you don't have the wall to mark the finish, and you don't have an exit strategy in the direction you are walking. A great exit strategy is a rollout, which requires a Forward Roll.

forward roll 01 Stand tall with your feet together, your body straight, and your arms straight overhead.

02 Hinge over as you reach your arms out in front of you, just like in the Old Man Squat (page 106).

03 Place your hands on the ground, allowing your legs to bend but keeping your hips higher than your knees and head. In the photo, my heels have come up off the ground, indicating that I'm about to jump in order to initiate the roll.

06 As you rotate, let the Hollow Rock carry over the momentum to drive you over so that you can stand up as you did in the Candlestick Roll (page 142).

The Forward Roll is a full 360-degree revolution performed in a forward motion. This is an important movement to learn, as it may be a useful exit strategy from a Handstand if you end up shifting too much of your weight forward.

Notice that when your hands reach the ground, the motion is the same as the negative phase of a Handstand Push-up. If your pushing mechanics, as seen in the Push-up section of chapter 5 (page 157), are off, a common fault is not reaching enough and not directing your shoulders in the right direction, causing you to lose control of the rotation as your center of mass remains on the starting side of your base of support rather than traveling over it. This is an example of how the Forward Roll requires the same pushing mechanics addressed in the Handstand Push-up chapter. The Push-up performed during the Forward Roll also looks more like the vertical Push-up seen in the Handstand Push-up than a horizontal Push-up. You can take this vertical orientation further as you progress to the Handstand Forward Roll.

04 Perform a jump, sending your hips over your head. Bend your arms slightly, adopting a position similar to a Handstand Push-up at shoulder level.

05 Transfer the momentum into a roll, tuck in your chin, and allow your elbows to come past your hands. It's important to adopt a hollow body position here and to fight to maintain straight legs for as long as possible.

07 As you finish the Hollow Rock, drive your heels to the ground, placing your feet flat on the ground in order to get your hips up. Reach your arms in front of you, allowing your hips to come up off the ground, and plant your feet firmly.

08 Start standing, lifting your chest to perform a proper Squat.

09 Finish in a full standing position with your arms overhead.

handstand forward roll

The Handstand Forward Roll is the act of performing a Handstand directly into a Forward Roll. You begin by performing the negative phase or descent of a Handstand Push-up until your head is about to touch the ground, and then you simply tuck your chin into your chest and perform the rolling mechanics outlined for the Forward Roll.

For advanced athletes, the Handstand Push-up seen in photos 1 and 2 is not required. You can simply drive your heels over your head, fall out of the Handstand, and adopt a more hollow body position in order to perform the roll, where the arm bend is no longer required.

This movement is a great exit strategy for any Handstand; plus, it's an effective way of developing a formal approach to forward rolling mechanics.

handstand forward roll 01 Start in a Handstand position.

02 Initiate the forward roll by starting to bend your arms as if you were performing a Handstand Push-up. As your hands are about to touch the ground, tuck in your chin, allowing yourself to adopt a more hollow body position, which will assist in the rotation.

03 Continue to perform your roll as you progress from the Handstand position into a piked roll.

04 Bend your legs into a tuck position in order to start directing your feet toward the ground. This knee bend increases your speed, shortens your body, and allows you to place your feet on the ground.

05 Perform an aggressive Sit-up.

06 Transition into a deep Squat with your feet together, pressing into the ground to start standing.

07 Finish completely standing with your arms overhead and fully extended.

As with any movement, it's beneficial to learn how to reverse the Handstand Forward Roll. When developing rolling mechanics, I believe it is important to learn the Backward Roll and the Back Extension Roll.

backward roll

If you go back to the Hollow Rock and start increasing the range of motion for it, the Candlestick Roll will eventually happen. But the Candlestick Roll (page 142) is a form of rolling mechanics that focuses mostly on the forward motion for completion rather than the backward motion. In this progression, an easy drill to bridge the gap into the Backward Roll is to perform a Candlestick Roll with your hands flat on the ground in the shoulder stance, flexing your shoulders and elbows until you can place your hands flat on the ground and close to your shoulders.

This drill helps you prepare to adopt the position required to push your body away from the ground in order to continue the backward rotation and allow your head to clear the ground and your hips to transition over your head. The pushing mechanics performed during the Backward Roll are very similar to those in the Handstand Push-up; the only difference is that the shoulder range of motion in flexion is greater in the Backward Roll. This position and the motion required to get your hands to the ground is similar to the motion seen in Olympic weightlifting while performing a Clean. In the Clean, the arms must flex and spring around the bar as the weight comes up in order for the athlete to adopt a rack position with the barbell on his shoulders and set up for the next movement.

Once you have mastered this movement and can perform it with control, without your head acting as a base of support during the transition, instead of simply placing your legs on the ground, you can use the transition position as a setup for a Handstand Push-up and progress the Backward Roll to a Back Extension Roll.

backward roll drill 01 Start in the beginning of the Hollow Rock Sit-up position or Forward Rock.

02 Rock backward as you would in a normal Hollow Rock, but with more speed, which you are going to use to lift your hips off the ground.

03 Place your hands flat on the ground next to your ears as you quickly lift your hips off the ground and point your toes toward the sky.

backward roll 01 Stand tall with your arms by your ears, your body straight, and your feet together.

02 Perform a partial Squat, maximizing hip flexion as you push your hips back behind you. You want to feel like you are falling off the back edge of your base of support.

03 As you reach this moment, place your hips gently on the ground as you adopt a rocking position. In this position, your back is rounded and your hips are far from your feet, allowing you to create more momentum.

04 Perform the backward rock of a Hollow Rock with your legs bent.

05 Quickly place your hands on the ground, performing the same Backward Roll drill explained earlier. Your elbows remain on top of your wrists, and you now have enough room to push away from the ground and ensure that your head doesn't touch.

06 Keeping your chin tucked in, press away from the ground, almost performing a Handstand Push-up or the stance of a Handstand Push-up, in order to clear your head and continue the roll. Keep your legs in flexion to carry that momentum and make this movement a little easier.

07 Place your feet on the ground with your hands remaining on the ground. This is similar to the Old Man Squat Touch position (page 107).

08 Lift your hands and start standing.

09 Finish with your feet together and your arms overhead.

back extension roll

The Back Extension Roll is the act of performing a Backward Roll into a Handstand Push-up, where the transition position for the Backward Roll acts as the starting position for the Handstand Push-up. In this position, your hands are on the ground, your spine is in flexion, and your legs are flexed, as seen in the bottom of the kipping motion for a Handstand Push-up. This is an opportunity to bring the Kipping Handstand Push-up mechanics into play and perform the kick of your legs straight up toward the sky followed by an arm extension until you reach a full Handstand.

Here are a couple of things to keep in mind during the Back Extension Roll:

back extension roll 01 Stand with your arms overhead.

02 Perform a Squat by pressing your hips back, just as you would for a Backward Roll.

1. Keep your feet and legs together throughout the entire motion for the best control, direction, and application of the kipping mechanics.
2. Due to the backward rotation, you must perform the kip of your legs at a slight forward angle, as seen in the Candlestick Roll, in order to find balance in the Handstand. This allows extension to occur as the momentum created by the roll pulls your body's center of mass onto the center of your base of support.

The same way the Backward Roll mechanics for the arms mimic the Olympic weightlifting movement pattern seen in the Clean, the kick up to Handstand during the Back Extension Roll resembles the movement required for the Jerk, which is the act of jumping a barbell from a shoulder position to an overhead position.

03 As you rock back, reach farther back with your hips than you would for a Backward Roll.

04 Continue to roll backward with your legs bent, and start driving your hands to the ground.

05 Once your hands reach the ground, start pushing away from the ground to clear your head.

06 Extend your hips and legs explosively toward the sky as if you were performing a Kipping Handstand Push-up.

07 Finish by fully extending your arms and holding the Handstand position.

shoulder roll

Once you have developed and feel comfortable with the Forward and Backward Roll, it's easier to understand the mechanics required to perform a Shoulder Roll, which is a more natural adaptation of rolling mechanics seen in martial arts and the art of freerunning.

The Shoulder Roll is the act of performing a Forward or Backward Roll as seen in the previous section, but over just one shoulder, clearing the head and neck laterally while rolling diagonally across the back.

The Shoulder Roll is commonly performed in a forward motion, as it is a natural adaptation of falling forward, rolling over, and saving the body from injury.

Just as the Candlestick Roll is a great way to develop the Forward and Backward Roll, the Shoulder Roll can use the Rolling Lunge as a progression. The best way to learn the beginning of the Shoulder Roll is to start in a Lunge position and initiate the movement by dropping the arm opposite your posting leg toward the ground laterally and slightly in front of you, while your other arm reaches in front of your body and internally rotates, with your fingers pointing toward the opposite hand or your back leg. Once your

shoulder roll 01 Start in a Lunge position. In the photo I have my left leg in front of me, which means that I'm going to roll over my left shoulder to my right hip. If you have your right leg in front of you, you will roll over your right shoulder to your left hip.

02 Place your right hand down to your side and reach forward with your left hand to initiate the roll. The shoulder of your reaching arm should be rotated so that your fingers are pointing toward you.

03 Pivot over your front leg by pushing your hips over your head with your back leg. Tuck your head in as if you were trying to look under your legs.

hands reach the ground, you must start to pick up your hips by pushing away from your front and back legs. As your hips come up, you tuck your chin in and off to the side as if you were looking behind you under your first arm. As the back of your shoulder reaches the ground, allow your body to follow the motion, which naturally tends to go across the back in a diagonal fashion. If you are rolling over your right shoulder, the roll finishes toward your left hip. This diagonal motion puts mostly soft tissue in contact with the ground, avoiding bone bruising and protecting your spine from impact. The finish is performed exactly like the Rolling Lunge, where you make a figure-four across with your back leg by flexing your knee and placing it behind the knee pit of your posting leg for the Lunge.

This roll is an effective way to develop rolling mechanics that can save you a lot of pain if you happen to fall.

Everyone should have rolling mechanics in their skill arsenal for life and sport—especially athletes who play team sports, which involve a fair amount of falling and getting back up as quick and safely as possible. Rolling isn't just for safety and better strategies for falling and getting up, but also enables you to perform cool movements such as the famous Bruce Lee Get-up and the Backflip.

04 Continue the roll into the figure-four leg position seen in Rolling Lunge (page 146).

05 Plant your right hand on the ground as your body pivots over the leg that started behind you (your right leg).

06 Plant your front (left) leg and finish in a Lunge position.

kip-up

There isn't much to say about this movement other than it is rad. It relates directly to the transition seen in the Kipping Muscle-up in chapter 6 (page 264).

The starting position looks exactly like the Candlestick Roll progression from the Backward Roll. The kick-up is the same motion that you perform for the Back Extension Roll, but with an exaggerated forward motion and direction of the legs. The heel drive by flexing the knees is exactly the same as the heel drive seen in the Muscle-up transition. The turnover for the forward rotation is the same motion performed in the Sit-up progression for the Muscle-up, not to mention the Candlestick Roll up. Finally, the landing is similar to the jumping and landing in the Burpee.

In this progression, my landing shape mimics the bottom of the Ring Dip seen in the Muscle-up progression, but you can adopt any shape you want. If you want a formal approach, the preferred landing position is the partial Squat seen in the landing portion of the Burpee.

kip-up progression 01 Start in a supine position with your hands flat on the ground. Flex your hips so that your legs are off the ground and pointing straight to the sky.

02 Continue to lift your hips, and reach with your toes over and past your head.

03 Without moving your hands, extend your hips violently up to the sky, performing a shoulder stance but allowing yourself to fall forward.

04 Bend your legs halfway through the kick-out and direct them to the ground. Maintain tension in your lower back by squeezing your butt.

05 Finish in a bridge. You need to have your hips off the ground in extension to maximize this effort and be able to perform the Kip-up.

kip-up 01 Start in a supine position with your feet together. Place your hands on the ground right by your head, adopting the same position as for the Backward Roll. Keep your elbows on top of your wrists and pressed in toward your head. Your belly should be tight and your legs straight.

03 Pick your legs up off the ground, flexing your hips without losing the position you adopted with your hands.

03 Flex your hips completely, reaching with your toes past your face.

04 Extend your hips violently up and forward, allowing you to create the same shoulder stance seen in the Candlestick Roll, Backward Roll, and Back Extension Roll.

05 Continue to drive your feet forward, almost getting into a bridge position with your feet off the ground. Continue to drive your heels toward the ground as you bend your legs, while violently pushing away from the ground with your arms.

06 While airborne, perform a fast Sit-up by driving your chest toward your thighs. As your feet touch the ground, you should be in the bottom of a Squat. Your arms could be in a Dip position to mimic the performance of a Muscle-up. This makes this movement a great drill to learn the Muscle-up transition with the kip.

07 Finish standing tall.

standing backtuck

The Standing Backtuck is a common movement in gymnastics and other acrobatic arts. It is another great movement that expresses the potential of the human body and shows how things that seem impossible can become possible.

The greatest thing about the Standing Backtuck is that it isn't that complicated. If you have the proper movement foundation, basic strength and skill, a good coach, and a good environment in which to learn it, it is achievable.

The Standing Backtuck is a vertical jump performed with a slight backward lean, followed by a knees-through-elbows (check the accessory work section on page 360), and finishing with a landing position as seen in the Burpee chapter and squatting mechanics as seen in the Pistol chapter.

standing backtuck 01 Stand with your arms straight overhead and your body in a straight line.

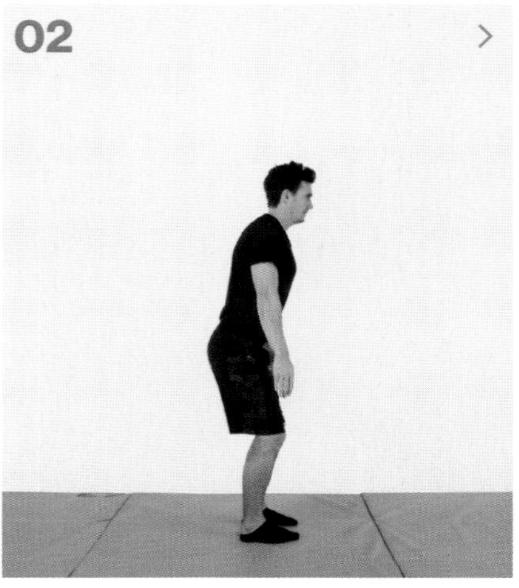

02 Start dipping into a partial Squat as you drop your hands down to your sides.

03 Allow your arms to swing back as you reach the partial Squat position, but with peak hip tension as your push your hips back. Try to keep your shins as vertical as possible, keep your chest up, and look straight ahead.

If you want it, you can have it. Be smart and take a calculated risk!

04 Explosively perform a straight jump as you reach up and back with your shoulders, creating a slight angle and slight global extension to facilitate the rotation.

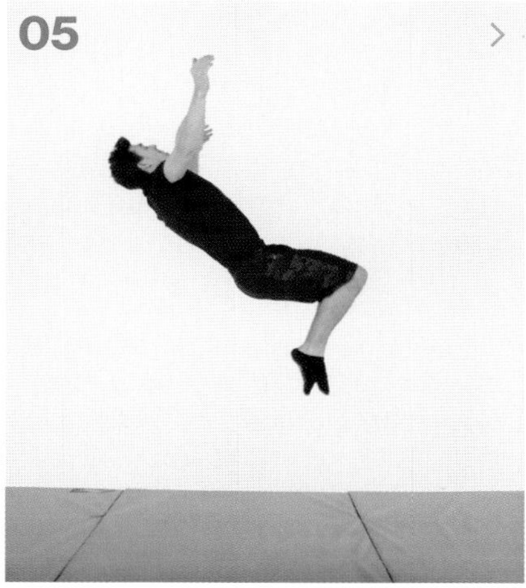

05 At this point, you are weightless. Perform the fastest Knees to Elbows you've ever done, pulling your legs off the ground and keeping your shoulders where you left them when you jumped.

06 Keep your hands and arms where they are as you pull your hips toward them, adopting the tuck position. You're not pulling your hands to your legs; you're pulling your legs to your hands. Grab your shins to facilitate the rotation.

07 Continue to rotate until your hips pass your head and you see the ground. Let go of your shins and start opening up your legs and hips, preparing for landing.

08 Stick the landing and adopt a partial Squat with your arms in front of you, absorbing all the energy by flexing your hips and knees.

09 Finish by standing tall, mimicking the starting position.

As discussed in my definition of functional movement in chapter 1 (page 40), I focus mostly on the longest-lasting versions of the most useful movement patterns. But, depending on your goals, you can often benefit from training on less-common movement patterns, such as the ones seen in this chapter, in order to focus on certain holes you have discovered in your movement ability.

In the feats of strength section of this chapter (page 318), you progressed the Push-up by moving your arms from a neutral position at midrange of motion for the shoulders to an abducted, flexed, or extended position. What eventually happens is that you run out of room to keep widening your arms. When you reach end range of motion, you can change the movement by changing your orientation in space and adding an external weight or adding equipment, which is the focus of this section.

These movements are just ways of adopting a simpler body shape (see the S-C-S progression method on page 91) while continuing to develop the pushing mechanics. The beauty of having an external load is that you can progressively develop these positions and build strength throughout different ranges of motion according to your own stage of development. In addition to adding external loads in this section, I will address different variations of Pull-ups and hip flexion mechanics that you can benefit from as well.

grips

As introduced in chapter 5, in any discussion of upper-body mechanics, it is important to cover grip strategy and strength.

Depending on the type and shape of the surface and your position in relation to the surface, there are a few common strategies to employ:

1. Hook grip under
2. Hook grip over
3. Gripping ground
4. Gripping odd surfaces
5. Gripping rings (page 252)

A hook grip is the act of strategically overlapping the fingers while grabbing or hanging from an object. The overlap of the fingers improves stability by increasing points of contact between hand and surface and increases physiological stability by interlocking the fingers and adding finger-to-finger contact.

The hook grip is not limited to hanging from a bar or a set of rings; it is also seen while holding a barbell. The difference is that when you hold a barbell, your thumbs fall under your index and middle fingers rather than over them. I remind my athletes of the over-over/under-under rule:

When you hang from a bar and your arms are ***over*** your head, your thumbs go ***over*** your index and middle fingers, and when the bar you are holding is ***under*** your head, your thumbs go ***under*** your index and middle fingers. You can see this difference clearly in the photos below.

The thumb position changes simply because the rotational forces put on your hand have changed. In the over-over, your thumb is the hook, and in the under-under, your index and middle fingers are the hook.

Depending on your position with respect to the surface you are holding as well as your ability to wrap your thumb around the surface, the number of fingers you can wrap around the surface, or the shape of the surface, you vary your grip according to a few basic principles. But the key point is that you are always reinforcing your fingers as best you can and perhaps increasing surface area.

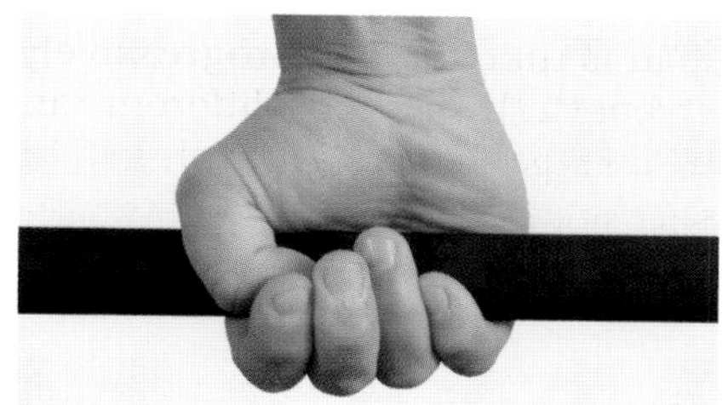

grip bar under center of mass When the bar is under your body or shoulders, which happens during all barbell work, you use a hook grip, but with your thumbs under your fingers.

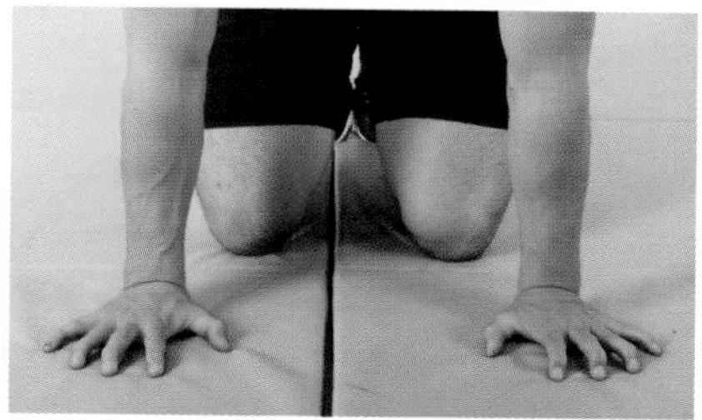

grip ground Squeeze your fingers into the ground and create muscular tension throughout your hands.

grip ledge 01 Place as much of your fingertips on the ledge as you can.

02 Press your fingers into the ledge, bending them to create a shelf.

03 Flex your thumb so that as much of the surface of your thumb as possible is in contact with the ledge.

04 Place your thumb over your index and middle fingers, creating a ledge hook grip.

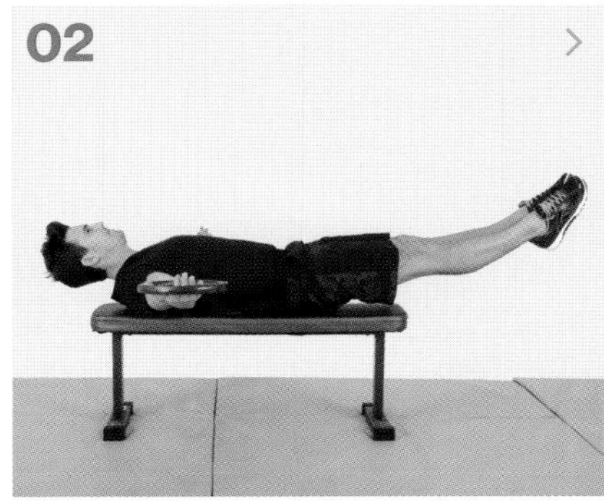

abduction/adduction 01 Start on a bench in a hollow body position. Hold two plates, dumbbells, or kettlebells directly above your shoulders, with your arms straight and your palms facing each other.

02 Drop your arms to the sides, in line with the frontal plane, without bending your elbows. Keep your shoulders and head off the bench and your feet in the same hollow body position.

plate work

plate abduction/adduction

The ideal way to set up this progression is to lie on a bench or platform so that you can adopt the hollow body position in order to maintain a strong midline as you perform the abduction, or spread of your arms. The majority of these movements can also be performed on a set of rings, but the benefit of performing them with weights is that you can progressively increase the load according to your movement ability. Notice that I allow my arms to reach past the frontal plane. Remember, you always want to develop movement strength through the fullest range of motion that allows you to maintain the proper mechanics.

plate flexion

The Plate Reach overhead is an interesting movement, as it is a product of progressing pushing mechanics but develops better pulling mechanics. Bringing your arms from a flexed position overhead and in line with your midline to a neutral starting position is an act of pulling. This movement is a great way to bridge the gap between pushing mechanics and their application to pulling mechanics.

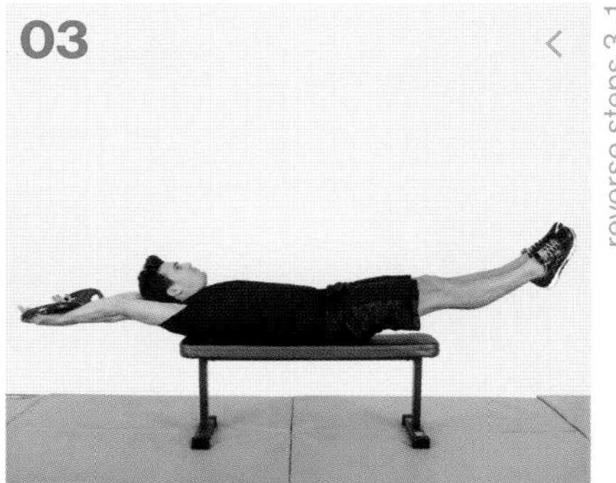

reverse steps 3–1

flexion 01 Start on a bench in a hollow body position. Hold two plates directly above your shoulders, with your arms straight. Your palms are where you can see them, and your shoulders are in external rotation.

02 Reach your arms overhead, rotating the plates to keep your palms facing up toward the sky.

03 Allow your shoulders to go into full flexion. Feel free to go farther than in the photo if you can, but make sure that you never lose the hollow body position.

03 Allow your hands to fall past the frontal plane and reach the ground. You may feel a little stretch in your shoulders. Your elbows remain locked out, and you maintain the hollow body position.

04 Press your arms through the frontal plane until they are straight in front of you, returning to the starting position.

plate extension

The Plate Extension is another great accessory movement, as it develops pushing mechanics in a position of shoulder extension. The mechanics developed here relate to many movements, such as lifting your arms over your head without weight, Push-up, Dip, Skin the Cat, Back Lever, and Planche.

This is the only section of the book that discusses carrying external loads. A big part of strength and conditioning is applying the fundamental mechanics learned in this book while sometimes under external load in order to progress certain aspects of movement ability. The movements you've learned in this book have very common loaded analogs in the gym. For example, for squatting and hip mechanics we see the Back Squat, Front Squat, and Overhead Squat, all variations of Deadlifts. For pushing mechanics we see the Bench Press, Military Press, and Push Press. For complex pushing and pulling combinations we see the Snatch and the Clean and Jerk. These common gym movements can also be viewed as great accessory work to the Freestyle Four movements. If you want to really tap into the potential of mastering the basic human movements, I highly recommend that you visit a gym and learn some of these techniques.

extension 01 Start on a bench in a hollow body position with your arms straight over your shoulders, two plates in your hands, and your palms facing each other.

02 Drop your hands toward your hips with your palms facing up.

03 Allow your shoulders to go into extension, where your arms are behind your back but your palms are still facing forward.

reverse steps 3–1

ring work

The same movements performed with plates on a bench can be performed on a set of rings. Here I present two of the many movements that you can perform on the rings to reinforce the basics outlined in this chapter:

1. Fly
2. Olympic Push-up

If you want to learn more about the rings, I highly recommend that you seek out a gymnastics facility in your area and take a couple of lessons.

Notice that the rings or ring straps are making an angle at the top and seem to be attached in a very narrow position. The narrower they are, the easier this movement is. The wider those straps are, the harder it gets. This is a good way to scale the load for the Fly on the rings.

The Olympic Push-up on the rings is a great way to further develop the strength required for the plank position applied to upper-body pulling movements. Returning from the fully locked-out Olympic position on the rings to the starting plank position requires an advanced movement ability of pulling mechanics at shoulder level.

fly 01 Start in plank position with your hands turned out, elbows locked out, and feet together.

02 Spread the rings out to the sides while maintaining a hollow body position.

03 As you reach the bottom position, your arms remain straight and as far out to the sides as possible with your wrists neutral. Your chest should not touch the ground. Press into the rings to maintain stability so that you don't collapse.

reverse steps 3–1

olympic push-up 01 Start in plank position with your hands turned out, shoulders above or slightly in front of your hands, and feet together.

02 Reach forward with your arms, maintaining a hollow body position. As your hands go past eye level, you will start to feel a lot of tension in your midline.

03 As you reach the bottom position, fight hard to keep the hollow body position by pressing down into the rings and keeping them close together.

reverse steps 3–1

kicking pull-up

As you now know, learning how to perform Pull-ups can give you an amazing degree of movement ability and help increase your overall physical health, fitness, and athleticism. Being able to do different styles of Pull-ups is a great way to keep your exposure to pulling mechanics varied and applicable to a greater number of movements seen in life and sport.

The Kicking Pull-up is an effective way to develop pulling mechanics in your lower extremities along with pulling mechanics for your upper body. It also mimics the kipping motion required to perform the Kipping Dip, as seen in chapter 5 (page 243).

kicking pull-up 01 Hang from a bar in a hollow body position.

02 Pull your knees up aggressively by bending your knees and flexing your hips. Use this momentum to drive your body up toward the bar.

03 Use the moment of weightlessness to start pulling with your arms by bending your elbows as if you were performing a Pull-up.

04 Extend your hips violently upward, never kicking your legs down, always thinking hips up to finish the Pull-up with your chin over the bar. Your position at the top is the same position that you adopt in any style of Pull-up—strict, kipping, etc.

butterfly pull-up

The Butterfly Pull-up is a great way to add speed and range of motion to your shoulders while performing pulling mechanics. Transitioning under the bar in a forward motion by taking your arms into flexion and your body into extension is an extremely technical movement and will benefit you greatly when you are learning how to pull yourself under an object, as seen in the Snatch in Olympic

butterfly pull-up 01 Start by performing the same kip you would in a Kipping Pull-up (page 236).

02 Snap your body into a hollow body position to set your shoulders behind the bar so that you can make visual contact with the bar.

03 Use this moment of weightlessness to initiate the pull. Pull until your chin is above the bar as your body adopts a more neutral global position.

weightlifting. The shoulder mechanics are not exactly the same, but they're very similar. I also appreciate the Butterfly Pull-up because it is a signature movement of CrossFit, where the strict Pull-up has adapted naturally into a style of Pull-up that allows athletes to perform them at high speeds, for long periods, and at a high number of repetitions.

04 Continue to pull your body toward and under the bar as you adopt a position of slight global extension.

05 Continue to pull the bar over and behind your head as push your chest and hips forward, furthering the global extension.

06 As you reach full extension in your elbows, bend your knees to finish the pull forward and prepare for the next kip.

07 Kick your feet down and forward, returning to the global extension of the original kip, but with more momentum.

08 Use this momentum plus a snap of your hips to carry you back into the hollow body position that sets you up for the next Pull-up repetition.

knees to elbows & toes to bar

Knees to Elbows and Toes to Bar are progressions of the Tuck-up, Straddle-up, and Pike-up. They combine the global shape changes with a change in orientation in space, local pulling mechanics at shoulder level, and kipping. The Knees to Elbows is a more complex movement pattern that requires more range of motion in the knees and hips and requires pulling at shoulder level. The Toes to Bar does not require pulling at shoulder level and is focused on pulling from the hips. I show two variations of each movement:

1. Kipping
2. Non-kipping

knees to elbows 01 Hang from a bar in a hollow body position.

02 Flex your hips and bend your knees to pull your lower body up. As you pull, keep flexing your hips until your thighs touch your chest.

03 Start pulling at your shoulders with your arms remaining straight in order to finish with your knees touching your elbows or even past them.

toes to bar 01 Hang from a bar in a hollow body position.

02 Flex your hips without pulling with your shoulders.

03 Continue to flex your hips until your feet touch the bar. If you can't reach the bar due to hip mobility, start pulling with your arms straight to finish the movement.

kipping For the kipping variations, you perform the same kip seen in a Kipping Pull-up (page 236). The kipping action shown here enables you to create momentum. This is a great drill to start practicing any kind of tumbling, like Backtucks, or any kind of double-back acrobatics.

kipping knees to elbows 01 As you kip into a hollow body position, you will have a moment of weightlessness. Take advantage of this moment of weightlessness to drive your knees up toward your chest.

02 Drive your knees through your elbows.

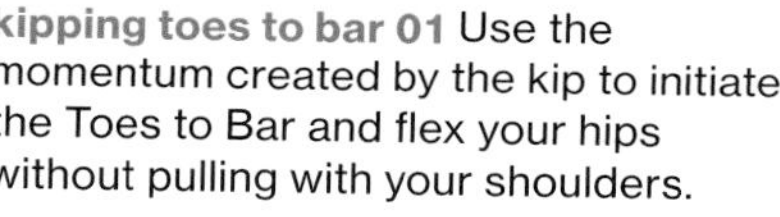

kipping toes to bar 01 Use the momentum created by the kip to initiate the Toes to Bar and flex your hips without pulling with your shoulders.

02 Continue to flex your hips until your feet touch the bar. If you can't reach the bar due to hip mobility, start pulling with your arms straight to finish the movement.

This chapter doesn't cover all the ways you can expand the Freestyle Four. It just scratches the surface of where you can go with your training and the options you have to further develop it. Stick to the basics and explore the natural paths that the basics have to offer by challenging them in any way you feel is right for you!

Fitness KB - 25/15
Wallball - 10/
Box - Step ups

Photo by Caragh Camera

programming

09

"Life can only be understood backwards; but it must be lived forwards." —Søren Kierkegaard

In the pursuit of optimal human performance, programming is a strategic plan to maximize your training efforts in order to achieve your unique goals. In other words, the plan should help you close the gap between where you are now and where you want to be.

While a progression defines the stages of advancement for a movement, programming strategically develops your body to handle that movement progression within the limits of your goals. In other words, you want to build a large base of movement ability but not lose track of the specific movement needs that will advance you toward your goals. If it didn't cost us anything, we would all prefer to be able to squat 500 pounds, perform an Iron Cross, and run a sub-4-minute mile. In reality, though, achieving each of those goals requires a significant investment in training, so we must have some focus toward the specificity that our goals require.

A special thank you to Jami Tikkanen for guiding and assisting me in writing this chapter.

Even though programming is backed by a rich scientific literature, solving for these constraints in order to reach your goals can be challenging because everyone responds differently to a training stimulus. The art of programming is aligning an individualized program with what your experience as a coach or an athlete tells you has worked before.

Individualizing a plan is challenging because it involves balancing your progress along an already established path for developing movement with exploring what is best for you as an individual. The exploration side is often hard to prioritize, as everyone naturally wants the straightest and fastest path to a goal. There is no secret sauce, however; programming is always a balance between following a plan that has worked before, assessing where you are, and patching the particular holes you have in your individual performance. This includes exploring the different types and styles of movement as well as the physiological demands. In other words, it's what I've been talking about throughout this book: Freestyle!

This balance relies heavily on developing an intuition for building the movement foundation required to reach your goals. The Freestyle Connection language outlined in part 1 can be very useful for this development, as it helps you take a specific movement problem and translate it into the most similar universal movements that can be effectively assessed and challenged in the gym.

Imagine you are a baseball pitcher, for example, coming to me for help with strength training because you have been experiencing pain in your shoulder. After you show me some throws, I ask you to perform a Push-up with your elbows against your body. You struggle to perform even one without flaring your elbows out as you press up. This elbow flaring indicates that your fundamental pushing mechanics at shoulder level may be deficient, and you should choose a program that focuses on eliminating that deficiency.

To me, it's essential for a pitcher to improve his shoulder mechanics in order to achieve his goals, despite the fact that it may not seem like the most direct path to better pitching. At this point in the book, you may readily agree that Push-up strength is important for a pitcher's shoulder mechanics, but what about the ability to do 100 Push-ups in two minutes or to hold 100 kilos overhead? How much fundamental movement proficiency is enough, and what holes are OK to leave? Some say that a good coach or athlete knows what works and what doesn't based on experience. While I think there is tremendous truth to that statement, there is always room for exploration. Your experience won't always tell you what to do. Try not to get caught up in one-size-fits-all solutions. Continue instead to excel at the fundamentals of movement so that you can explore and solve problems as efficiently as possible.

Now that I've established how important programming is, I want to get one more important point across before I start explaining programming further: you don't actually need a plan to succeed. That's right, you can succeed just fine without a program or structure in place. Establishing goals and organizing your training are good exercises in that these tools are used by the most successful athletes, coaches, and people. I am fairly certain, however, that a plan is good only so far as it facilitates the important things: consistency, a positive mental attitude, and the pursuit of quality. Essentially, your plan helps you approach your goals and life with character. The moment your plan fails to do so, switch it up, as it isn't working for you.

In chapter 3, I explained a fundamental approach to help you explore which movement ability may relate to your particular goals. That approach should help guide your exploration of movement as you develop a structured way to pursue your goals through programming. I also gave you a basic foundation and vocabulary for what I see as the most common human movement patterns within the Freestyle Four. This chapter gives you several principles that you can use to produce programs that balance exploration with advancement toward defined goals in order to get the most out of your programming. Then I demonstrate those programming principles with case studies.

To develop and follow a systematic plan for improving movement ability, I use several programming principles.

movement sandwich

Optimal programming starts and ends with movement. I find it essential for any training plan to start with a movement as its principal objective. From there, it should use that movement as a focus to challenge the body. In other words, the plan should concentrate on movement patterns to develop how you want to move and then challenge those patterns based on your physiological goals. For example, if I wanted to learn how to throw better, I would work on the essential patterns of throwing and then challenge those fundamental movements in the gym from many directions.

With this principle, you take a task that you want to get better at and transform it into a related movement in the gym. Only after you have a handle on the basic movement patterns that you need to get closer to your goal do you add on demands that will develop physiological adaptations that are useful for bringing that task back out onto the field and hopefully performing it better.

Programming generally proceeds through what I call a "movement sandwich," as follows:

1. You take a specific movement pattern.
2. You translate that specific movement pattern into a fundamental movement pattern that is easier to control and develop in the gym.
3. You train the fundamental movement pattern to achieve the desired physiological adaptation.
4. You go back to your specific movement pattern and measure your performance after adaptation and repeat the sandwich.

Let's take a track and field athlete who specializes in the 100-meter sprint, for example. The movement required to perform this specific task is simply running. Running mechanics can be translated into squatting mechanics in the gym. The squatting mechanics can be challenged by varying the style, load, speed, and volume. This causes a mechanical and physiological adaptation that can be measured with the next 100-meter sprint.

Performing a movement also gives you a chance to observe or assess your physiology—that is, the systems your body has to support movement.

You can always examine physiology in terms of these components:

1. ***Biology:*** Energy systems, or the aerobic and anaerobic capacity needed to perform a movement
2. ***Strength:*** From a physiological standpoint; for example, creating bigger, faster, longer-lasting muscles
3. ***Mobility:*** Health of soft tissues and joints

Programming should consider all three of these components. But I always start with movement or within a movement sandwich; find fundamental movement patterns that are most relevant to the desired specific movement, apply challenges to that relevant movement, and move again. So, even though you know that the physiology concerns are complex, you are always looking at assessing and developing the movement pattern itself. Then you introduce the challenge needed to get you closer to your purpose.

movement quality

The best programming prioritizes making the movement you care about bulletproof. Doing so requires training with high-quality, relevant movements. By "high-quality," I mean properly executed; and by "relevant," I mean that the movement relates to your goals or is otherwise functional. Even if the focus of your training day is aerobic adaptation, the movement you perform must be functional and well executed.

Suppose you have only performed a Muscle-up in a few practice situations. A program that prescribes a training session with Muscle-ups and other movements that stress the cardiovascular system would not make sense, then, because it would require Muscle-ups to be performed under fatigue despite your lack of movement ability. This is not an effective way to develop capacity for Muscle-ups. Effective programming always uses movements that can be performed with proper mechanics and with the desired intensity of the session.

If your movement quality degrades to the point where it is no longer helping your purpose, then there is little value in challenging the movement. Rather than worry about challenging the physiological system required for this movement, it would be more efficient for you to fix the mechanical errors and make this movement pattern more relevant to your goals. Make sure that your movement is of high quality so that your adaptations relate closely to your purpose.

map the gap

Any structured training program must have a definitive starting point and consider specific goals in order to be complete. These points define a map that you can use to explore ways to close the gap between your current abilities and your goals.

Keeping your current abilities and ultimate goal in mind when planning your training is important for two primary reasons:

1. Knowing your ultimate goal keeps you on track and focused.
2. Trying to understand your current abilities enough to plot them on your map encourages you to do a useful amount of exploration and self-assessment.

When looking for an optimal route on your map, it is important to remember that while different athletes may start at similar points on the map, their abilities to negotiate the terrain can be quite different. Even knowing that the fastest route between points A and B is a straight line, you may not be able to take that route if you don't have the ability to traverse the terrain you would encounter along the way.

You must consider your individual abilities and differences to know what "terrain" makes sense for you. The key to programming is to find the plan that is optimal for you, rather than to find a plan that may be optimal in some statistical or theoretical sense but ignores the significant differences between individuals.

Good programming uses empirical evidence to suggest the next steps on the map, but in practice you should equally consider an individualized approach.

be realistic

A plan may look perfect on paper, but if it doesn't account for your lifestyle, it may be inefficient or even completely ineffective. When you are creating a plan, it's very important to keep in mind that the plan is for you. Try not to limit your gaze to your current movement ability, but also look at your behavior and mindset. The goal is to create a plan that you are able to follow because you enjoy it and it works for you within your life.

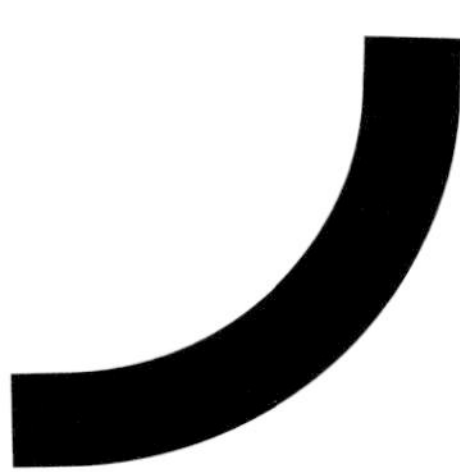

the psychological approach

My friend and fellow coach Kenny Kane has a great approach to help address mindset during training. He divides his programming into three focuses:

1. Movement quality rather than intensity
2. Mental toughness and decision-making under pressure and stress
3. Application to competition

The first focus helps the athlete learn the proper mechanics for efficient and safe movement. The second focus develops the athlete's ability to keep pushing through fear or extreme fatigue, regardless of how uncomfortable the challenge may be. The third focus helps the athlete tap into a state of mind that allows him to be strategic at the highest level of performance. The focuses work together in that the first two need to carry over to the competition mindset.

These focuses are best integrated into training when achieved through a common community-supported mindset, where working together with teammates and others develops a dynamic of support and constant progress.

next steps

Your plan is only as good as your next steps. The main purpose of seeing far, or all the way out to your ultimate goal, is to define what those next steps are. Your plan must always produce the next steps that keep you moving toward your goals. Revisiting the program is part of the game, so don't plan too many steps ahead; as long as you have the next few steps laid out, you are golden.

The general process of programming is to reverse-engineer where you would like to be based on your best assessment of where you currently are, and then use that assessment to determine what the next steps should be. By defining those next steps, you create a process that introduces physical challenges that will get you closer to your goal.

move, measure, and repeat

Good programming can be applied repeatedly. By this, I mean that programming is the process of constantly exposing deficiencies in order to make informed decisions based on the available data.

The programming process should be repetitive, but the actual steps of the program are always a unique blend and balance of your current fitness level, stage of development, and purpose for training. Those specific steps can be uncovered only by focusing on which areas need further development and what needs to be improved in order to progress to the next level of movement.

Even though the steps of programming should be repeated, the actual movement progressions you perform at these stages need to be tailored to your specific movement ability and goal. Take the Pistol, for example—one of the Freestyle Four movements. Before you challenge the Pistol with repetitions or speed, you need to develop the capacity to perform one Pistol with the appropriate mechanics. After you have achieved that initial level, then it's time to look more specifically at how you can challenge the movement to get closer to your goal.

expose holes

A plan allows you to make informed decisions according to your performance, so the best plans are derived from the best information. Aggressively gather that information.

One of the most essential aspects of programming is that holes in your movement ability will eventually be exposed. This is a problem in high-level athletics, where these holes are often masked and appear in ways that are difficult to diagnose. Translating a movement into more fundamental movement patterns allows you to more easily identify these holes and find ways to correct them. The more fundamental the movement pattern you are missing, the more certain it will limit your performance of advanced movements.

For example, the Push-up is one of the stages in the progression to a Handstand Push-up. It is crucial for understanding pushing mechanics at shoulder level and must be developed to a useful level before you move on to challenge it vertically. Sometimes an athlete is rushed to close the gap or is just excited about the Handstand and jumps to the vertical orientation before developing an adequate amount of basic pushing mechanics.

Unfortunately, if you try to go too fast, holes in your ability are often exposed later on as a lack of capacity in the volume of pushing (for example, repetitions or load), or sometimes as an injury. If you try to adapt too quickly without the proper foundations in place, you won't be able to sustain quality movement. Developing the right foundation while still challenging yourself is always a puzzle. And just because you are able to succeed at performing some advanced movements does not mean you have developed the fundamental movement patterns that allow you to last the longest.

Programming always fluctuates between assessing your abilities and developing those abilities based on the information you gathered during your assessment. These are not usually separate steps, however. Assessment and development are ongoing and happen every time you train. The cycle of assessment and development usually proceeds by creating movement goals, developing movement progressions that help you get from where you are to where you want to go, and administering tests that allow you to find deficiencies and create new goals based on your new abilities.

The better the information you have about where you are and where you're going, the better your estimates of when you will arrive will be—although life is good at messing up even the best-laid plans.

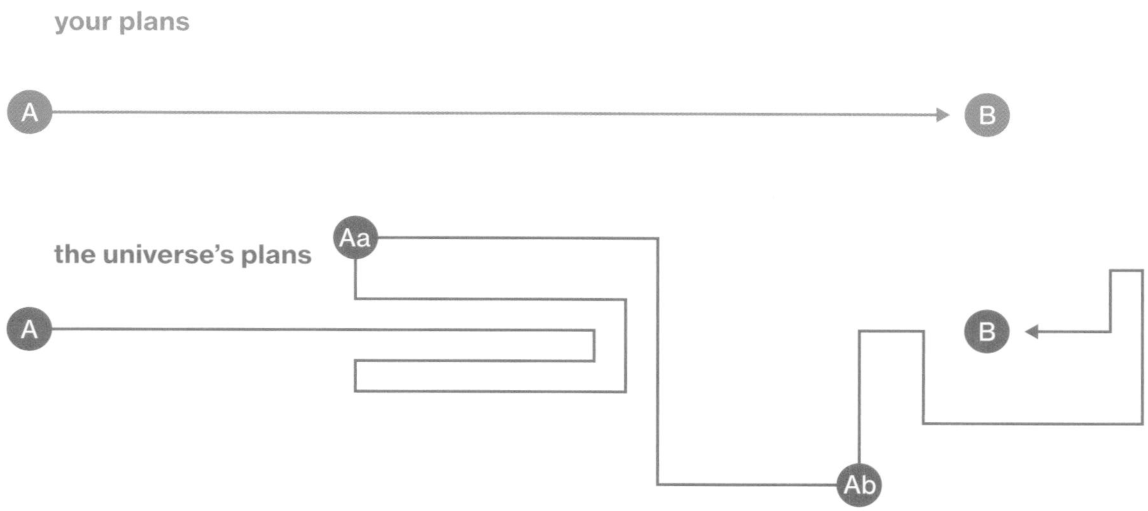

your plans

the universe's plans

Movement progressions are useful programming tools because they are both the tests that expose the holes and the exercises that fill them. Where you are in a progression is a great way to describe your current movement ability. So step 1 is to find out where you are in the progression and what your limitations are. Once you find this out, the progression gives you obvious ways to address your current limitations and prepares you to advance to the next stage.

Good programming tests movement from as many directions as possible. You want to be bulletproof, specifically according to your purpose. If you want to pitch, you don't necessarily need to snatch 200 kilos, but you do need to throw as fast as hell and for as long as possible—that is, you must be fit for throwing. In other words, "hole-finding" should be specific to your goals.

weakness of strength

Finding your weakest link and then fixing it enables you to move optimally toward your goals. This is important to remember even when you're working to further develop a strength. There is a lot of overlap here with the principle of exposing holes, but applying this focus equally to your strengths is important enough to merit its own section.

For example, if you're trying to get better at Muscle-ups, sometimes the most efficient strategy is not to do more of the same old Muscle-ups, but instead to find the weakest part of your Muscle-up and develop that part. Your weakest link could be your mobility, or your understanding of the transition position, or your understanding of the shift of your center of mass, or maybe you lack the peripheral adaptations that support the muscular endurance to perform multiple repetitions. This book is dedicated to helping you observe and describe movement in a language that also helps you build or progress a movement from simpler movements. These skills are vital for exposing the specific holes that are limiting you. Rather than vaguely working on the Muscle-up, you can more specifically work on the limiting component of that Muscle-up, thus making your programming more specific and efficient.

This technique is useful for developing strengths as well as weaknesses because the most effective way to enhance a strength is often through weaknesses. This goes back to the concept of a movement blanket, or the idea that your movement foundation needs to support various challenges to or variations of even your strongest movement. You won't find your weaknesses by doing only what you're strong at. The bottom line is that if programming includes the right selection of movements, those movements will help you assess your entire movement foundation.

movement ability and plan specificity

The more advanced your movements become, the more specific your goals become, and the more specific your programming must become. There is a natural evolution of and correlation between these elements. For example, someone coming off the couch to work out for the first time in years doesn't need and won't benefit from the specificity that an elite athlete looking to reach a particular goal needs. In fact, the optimal programming is likely not the same.

For a beginner, almost any plan is going to work. If you are mostly sedentary, simply practicing the movements and going through the progressions will improve your capacity to move in every way, because your current movement ability is so low that there is no need for a highly structured or specific program. That said, giving some thought to a beginner-level program can make it more effective than not planning at all.

Movement progression is so important to athletes' development because movement ability correlates very well with the specificity of their programming. The more capacity you have to move, the more specifically you can program for your development. Thus, depending on movement ability, your assessment varies from rough or general to very specific. You can then use these assessments to create the appropriate challenges to adapt to the next stage. Once you have figured out what these challenges are, you can create a program that systematically introduces those challenges so that your movement can become more robust.

movement efficiency

Because programming depends on physical movement, one of the first things you should think about is how you move. As described in chapter 2, your tissue and joint health plays a significant role in how well you move, and therefore how prepared you are to develop aspects of your physiology, such as power and capacity.

A good example of this is to compare an athlete who has significant limitations to her overhead mobility, maybe due to stiffness in her upper back, with an athlete who doesn't have the same restrictions. The passive tissue resistance is like moving a heavier load. An athlete moving a lighter load inherently has more potential to succeed.

Passive tissue resistance decreases the efficiency of movement and incurs a higher energy cost. And that passive tissue resistance is a form of increasing the load on your movements, thus reducing the effectiveness of your movements. Improving your movement efficiency will get you closer to expressing your physiological potential.

movement potential

Depending on your movement ability within a particular movement style, the type of physiological adaptations you can achieve using that movement may be limited. It is important to understand where you stand in a movement progression in order to get the desired physiological adaptation out of it.

Movement ability is the most effective way to use your current physiological (aerobic and anaerobic) capacity. Whereas the movement efficiency principle refers to the need for healthy tissue in order to have the most movement efficiency, this principle refers to the ability to exploit the correct physiological systems in order to perform a movement optimally.

I like to think of it as an athlete's ability to efficiently shift gears. Two people may have similar body architectures and even similar physiological capacities, but simply by improving the mechanics of a movement, I can get a person closer to her movement potential regardless of her fitness level.

Take a beginner starting a new training discipline, for example. When the beginner starts training, his potential to do work at a physiological level is significantly higher than his ability to exploit that potential through movement. The fastest way to close the gap is not necessarily to develop his physiology or mobility, but to expose and train him on the movement mechanics so that he can start tapping into the potential that is already available to him.

Once you narrow the gap between your movement potential and your ability to express it, you can begin to challenge that ability further by introducing higher levels of intensity together with more varied challenges.

I noticed this at the 2013 CrossFit Games. On the Thruster/Legless Rope Climb event, only two women finished the challenge within the time limit. The main challenge of this event was the Legless Rope Climb, which most of the athletes were not very familiar with. Most of them used very inefficient techniques, muscling the movement (see the strict Muscle-up style on page 254), which quickly fatigued them. The only two women who finished the event used a more effective movement style, performing a Kipping Legless Rope Climb (see the Kipping Muscle-up on page 264). None of these athletes were beginners per se, but in this particular event, almost everyone performed like a beginner because they were not comfortable with the most efficient movement mechanics. The two who did finish were better able to tap into their movement capacity than the other competitors.

Movement ability plays a crucial role in learning any new task. Often, what seems to be a conditioning deficit is actually a lack of movement ability that places an extra burden from a conditioning perspective.

order of aerobic adaptations

When developing aerobic adaptations, most athletes find that their central adaptations are worse off than their peripheral adaptations.

I simply consider aerobic adaptations to be the ones that improve your ability to distribute and use oxygenated blood throughout your entire body. I think of the central system as the strength of your heart and its ability to pump blood to all your tissues. Then I think of the peripheral system as your metabolism, or your ability to use the blood in your peripheral tissues to do work. Let's say that either system can be independently rated on a scale of 1–10, with 10 being the best. Most athletes would rate a 2 in central adaptations and a 4 in peripheral adaptations. This score difference basically means that you can't sustain a high enough output of blood and oxygen to your tissues to push your peripheral adaptations further. (Your scores might be flipped if you come from an endurance background.)

Training both of these systems is important, and often it's best to focus on one at a time. You typically start by pushing the central adaptations. Once your central adaptations improve to a rating of, say, 3, 4, or 5, your central system is able to feed the peripheral enough for you to go after the peripheral adaptations.

Depending on your level of adaptation, you probably won't need to focus on central adaptation for very long before you have enough to start focusing on the peripheral—think months rather than years. This is especially true for beginners, who can make central adaptations relatively quickly. The further along you are in your training, however, the more time this is going to take. A comprehensive adaptation of both systems can be a very long, or even a lifetime, endeavor.

Let's take the example of training for a 5k run. You might start by simply running a 5k. If you can't complete it because your legs are burning and cramping and you run only 1k, then your peripheral adaptation seems to be the limiting factor. Therefore, you cannot use the 5k run as a test of your central adaptation.

So maybe you change the movement style of the test to explore the adaptation differences further. You could test a 5k bike and perhaps find that you can complete it. Then you can use the bike to push your central adaptations to eventually be able to handle the 5k run from a central system perspective. This is a great motivation for what the fitness industry considers cross-training. Once you are satisfied with your central adaptations, you may switch back to the run or perhaps even add Squats to develop the peripheral adaptation necessary to sustain the 5k. And this priority order can be repeated, with central adaptation always leading peripheral.

A lot of run coaches use "run/walk" programs, a type of interval training in which a run (active) component is paired with a walk (active recovery) component. These programs target the central engine by keeping the athlete in constant motion for a predetermined distance or time.

training specificity

The human body is an integrated system; you cannot train a piece of it in isolation. Training often involves focus, and that is important for central and peripheral adaptations. You need to focus on one aspect at a time, but this does not mean that only the central system benefits while you are training the peripheral or vice versa.

In real life, regardless of the adaptation you're trying to achieve through training, these are just ways of understanding what happens in physiology. They are not absolute truths; they are just theories based on both empirical and research evidence so that, based on those findings, you can say, "X is my goal, and I aim to develop this adaptation to come closer to my goal."

Now, you might be developing several other adaptations, but based on experience, it is possible to do some targeting of these adaptations. Therefore, in order to be systematic and make sure that you expose all the holes in the game, you should go after these adaptations. Try to be as specific as you can, remembering that nature makes no distinctions for these things.

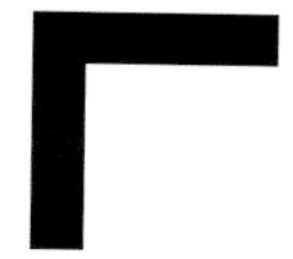

programming examples

In this section, I lay out a few sample training scenarios in order to demonstrate the programming principles in action, focusing mostly on the Freestyle Four movements. I do not intend to suggest that these are the only movements you need to do to reach your goals, and I certainly don't suggest that you should follow this specific program. Instead, I focus on providing insight with these programming snapshots that you can use to understand how you can successfully implement a real programming plan with the progressions presented in this book.

I cover beginner, intermediate, and advanced athlete scenarios. Each scenario includes:

1. ***Athlete profile:*** A brief intro of the athlete and his or her goals.
2. ***Assessment:*** An analysis of the athlete's current movement ability. I do this assessment by taking the athlete through the Freestyle Four movement progressions regardless of his or her ability to perform the complete movement. I'm looking for any steps where he or she might have deficiencies as opportunities to improve movement quality and efficiency.
3. ***Training plan:*** A sample programming snapshot based on the athlete's assessment and goals.

Photo by Chris Greer

how to read a training plan

Each training plan includes a sample training day, with one or more training sessions per day. The beginner and intermediate plans spell out one or more weeks, while the advanced plan simply describes potential training days that are not put together in a particular sequence.

A training session includes one or more blocks. Each block includes one or more movements. When there are at least two movements in a block, you perform the block as a superset. In a superset, you alternate between movements, doing the repetitions prescribed for one movement, resting before the next movement, doing the repetitions prescribed for the next movement, and then resting before starting again with the first movement. When no rest is prescribed, you move continuously through all the movements in the block.

For some movements I include a tempo prescription, which tells you how much time you have to perform each phase of the movement. The movement is broken down into four phases, with a digit that represents the number of seconds:

1. Moving between the start and transition positions
2. In the transition position
3. Moving between the transition and finish positions
4. In the finish position

Take a Squat with a tempo prescription of 2010, for example. You would start standing and take two seconds to reach the bottom of the Squat. You would immediately (zero seconds) start the ascent from the bottom back to the top and take one second to reach the top position. As soon as you reached the top position, you would immediately (zero seconds) initiate the next descent. This tempo repeats for however many repetitions are prescribed.

Jami Tikkanen (pictured at left) is a master at programming strength and conditioning for athletes of all levels. He has been my mentor, colleague, and friend. In addition, he has been coaching elite-level CrossFit athletes since 2010, when he first worked as an osteopath to Mikko Salo (crowned the World's Fittest Man in 2009, fifth in 2010) and as a coach to Annie Thorisdottir (second Fittest Woman on Earth in 2010, Fittest Woman on Earth in 2011 and 2012). In 2013, Jami coached Team Europe against Team USA at the first-ever CrossFit Invitational. He travels the world teaching strength and conditioning, movement, and mobility.

athlete profile

Stacy is a mother of two young boys and enjoys jogging up and down the hills of San Francisco and going to the gym when she can find time to exercise. Although she is fairly active, she doesn't feel very athletic and is interested in improving her overall fitness and athleticism to keep up with her young family.

assessment

I used the Freestyle Four movements and progressions to assess Stacy's current movement ability. For each of the Freestyle Four, we proceeded through the progression in order to find a movement that was close to the limit of Stacy's ability. With that movement, we could test her movement strength. When doing the assessment, my main focus was how she executed each movement and not necessarily the number of repetitions she did, although the numbers also provided some insight.

	diagnostics	test	score
pistol	0 Pistols, couldn't balance, limited ankle/hip range of motion	Max reps Squats in 60 seconds	30 (poor mechanics)
handstand push-up	Headstand, no Handstand or kick to Handstand (against a wall), difficulty in overhead position	Max reps Push-ups in 60 seconds	11 Push-ups
muscle-up	Poor pulling mechanics in Pull-up, but good Ring Rows; no kipping ability	Max reps Pull-ups and Dips	2 Pull-ups 2 Ring Dips
burpee	Squatting and pushing mechanics poor; limited by ankle and hip mobility	Max reps	13 Burpees

The assessment showed that Stacy was unable to perform a Pistol but was able to perform a Squat, although her form and control needed work. She was able to perform several basic Push-ups, but when I brought her arms closer to her midline, she was unable to maintain her global position. When I tested her on Dips, the same poor mechanics seen in the Push-up appeared. She was able to perform a few Pull-ups, and her Ring Rows looked pretty solid. Unfortunately, the poor mechanics in the Squat and Push-up were apparent in the Burpee as well.

training plan

We set out to build a better foundation of movement ability by focusing on the biggest gaps in Stacy's basic pushing and squatting mechanics. She already had a pretty good engine, and she could do a fair amount of work, so I started by improving her movement quality and then used the new movement ability to challenge her engine further. In addition, I hoped that she would be able to progress into higher levels of performance on the progressions. Getting closer to the Pistol and improving her pushing mechanics would be great benefits to the activities she enjoys most.

week 1

day 1

superset 1

1. Blocked/regular Push-up 4 x 6 (60% effort), tempo 2111, rest 30 seconds

2. Tripod 4 x 15 seconds, rest 60 seconds

superset 2

1. Hinge & Touch 1 x 10, rest 30 seconds

Hinge, Touch, & Drop 1 x 10, rest 30 seconds

Hinge, Touch, Drop, & Lift 2 x 10, rest 30 seconds

2. Burpee feet-together with hands in anatomical position 4 x 10, rest 60 seconds

superset 3

1. Ring Row 4 x 8, tempo 1011, rest 60 seconds

2. Hollow Rock 4 x 30 seconds, rest 30 seconds

conditioning

day 2

superset 1

1. Blocked/regular Push-up 4 x 6 (60% effort), tempo 3111, rest 30 seconds

2. Tripod 4 x 18 seconds, rest 60 seconds

superset 2

1. Hinge, Touch, & Drop 1 x 10 + Hinge, Touch, Drop, & Lift 1 x 10, rest 30 seconds

Plate Squat 3 x 8–10, tempo 2111, rest 30 seconds

2. Burpee feet-together with hands in anatomical position 4 x 12, rest 60 seconds

superset 3

1. Ring Row 4 x 6, tempo 1021, rest 60 seconds

2. Superman Rock 4 x 30 seconds, rest 30 seconds

conditioning

day 3

superset 1

1. Blocked/regular Push-up 4 x 6 (60% effort), tempo 3111, rest 30 seconds

2. Tripod 4 x 18 seconds, rest 60 seconds

superset 2

1. Hinge, Touch, & Drop 1 x 10 + Hinge, Touch, Drop, & Lift 1 x 10, rest 30 seconds

Plate Squat 3 x 8–10, tempo 2111, rest 30 seconds

2. Burpee feet-together with hands in anatomical position 4 x 12, rest 60 seconds

superset 3

1. Ring Row 4 x 6, tempo 1021, rest 60 seconds

2. Superman Rock 4 x 30 seconds, rest 30 seconds

conditioning

During Stacy's three training sessions for week 1, her focus was on improving her overall pushing strength and mechanics combined with Tripod practice. This prepared her to gain the movement ability required to eventually perform a Handstand Push-up. In addition, she developed better squatting mechanics by working on the Old Man Squat progression and continued to apply her pushing mechanics by performing Burpees. Lastly, she focused on improving her overall pulling strength and mechanics combined with the Hollow and Superman rocks that required to perform a swing and the Pull-up required for performing a Muscle-up.

week 2

day 1

superset 1

1. Wall Climb to Handstand 4 x 3–4, rest 60 seconds

2. Tripod Leg Lift 4 x 4–6, rest 60 seconds

superset 2

1. Lunge 4 x 8 (per side), tempo 2011

2. Hollow Rock 4 x 30 seconds, rest 30 seconds

superset 3

1. Kipping Ring Row 4 x 8, rest 40 seconds

2. Kipping Swing 4 x 8, rest 60 seconds

3. Muscle-up progression, rest 60 seconds
Stage 1: 1 x 6
Stage 2: 1 x 4
Stage 3: 2 x 4

conditioning

day 2

superset 1

1. Handstand 4 x 30 seconds, rest 60 seconds

2. Tripod Kick, Pause, & Press 4 x 4–6, rest 60 seconds

superset 2

1. Lunge with toe point 4 x 8 (per side), tempo 2011

2. Hollow Rock to shoulder stance 4 x 8–10, rest 30 seconds

superset 3

1. Band Pull-up 4 x 8, rest 60 seconds

2. Kipping Swing 4 x 8, rest 60 seconds

3. Muscle-up progression, rest 60 seconds
Stage 2: 2 x 4
Stage 3: 2 x 4

conditioning

day 3

superset 1

1. Handstand 4 x 30 seconds, rest 60 seconds

2. Tripod Kick, Pause, & Press 4 x 4–6, rest 60 seconds

superset 2

1. Lunge with foot off ground 4 x 8 (per side), tempo 2011

2. Hollow Rock to shoulder stance 4 x 8–10, rest 30 seconds

superset 3

1. Kipping Pull-up 4 x accumulate max high-quality reps in 60 seconds, rest 60 seconds

2. Muscle-up progression
Stage 1: 4 x 6, rest 60 seconds

3. Muscle-up progression, rest 60 seconds
Stage 1: 1 x 6
Stage 2: 1 x 4
Stage 3: 2 x 4

conditioning

In week 2, Stacy took inversion to the next level by starting to perform a Handstand against a wall. She combined the Handstand position with some early stages of the Handstand Push-up progression. She also started including some basic unilateral loading for the lower body to further prepare her to perform a Pistol and improve her overall locomotion for running. Lastly, Stacy included a more dynamic style of pulling mechanics by progressing her Ring Row into a kipping Ring Row and eventually applied it to vertical pulling mechanics with the Pull-up. All these elements are helping her get closer to a complete Muscle-up.

week 3

day 1

superset 1

1. Kick to Push-up 4 x 6, rest 45 seconds

2. Step-up and Pistol Swing 4 x 5 (per side), tempo 21X1, rest 45 seconds

superset 2

1. Headstand 4 x 10 seconds

2. Band Dip 4 x 6, tempo 2121

superset 3

1. Candlestick Roll 3 x 6

2. Muscle-up progression
Swing on high rings 1 x 6
Stage 4: 1 x 5
Stage 5: 1 x 4

conditioning

Conditioning builds on movement patterns from week 2—for example, Wall Climbs

day 2

superset 1

1. Kick to Olympic Plank 4 x 6, rest 45 seconds

2. Box Pistol 4 x 5 (per side), tempo 2121, rest 45 seconds

superset 2

1. Handstand 4 x 30 seconds, rest 90 seconds

2. Kipping Pull-up 4 x accumulate max high-quality reps in 60 seconds, rest 60 seconds

superset 3

1. Rolling Lunge 4 x 5 (per side)

2. Muscle-up progression
Swing on high rings 1 x 6
Stage 5: 2 x 5
Swing on high rings 1 x 6

conditioning

Conditioning builds on movement patterns from week 2—for example, Wall Climbs

day 3

superset 1

1. Kick to 45° (wall) 4 x 6, rest 45 seconds

2. Plate Pistol to box 4 x 5 (per side, alternating), tempo 20X1

superset 2

1. Handstand Push-up descent (wall facing) 4 x 3–4, tempo 20 (climb up) 1, rest 2 minutes

2. Chest-to-Bar Pull-up 4 x max high-quality reps in 60 seconds, rest 60 seconds

superset 3

1. Pistol to Candlestick Roll to Lunge, tempo 20X1, rest 30 seconds

2. Muscle-up progression
Swing on high rings 1 x 6
Stage 5: 2 x 5
Swing on high rings 1 x 6

conditioning

Conditioning builds on movement patterns from week 2—for example, Wall Climbs

In week 3, Stacy is starting to advance into higher levels of inversion by practicing her kick up to Handstand and taking her Handstand Push-up progression to a higher level by performing the kipping Handstand Push-up to a stage closer to the complete movement. Plus, Stacy has now included another variation of pushing mechanics, such as the Dip, that will be required for her Muscle-up. For her lower body, Stacy has started advancing into a higher-level performance for her squatting by doing step-ups and adding speed and change of orientation in space through the Candlestick Roll. In this stage of her training, Stacy is able to superset upper-body movements with some lower movements as she is now performing higher levels stages of each progression. This is beneficial because it gives her a more integrated approach to her training.

week 4

day 1

superset 1

1. Chest-to-Wall Kipping Handstand Push-up 4 x by feel, rest 45 seconds

2. Lunge variation
Rest 90 seconds
Lunge with toe point 1 x 8 (per side)
Lunge with foot off ground 1 x 6 (per side)
Candlestick Roll to Lunge 2 x 4 (per side)

superset 2

1. Plate Pistol 4 x 4, tempo 20X1, rest 60 seconds

2. Muscle-up progression, rest 60 seconds
Stage 1: 1 x 4
Stage 3: 1 x 4
Stage 5: 1 x 4
Stage 3: 1 x 4

superset 3

1. Kipping Hip-to-Bar Pull-up 4 x by feel, rest 60 seconds

2. Dip Balance, extend legs, Kipping Dip 4 x 3–4, rest 90 seconds

conditioning

day 2

superset 1

1. Back-to-Wall Kipping Handstand Push-up 4 x by feel, rest 45 seconds

2. Lunge variation
Rest 90 seconds
Lunge with toe point 1 x 8 (per side)
Lunge with foot off ground 1 x 6 (per side)
Candlestick Roll to Lunge 2 x 4 (per side)

superset 2

1. Slow Plate Rolling Pistol 4 x 4, tempo 23X1, rest 60 seconds

2. Muscle-up progression
Rest 60 seconds
Stage 1: 1 x 4
Stage 3: 1 x 4
Stage 5: 1 x 4
Stage 3: 1 x 4

superset 3

1. Kipping Chest-to-Bar Pull-up 1 x by feel, rest 60 seconds
Kipping Hip-to-Bar Pull-up 1 x by feel, rest 60 seconds
Swinging hip to rings 2 x by feel, rest 60 seconds

2. Dip Balance, extend legs, Kipping Dip 4 x 3–4, rest 90 seconds

conditioning

day 3

superset 1	superset 2	superset 3	conditioning
1. Kipping Handstand Push-up progressions (review all)	**1.** Pistol progressions (review all)	**1.** Kipping Muscle-up progressions (review all)	
2. Kipping Handstand Push-up—test max reps	**2.** Rolling Pistol—test max reps	**2.** Kipping Muscle-up—see how close you are to the full movement if confident	

Week 4 of Stacy's training is an extension of the previous weeks, with an emphasis on guaranteeing that she has achieved the movement ability required to perform movements such as the Handstand Push-up, Pistol variations, and Muscle-up. These movements are all tested on the third training day of the week.

The beginner plan uses the Freestyle Four to develop the foundation of pushing, pulling, squatting, swinging, and changing orientation in space at the same time. For example, the Burpee develops both pushing and squatting mechanics. The snap performed on the ascent of the Burpee mimics the snap required to perform a kipping Muscle-up. The Hollow and Superman rocks are the foundation of the swing for the Muscle-up and also are applicable to the Candlestick Roll used in the Rolling Pistol. The Candlestick Roll is the essence of the transition from the bottom of the rings to the support.

athlete profile

Ivan is a young, determined former college lacrosse and hockey player and current CrossFit athlete who is preparing for a local competition in two weeks. He is looking to supplement his normal training with a few extra sessions in the next two weeks in order to prepare for the event.

assessment

Again, I used the Freestyle Four movements and progressions to assess Ivan's movement ability. The resulting numbers of Ivan's test are more important than in Stacy's beginner test, although I focused on movement quality in order to interpret the results.

	diagnostics	test	score
pistol	Lacking ankle range of motion	Max reps on each leg	5 right, 3 left
handstand push-up	Hard time locking out elbows at top of Handstand; lack of kipping ability	Max reps	4
muscle-up	Very crude kip	Max reps	2
burpee	Seems to lack transition efficiency	Max reps in 30/60/90 seconds with full recovery between efforts	16/28/34

The assessment highlighted a left/right imbalance and an ankle mobility issue in the Pistol, overhead mobility restriction in the Handstand Push-up, and a lack of kipping skill in the Handstand Push-up as well as the Muscle-up. Ivan also had relatively high lactic power in relation to lesser lactic endurance in the Burpee. After this rudimentary assessment, I took him through the progressions for each movement in order to find the best starting point for the program.

pistol

Ivan could perform the Lunge and the Box Step-down but was very knee dominant. He had difficulties with the Rolling Pistol, and it was obvious that the range of motion of his left ankle was restricted.

handstand push-up

Ivan was inefficient throughout the Kipping Handstand Push-up progressions. He was pressing too early with his arms and trying to muscle his way up rather than catching the fall. Furthermore, he was unable to reach full lockout at the top of the Handstand.

muscle-up

Ivan was able to do multiple Chest-to-Bar Pull-ups but was unable to perform a single Hip-to-Bar Pull-up. I noticed that his Pull-ups were very upper-body dominant with minimal hip use. While Ivan could do Ring Dips, his movement pattern was inefficient because he was leading with his elbows. In addition, he had considerable difficulty with the blocked Push-up. He could do chin-over Pull-ups on the rings but was unable to pull low enough on Chest-to-Rings Pull-ups.

burpee

Ivan had trouble controlling his lower body during the transition from the ground to standing in the Burpee. Specifically, his hip mobility seemed to cause him to widen his stance on the way up while losing some movement control.

training plan

Based on the short preparation time available as part of Ivan's goal, I decided to focus primarily on maximizing his skill. This meant working on his Kipping Handstand Push-up and Muscle-up, cleaning up his shoulder mechanics for pushing for the Handstand Push-up and Dip, transitioning from pulling to pushing for the Muscle-up and Pistol, and addressing the mobility issues of his ankles and shoulders.

day 1

superset 1

1. Kipping Ring Row 3 x 8

2. Blocked Push-up 3 x 1–8

3. Shoulder overhead mobility—at end of each set

superset 2

1. Low ring kipping progressions 5 x 5–10 to get a feel for the progression; each set move to the next step in the progression

2. Ring Swing 5 x 5

3. Shoulder internal rotation mobility—at end of each set

superset 3

1. Candlestick Roll 5 x 5

2. Hip-to-Rings Pull-up + Muscle-up 5 x 1 + 1

3. Ankle mobility—at end of each set

conditioning

Ivan started the week by addressing pulling mechanics combined with some strict pushing mechanics to improve his overall shoulder mechanics assisted by overhead mobility work. This session emphasizes the foundation for performing better Muscle-ups. Even though a Candlestick Roll is programmed, it is intended to assist in the transition required to perform the Muscle-up. Notice how pushing and pulling mechanics are performed in superset fashion to maximize movement ability at shoulder level and combined with mobility to improve range of motion and best application of the foundation of the movement. This quality of movement will benefit Ivan by allowing him to perform at the highest level under the stress of competition.

day 2

superset 1

1. Kipping Handstand Push-up progression 6 x 3–5 to get a feel for the progression; each set move to the next step in the progression

2. Kipping Muscle-up band progressions 5 x 3–5 to get a feel for the progression; each set move to the next step in the progression

superset 2

1. Kipping Handstand Push-up 5 x 4–8, broad rep range to challenge Ivan but allow him to feel OK if he doesn't reach the higher end of the rep scheme. As he's learning the kipping, the number of reps might vary a lot from set to set based on form.

superset 3

1.Candlestick Roll to Lunge 5 x 5 each side + ankle mobility

2. One-Leg Burpee 5 x 5 each side + ankle mobility

conditioning

Ivan continued to develop the quality of his movement by focusing on the Freestyle Four progressions, but during this session he focused on the Handstand Push-up progression in conjunction with the Muscle-up and some variations of get-ups such as the Candlestick Roll and Burpee. The Handstand Push-up emphasizes developing strength and stamina, whereas the Muscle-up focuses more on developing technique by working on the specific transition drills through the Kipping Muscle-up. The get-up provides some drills for the transition for the Muscle-up seen in the Candlestick Roll, and the Burpee provides an increase of movement ability at hip level.

day 3

superset 1

1. Kipping Ring Row 3 x 8 + shoulder overhead mobility

2. Blocked Push-up 3 x 1–8 reps + shoulder overhead mobility

superset 2

1. Low ring kipping progressions 5 x 5–10 to get a feel for the progression, each set move to the next step in the progression + shoulder internal rotation mobility

2. Ring Swing 5 x 5 + shoulder internal rotation mobility

superset 3

1. Pistol down (1 foot descent), Candlestick Roll 2 feet up 5 x 3 (each side, alternating legs) + ankle mobility

2. Hip-to-Rings Pull-up + Muscle-up + hip-to-rings Pull-up 5 x 1 + 1 + 1 + ankle mobility

conditioning

Ivan continued to progress his Muscle-up by refining his technique through the basic pulling mechanics seen in the Ring Row and assisting the mechanics by working on strict pushing mechanics to make sure that his shoulder mechanics are maximized. In addition to working on all the progressions, integrating mobility to assist these movements and the positions the joint goes through are continuing to improve his movement ability.

day 4

superset 1

1. Handstand Push-up progression

2. Kipping Handstand Push-up: 3 x as many reps as possible with good mechanics, with as much recovery as needed between sets

superset 2

1. Kipping Muscle-up progression

2. Kipping Muscle-up: 3 x as many reps as possible with good mechanics, with as much recovery as needed between sets

superset 3

1. 6 x 90 seconds on, 3 minutes off
2 Muscle-ups
4 Handstand Push-ups on wall
6 Rolling Pistols (alternating legs)
Max rep Burpee (all-out effort)

conditioning

In this session, Ivan used the Handstand Push-up and Muscle-up progressions to warm up and prepare for a maximum-effort test to measure his improvement. Programming a combination of the Handstand Push-up, Muscle-up, and Pistol progressions gave him a chance to test how he performs under the pressure of having to switch from one movement to another, as he will experience in competition.

As discussed in the programming principle of specificity versus ability (page 382), advanced athletes typically require very specific programming. Rather than lay out one very specific example, I think it is more useful to give you examples of how to work on specific gaps in movement strength. I consider advanced athletes to be those who are highly proficient in the progressions presented in this book, or in whichever specific movements relate to their sports. This section is about how you can go back to the basics to continue to improve your ability while still challenging different aspects of your movement strength. These templates simply serve as examples of how you can target an energy system based on a measured level of ability.

aerobic power interval

The aerobic system represents a significant opportunity in terms of the variety of physiological adaptations that can be achieved through systematic training—everything from cardiac output to peripheral vascular density and oxidative capacity of fast-twitch muscle fibers to the number of mitochondria (where the energy is produced) in the cells available for development through various training methods.

Aerobic power intervals are a great way to increase the contractility of the heart together with its mitochondrial density, allowing for higher power outputs being sustained aerobically (that is, higher power outputs sustained for longer periods). Essentially you are developing a "stronger" heart. This kind of work presumes a certain amount of base cardiorespiratory endurance being developed (higher cardiac output allows you to work harder during the aerobic power intervals) to support the adaptations achieved through the utilization of this method.

This template engages in very-high-intensity intervals followed by sufficient rest to return the heart rate to conversational level (less than 130 BPM is a good starting point). This often equates to a 1:1 work:rest ratio, with the number of intervals based on your ability to recover and the duration of the intervals. Aerobic power intervals can range from 30 seconds to 10+ minutes. The intensity of effort will of course decrease as the work time increases (you can't sustain the same rate of work for 2 minutes as you can for 30 seconds). Longer intervals provide an opportunity to learn how to sustain a high pace without "tipping over" to the lactic, unsustainable realm. A coach's job is to find the right balance of duration, load, and movement selection based on the athlete's needs and capabilities to allow for optimal results from this method.

aerobic power interval – short

superset 1

1. 7–10 x 30 seconds on, 30 seconds off
3 Muscle-ups
7 Burpees
Rest 10 minutes

superset 2

1. 4–6 x 60 seconds on, 60 seconds off
14 Squats
7 Kipping Pull-ups
14 Squats
7 Handstand Push-ups

or

7 Kipping Pull-ups
21 Squats
7 Handstand Push-ups

aerobic power interval – medium

superset 1

1. 6–10 x 2 minutes on, 2 minutes off
6 Pistols (each leg)
8 Chest-to-Bar Push-ups

conditioning

Max rep Burpee (sustainable pace, 90% effort)
Aim to hit same number of reps in each interval.

With lactic there are also engine and capacity concerns or power and endurance.

tempo method

Tempo is an extremely useful training variable. It can be used not only to improve form, but also to target specific physiological adaptations. A longer eccentric phase (the negative or "down" portion of a movement) tends to promote more tissue damage (soreness, but also potentially hypertrophy), increased strength, allowing the athlete to control a more significant load than the concentric counterpart, while isometric (static) holds within a repetition allow targeting of desired strength adaptations. Overall time under tension is an important consideration in any training plan. Without getting too deep into the intricacies of various tempo prescriptions, I will discuss the benefits of the 2020 tempo used in the case study shortly.

Tempo prescriptions are always read: eccentric phase / bottom position / concentric phase / top position (e.g. for a Pistol, a tempo of 2020 is read: 2 seconds down / no pause at bottom / 2 seconds up / no pause at top). A tempo of 2020 for 8–12 repetitions means a total time under tension of 36–48 seconds, which allows you to target slow-twitch muscle fibers and specifically their size and the amount of mitochondria found in the muscles. The main benefit is that slow-twitch fibers oxidize the lactate produced during high-intensity workouts, allowing you to continue moving longer with higher power outputs.

tempo method

superset 1

1. Muscle-up complex
Kipping Muscle-up + slow return (6 seconds)
3–4 x (1 + 1), rest 2 minutes between sets

2. Blocked Push-up 3 x 1–8 reps + shoulder overhead mobility

superset 2

1. Parallette Handstand Push-up 5 x 2–4, tempo 4011, go straight to 2

2. Pistol 4 x 6–8 (per side, finish one side before doing the other), tempo 2020, rest 1 minute before B1

superset 3

1. Kipping Ring Row 4 x 8, rest 40 seconds

2. Kipping 4 x 8, rest 60 seconds

3. Muscle-up progression, rest 60 seconds
Stage 1: 1 x 6
Stage 2: 1 x 4
Stage 3: 2 x 4

conditioning

lactic power intervals

The anaerobic lactic pathway allows for a higher rate of energy production than the aerobic pathway discussed previously. Lactic energy production is an important part of many sports (those requiring higher power outputs for relatively short periods) but needs to be carefully balanced with sufficient aerobic adaptations for optimal performance, as it's the aerobic system that ultimately allows the "recovery" of the lactic pathway.

Lactic power in particular refers to the rate of energy production by this pathway (as compared to capacity, which is more about duration, or how long the energy production can be sustained) and therefore is especially important for athletes in sports where the duration of effort is short but the demand on power output is high.

With this in mind, lactic power intervals consist of relatively short bouts of very-high-intensity effort (20–40 seconds) followed by a significant amount of rest (a 1:5–10 work:rest ratio) to allow for sufficient recovery to keep working at high intensity during the next interval. An increased work duration and a shortened rest time would lead to increased fatigue over the intervals and change the expected adaptation from power to capacity.

lactic power intervals

superset 1	superset 2	superset 3	conditioning
1. 6 x 40 seconds on, 4 minutes off 12 strict Pull-ups in 1 set Aim to hit same or higher X each interval (compare right to left) Rest 12 minutes	**1.** 5 x 40 seconds on, 4 minutes off Max rep Burpees (all-out effort = 21+ reps) **2.** Hollow Rock to shoulder stance 4 x 8–10, rest 30 seconds	**1.** Kipping 4 x 8, rest 60 seconds **2.** Muscle-up progression, rest 60 seconds Stage 2: 2 x 4 Stage 3: 2 x 4	

alactic endurance intervals

The alactic system produces extremely high power outputs but lasts for a very limited time. It works closely with the aerobic system, which allows for recovery of the alactic pathway. Development of this energy system is fairly limited and is even more predetermined by genetics than the lactic pathway. However, sometimes the smallest changes make the biggest difference in performance, and neglecting potential adaptations is not an option here.

Alactic endurance (capacity, or duration of energy production) can be developed with short intervals (10–15 seconds) followed by a moderate amount of rest (a 1:5+ work:rest ratio). The aim is to perform as many repetitions as possible of a maximally explosive exercise with the best possible mechanics over the given time and then allow the aerobic system to recover before the next interval.

As you work on the endurance aspect, it is normal to feel fatigue accumulate over the intervals and see the repetitions slow down a bit. However, it's important to understand that you want to be as explosive as possible when performing this kind of work.

alactic endurance levels

superset 1	superset 2	superset 3	conditioning
1. Clapping Push-up 10 x 10 seconds on, 50 seconds off, each rep as explosive as possible 8 minutes active recovery	**1.** Jumping Squat 10 x 10 seconds on, 50 seconds off, each rep as explosive as possible. Wear a weighted vest if you have one. 8 minutes active recovery	Chest-to-Bar Pull-up 10 x 10 seconds on, 50 seconds off, each rep as explosive as possible 5 rounds for time 6 Muscle-ups 12 Rolling Pistols (6 per side)	

lifestyle

10

Practice, train, apply, create.

Up to this point, I have explained how I approach observing and describing movement, how I define the ability to move, and how I approach progressing movement to improve human performance. Then I presented the Freestyle Four, which are the movements I have found to be the most useful for building a blueprint for all movement in sport and life. Next, I taught you some movements that can assist you in developing the Freestyle Four movements and help you bridge the gap from the Freestyle Four to your own movements and goals. Finally, I covered the basics of programming and the process of implementing the progressions seen in this book. But this material will ultimately be useless unless it finds a place within your lifestyle.

In this chapter, I want to share with you a few examples of what the human body is capable of. Here I introduce you to a few people whom I look up to and whose crafts I draw inspiration from to create my own athletic expression and lifestyle.

Jon Olsson—Photo by Oskar Bakke

Red Bull

"To be an athlete, you must think, feel, and live like one."

why strength and conditioning?
After having to back out of competing at the Ironman World Championships in Kona due to a nagging hamstring injury and not getting a clear answer from my doctors and physical therapists, through strength and conditioning I healed, relearned what it meant to be an athlete, and came back stronger than ever before. Ever since, I have been committed to collaborating with other coaches in the field to help make all endurance athletes in the world more resilient.

what makes a professional coach?
It is very similar to being a professional in a lot of other spheres. You have to have passion, experience, and knowledge. You must live in a constant state of growth, where being comfortable with uncertainty and being able to say, "I don't know, but I can figure it out," is normal. This state of uncertainty is where you start developing your theories and philosophy and come up with universal solutions that can benefit everyone.

3 focuses of your practice:

1. Posture, by developing the form required to spend long periods working really hard in one position.

2. Strength and mobility, by challenging fundamental movements from a load and speed perspective in addition to helping athletes achieve the positions required for those movements.

3. Gymnastics, by developing basic tumbling skills to better understand the body and space and give athletes an exit strategy in case of a fall while riding a bike or even performing a flip turn during swim practice and competition.

Nathan Helming

Boston, Massachusetts

Athletic history: sailing, soccer, tennis, mountain biking, lacrosse, basketball, T-ball, cross-country, marathon running, and triathlon

Nathan was always involved in sailing and traditional team sports. His first memory as an athlete is of playing goalie for a local soccer team at age 6, with his dad on the sidelines cheering him on and coaching him. When Nathan failed to make the varsity soccer team in high school, he shifted gears into endurance sports, starting with cross-country, marathons, and eventually ultramarathons and triathlons.

Even though Nathan was setting good times in training and racing, he never considered himself an athlete. In Boston, being an athlete meant that you played a ball sport such as football or baseball. After one of his races, he went to a local running shoe store and bought himself a Nike running hat. Once he put that hat on, he started feeling like an athlete and eventually realized that to be an athlete, you must think, feel, and live like one.

Nathan moved to San Francisco and worked at a sporting goods store and as a physical therapy aid to sponsor his training and racing, and he earned a spot at the Ironman World Championships in Kona, Hawaii. Unfortunately, a nagging hamstring became an injury and left him on the sidelines. As he consulted with orthopedic surgeons, physical therapists, and chiropractors on how to heal his hamstring, he grew desperate when nobody could give him a straight answer to solve his problem. After Nathan ran out of funds to cover his treatment, a local strength and conditioning coach who specialized in endurance athletes decided to pick him up as a client for free to train and mentor him.

It was when he performed a deadlift for the first time that the light bulb went off for Nathan. His hamstring felt like it had started to wake up, and shortly thereafter he was back to competing and feeling stronger than ever. In addition to competing, he now has a private practice as a strength and conditioning coach specializing in endurance sports.

Nathan's experience as a high-level competitor, his passion and enthusiasm to provide the endurance community with solutions to improve performance, and his ability to collaborate with innovative thinkers to challenge his ideas and philosophy on a daily basis have made him a force and an inspiration to coaches and athletes around the world.

3 benefits of strength and conditioning:

1. Fun. This is like recess for adults; it's a time to play and discover what their bodies can do.

2. Injury healing and prevention. Through training I can teach athletes how to find what is missing in their performance and how to build it back up.

3. Through strength and conditioning I can make all movement relevant and help athletes understand how all human movement connects and translates to their specific goals.

“Skills talk, no hype needed.”

why b-boying?
I can’t say exactly why, but I can just feel it. Growing up you go through the process of exploring the world and yourself. I found b-boying, which allowed me to do exactly that through dance. In high school, you were either into sports or not, and for me breaking fell right in the middle of being athletic and being a regular dude. B-boying allowed me to become an artist but with an athletic expression.

does b-boying define you, or do you define b-boying?
You can say it defines me, but it comes down to how you represent and approach the dance. I feel like if it truly defined me, it would define everyone else the same way, but it doesn’t. Every b-boy is different, and that is what helps define the craft itself. You become what you make of it.

3 benefits of b-boying:

1. You learn to appreciate music through movement, use your body as a tool to express it, and make the music your own.

2. It builds a great foundation for fitness and health.

3. You learn and appreciate the history and art of hip-hop.

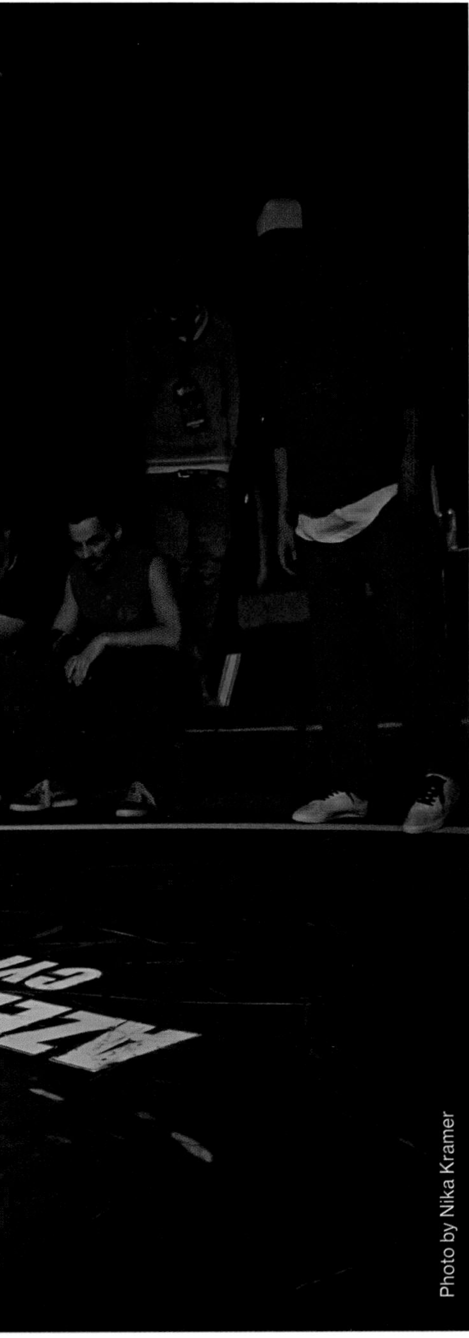
Photo by Nika Kramer

3 focuses of your training and practice:
1. Music is number one. Through music I get in the mood and allow it to push me.

2. I train the way I compete, in intervals as seen in b-boy battles, making sure to constantly vary my movements. Even though it is physical, it is a more of a mental challenge, where you must focus on thinking fast and strategic on the fly. You can't draw a blank. When you draw a blank you lose.

3. I focus on execution, control, and speed of my movement.

RoxRite

Guadalajara, Mexico

Winner of the 2011 Red Bull BC ONE
85 international titles

RoxRite was born in Guadalajara, Mexico, and grew up in very humble surroundings. Both his parents had limited education and worked on a farm to provide food and shelter for RoxRite and his older brother. The economic decline in the late 1980s caused a rise in the unemployment rate, forcing RoxRite and his family to emigrate to Los Angeles. After two years in southern California, work opportunities finally landed RoxRite and his family up in the Bay Area, where his father and brother worked in the vineyards picking grapes.

The family's financial stability allowed RoxRite to go to school and get an education. It was at school, when a group of high school kids came to perform a dance show with breaking, that RoxRite first discovered what would one day become his profession. He started trying and practicing the moves at home, and when he could he would practice together with his friends. Eventually, he started attending local contests, which quickly earned him a spot in a well-established crew in San Francisco called the Renegade Rockers.

It was RoxRite's older brother who inspired him most. His brother ran cross-country and track in high school, held all the school records, and went on to run as a sponsored athlete for Adidas. This success fueled RoxRite to believe that it is possible to become a professional doing what you love.

Even though RoxRite competed for several years, it wasn't until he was 25, when he was at a contest and went to perform one of his signature moves and couldn't, that he realized his body was his tool and he needed to take care of it. This moment in his career marks his transition from being an artist who danced to being an artist who trains to express himself in an athletic fashion.

To elevate his game, RoxRite started training like an athlete and made sure that he always had the mobility, endurance, and power to perform his moves at any moment. He explains that in breaking, when your body doesn't feel right, your mind feels off and your creativity dries up.

RoxRite now holds 85 international titles and travels around the world competing, judging contests, and teaching workshops to all levels of b-boys. Inspired by athletes like Michael Jordan, Mike Tyson, and Muhammad Ali, he continues to approach his craft as an athlete mixed with an artistry that makes him a living legend and a driving force in the future of b-boying and hip-hop.

Marc Morisset

Montreal, Canada

First person to land a Frontside Rodeo 1080

Marc grew up in a big family in Canada. He was always very active, but it wasn't until the Canadian government launched a campaign to test and promote physical fitness that Marc discovered he had athletic qualities. Even though he practiced a wide variety of sports, he was especially attracted to the mountain lifestyle as he trained and practiced ski racing. Everything really came together when he discovered skateboarding and eventually connected the skills he learned in skateboarding to snowboarding.

As snowboarding was growing in the 1990s, so was Marc. Although snowboarding was his focus, other expressions of physical activity were never far from his mind. It was obvious to Marc that taking care of his body was important to perform better in a sport, but how to do that was not yet clear. He knew that through training and developing the body, an athlete could become seamless in the way he exerted himself while practicing his sport.

For a few years Marc used a road bike to build his endurance by climbing a steep 12-kilometer hill near his house. Later he discovered the world of functional training through CrossFit. After eight months of training, he decided to go back to the hill for the first time, and his time improved by 25 percent. Marc explains that it felt like he was pedaling with his entire body, not just with his legs. This is when his philosophy of baseline training solidified and truly brought full circle the notion that good training will fill the gaps in your sport-specific performance.

Now retired from snowboarding and living close to the mountains of Whistler in British Columbia, Marc continues to live an athletic lifestyle and has become a wise businessman dedicated to developing shoes and apparel for functional athletes with the belief that we are all united by motion.

Photo by Sean Sullivan

athletic history
Soccer, ski racing, speed skating, swimming, yoga, skateboarding, and snowboarding

why snowboarding?
I grew up freestyle skiing. When my family and I moved, I didn't have access to good ski hills, so I ended up enrolling in speed skating. Besides speed skating, I really started getting into skateboarding and eventually fell in love with the then-booming sport of snowboarding when I moved back to the mountains. I didn't choose snowboarding; it chose me. I had no choice but to go and do it. Snowboarding became my physical and creative outlet, and it represented more than just a sport; it was a lifestyle.

does snowboarding define you, or do you define snowboarding?
I'm a truly a skate kid who grew up going to punk rock shows, which originally defined me. When I discovered snowboarding and became a professional in the '90s, I know I played small part in the great things that were happening with the sport, but I would stop well short of claiming that I defined it in any way.

3 benefits of snowboarding:

1. Learning to let go of other people's expectations

2. Sharing experiences with friends and pushing each other to succeed

3. Freedom

3 focuses of your training and practice:

1. Baseline fitness. Being able to go outside and feel unlimited and able to perform at a relatively high level is what a good foundation of fitness gives me.

2. Mobility. Being able to improve the way I move has been essential to performing well, especially after dealing with some old injuries.

3. Prioritize bodyweight movement over lifting. Without good control and awareness of your body, the application of muscular strength is limited.

"Understanding diet, movement, and good training are keys that will fill the gaps you have in your sport-specific performance."

Photo courtesy of Manuel Carballo

Manuel Carballo

Madrid, Spain

Member of the Spanish national team for 13 years

Manuel grew up in Madrid, Spain, in a family with deep roots in the world of gymnastics. Both of his parents were gymnasts. His dad was the head coach of the Spanish men's national team for ten years and the women's national team for twenty years. Both of his brothers were gymnasts, one of them a two-time world champion. In addition, Manuel's sister was a rhythmic gymnastics coach. Coming from such a family, it is obvious why gymnastics is such a big part of Manuel's life.

Although Manuel's family lives and breathes gymnastics, Manuel combined it with swimming and judo when he first started. Eventually gymnastics took over and became his full-time sport. His first memory of practicing gymnastics is the excitement of feeling suspended in the air as he swung around the rings and bars. The fact that gymnastics has signature movements that can only be learned by doing gymnastics also made him feel special, and the high degree of risk management brought a sense of responsibility that further developed his confidence.

Manuel made the Spanish national team at a young age and was determined to make it to the Olympics. On his journey, he faced many moments of weakness due to constant nagging pains, injuries, and the fact that he wasn't growing up like a "normal" kid. Thankfully he had a great family, coaches, and friends who supported him along the way until he fulfilled his dream of making it to the 2008 Olympic Games in Beijing.

Manuel explains that a lifetime commitment to making it to the Olympics can be really tough and lonely at times, especially when you try to explain why you are putting yourself through the torture. Thankfully you get to a point in your profession and life where no matter the outcome, the determination to push your body as far as it can go and to channel the values fostered by your family and expressed through your body brings an indescribable sense of reward.

Manuel continues to practice gymnastics but has retired from the competitive circuit. He is committed to educating the world about the beauty and power of his sport, not just through competitive gymnastics but also through health and fitness.

athletic history
Judo, swimming, and gymnastics

why gymnastics?
My two older brothers were gymnasts, and looking up to them made becoming a gymnast very natural. But what truly drew me to gymnastics was that feeling you get when you first learn to do an unassisted handstand or a flip. The few seconds in a handstand or fraction of a second while flipping where your body feels suspended in the air is a feeling that can't be explained, it is just a very unique, special feeling. Gymnastics is a sport where you get to know yourself better than any other. Your body is your working tool, and you create a very tight bond between your mind and your body, which translates into life. I have no doubt that gymnastics gives you many advantages, such as helping you make better decisions and live a more fulfilled life.

does gymnastics define you, or do you define gymnastics?
Gymnastics totally defines me. You get to a point where the prolonged practice turns into a lifestyle and the habits of your life, such as eating and sleeping, become a mold for who you are and how you live. In order to pair up gymnastics with your life, you must make your daily routine match the demands of your sport. When I look back at my history with gymnastics, the internal and external transformations in myself are radical.

3 benefits of gymnastics:

1. You develop quick reflexes, overall agility, and extreme proprioception.

2. The challenges presented are hard, but once you overcome them, the reward is beyond satisfying.

3. The relationships you build with your teammates and coaches go beyond the practice of the sport. They become family.

3 focuses of your training and practice:

1. Consistency is king, especially when practicing such a complicated sport.

2. Always go back to the basics, break down each movement into a progression, and train each progression separately before putting them all together.

3. Never waste time. Every moment you have for training must be utilized even if it is in small doses.

why weightlifting?

On the surface, weightlifting is just two movements, but if you take a closer look and start peeling off the layers, you realize that there is an infinite number of layers to the sport and practice of Olympic-style weightlifting. Weightlifting puts me in a constant state of exploration, and the more I peel away the layers, the more I realize that I just want to hang out here.

does weightlifting define you, or do you define weightlifting?

I define it, but when I first started I truly believed that the way I was originally taught was the only way. I believed in one style of lifting, and I trained and practiced only that style. It wasn't until I began coaching that I discovered that everyone has a slightly different approach, even though the essence of lifting is the same for everyone. Ever since, I have been determined to help define what is behind the universal style of lifting and how it has a unique application to all styles of weightlifting.

3 benefits of weightlifting:

1. Self-reflection and meditation.

2. Power production.

3. Developing overall fitness, athletics, or even becoming an athlete.

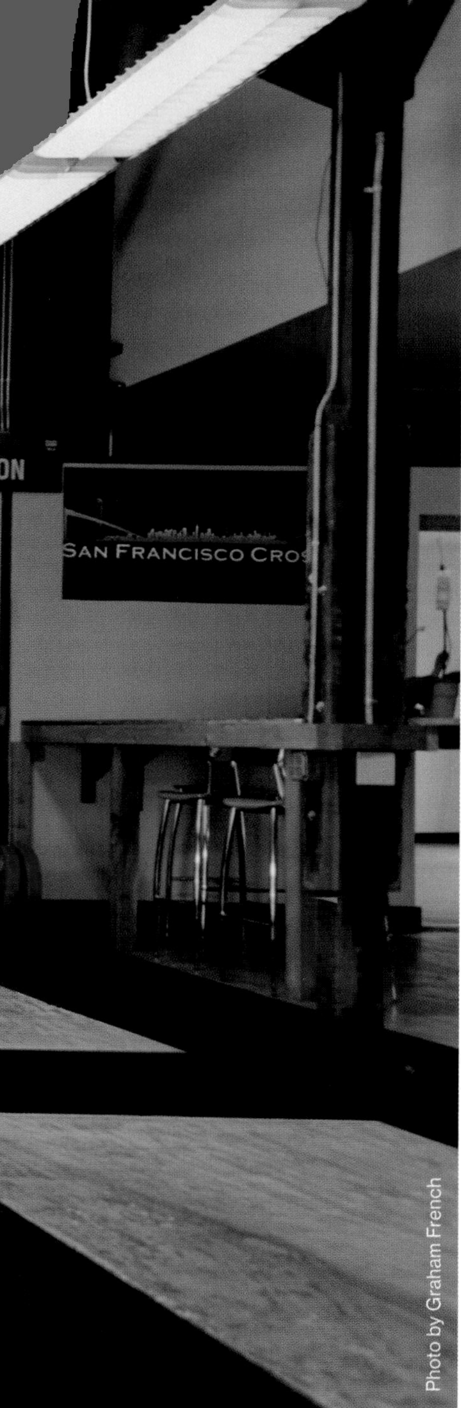

Photo by Graham French

Diane Fu

Monterey, California

Athletic history: basketball, badminton, fitness, personal training, CrossFit, and weightlifting

Diane grew up in the Midwest in a family that prioritized academics over athletics, but that didn't stop her from pursuing her dream of becoming a basketball player. When she started high school, she made it a point to start practicing in her backyard and eventually built up the courage to try out for the team. Unfortunately, as she likes to put it, she got murdered. It turned out that Diane was terrible at basketball. Every student in her high school who didn't make a team was sent to play badminton. Even though she ended up pursuing a sport that wasn't part of her dream, it helped pave who she is today as an athlete and a coach.

When Diane started spending time at the gym, she stood out like a sore thumb: she was the only skinny Asian girl hanging out with the football players doing bicep curls and learning to lift heavy. At age 16, she got a pair of dumbbells and a mirror to build her home gym and continued to pursue her training in her parents' basement.

After high school she moved San Francisco to study kinesiology, where she also got a job working the front desk at a local health club. Impressed by the personal trainers she worked with, she decided to pursue becoming a personal trainer, which eventually became her full-time job. She explored different avenues of physical performance, one of them being CrossFit. Through CrossFit, she discovered Olympic-style weightlifting.

Weightlifting sparked a new drive in Diane to learn everything about the sport and about human movement. She reached out to a local Olympic weightlifting coach and started training under his supervision. Her first experience was humbling, to say the least: a girl in her late teens was snatching for doubles what Diane could clean and jerk for one repetition on a good day.

Her first three years of lifting were all about training and chasing the numbers. She took her body from 130 to 160 pounds in order to compete in the U.S. Nationals. Even though she felt like she could have been competitive in the sport, she had come into it late and realized that where she was starting to shine was in coaching. She has the ability to communicate with athletes who are more advanced than she is and help them pursue their dreams as lifters.

Since Diane started coaching, she has dedicated all her time to developing her craft, creating a place for all levels of athletes to train and practice in order to help athletes and coaches all around the world better understand why weightlifting has such a great number of styles but still shares a universal approach that is inclusive to everyone.

3 focuses of your practice:

1. Movement quality. The line has to be clean; the body has to fit different shapes, flow and fluidity.

2. Attitude. No wild antics. I like keeping the group dynamics light.

3. Fun.

Jon Olsson

Mora, Sweden

Winner of nine X-Games medals and inventor of several double flips, including a D-spin 720 into a flatspin 540 (DJ flip), a switch double rodeo 1080 (hexo flip), a double flatspin 900 (kangaroo flip), and a switch cork 720 to flatspin 540 (the tornado)

Jon Olson was born in Mora, Sweden. From a young age, he loved winning and taking on new challenges. More than loving to win, he hated losing. At his first competition in ski racing, he took third and remembers riding home in his parents' car feeling devastated at not winning a trophy. Jon continued to practice alpine skiing until he was 16. This is when he started seeing these guys riding backward and flipping on their skis and decided to pursue this style of skiing.

His eagerness to win carried over to all aspects of his life. Even at school when he was assigned to write a paper, he would make sure that his paper was the longest. Everything Jon did had to be extreme. He made sure that he always had the best trick and that he worked the hardest to be the best. When everyone left to go home for the day, he would stay on the mountain, hiking up the jump to get another 20 attempts in before calling it a day.

Jon's determination to become the best in the world paid off and brought him to the top of the world rankings, earning him a gold medal at the winter X-Games, among many other world international titles. Not only did win contests, but he also pushed the sport to a new level by creating several new tricks that became signatures of freestyle skiing.

After performing at the highest level for several years, Jon decided that he was going to try his luck again at alpine ski racing. As he returned to ski racing, he realized that his satisfaction for winning had changed, and now he started to appreciate his performance less through winning and more through knowing that he tried his best and worked his hardest to get a step closer to his goals.

Jon now spends most of his time in Europe, training, racing, and further developing his practice as a freestyle skier as his ski-racing training and season allows. He doesn't just compete, but also hosts one of the most popular Big Air events in Sweden. In addition, he is a young and rising business mogul.

Photo by Oskar Bakke

why skiing?
My first memory as a kid was on skis, and it is second nature to me. Whenever I feel stressed, life is moving too fast, or things start to feel too serious, getting to the mountains and getting on the lift gives me instant relief—not to mention that being surrounded by nature changes your state of mind.

does skiing define you, or do you define skiing?
Skiing definitely defined my lifestyle growing up, but as I grew older I started creating the lifestyle I wanted. Skiing led to a million other ventures outside of skiing that I have been able to use to further define the sport.

3 benefits of skiing:

1. Constant growth. No matter how long you have been skiing, there is always room for improvement.

2. Freedom.

3. Fresh air and a beautiful view does anyone good.

3 focuses of your training and practice:

1. Leg strength. I want my lower body to be strong and explosive to push myself further on the slopes.

2. Movement technique. I am always trying to refine my technique.

3. Core strength, as it is the base of all my movement.

"It was never a matter of if I was going to be the best, but more like when I grow old I will be the best skier in the world"

athletic history
Gymnastics, ballet, pole vaulting, boot camp, yoga, and CrossFit

why CrossFit?
Growing up as an athlete my entire life and having had the chance to explore different disciplines of sport, I never felt like any of those sports allowed me to truly dig deep into who I truly am as an athlete. I love to win, but focusing solely on one thing has never been my style. CrossFit's versatile approach to developing athleticism keeps me in a state where I constantly feel challenged, and for me that is fun, as I feel like I am never done.

does CrossFit define you, or do you define CrossFit?
CrossFit is my sport and has defined part of how I live my life today. I was fortunate enough to step into the sport right as it started to blow up, and I have grown with it. Seeing how all the athletes and coaches that are part of the sport and the CrossFit community have contributed to the growth inspires me every day to continue to push forward and help define how future generations will experience this approach to fitness and lifestyle.

Annie Thorisdottir

Reykjavik, Iceland

First two-time winner of the CrossFit Games

"Train, win, smile, repeat."

Annie grew up in Iceland with her parents and three older brothers. Besides being a very active girl growing up, the competitive dynamics with her older brothers fueled her fire to win. If you ask any of her family members, you will quickly learn that Annie does not like to lose and will do whatever it takes to come out victorious in any competitive setting. It doesn't matter whether it is a sport, a pull-up contest, or a video or board game, Annie always brings her champion mentality with her.

Annie picked up gymnastics at a young age and pursued it competitively for several years. In addition to gymnastics, ballet became an important part of her physical expression until she noticed that she didn't have the typical dancer's body and eventually decided to focus just on her gymnastics career. Even though she was good at gymnastics, her stature, athleticism, and powerful athletic ability led her to pole vaulting in the world of track and field, where she spent several years training and was on track to represent her country on the international circuit.

Annie's curious nature and drive to constantly test herself was heightened when she attended a local boot camp class as part of her strength and conditioning program. She became a regular at the boot camp classes and was approached there by one of the coaches who mentioned that she should try her luck at CrossFit competition. Without knowing what CrossFit was, Annie attended the competition and won. The victory earned her a spot in the CrossFit Games in Aromas, California, in 2009. Even though she didn't podium at the Games in 2009, she returned in 2010 to take second, and then took first place in 2011 and 2012, becoming the first two-time Fittest Woman on Earth with back-to-back victories.

Annie continues to pursue and train CrossFit and is co-owner of a gym in her hometown, Reykjavik, where she coaches and educates members on the benefits of living a fit lifestyle. She has become a role model for women around the world.

Photo courtesy of *The Box Magazine*

3 benefits of CrossFit:

1. You become cultured, as you get to interact with a very diverse group of people that you maybe would never get a chance to outside of the gym and sport.

2. The group dynamics and challenges are always fun.

3. You gain a new appreciation for what health really means and what the body is capable of doing.

3 focuses of your training and practice:

1. Positive attitude. No matter how hard the problem, there is always something good to be gained.

2. Challenge myself. I push myself to find the new me as an athlete. I thrive to become who I want to be tomorrow.

3. Make things look good. I believe that beauty is an expression of strength.

"Work as hard as you can, but always make sure to feel proud of the work you do."

athletic history
Hockey, BMX, skateboarding, inline skating, snowboarding, motocross, basketball, baseball, rugby, and wakeboarding

why wakeboarding?
I fell in love with it. It consumed me. Before becoming my job, wakeboarding was a complete obsession that eventually became part of my life, like a life partner.

Rusty "Bone Crusher" Malinoski

Humboldt, Saskatchewan, Canada

World champion
First person to land a 1080 in competition

Rusty grew up in a small town in Canada. He and his brothers were known for participating in a variety of team and individual sports, such as hockey, basketball, baseball, rugby, and motocross. It was wakeboarding, though, that ended up defining Rusty as a professional athlete. One of the steps toward becoming a professional required him to spend time developing his body to further his craft. He had already been hitting the gym, but by the age of 18 training had become an important part of his approach to wakeboarding. It was the individualism of the sport of motocross that made him understand how important it was to develop his body, which carried over to his wakeboarding career.

The first three years of wakeboarding, all Rusty wanted to do was ride. He didn't realize that wakeboarding could become a career until his friends and the people around him noticed his talent and pushed him to pursue wakeboarding professionally. In order to do that, the first step was to move to the mecca of wakeboarding: Orlando, Florida.

Ten years into his career, Rusty ranked among the top ten athletes every year, but now holds the title of World Champion. He says one of the things that made a big difference in his career was starting CrossFit. Not only did he learn how to master the basics of human movement and performance, but he also took his body from a 220-pound top rider in the world to a 190-pound ripper who was faster, stronger, and more mobile than ever before. This change lit a fire in Rusty's training regimen, and he has since become committed to learning how to move his body in the most basic ways in order to truly maximize his effort and the hours dedicated to practicing his sport as he juggles life as a business and family man with his wife and son.

does wakeboarding define you, or do you define wakeboarding?
When you are trying to get to a certain level, you stick to the game plan that wakeboarding has for you, and once you become someone in the world, then you start setting the new standard for yourself and your surroundings and help create a new game plan for the sport of wakeboarding.

3 benefits of wakeboarding:

1. Exploration and discovery. (Rusty went around the world.)

2. Relationships. (He met his wife.)

3. Overcoming adversity. (Mindset and work ethics.)

3 focuses of your training and practice:

1. Mobility. Remove all restrictions and step out of the main positions you spend most of the time in your sport.

2. Jumping and landing mechanics. Olympic weightlifting.

3. Increasing work capacity. More endurance, stamina, and strength, which allows Rusty to practice harder, compete, and feel fresh.

Chris "Stouty" Stoutenburg

Collingwood, Ontario, Canada

Two-time Olympic Gold medalist in wheelchair basketball

Stouty grew up in small town in Canada, where sports were a big part of his family's roots. His mother was the coach of a junior girls' basketball team that went on to win eleven county championships, and his dad played for the Toronto Marlies and was known for raising money for cystic fibrosis by riding his bike across Ontario. With such a sports-driven family, it wasn't surprising that Stouty learned how to skate and play hockey at the age of 3.

Stouty played multiple sports, but football captured his attention. He remembers being a 5-foot-6-inch, 105-pound kid standing on the field wanting to play and hearing the coaches debate whether they would let him participate due to his small size. Stouty would say, "Coach, put the biggest guy in front of me and I will tackle and stop him." His determination kept him in football, and he grew up to become a 6-foot-4-inch, 200-pound athlete who was set to play college ball.

One day while hanging out on the balcony at a friend's house, Stouty's life took a 180-degree turn. He leaned against a railing that couldn't support his weight, which caused him to plummet to the ground and break his back. After the accident, he woke up in the hospital, where he realized that he would never walk again. Even though this realization came with huge amounts of fear and depression, it was a defining moment in his life. He told himself, "Either I am in it to go on with my life or I am not, but whatever I do, I will put everything I have in it." Stouty decided that he would go on with his life and set out on the road to recovery.

The doctors told him that it would take six months of rehab before he would be released, but Stouty told them that he couldn't stay that long, as he had plans to start college three months later. After multiple surgeries, he asked a nurse for a wheelchair. The nurse told him that he wasn't ready yet, and Stouty replied by swinging his legs off the side of the bed and saying, "If you don't give me a chair, I will get out of the bed myself!" She ran to grab a chair, and the road to recovery began. The scheduled daily one-hour therapy session turned into a full day of training for Stouty, as he listened in on other people's sessions and trained himself to be ready for college. Two months later, he was released from the hospital.

Photo by Jennifer Nichol

athletic history
Hockey, baseball, soccer, basketball, track and field, football, wheelchair tennis, wheelchair football, and wheelchair basketball

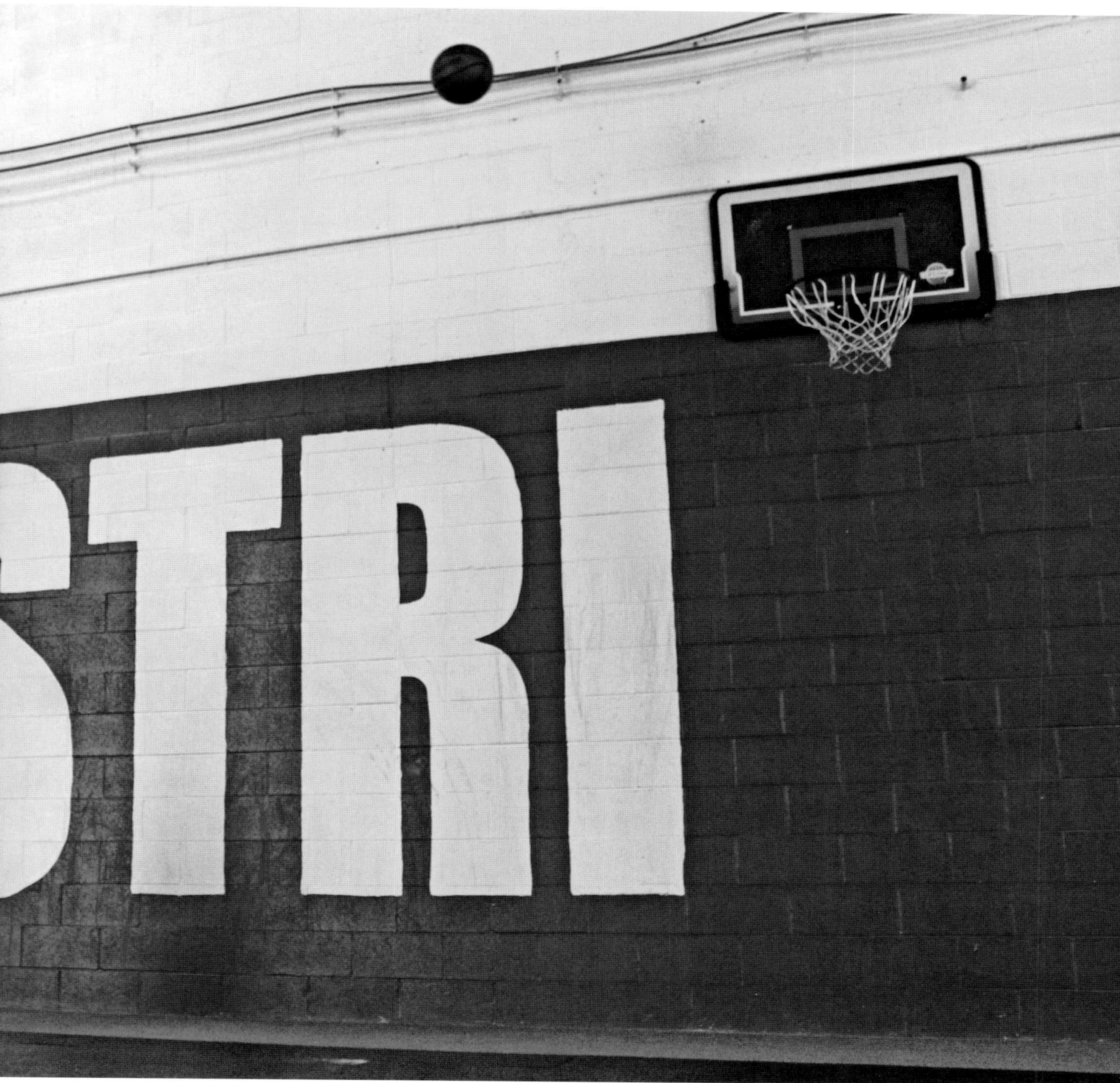

why basketball?
When you are in a wheelchair, people see the chair first and the person second. This, unfortunately, is human nature, and it can be really discouraging to someone in my situation. Through basketball, I have built the courage to interact socially and physically with others while in a wheelchair and express who I am and what I am capable of. I would still be who I am without basketball, but it has helped me develop the tools to become a better me.

3 benefits of training as an adaptive athlete:

1. I became an able father. I can interact and play with my child.

2. I became an independent individual. I can get around without my wheelchair or anyone's help.

3. I developed the most basic human functions—things we take for granted, such as bladder and bowel control.

3 focuses of your training:

1. Preparation. I always have a plan and a strategy.

2. Fitness. I train for more than just basketball; I train for life.

3. Mental training. I focus on developing the right mindset.

Once released, he pursued several adaptive sports, such as tennis, football, and track. It was basketball, though, that made him feel at home and gave him the courage to feel like himself again. Most important, Stouty wanted a family of his own. He struggled with the fact that there were basic functions he couldn't serve as a father, such as being able to pick something up off the ground and put it in his lap without using both his arms to get himself up from a bent-over position to seated. The doctors said that he would never be able to do this, but Stouty was determined to learn it in order to be able to pick up his kid and put him in his lap. After months of training and practicing, he got it, and he can now pick his kid up off the ground and place him in his lap.

Stouty now lives with his wife and son in Collingwood, Ontario, where he plays and coaches basketball, trains daily to stay in shape for life, and is on a mission to help and inspire adaptive athletes around the world to reach levels of performance that they never thought possible.

"Losing is part of life. I actually don't mind losing; it just makes me want to work harder."

Having the opportunity to write a book and get it published is not something that happens every day. Think about the number of people out there who have "writing a book" on their bucket list, not to mention how many great writers go a lifetime without getting any of their work published.

After spending more than half my life in a gymnastics gym as an athlete and a coach, it seemed obvious to me that I should write about the sport of gymnastics—specifically about using gymnastics to improve strength and conditioning and fitness. So I called my friend and former client, Anthony Sherbondy, and asked him to be my co-author. This partnership seemed appropriate, as we had discussed the idea of collaborating on writing articles on gymnastics and its application to fitness and sports performance a few years earlier.

When we first started getting together, we would meet at a café in Palo Alto and talk for hours. We made notes on notepads and napkins and recorded our conversations for reference and future transcription. The more we talked about the book and tried to get our ideas down on paper, the more the concept of the book changed. It was hard for us to stick to the topic of gymnastics. We kept deviating from gymnastics to talk about action sports, CrossFit, and even philosophical questions. After a few months of going back and forth, we felt a little lost.

During one of our meetings, Tony suggested that it would be great to go back and forth between different topics and try to start by writing a manual for the seminars I was teaching. This manual would not take the form of a traditional book, but rather the form of an interactive e-book. We both believed that it would give my audience a unique experience for consuming and digesting the material.

We were both excited about this idea and got to work. After just a few days, we had managed to put together more content than we had in the previous six months. We were finally rolling, and we had a clear idea of what we were writing and who would want to read it. It didn't take long, though, before we realized that a physical book with real pages had to happen, as it was the opportunity of a lifetime. We also realized that the book was no longer about gymnastics. It was about life, about sport, about living long and healthy. It was about a topic we really care about: self-expression through movement.

The book was no longer a manual; it was a manifesto of a lifestyle we both believed in and agreed should be shared with the world. A lifestyle is not something you do, but something you ***live.***

I grew up with an athletic lifestyle—a lifestyle dedicated to constant practice, training, exploration, and focus on developing the body and mind. The greatest lesson I learned was that your lifestyle is only as valuable as the people you surround yourself with. These people are more than your teammates, coaches, doctors, and therapists. They become your friends, extended family, and the most amazing support group and source of inspiration you will ever find.

Growing up, I was so obsessed with my lifestyle of gymnastics training that I would eagerly go to bed at night so I could close my eyes and dream of winning the Olympics. In my dream I could see myself standing on the podium, receiving a medal, and looking up at a stadium filled with cheering spectators and flashing lights. Still to this day I think of this dream, but now I sometimes imagine what it would be like if, instead of looking up at a stadium of flashing lights, I looked up at an empty and silent stadium with no flashing lights and no family or friends to celebrate with. In this version of the dream, winning the Olympics would obviously mean nothing.

I tell you about this dream because it taught me that no matter what you accomplish in life, unless you share that accomplishment with the world, your stadium will be empty. Writing this book is one of my life accomplishments, so I share it with you. If while reading this book you learn one thing or have a moment when a light bulb goes off in your head, that moment is a win. No matter how big or small the win, you can always consider a win an accomplishment.

So I now leave you and encourage you to embrace what you've learned and go share it with others. The moment you do, you will see progress, and if you ask me, progress is always success.

abduction: A type of movement that draws the extremities away from the midline of the body.

adduction: A type of movement that draws the extremities toward the midline of the body.

anatomical position: A position in which the human body is standing erect and at rest, with feet together and arms rotated outward so that the palms are facing forward and the thumbs are pointed away from the body.

anterior: Nearer the front, especially situated at the front of the body.

base of support: The area under the body that is composed of every point of contact that the body makes with the supporting surface. These points of contact may be body parts, such as feet or hands, or they may include things like crutches or the chair in which a person is sitting.

center of mass (COM): The hypothetical point around which the force of gravity appears to act. It is the point at which the body's combined mass appears to be concentrated. Because it is a hypothetical point, the COM does not need to lie within the physical bounds of a person or object.

concentric phase: The phase of a movement in which a concentric contraction occurs and the muscle length decreases in order to perform a movement. In a Squat, for example, this would be the phase in which you push away from the ground to stand back up.

contralateral: Refers to a movement occurring on opposite sides of the body.

dorsiflexion: Flexion of the foot in an upward direction.

eccentric phase: The phase of a movement in which an eccentric contraction occurs, and the muscle length increases in order to perform a movement. In a Squat, for example, this would be the phase in which you lower yourself toward the ground.

end range of motion: The extreme end limit of a movement at a global (body shape) or local (joint) level.

extended plank position: A plank position in which the hands are no longer underneath the shoulders but rather in front of them, with the shoulders in flexion and creating a hollow body position from hands to feet.

extension: A straightening movement that increases the angle between body parts. When standing, for example, the knees are extended. Extension of the hip or shoulder moves the leg or arm down and backward. The opposite of flexion.

flexion: A bending movement that decreases the angle between body parts. Flexion of the shoulder or hip moves the arm or leg forward and up. For example, bending your elbow is an example of elbow flexion, and reaching your arms overhead is an example of shoulder flexion. The opposite of extension.

frontal plane: The vertical plane that divides the body into front and back sections.

global: Refers to the complete body shape adopted during movement or at rest. For example, standing is a neutral global position, and swinging on the rings is a movement in which the body flexes and extends globally.

hinge: The act of a joint performing a function similar to a hinge. For example, bending over to pick something up off the ground requires a hinge at the hips.

hollow body position: A term adopted from gymnastics that refers to a position in which the body adopts global flexion, commonly while supine or faceup on the ground.

inversion: The act of changing the body's orientation to the point of being inverted or upside down.

kip: An explosive kicking or swinging motion.

local: Refers to a joint position adopted during movement or at rest. For example, a Handstand requires the shoulders to be in flexion.

locomotion: Movement from one place to another. The most common forms of locomotion are crawling, walking, and running.

lumbar curve: Also known as lordosis, the normal inward curvature of the lumbar (lower) and cervical (upper) regions of the spine.

midline: An imaginary line that runs from the top of your head down to your feet. The midline is usually associated with the sagittal pane, which divides the body into right and left halves.

movement control: The ability to control your form at a global and local level during movement or in a static position.

multi-joint movement: A movement that involves several joints flexing and extending at the same time, also referred to as a compound movement in the fitness industry.

negative phase: The eccentric phase or lowering phase of a movement. See also eccentric phase.

neutral: Refers to the body being as close to the anatomical position as possible at a global and local level.

plank position: A static hold used as a strength exercise that involves maintaining a neutral global body position while supporting yourself with your arms and legs. The most common plank, or front plank, is held in a Push-up position, where your weight is supported over the base of support created by your hands and feet, but a plank can also be supported by your forearms, elbows, and toes.

plantarflexion: Extension of the foot in a downward direction.

positive phase: The concentric or rising phase of a movement. See also concentric phase.

posterior chain: A group of muscles consisting predominantly of tendons and ligaments on the back side of the body.

progression: The act of placing progressively more challenging demands on a movement pattern in order to develop a specific movement or work toward a specific task-completion goal.

prone/pronated position: Lying facedown on your belly.

proprioception: The sense of the relative position in space of your different body parts during movement.

receive: To catch an object, such as a barbell landing on your shoulders during a Clean in Olympic-style weightlifting. Also, to control movement into a specific position, such as to perform a Kipping Muscle-up and catch yourself with control in the Dip position.

sagittal plane: The vertical plane that divides the body into right and left halves.

single-joint movement: A movement that involves one joint flexing and extending, also referred to as an isolation movement in the fitness industry.

skill transfer: The ability to convey the movement ability acquired from practicing and training one specific movement technique to another movement technique.

square: Refers to keeping the hips and shoulders aligned with the frontal plane.

strict: Refers to a type of movement that does not involve kipping. Strict movements are usually performed slowly and with minimal changes in global shape.

Superman position: A term adopted from gymnastics that refers to a position in which the body adopts global extension, commonly while prone or facedown on the ground with the arms overhead and in adduction.

supine/supinated position: Lying faceup on your back.

traction: Control and stability while performing a movement. Think of it as the grip that tires on a car would have on the road.

transition position: The last position the body adopts before changing direction during movement.

transverse plane: An imaginary plane that divides the body into upper and lower halves. It is perpendicular to the frontal and sagittal planes.

tuck: A position in which the knees are bent and held close to the chest, often with the hands clasped around the shins.

unilateral loading: Most of the load is placed on one side of the body during movement or while holding a position.

First and foremost, I want to thank my wife-to-be, Tonya White, for giving me the unconditional love, support, encouragement, and guidance I needed to get through the process of writing this book. Not to mention being a trooper while dealing with a stressed, tired, and mentally absent self. Thank you for being my best friend, my inspiration, and the best reason to keep pushing forward in life.

To my family for always believing in me and helping me become who I am today. Thank you to my mom, for showing me the importance of family and how powerful it is to carry your values and integrity to all aspects of your life and career. Thank you to my dad, for teaching me the importance of having initiative and how to make hard work look easy. Thank you to my sister Helena, for teaching me how to dream big, blaze your own path, and not be scared to break the mold. To my brother John, for being my role model and showing me who I wanted to grow up to be. To my brother Oscar, for always being by my side during the good and bad and always being willing to sacrifice himself for my well-being. To my baby sister Cristina, for always bringing happiness into my life and showing me that we are all equal and deserve to be treated with respect and integrity.

Thank you to my coauthor and now good friend, Tony, for not thinking twice about jumping on this project and making it the greatest learning experience of my professional career. Thank you for teaching me how to become a better communicator and team player and how to execute and solve the most difficult problems. Without you this book would have never happened, and for that I am forever grateful.

Thank you to Ryan Smith and Nick D'Amico for helping me bring to life my ideas and teachings on the pages in this book. Thank you for teaching me how to create the most unique and complete experience for my audience and for constantly reminding me to not be scared of being different.

Thank you to Kelly Starrett for taking me under his wing and being my mentor. Thank you for showing me that to become a master at communication you must first master being a teacher, and that innovation is as simple as making ideas and concepts relevant to everyone.

Thank you to Nathan Helming for reminding me that there is always more room for growth. Not to mention for helping with reading, editing, organizing, and writing this book.

Thank you to Jami Tikkanen for believing in me since day one, giving me the opportunity to work with a fantastic athlete such as Annie Thorisdottir, and being an example of what a true coach should be. Thank you for sharing your knowledge in this book and helping me bring my ideas full circle.

Thank you to AcroSports for giving me a home and the opportunity to return to gymnastics. Thank you for helping me see and respect all performance arts and disciplines.

Thank you to Juliet Starrett for always accommodating for me and helping me continue to pursue my career. Thank you to all the coaches at San Francisco CrossFit for being excellent role models, colleagues, and friends.

Thank you to Gabriel Jaochico, aka BBoy Wicket, for showing me the power of dance and how to express art through movement. Thank you to Miles Pinneda, for being my teacher and showing me the true meaning of Freestyle.

Thank you to Annie Thorisdottir for trusting me in helping guide you to achieve your goals and showing me what the human body is truly capable of.

Thank you to my publisher, Victory Belt, for guiding and supporting along the way and for believing that I had something valuable enough to say to give me a shot. A special thank you to Glen Cordoza for taking all the technique pictures.

Thank you to Rusty Malinoski, Jon Olsson, Omar Delgado (RoxRite), Annie Thorisdottir, Chris "Stouty" Stoutenburg, Marc Morisset, Manuel Carballo, Brian Orosco, Diane Fu, and Lindsey Mathews for taking time out of your busy careers to talk to me and allow me to tell your stories.

Thank you to Caragh Camera, Graham French, Oskar Bakke, Paolo Sanchez, Sean Sullivan, Aaron Katen, Jennifer Nichol, Nika Kramer, Chris Greer, Kid David, and Maria Davey for providing me with beautiful photos to help bring to life the lifestyle I believe in. Thank you to Jeanie Mordukhay for supporting and helping with the layout of the book.

Thank you to every person who has personally trained with me, watched one of my videos, or simply reached out to support my work. Your kind words are what keep me going, so I dedicate this book to you.